On the cover: Gold weight in the form of a portrait mask (Asante)

Third Edition, First Printing, 1995.

Library of Congress Cataloging-in-Publication Data

Ghana : a country study / Federal Research Division, Library of Congress ; edited by LaVerle Berry.—3rd ed.
p. cm. — (Area handbook series, ISSN 1057–5294) (DA Pam ; 550–153)
"Supersedes the 1971 edition of Ghana : a country study, coauthored by Irving Kaplan et al."—T.p. verso.
"Research completed November 1994."
Includes bibliographical references (pp. 319–349) and index.
ISBN 0–8444–0835–2 (hc : alk. paper)
1. Ghana. I. Berry, LaVerle Bennette, 1942– . II. Library of Congress. Federal Research Division. III. Series. IV. Series: DA Pam ; 550–153
DT510.G44 1995 95–18891
966.7—dc20 CIP

Reprinted without on recycled acid-free paper.

Bernan
Lanham, Maryland
December 1995

W9-BZK-816

C
a country

Federal Re
Lib

Rese

Foreword

This volume is one in a continuing series of books prepared by the Federal Research Division of the Library of Congress under the Country Studies/Area Handbook Program sponsored by the Department of the Army. The last two pages of this book list the other published studies.

Most books in the series deal with a particular foreign country, describing and analyzing its political, economic, social, and national security systems and institutions, and examining the interrelationships of those systems and the ways they are shaped by cultural factors. Each study is written by a multidisciplinary team of social scientists. The authors seek to provide a basic understanding of the observed society, striving for a dynamic rather than a static portrayal. Particular attention is devoted to the people who make up the society, their origins, dominant beliefs and values, their common interests and the issues on which they are divided, the nature and extent of their involvement with national institutions, and their attitudes toward each other and toward their social system and political order.

The books represent the analysis of the authors and should not be construed as an expression of an official United States government position, policy, or decision. The authors have sought to adhere to accepted standards of scholarly objectivity. Corrections, additions, and suggestions for changes from readers will be welcomed for use in future editions.

Louis R. Mortimer
Chief
Federal Research Division
Library of Congress
Washington, DC 20540–5220

Acknowledgments

The authors wish to acknowledge the contributions of the coauthors of the 1971 edition of *Ghana: A Country Study.* Their work provided general background for the present volume.

The authors also gratefully acknowledge the numerous individuals in various government agencies and private institutions who gave of their time, research materials, and expertise in the production of this book. These individuals include Ralph K. Benesch, who oversees the Country Studies/Area Handbook program for the Department of the Army.

The staff of the Federal Research Division who contributed directly to preparation of the manuscript also deserve recognition. These people include Sandra W. Meditz, who reviewed all drafts and served as liaison with the sponsoring agency; Marilyn L. Majeska, who managed editing and production; Andrea T. Merrill, who edited tables and figures; Ramón Miró and Tim L. Merrill, who provided research support; and Barbara Edgerton and Izella Watson, who did word processing. Stephen C. Cranton, David P. Cabitto, and Janie L. Gilchrist prepared the camera-ready copy.

Also involved in preparing the text were Peter J. Tietjen, who edited the text; Helen Chapin Metz, who helped with editing; and Carolyn Hinton, who performed the prepublication editorial review. Joan C. Cook compiled the index.

David P. Cabitto prepared the graphics. Harriett R. Blood prepared the topography and drainage map; Thomas D. Hall drafted the remaining maps. David P. Cabitto and the firm of Greenhorne and O'Mara prepared the final maps. Special thanks go to Teresa Kamp, who prepared the illustrations on the title page of each chapter and the cover art.

The editor and the authors acknowledge the generosity of the Embassy of Ghana, the White House, James Sanders, and Brook, Rose, and Cooper Le Van, who allowed their photographs to be used in this study. Staff of the Embassy of Ghana in addition provided invaluable guidance in the drafting of the rank and insignia charts. Finally, the editor wishes to acknowledge the support given by authors David Owusu-Ansah, Maxwell Owusu, and Thomas P. Ofcansky to this volume. Their devotion clearly exceeded the normal call of duty.

Contents

List of figures

Preface

This study replaces *Ghana: A Country Study,* which was completed in 1971 during the second effort to establish republican government in Ghana under Kofi Abrefa Busia. Since then, Ghana has experienced four military governments and a third attempt at representative democracy before the inauguration of the Fourth Republic in January 1993. Since the early 1980s, the dominant developments in Ghana have been the adoption of an economic structural adjustment program backed by international lending agencies and a prolonged transition to a new form of elective government, both presided over by a military government headed by Flight Lieutenant Jerry John Rawlings. Rawlings continues to dominate political life, having been elected president in national elections in November 1992, one of the crucial steps in the latest attempt at representative government.

This edition of *Ghana: A Country Study* examines the record of the military government after 1981 and of the first two years of the Fourth Republic, 1992–94. Subsequent events are discussed in the Introduction.

This study is an attempt to treat in a concise and objective manner the dominant historical, social, economic, political, and national security aspects of contemporary Ghana. Sources of information used in preparing this volume include scholarly books, journals, and monographs; official reports of governments and international organizations; Ghanaian newspapers; the authors' previous research and observations; and numerous periodicals. Chapter bibliographies appear at the end of the book; brief comments on some of the more valuable sources recommended for further reading appear at the end of each chapter.

All measurements in this book are given in the metric system. A conversion table is provided to assist those readers who are unfamiliar with metric measurements (see table 1, Appendix). A Glossary is also included to explain terms with which the reader may not be familiar.

Place-names follow the system adopted by the United States Board on Geographic Names (BGN). The authors have followed current and more accurate usage by using the term *Asante* rather than *Ashanti* in referring to one of the most prominent of Ghana's peoples and indigenous states. The term *Ashanti*, which was generally employed during the pre-independence period, does, however, still appear in some geographic and commercial contexts. The reader should refer to the Glossary for further explanation.

The body of the text reflects information available as of November 1994. Certain other portions of the text, however, have been updated. The Introduction discusses significant events that have occurred since the completion of research, the Country Profile and Chronology include updated information as available, and the Bibliography lists recently published sources thought to be particularly helpful to the reader.

Table A. Chronology of Important Events

Period	Description
EARLY HISTORY	
ca. 10,000 B.C.	Earliest recorded probable human habitation within modern Ghana at site on Oti River.
ca. 4000 B.C.	Oldest date for pottery at Stone Age site near Accra.
ca. 100 B.C.	Early Iron Age at Tema.
FORMATIVE CENTURIES	
ca. A.D. 1200	Guan begin their migrations down Volta Basin from Gonja toward Gulf of Guinea.
ca. 1298	Akan kingdom of Bono (Brong) founded. Other states had arisen or were beginning to rise about this time.
1471–82	First Europeans arrive. Portuguese build Elmina Castle.
1500–1807	Era of slave raids and wars and of intense state formation in Gold Coast.
1697–1745	Rise and consolidation of Asante Empire.
NINETEENTH CENTURY	
1843–44	British government signs Bond of 1844 with Fante chiefs.
1873–74	Last Asante invasion of coast. British capture Kumasi.
1874	Britain establishes Gold Coast Colony.
1878	Cocoa introduced to Ghana.
1896	Anglo-Asante war leads to exile of *asantehene* and British protectorate over Asante.
TWENTIETH CENTURY	
1900	First Africans appointed to colony's Legislative Council.
1902	Northern Territories proclaimed a British protectorate.
1914–18	Gold Coast Regiment serves with distinction in East Africa.
1919	German Togo becomes a mandate under Gold Coast administration.
1925	Constitution of 1925 calls for six chiefs to be elected to Legislative Council.
1939–45	Gold Coast African forces serve in Ethiopia and Burma.

Table A. Chronology of Important Events

Period	Description
1947	United Gold Coast Convention founded.
1949	Kwame Nkrumah breaks with United Gold Coast Convention and forms Convention People's Party.
1951	New constitution leads to general elections. Convention People's Party wins two-thirds majority.
1954	New constitution grants broad powers to Nkrumah's government.
1956	Plebiscite in British Togoland calls for union with Gold Coast.
	Convention People's Party wins 68 percent of seats in legislature and passes an independence motion, which British Parliament approves.
1957	British Colony of the Gold Coast becomes independent Ghana on March 6.
1958	Entrenched protection clauses of constitution repealed; regional assemblies abolished; Preventive Detention Act passed.
1960	Plebiscite creates a republic on July 1, with Nkrumah as president.
1964	Ghana declared a one-party state. Completion of Akosombo Dam.
1966	While Nkrumah is in China, army stages widely popular coup. National Liberation Council comes to power.
1969	Progress Party, led by Kofi Abrefa Busia, wins National Assembly elections.
1972	Lieutenant Colonel Ignatius Acheampong leads a military coup in January that brings National Redemption Council to power.
1978	Fellow military officers ease Acheampong from power.
1979	Junior officers stage Ghana's first violent coup, June 4. Armed Forces Revolutionary Council formed under Flight Lieutenant Jerry John Rawlings. Hilla Limann elected president in July.
1981	Rawlings stages second coup, December 31. Provisional National Defence Council established with Rawlings as chairman.
1983	First phase of Economic Recovery Program introduced with World Bank and International Monetary Fund support.
1985	National Commission for Democracy, established to plan the democratization of Ghana's political system, officially inaugurated in January.
1988–89	Elections for new district assemblies begin in early December and continue through February 1989.
1990	Various organizations call for return to civilian government and multiparty politics, among them Movement for Freedom and Justice, founded in August.

Table A. Chronology of Important Events

Period	Description
1991	Provisional National Defence Council announces its acceptance, in May, of multipartyism in Ghana. June deadline set for creation of Consultative Assembly to discuss nation's new constitution.
1992	National referendum in April approves draft of new democratic constitution. Formation and registration of political parties become legal in May. Jerry John Rawlings elected president November 3 in national presidential election. Parliamentary elections of December 29 boycotted by major opposition parties, resulting in landslide victory for National Democratic Congress.
1993	Ghana's Fourth Republic inaugurated January 4 with the swearing in of Rawlings as president.
Late 1994–early 1995	Ghana hosts peace talks for warring factions of Liberian civil war.
1995	President Rawlings pays official visit to the United States, March 8–9, first such visit by a Ghanaian head of state in more than thirty years.

Country Profile

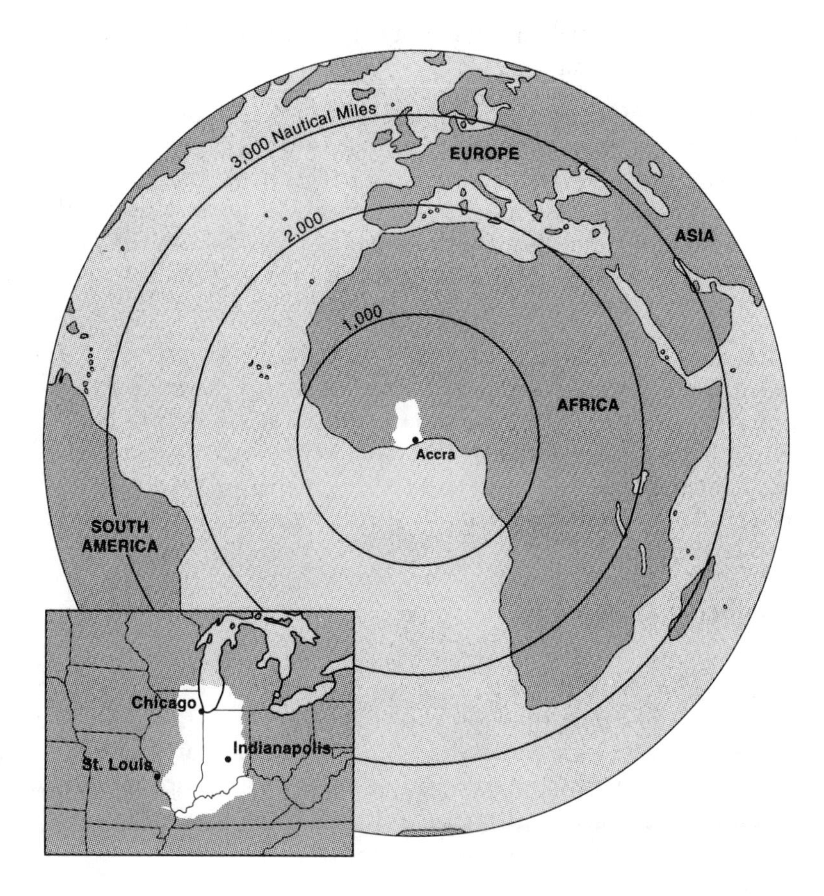

Country

Formal Name: Republic of Ghana.

Short Form: Ghana.

Term for Citizens: Ghanaian(s).

Capital: Accra.

Date of Independence: March 6, 1957.

Note—The Country Profile contains updated information as available.

Geography

Size: 238,533 square kilometers, roughly the size of the states of Illinois and Indiana.

Topography: Generally low physical relief except in the east. Five distinct geographical regions: low plains inland from Atlantic coast; northern plateau stretching from western border to Volta River Basin averaging 450 meters in height; mountainous uplands along eastern border, bisected in south by Volta River Gorge; Volta River Basin in center; and dissected plateau up to 300 meters high in north.

Climate: Tropical climate governed by interaction of dry continental airmass from the northeast and moist southwest equatorial system. Annual mean temperature between 26°C and 29°C. Annual rainfall varies from more than 2,100 millimeters in southwest to 1,000 millimeters in north. Vegetation heaviest in south, thinning to savanna and dry plains in north.

Society

Population: Estimated at 17.2 million in mid-1994, up from about 6.7 million in 1960; approximately half under age fifteen. Growth rate more than 3 percent per year since 1980. 1990 population density sixty-three persons per square kilometer; density highest in southwestern third of country, thinnest in center, higher in north. About 33 percent urban in 1992.

Ethnolinguistic Groups: Approximately 100 ethnolinguistic groups, all further subdivided into numerous cultural and linguistic units. Major ethnic groups are the Akan, Ewe, Mole-Dagbane, Guan, and Ga-Adangbe. Languages belong either to Kwa or to Gur subfamily of Niger-Congo language family. Kwa speakers, found to south of Volta River, include the Akan, Ewe, and Ga-Adangbe. Gur speakers live north of Volta River and include the Grusi, Gurma, and Mole-Dagbane. English is official language used in government, large-scale business, national media, and school beyond primary level. Akan, Ewe, Ga, Nzema, Dagbane, and Hausa (a trade language from Nigeria) also used in radio and television broadcasting.

Religion: According to 1985 estimate, 62 percent Christian, 15 percent Muslim, 22 percent indigenous or nonbelievers. Christians composed of Protestants (25 percent, Methodists and Presbyterians especially numerous), Roman Catholics (15 percent), Protestant Pentecostals (8 percent), and Independent African Churches (about 14 percent). Muslims mostly Sunni. Christianity predominates in center and south, Islam in north.

Health: Large number of infectious diseases endemic to tropics, including cholera, typhoid, tuberculosis, anthrax, pertussis, yellow fever, hepatitis, trachoma, and malaria. Other diseases include schistosomiasis, guinea worm, dysentery, onchocerciasis, venereal diseases, and poliomyelitis. Malnutrition also widespread. Average life expectancy fifty-six years in 1993. Severe shortage of hospital beds and doctors. Since late 1980s, government has emphasized immunization and primary health care programs. Incidence of acquired immune deficiency syndrome (AIDS) second highest in West Africa and rising.

Education: Education system consists of primary (six years), junior secondary (three years), and senior secondary (three years) after reforms of mid-1980s eliminated former middle schools; polytechnic institutions; and four universities. Universal education remains an unrealized goal, but most children have access to primary and junior secondary schools. Local vernacular is language of instruction on primary level, English thereafter. All students pay textbook fees. Enrollments for 1990–91: primary 1.8 million, junior secondary 609,000, senior secondary 200,000. In 1989–90 about 11,500 students attended polytechnic schools. Enrollment in universities at Legon, Kumasi, and Cape Coast totaled 9,251 in 1989–90; in 1993 a fourth university opened at Tamale. In early 1990s, the government instituted fees for boarding and lodging, provoking student demonstrations. Adult literacy rate reportedly about 40 percent in 1989.

Economy

General Character: At independence, economy based on cocoa and gold; country relatively prosperous. After mid-1960s, economy stagnated, characterized by weak commodity demand, outmoded equipment, overvalued currency, smuggling, and foreign debt. Since 1983 Economic Recovery

Program (a structural adjustment program) has resulted in new investment and rising exports of cocoa, gold, and timber, but also in high foreign debt and little improvement in general standard of living.

Gross Domestic Product (GDP): In 1992 GDP was US$6.1 billion; per capita income US$380.

Budget: In 1993 about ¢667 billion, including ¢119 billion deficit (roughly US$1.1 billion and US$187 million, respectively, based on mid-1993 exchange rate).

Agriculture, Forestry, and Fishing: In 1991 agriculture most important sector of economy, constituting just under half of GDP, down from 60 percent in 1983. Production of exports and food crops fell steadily after mid-1960s; major recovery began in 1980s. Cocoa most important cash crop; Ghana world's third largest cocoa producer as of 1992–93 crop year. Other cash crops—palm oil, cotton, tobacco, sugarcane, rubber, and kenaf (used in fiber bags)—much less important. Major food crops: yams, corn, cassava, and other root crops. Forests cover southern third of country. Commercial forestry major industry; deforestation serious problem. Livestock production negligible outside far north. Limited commercial fishing industry.

Industry: In 1960s largest manufacturing industries included aluminum, saw mills and timber processing, cocoa processing, breweries, cement, oil refining, textiles, and vehicle assembly. Factory output fell as low as 21 percent of capacity by 1982 but recovered to average of 40 percent in 1989. In early 1990s, many textile, pharmaceutical, leather, and electronics factories reportedly closed because of economic liberalization and foreign competition.

Mining: Major minerals are gold, bauxite, manganese, and diamonds. Mineral production fell precipitously during 1970s, recovered during 1980s. Minerals second highest export earner in early 1990s. Gold most important mineral, long associated with ancient and contemporary Ghana. Production in 1992 more than 1 million fine ounces and rising, surpassing cocoa as chief export earner. One of world's leading producers of manganese, but early 1990s production less than half mid-1970s output. Diamonds mostly industrial grade; 1992 production 694,000 carats and increasing. Large bauxite reserves little exploited.

Energy: Commercial quantities of petroleum offshore, but output negligible in early 1990s. Hydroelectric generating capacity nearly 1.2 megawatts, mostly at Akosombo Dam on Volta River; 60 percent consumed by Volta Aluminum Company, remainder consumed domestically or sold to Togo and Benin. Significant expansion planned. Northern regions being connected to national power grid.

Foreign Trade: Major exports—cocoa, gold, timber, and industrial diamonds—mainly to Germany, Britain, United States, and Japan. Major imports—capital goods, oil, consumer goods, and intermediate goods—mostly from Britain, Nigeria, United States, and Germany. Ghana's trade balance, negative since 1980s, estimated at –US$190 million for 1994.

External Debt: US$4.6 billion in 1993.

Currency and Exchange Rate: Cedi(¢), divided into 100 pesewas. In April 1995, US$1.00 = ¢1,105.

Fiscal Year: Calendar Year.

Transportation and Telecommunications

Roads: Most regions accessible by road network of more than 32,000 kilometers; 12,000 classified as main roads. About 6,000 kilometers paved, remainder gravel or earth. Since 1985 major repairs under way on all main and some feeder roads.

Railroads: 953 kilometers of narrow gauge (1.067 meter) track; only thirty-two kilometers double-tracked. Serve only southern industrial/commercial centers, mainly connecting Accra, Sekondi-Takoradi, and Kumasi. Limited renovation under way as part of Economic Recovery Program.

Civil Aviation: Eleven airfields, including Kotoka International Airport at Accra and major domestic airports at Sekondi-Takoradi, Kumasi, and Tamale. Ghana Airways operates small fleet on domestic and international routes. In early 1990s, runways, lighting, and freight and terminal buildings upgraded at Kotoka.

Ports and Waterways: Two deep artificial harbors—Tema (2.7-million-ton capacity) and Takoradi (projected 1.6-million-ton capacity). More than 1,100-kilometer navigable network on Lake Volta, with additional ports planned; 168 kilometers of

Ankobra River, Tano River, and Volta River navigable. Small merchant marine of one refrigerated and five cargo ships.

Telecommunications: Relatively limited telecommunications system. About 45,000 telephones in 1993, concentrated in Accra. Two domestic radio-relay systems, one east-west serving coastal cities, one north-south connecting Accra with Burkina Faso. International telecommunications via link with International Telecommunications Satellite Corporation (Intelsat) Atlantic Ocean Satellite. Four AM and one FM radio stations; four television stations; two domestic shortwave transmitters broadcast in English and six local languages; one international transmitter broadcasts in English, French, and Hausa.

Government and Politics

Government: A parliamentary democracy at independence in 1957, followed by alternating military and civilian governments. In January 1993, military government gave way to Fourth Republic after presidential and parliamentary elections in late 1992. The 1992 constitution divides powers among a president, parliament, cabinet, Council of State, and an independent judiciary. Government elected by universal suffrage.

Administrative Divisions: Ten administrative regions divided into 110 districts, each with its own District Assembly. Below districts are various types of councils, including fifty-eight town or area councils, 108 zonal councils, and 626 area councils. 16,000 unit committees on lowest level.

Judicial System: Legal system based on Ghanaian common law, customary (traditional) law, and the 1992 constitution. Court hierarchy consists of Supreme Court of Ghana (highest court), Court of Appeal, and High Court of Justice. Beneath these bodies are district, traditional, and local courts. Extrajudicial institutions include public tribunals, vigilante groups, and *asafo* companies. Since independence, courts relatively independent; this independence continues under Fourth Republic. Lower courts being redefined and reorganized under Fourth Republic.

Politics: Since mid-1992 political parties legal after ten-year hiatus. Under Fourth Republic, major parties are National Democratic Congress, led by Jerry John Rawlings, which won presidential and parliamentary elections in 1992; New Patriotic Party, major opposition party; People's National Convention, led by former president Hilla Limann; and (new) People's Convention Party, successor to Kwame Nkrumah's original party of same name.

Foreign Relations: Since independence, fervently devoted to ideals of nonalignment and Pan-Africanism, both closely identified with first president, Kwame Nkrumah. Favors international and regional political and economic cooperation. Active member of United Nations and Organization of African Unity. In 1994 President Rawlings elected chairman of Economic Community of West African States.

National Security

Armed Forces: In 1994 armed forces totaled about 6,850 active personnel, consisting of army, 5,000; air force, 1,000; and navy, 850. Missions are to protect against foreign aggression and to maintain internal security. Armed forces aided in these missions by various paramilitary forces.

Major Military Units: Army largest and best-equipped service and primary unit of defense. Air force and navy both smaller and subordinate to army. All three services hindered by equipment maintenance problems and low states of combat readiness.

Military Equipment: Army equipment mostly older and poorly maintained weapons, largely of British, Brazilian, Swiss, Swedish, Israeli, and Finnish manufacture. Air force equipped with combat, transport, and training aircraft. Navy possesses eight sizable ships, including two corvettes and four fast-attack craft. All three services experience budgetary and maintenance problems.

Defense Budget: Defense spending high in 1960s, declined in 1970s and 1980s. In 1992 defense budget about US$105 million, less than 2 percent of budgetary expenditures.

Foreign Military Relations: During colonial and early independence periods, military training and equipment came from Britain. In 1960s and after, military relations diversified to include Soviet Union, China, German Democratic Republic (East Germany), and Libya. In 1990s Ghana revived military ties with Britain, United States, and other Western countries. Ghana also providing military units for peacekeeping operations in Liberia and Rwanda and observers and police for several United Nations missions.

Internal Security Forces: Consist of more than 16,000 General Police, 5,000-member People's Militia, and National Civil Defence Force composed of all able-bodied citizens. Since independence, stature of police has varied according to role in suppression of dissent, extortion, and bribery. In 1990s police involved in various United Nations international peacekeeping operations.

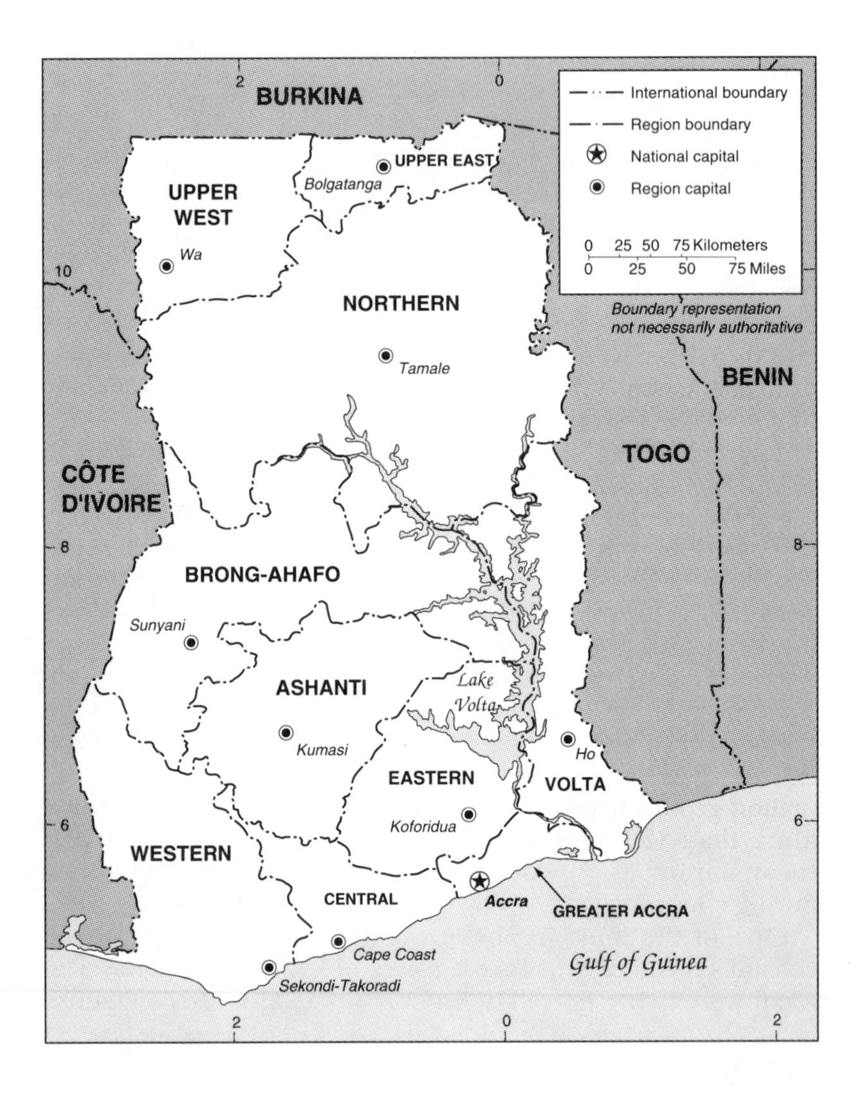

Figure 1. Administrative Divisions of Ghana, 1994

Introduction

WHEN GHANA ACHIEVED INDEPENDENCE from colonial domination in 1957, the first country in sub-Saharan Africa to do so, it enjoyed economic and political advantages unrivaled elsewhere in tropical Africa. The economy was solidly based on the production and export of cocoa, of which Ghana was the world's leading producer; minerals, particularly gold; and timber. It had a well-developed transportation network, relatively high per capita income, low national debt, and sizable foreign currency reserves. Its education system was relatively advanced, and its people were heirs to a tradition of parliamentary government. Ghana's future looked promising, and it seemed destined to be a leader in Africa.

Yet during the next twenty-five years, rather than growth and prosperity, Ghanaians experienced substantial declines in all of the above categories, and the country's image became severely tarnished. Beginning in the early 1980s and continuing into the mid-1990s, efforts were undertaken to rebuild the government and the economy and to restore the luster of Ghana's name. It is this attempt at reconstruction that constitutes the major focus of the present volume.

The region of modern Ghana has been inhabited for several thousand years, but little is known of Ghana's early inhabitants before the sixteenth century. By then, however, the major population groups were on the scene and in their present locales. More than 100 separate ethnic groups are found in Ghana today, a number of which are immigrant groups from neighboring countries.

One of the most important is the Akan, who live in the coastal savannah and forest zones of southern Ghana. The Akan were living in well-defined states by the early sixteenth century at the latest. By the end of that century, the states of Mamprusi, Dagomba, and Gonja had come into being among the Mole-Dagbane peoples of northern Ghana. These peoples and states were significantly influenced by Mande-speaking peoples from the north and the northeast. In the extreme north of present-day Ghana are a number of peoples who did not form states in pre-colonial times. These peoples, such as the Sisala, Kasena, and Talensi, are organized into clans and look to the heads of their clans for leadership. Like the Mole-

Dagbane, they have been heavily influenced by Islam, introduced into the region centuries ago by trans-Saharan traders or by migrants from the north.

The best-known of the indigenous states of Ghana is without doubt Asante, a term that applies to both people and state. Beginning in the mid-seventeenth century, this Akan-based society began to expand from the area around Kumasi, its capital, allying with or subduing neighboring Akan states such as Denkyira and Akwapim. Eventually, Asante incorporated non-Akan peoples and kingdoms, including Gonja, Dagomba, and Mamprusi, into an empire that encompassed much of modern Ghana and parts of neighboring Côte d'Ivoire. Along a network of roads radiating from Kumasi flowed communications, tribute, and, above all, gold, over which the Asante held a monopoly.

Gold is found in several regions of West Africa, including the headwaters of the Niger River and the forest zone of modern Ghana. The West African gold trade was well-established in antiquity, and it helped tie the peoples of Ghana into a trans-Saharan commercial network that stretched from the West African forest zone across the Sahara to ports on the Mediterranean. Aside from providing material benefits, trade seems to have been one of the major factors in state formation in Ghana.

Gold drew European traders to the Gulf of Guinea. The first to arrive in the late fifteenth century were the Portuguese, who set up an outpost on Ghana's coast. During the next century, the lure of gold gave way to the slave trade because of the demand for labor in the Americas. Trading in slaves as well as gold, the Dutch, the Danes, the English, and the Swedes eventually joined the Portuguese on what had come to be known as the "Gold Coast." By the early nineteenth century, the British were the most important European power on the Gold Coast. Thereafter, the British extended their control inland via treaties and warfare until by 1902 much of present-day Ghana was a British crown colony. Ghana's current borders were realized in 1956 when the Volta region voted to join Ghana.

British colonial government, while authoritarian and centralized, nonetheless permitted Ghanaians a role in governing the colony. This was true not only of central governing bodies such as the Legislative Council and later the Executive Council, but of local and regional administration as well. The British policy of indirect rule meant that chiefs or other local leaders became agents of the colonial administration. This system of rule gave Ghanaians experience with modern, representative government to a degree unparalleled elsewhere in sub-Saharan Africa.

During the colonial period, the Gold Coast began to develop economically. Roads, railroads, and a harbor at Takoradi were constructed. In 1878 a Ghanaian brought cacao pods into the country, introducing what eventually became the country's major cash crop. Large-scale commercial gold mining began, and Western-style education was introduced, culminating in the founding of the University College of the Gold Coast in 1948. The education system trained a class of Ghanaians that found employment in the colonial administration. In the twentieth century, this same class increasingly sought economic, political, and social improvements as well as self-government, and, eventually, independence for Ghanaians.

After World War II, the drive for independence began in earnest under the auspices of the United Gold Coast Convention and the Convention People's Party, the latter founded by Kwame Nkrumah in 1949. Britain granted independence on March 6, 1957, under a governor general as representative of the crown and Nkrumah as prime minister. In 1960 a new constitution created the Republic of Ghana, the same year that Nkrumah was elected president.

Nkrumah saw Ghana as the "Star of Black Africa." He believed that Ghana should lead the effort to free Africa from the shackles of Western colonialism and envisioned a union of independent African states that would command respect in the world. Nkrumah also helped found the Non-Aligned Movement, a grouping of world states that attempted to pursue policies independent of East and West. His ideas about African unity proved immensely appealing in the late 1950s and early 1960s; indeed, the Pan-Africanist dream still resonates across Africa in the 1990s.

Nkrumah's pursuit of Pan-Africanism proved expensive and ultimately futile, and it partially accounts for the economic problems that Ghana encountered during the early 1960s. More important, however, were Nkrumah's domestic policies. He believed in centralization, both political and economic. Constitutional safeguards against authoritarianism were abolished, political opposition was stifled, and, shortly after the 1960 elections, Nkrumah was declared president for life. By the mid-1960s, Ghana had become a one-party state under a powerful president.

Nkrumah also believed in a rapid transformation of the Ghanaian economy along socialist lines. He channeled investment into new industrial enterprises and agricultural projects, nationalized foreign-owned enterprises, and wherever possible "Ghanaianized" the public and private sectors. State-sponsored enterprises such as the Akosombo Dam and the Volta Aluminum Company were undertaken, roads were built, and schools and health services were expanded. The former Northern Territories, the northernmost third of the country which had been neglected by the British, received special attention in an attempt to address the imbalance in infrastructure and social services between North and South.

Ghana, however, lacked sufficient resources to finance the public-sector projects that Nkrumah envisioned. When foreign currency reserves were exhausted, the government resorted to deficit financing and foreign borrowing to pay for essential imports. Trained manpower to allocate resources and to operate old and new state enterprises was equally in short supply, and internal financial controls necessary to implement development led almost naturally to corruption. Despite obvious gains from investment in roads, schools, health services, and import-substituting industries, by the mid-1960s Ghana was a nation ensnared in debt, rising inflation, and economic mismanagement, the result of Nkrumah's ill-conceived development policies. An overvalued currency discouraged exports, corruption was increasingly a fact of life, and the political system was intolerant of dissent and authoritarian in practice.

In 1966 Nkrumah was overthrown and a military government assumed power. But neither military nor civilian governments during the next fifteen years were able to deal successfully with the host of problems that Nkrumah had bequeathed. In particular, under the Supreme Military Council (1972–79), Ghana's economy and political institutions deteriorated at an alarming rate. The 1970s were a period of steadily falling agricultural production, manufacturing output, and per capita income. Declining cocoa production and exports were accompanied by a corresponding rise in smuggling of the crop to neighboring countries, especially Côte d'Ivoire, and largely accounted for chronic trade deficits. Personal enrichment and corruption became the norm of government.

Beyond these serious problems loomed much larger issues that needed to be addressed if Ghana were to resume its position at the forefront of Africa's leading nations. Among these were the fear of an overly centralized and authoritarian national executive, the burden of accumulated foreign debt, and the need to forge a nation from Ghana's diverse ethnic and regional interests. In particular, the challenge was to devise a system of government that would bridge the enormous gap that had developed between the political center and society at large. For most Ghanaians, the nation-state by the late 1970s had become a largely irrelevant construct that had ceased to provide economic benefits or opportunities for meaningful political participation. As a consequence, local, ethnic, and regional interests had become much more prominent than those of Ghana as a whole.

Such were the challenges that lay before the group of military officers who seized power at the end of 1981. During its first year, the Provisional National Defence Council (PNDC) spoke vaguely about socialism and established people's and workers' defence committees and extra-judicial public tribunals as a way to involve Ghanaians in public administration. In 1983, however, the council, under its leader, Jerry John Rawlings, abandoned its socialist leanings and negotiated a structural adjustment program with the World Bank and the International Monetary Fund as the best and perhaps only method of rejuvenating the economy. Called the Economic Recovery Program, it was designed to stimulate economic growth and exports, to enhance private initiative and investment, and to reduce the role of the state in economic affairs.

On the one hand, Ghana's structural adjustment program was and continues to be one of a half dozen models for such programs backed by international lending agencies. It succeeded in reversing the downward trend in production and exports, especially in the cocoa, mining, and timber industries. During the 1980s, gross national product grew at annual rates of 5 percent or more a year, per capita income slowly began to rise, and inflation abated. Since 1990, economic growth has slowed, but trends in the economy remain positive.

On the other hand, Ghana has incurred new debts to finance its Economic Recovery Program, unemployment has risen, and new fees for basic services such as education and health care have added to the burdens of ordinary citizens. Indeed, for many Ghanaians, structural adjustment has not yet significantly improved their lives. Additionally, per capita income, while continuing to rise, is unevenly distributed throughout the population, and private overseas investment has largely failed to materialize. In Ghana's case, structural adjustment is clearly a long-term process. Despite problems and shortcomings, the government of the present Fourth Republic, which succeeded the PNDC in 1993, remains committed to it.

Equally significant were steps to devise new political institutions that would allow a large number of Ghanaians to participate in governing the country. The creation of defence committees and public tribunals in the early 1980s was a step in this direction. In 1988 and early 1989, nonpartisan elections were held to fill seats in representative assemblies constituted in each of Ghana's ten administrative regions; similar bodies were eventually seated in cities, towns, and villages. Thereafter, the overriding question was what form the national government would take. After initial reluctance to commit themselves to a multiparty political system, Rawlings and the PNDC yielded in the face of domestic and international pressures. In April 1992, a new constitution that called for an elected parliament and chief executive won overwhelming approval in a national referendum. Political parties, banned since 1982, were the mechanism by which the system was to work.

Presidential elections were held in November 1992, followed in December by elections for the 200-member national parliament. After a heated campaign, Jerry Rawlings was elected president. His party, the National Democratic Congress (NDC), won control of parliament. In January 1993, Rawlings and the new parliamentarians were sworn into office, thereby launching Ghana's fourth attempt at republican government since independence.

The new political order in Ghana, unfortunately, did not get off to a happy start. The four opposition parties that had candidates running in the presidential race charged that fraud and voting irregularities accounted for Rawlings's victory. When their demands for a revised voters register were rejected because of cost and time factors, they boycotted the parliamentary elections. This stance by the opposition resulted in what is in effect a one-party republic, which imparts a hollowness to Ghana's latest effort at democratic government. Although the opposition parties have accepted the status quo for the time being and have taken on the role of watchdog even though they are not represented in parliament, they have continued to press for a new voters list before elections scheduled for 1996 and remain basically unreconciled to NDC rule. As a result, the first two years of the Fourth Republic were marked by a series of skirmishes and quarrels between the government and the opposition.

In its campaign against the NDC government, the opposition, resorting to the courts, won several cases against the government in 1993 and early 1994. Since 1993 a small but vigorous independent press has developed, which the opposition has used to publicize its views. Despite publication of what at times have been sensational or even libelous charges against members of the NDC, including Rawlings, the government has made no move to censor or suppress independent newspapers and magazines. Official spokesmen, however, have repeatedly denounced what they consider irresponsible reporting in the private press.

In late 1994 and early 1995, controversy over the media continued unabated. The most contentious issue involved the attempt to establish a private radio station as an alternative to the official Ghana Broadcasting Corporation. Known as "Radio Eye" and dedicated to providing a wider range of political opinion and information than the government network, it began broadcasting in November 1994. The government promptly shut it down and seized its equipment, charging that Radio Eye had not been licensed. The opposition parties protested that the government's action was an affront to democratic procedures and turned once more to the courts, challenging the government's licensing practices and the constitutionality of its actions.

By early 1995, the case was before the Supreme Court of Ghana. Meanwhile, in early February the government announced that properly authorized private radio stations would begin broadcasting in February. The large number of license applications received by the government—more than sixty—indicated the interest in private, independent radio broadcasting.

Prospects for abatement in the media battles between the government and its critics were nil, given the degree of antipathy between the two sides and preparations for national elections in 1996. Even so, both appeared to accept the basic rules of democratic procedure. In a statement marking the second anniversary of the Fourth Republic, the New Patriotic Party called on Rawlings (and the NDC) to respect the 1992 constitution to ensure that this latest exercise in democracy would succeed. Most significantly, the statement added, "Let us recognise that the eras of violent and revolutionary change of government in Ghana are over."

Aside from freedom of the press and speech, other basic human rights also appeared to enjoy increased respect in mid-1995. There were persistent reports of police abuse, especially in areas distant from Accra, as well as of unwarranted detentions, beatings, and similar infringements of rights, but, in general, the number and severity of human rights violations continued to decline. The judiciary in particular showed clear evidence of preserving its independence, in keeping with Ghanaian tradition and the requirements of democratic governance.

Such a state of affairs was encouraging, given the role of the armed forces and the police in Ghana's postindependence history. Of the ten governments since 1957, six were composed of military officers who came to power via coups. The PNDC was one such regime, and even though it handed over power to a civilian, constitutional government in 1993, the question of the role of Ghana's military in the Fourth Republic was still an important one. Under the Economic Recovery Program, funding of the armed forces was reduced, and equipment and facilities were allowed to deteriorate. In recognition of this fact and of the continuing mission of the armed forces in matters of defense and international peacekeeping, Rawlings called for renewed attention to the needs of the armed forces in his speech marking the second anniversary of the Fourth Republic in January 1995.

On the economic scene, the government was determined to continue with structural adjustment. Tight fiscal controls in central and local government accounts, an essential element in structural adjustment, had been relaxed as the 1992 elections approached, leading to an increase in the government deficit, inflation, and interest rates. Indications were that this situation had not been brought under control in mid-1995.

Ghana faced other major problems with its Economic Recovery Program in the mid-1990s as well. These included the progressive fall in the value of the cedi, the national currency; a high rate of inflation (more than 30 percent in mid-1995); the lack of private-sector investment, especially in manufacturing; and rising levels of unemployment as a result of international competition, domestic factory closings, and downsizing of parastatals and the government bureaucracy. Added to these problems were the difficulty of reconciling the rigors of free-market economic reforms with popular demands for improved public services and living standards, and a population growing by well over 3 percent a year.

Preliminary data for the whole of 1994 showed that the country had achieved a budget surplus, with another anticipated for 1995, and that gross domestic product adjusted for inflation amounted to 3.8 percent, short of the target of 5 percent but still commendable. Ghana's trade deficit, however, amounted to US$200 million, with a similar figure projected for 1995. Total international debt for 1993, the most recent year for which revised figures were available, stood at US$4.6 billion; its rate of increase, however, showed signs of slowing. In January 1995, the government granted a 52 percent increase in the minimum wage under pressure from the Trade Union Congress.

On the whole, Ghana's economy seemed to be headed in the right direction in the mid-1990s, even if sustained economic recovery was not yet a reality more than a decade after introduction of the Economic Recovery Program and even if the country continued to rely on cocoa, gold, and timber for most of its foreign currency earnings. Nonetheless, in spite of real problems, Ghana was still the model for structural adjustment in Africa in the eyes of Western lending institutions.

The fragility of the economic and political transition underway in Ghana was evident from events in the spring of 1995. On March 1, the government introduced a new value-added tax to replace the national sales tax. Set at 17.5 percent of the price of many commodities and services, the new tax immediately resulted in rising prices and contributed to an already high rate of inflation. It thereby added to the deprivation many Ghanaians had been experiencing for more than a decade under the Economic Recovery Program. For many, it was simply too much. Discontent among civil servants, teachers, and others led to street demonstrations and finally, on May 11, to the largest protest demonstration in Accra against government policies since Rawlings and the PNDC came to power. Five people were killed and seventeen injured in clashes between supporters and opponents of the government. Demonstrators not only criticized what they considered harsh economic policies, but some also called openly for Rawlings to step down.

The protests, organized by opposition parties, provided Rawlings's opponents with a rallying cry. For the first time since 1993, the Rawlings government appeared politically vulnerable. In the face of continued protests and increasing doubts about the viability of the value-added tax, the government in early June announced plans to replace it with a new national sales tax. In the meantime, one of the NDC's partners in the Progressive Alliance, the National Convention Party, withdrew from the alliance in late May. The party's leaders claimed that it had not been allowed to participate in affairs of government as had been promised when the alliance was formed to contest the 1992 elections. The National Convention Party, therefore, would no longer be bound by the agreement, and it would feel free to associate with the opposition if it chose to do so.

In early 1995, Rawlings, as chairman of the Economic Community of West African States (ECOWAS), continued his efforts to find a solution to the civil war in Liberia. At a December meeting in Accra, the major combatants agreed to form a new governing council and to implement a cease-fire. As of April, however, the combatants had not been able to agree fully on the new council's membership despite another meeting in Accra in January, and even the cease-fire threatened to come unraveled as renewed fighting broke out in Liberia. So disappointed were Rawlings and other West African leaders that they threatened to withdraw their peacekeeping troops if the Liberians continued to obstruct the ECOWAS peace process.

In support of another peacekeeping mission, on March 1, 1995, Ghana dispatched a contingent of 224 officers and men as part of its long-term commitment to the United Nations peacekeeping forces in Lebanon. Other Ghanaians continued to serve as military observers, police, or soldiers in international peacekeeping missions in Western Sahara, the former Yugoslavia, Mozambique, and Rwanda. The warming in relations with neighboring Togo also continued. After the arrival of a new Ghanaian ambassador in Lomé in mid-November, Togolese authorities reopened their western border in December and were expected to name an ambassador to Accra during 1995.

As the home of Pan-Africanism, Ghana hosted the second Pan-African Historical and Theatre Festival (Panafest) from December 9 to 18, 1994. As with the first Panafest in Accra in 1992, the 1994 festival was designed to foster unity among Africans on the continent and abroad. Unfortunately, attendance at Panafest 94 was lower than expected, one reason the festival was a disappointment to its sponsors.

Finally, in early March 1995, Rawlings paid an official visit to Washington, where he met with President Bill Clinton. The two presidents discussed a variety of topics, including regional stability in West Africa and trade and investment in Ghana. Clinton noted Ghana's prominence in international peacekeeping missions, especially in Liberia, and pledged continued United States support for Ghanaian efforts at regional conflict resolution. Rawlings's visit was the first to the United States by a Ghanaian head of state in at least thirty years.

By mid-1995, Ghana had emerged at the forefront of change in sub-Saharan Africa. Its structural adjustment program was a model for other developing nations on the continent, and its pursuit of popular, representative government and democratic institutions made it a pacesetter in the political realm. Endowed with both human and natural resources and with a political leadership seemingly determined to reverse decades of economic and political decline, Ghana had the potential to become one of Africa's leading nations once again. Whether Ghana would resume its status as the "Star of Black Africa" envisioned by Kwame Nkrumah, however, remained to be seen.

August 1, 1995 LaVerle Berry

Chapter 1. Historical Setting

A pectoral of cast gold (Akan)

ACCORDING TO TRADITION, most present-day Ghanaians are descended not from the area's earliest inhabitants but from various migrant groups, the first of which probably came down the Volta River Basin in the early thirteenth century. By the sixteenth century, most ethnic groups constituting the population of Ghana (formerly the British colony of the Gold Coast) had settled in their present locations. Prior to British control in the nineteenth century, political developments in the area largely revolved around the formation, expansion, and contraction of a number of states—a situation that often entailed much population movement. Some people, however, lived in so-called segmentary societies and did not form states, particularly in northern Ghana.

Early states in Ghana made every effort to participate in or, if possible, to control, trade with Europeans, who first arrived on the coast in the late fifteenth century. These efforts in turn influenced state formation and development. Much more important to the evolution of these states, however, were their responses to pre-European patterns of trade. This was particularly true of commercial relations between the Akan states of southern Ghana and trading centers in the western Sudan. Competition among the traditional societies ultimately facilitated British efforts to gain control of what Europeans called the "Gold Coast." Traditional authorities, who with their elders had hitherto exercised autonomous control over their territories, became agents of the British colonial government under the policy of indirect rule.

As was the case in many sub-Saharan African countries, the rise of a national consciousness in Ghana developed largely in the twentieth century in response to colonial policies. The call to freedom came from a few elites, but it was only after World War II that the concept of independence captured the imagination of large numbers of people and gained popular support. Differences existed between the two leading political parties, however, on such issues as the timetable for independence and the powers to be vested in the modern state.

Ghana's first independent administration was inaugurated on March 6, 1957, with Kwame Nkrumah as prime minister. On July 1, 1960, Ghana was declared a republic, with Kwame Nkrumah as its president. Earlier, parliament had passed the Preventive Detention Act of 1958, which granted authority to the head of state to detain without trial those who were considered a threat to the nation. By means of such measures, Nkrumah and his party intimidated leading members of the opposition. Some opponents were co-opted; others were either exiled or jailed. As leader of Ghana at the time of the Cold War, Nkrumah forged alliances that increasingly placed him in the camp of the Eastern Bloc. Western governments understood Nkrumah's agenda to be socialist and worried about his influence on other African leaders. Some observers believed that Nkrumah's obsession with what he called the "total liberation of Africa" compelled him to create an authoritarian political system in Ghana. Critics of the regime accused Nkrumah of introducing patterns of oppression into Ghanaian politics and of tolerating widespread corruption among party leaders. The regime paid too much attention to urban problems at the expense of the more productive rural sector, they felt, and it embraced unrealistic economic and foreign assistance policies that led the nation to accrue huge foreign debts. The Nkrumah administration was overthrown by the military in February 1966. Many analysts maintain that the political instability and economic problems faced by the country since the mid-1960s are by-products of the Nkrumah era.

By 1981 Ghana had undergone seven major changes of government since the fall of Nkrumah. Each change was followed by alienation of the majority of the population and by military intervention, touted to end the rule that was responsible for the country's problems. Each time, the new government, civil or military, failed to stabilize the political and economic conditions of the country.

As its fourth decade of independence began in 1987, Ghana was under the administration of the Provisional National Defence Council, a military government led by Flight Lieutenant Jerry John Rawlings that had come to power in December 1981. Like the Nkrumah administration three decades earlier, the Provisional National Defence Council and Rawlings were criticized for their populism and desire for radical change. Despite the difficult early years of the Rawlings regime, Ghana's economy had begun to show signs of recovery by the late 1980s, and preparations were underway to return the country to some form of democratic government.

The Precolonial Period

By the end of the sixteenth century, most ethnic groups constituting the modern Ghanaian population had settled in their present locations. Archaeological remains found in the coastal zone indicate that the area has been inhabited since the early Bronze Age (ca. 4000 B.C.), but these societies, based on fishing in the extensive lagoons and rivers, left few traces. Archaeological work also suggests that central Ghana north of the forest zone was inhabited as early as 3,000 to 4,000 years ago. Oral history and other sources suggest that the ancestors of some of Ghana's residents entered this area at least as early as the tenth century A.D. and that migration from the north and east continued thereafter.

These migrations resulted in part from the formation and disintegration of a series of large states in the western Sudan (the region north of modern Ghana drained by the Niger River). Prominent among these Sudanic states was the Soninke kingdom of Ghana. Strictly speaking, *ghana* was the title of the king, but the Arabs, who left records of the kingdom, applied the term to the king, the capital, and the state. The ninth-century Arab writer, Al Yaqubi, described ancient Ghana as one of the three most organized states in the region (the others being Gao and Kanem in the central Sudan). Its rulers were renowned for their wealth in gold, the opulence of their courts, and their warrior-hunting skills. They were also masters of the trade in gold, which drew North African merchants to the western Sudan. The military achievements of these and later western Sudanic rulers and their control over the region's gold mines constituted the nexus of their historical relations with merchants and rulers of North Africa and the Mediterranean.

Ghana succumbed to attacks by its neighbors in the eleventh century, but its name and reputation endured. In 1957 when the leaders of the former British colony of the Gold Coast sought an appropriate name for their newly independent state—the first black African nation to gain its independence from colonial rule—they named their new country after ancient Ghana. The choice was more than merely symbolic because modern Ghana, like its namesake, was equally famed for its wealth and trade in gold.

Although none of the states of the western Sudan controlled territories in the area that is modern Ghana, several small kingdoms that later developed in the north of the country were ruled by nobles believed to have immigrated from that region. The trans-Saharan trade that contributed to the expansion of kingdoms in the western Sudan also led to the development of contacts with regions in northern modern Ghana and in the forest to the south. By the thirteenth century, for example, the town of Jenné in the empire of Mali had established commercial connections with the ethnic groups in the savanna-woodland areas of the northern two-thirds of the Volta Basin in modern Ghana. Jenné was also the headquarters of the Dyula, Muslim traders who dealt with the ancestors of the Akan-speaking peoples who occupy most of the southern half of the country.

The growth of trade stimulated the development of early Akan states located on the trade route to the goldfields in the forest zone of the south. The forest itself was thinly populated, but Akan-speaking peoples began to move into it toward the end of the fifteenth century with the arrival of crops from Southeast Asia and the New World that could be adapted to forest conditions. These new crops included sorghum, bananas, and cassava. By the beginning of the sixteenth century, European sources noted the existence of the gold-rich states of Akan and Twifu in the Ofin River Valley.

Also in the same period, some of the Mande, who had stimulated the development of states in what is now northern Nigeria (the Hausa states and those of the Lake Chad area), moved southwestward and imposed themselves on many of the indigenous peoples of the northern half of modern Ghana and of Burkina Faso (Burkina—formerly Upper Volta), founding the states of Dagomba and Mamprusi. The Mande also influenced the rise of the Gonja state.

It seems clear from oral traditions as well as from archaeological evidence that the Mole-Dagbane states of Mamprusi, Dagomba, and Gonja, as well as the Mossi states of Yatenga and Wagadugu, were among the earliest kingdoms to emerge in modern Ghana, being well established by the close of the sixteenth century. The Mossi and Gonja rulers came to speak the languages of the peoples they dominated. In general, however, members of the ruling class retained their traditions, and even today some of them can recite accounts of their northern origins.

Although most rulers were not Muslims, they either brought with them or welcomed Muslims as scribes and medicine men, and Muslims also played a significant role in the trade that linked southern with northern Ghana. As a result of their presence, Islam substantially influenced the north. Muslim influence, spread by the activities of merchants and clerics, has been recorded even among the Asante (also seen as Ashanti—see Glossary) to the south. Although most Ghanaians retained their traditional beliefs, the Muslims brought with them certain skills, including writing, and introduced certain beliefs and practices that became part of the culture of the peoples among whom they settled (see Christianity and Islam in Ghana, ch. 2).

In the broad belt of rugged country between the northern boundaries of the Muslim-influenced states of Gonja, Mamprusi, and Dagomba and the southernmost outposts of the Mossi kingdoms lived a number of peoples who were not incorporated into these entities. Among these peoples were the Sisala, Kasena, Kusase, and Talensi, agriculturalists closely related to the Mossi. Rather than establishing centralized states themselves, they lived in so-called segmented societies, bound together by kinship ties and ruled by the heads of their clans. Trade between the Akan states to the south and the Mossi kingdoms to the north flowed through their homelands, subjecting them to Islamic influence and to the depredations of these more powerful neighbors.

Of the components that would later make up Ghana, the state of Asante was to have the most cohesive history and would exercise the greatest influence. The Asante are members of the Twi-speaking branch of the Akan people. The groups that came to constitute the core of the Asante confederacy moved north to settle in the vicinity of Lake Bosumtwi. Before the mid-seventeenth century, the Asante began an expansion under a series of militant leaders that led to the domination of surrounding peoples and to the formation of the most powerful of the states of the central forest zone.

Under Chief Oti Akenten (r. ca. 1630–60), a series of successful military operations against neighboring Akan states brought a larger surrounding territory into alliance with Asante. At the end of the seventeenth century, Osei Tutu (d. 1712 or 1717) became *asantehene* (king of Asante). Under Osei Tutu's rule, the confederacy of Asante states was transformed into an empire with its capital at Kumasi. Political and military consolidation ensued, resulting in firmly established centralized authority. Osei Tutu was strongly influenced by the high priest, Anokye, who, tradition asserts, caused a stool of gold to descend from the sky to seal the union of Asante states. Stools already functioned as traditional symbols of chieftainship, but the Golden Stool of Asante represented the united spirit of all the allied states and established a dual allegiance that superimposed the confederacy over the individual component states. The Golden Stool remains a respected national symbol of the traditional past and figures extensively in Asante ritual.

Osei Tutu permitted newly conquered territories that joined the confederation to retain their own customs and chiefs, who were given seats on the Asante state council. Osei Tutu's gesture made the process relatively easy and nondisruptive because most of the earlier conquests had subjugated other Akan peoples. Within the Asante portions of the confederacy, each minor state continued to exercise internal self-rule, and its chief jealously guarded the state's prerogatives against encroachment by the central authority. A strong unity developed, however, as the various communities subordinated their individual interests to central authority in matters of national concern.

By the mid-eighteenth century, Asante was a highly organized state. The wars of expansion that brought the northern states of Mamprusi, Dagomba, and Gonja under Asante influence were won during the reign of Asantehene Opoku Ware I (d. 1750), successor to Osei Tutu. By the 1820s, successive rulers had extended Asante boundaries southward. Although the northern expansions linked Asante with trade networks across the desert and in Hausaland to the east, movements into the south brought the Asante into contact, sometimes antagonistic, with the coastal Fante, Ga-Adangbe, and Ewe peoples, as well as with the various European merchants whose fortresses dotted the Gold Coast (see fig. 2).

Arrival of the Europeans

Early European Contact and the Slave Trade

When the first Europeans arrived in the late fifteenth century, many inhabitants of the Gold Coast area were striving to consolidate their newly acquired territories and to settle into a secure and permanent environment. Several African immigrant groups had yet to establish firm ascendancy over earlier occupants of their territories, and considerable displacement and secondary migrations were in progress. Ivor Wilks, a leading historian of Ghana, has observed that Akan purchases of slaves from Portuguese traders operating from the Congo region augmented the labor needed for the state formation that was characteristic of this period. Unlike the Akan groups of the interior, the major coastal groups, such as the Fante, Ewe, and Ga, were for the most part settled in their homelands.

The Portuguese were the first to arrive. By 1471, under the patronage of Prince Henry the Navigator, they had reached the area that was to become known as the Gold Coast. Europeans knew the area as the source of gold that reached Muslim North Africa by way of trade routes across the Sahara. The initial Portuguese interest in trading for gold, ivory, and pepper increased so much that in 1482 the Portuguese built their first permanent trading post on the western coast of present-day Ghana. This fortress, Elmina Castle, constructed to protect Portuguese trade from European competitors and hostile Africans, still stands.

With the opening of European plantations in the New World during the 1500s, which suddenly expanded the demand for slaves in the Americas, slaves soon overshadowed gold as the principal export of the area. Indeed, the west coast of Africa became the principal source of slaves for the New World. The seemingly insatiable market and the substantial profits to be gained from the slave trade attracted adventurers from all over Europe. Much of the conflict that arose among European groups on the coast and among competing African kingdoms was the result of rivalry for control of this trade.

The Portuguese position on the Gold Coast remained secure for almost a century. During that time, Lisbon leased the right to establish trading posts to individuals or companies that sought to align themselves with the local chiefs and to exchange trade goods both for rights to conduct commerce and for slaves provided by the chiefs. During the seventeenth and eighteenth centuries, adventurers—first Dutch, and later English, Danish, and Swedish—were granted licenses by their governments to trade overseas. On the Gold Coast, these European competitors built fortified trading stations and challenged the Portuguese. Sometimes they were also drawn into conflicts with local inhabitants as Europeans developed commercial alliances with local chiefs.

The principal early struggle was between the Dutch and the Portuguese. With the loss of Elmina in 1642 to the Dutch, the Portuguese left the Gold Coast permanently. The next 150 years saw kaleidoscopic change and uncertainty, marked by local conflicts and diplomatic maneuvers, during which various

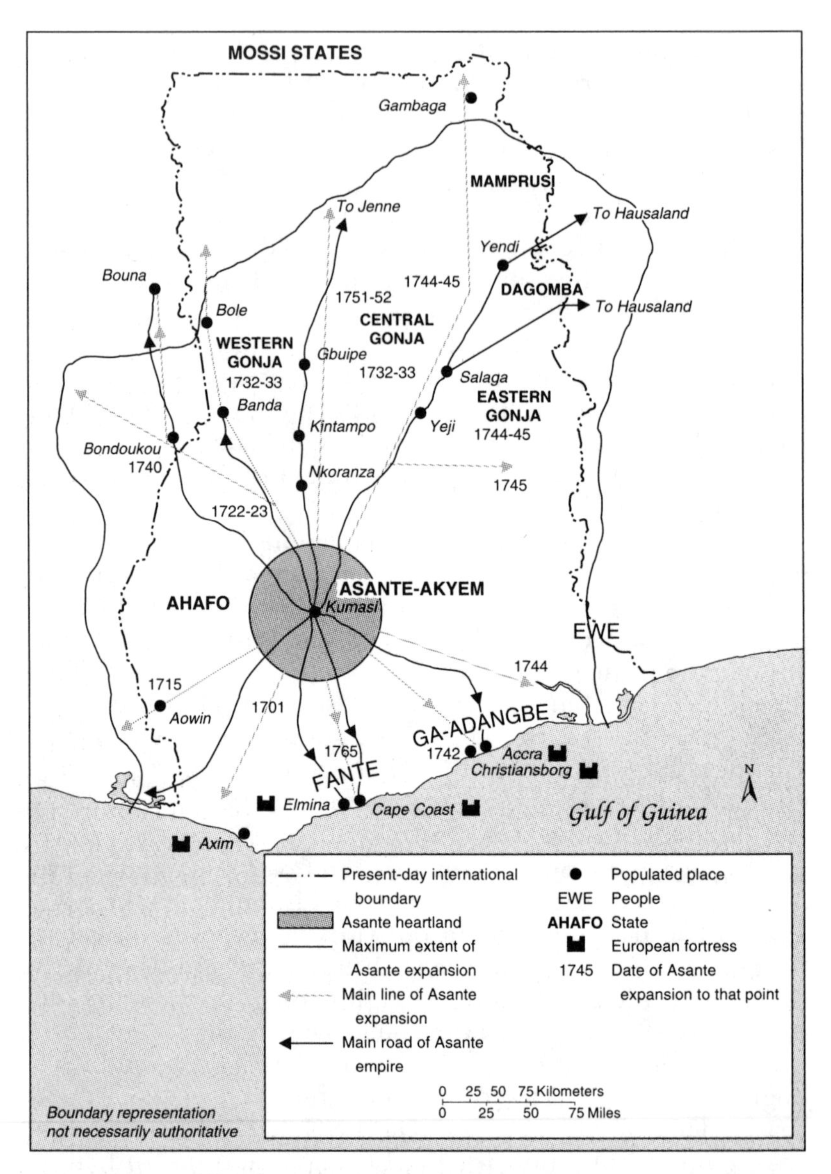

Source: Based on information from Daryll Forde and P. M. Kaberry, eds., *West African Kingdoms in the Nineteenth Century*, London, 1967, 208; and Ivor G. Wilks, *Asante in the Nineteenth Century*, London, 1975, 19.

Figure 2. Asante Expansion and Major European Fortresses in the Eighteenth Century

European powers struggled to establish or to maintain a position of dominance in the profitable trade of the Gold Coast littoral. Forts were built, abandoned, attacked, captured, sold, and exchanged, and many sites were selected at one time or another for fortified positions by contending European nations.

Both the Dutch and the British formed companies to advance their African ventures and to protect their coastal establishments. The Dutch West India Company operated throughout most of the eighteenth century. The British African Company of Merchants, founded in 1750, was the successor to several earlier organizations of this type. These enterprises built and manned new installations as the companies pursued their trading activities and defended their respective jurisdictions with varying degrees of government backing. There were short-lived ventures by the Swedes and the Prussians. The Danes remained until 1850, when they withdrew from the Gold Coast. The British gained possession of all Dutch coastal forts by the last quarter of the nineteenth century, thus making them the dominant European power on the Gold Coast.

During the heyday of early European competition, slavery was an accepted social institution, and the slave trade overshadowed all other commercial activities on the West African coast. To be sure, slavery and slave trading were already firmly entrenched in many African societies before their contact with Europe. In most situations, men as well as women captured in local warfare became slaves. In general, however, slaves in African communities were often treated as junior members of the society with specific rights, and many were ultimately absorbed into their masters' families as full members. Given traditional methods of agricultural production in Africa, slavery there was quite different from that which existed in the commercial plantation environments of the New World.

Another aspect of the impact of the trans-Atlantic slave trade on Africa concerns the role of African chiefs, Muslim traders, and merchant princes in the trade. Although there is no doubt that local rulers in West Africa engaged in slaving and received certain advantages from it, some scholars have challenged the premise that traditional chiefs in the vicinity of the Gold Coast engaged in wars of expansion for the sole purpose of acquiring slaves for the export market. In the case of Asante, for example, rulers of that kingdom are known to have supplied slaves to both Muslim traders in the north and to Europeans on the coast. Even so, the Asante waged war for purposes other than simply to secure slaves. They also fought to pacify territories that in theory were under Asante control, to exact tribute payments from subordinate kingdoms, and to secure access to trade routes—particularly those that connected the interior with the coast.

It is important to mention, however, that the supply of slaves to the Gold Coast was entirely in African hands. Although powerful traditional chiefs, such as the rulers of Asante, Fante, and Ahanta, were known to have engaged in the slave trade, individual African merchants such as John Kabes, John Konny, Thomas Ewusi, and a broker known only as Noi commanded large bands of armed men, many of them slaves, and engaged in various forms of commercial activities with the Europeans on the coast.

The volume of the slave trade in West Africa grew rapidly from its inception around 1500 to its peak in the eighteenth century. Philip Curtin, a leading authority on the African slave trade, estimates that roughly 6.3 million slaves were shipped from West Africa to North America and South America, about 4.5 million of that number between 1701 and 1810. Perhaps 5,000 a year were shipped from the Gold Coast alone. The demographic impact of the slave trade on West Africa was probably substantially greater than the number actually enslaved because a significant number of Africans perished during slaving raids or while in captivity awaiting transshipment. All nations with an interest in West Africa participated in the slave trade. Relations between the Europeans and the local populations were often strained, and distrust led to frequent clashes. Disease caused high losses among the Europeans engaged in the slave trade, but the profits realized from the trade continued to attract them.

The growth of anti-slavery sentiment among Europeans made slow progress against vested African and European interests that were reaping profits from the traffic. Although individual clergymen condemned the slave trade as early as the seventeenth century, major Christian denominations did little to further early efforts at abolition. The Quakers, however, publicly declared themselves against slavery as early as 1727. Later in the century, the Danes stopped trading in slaves; Sweden and the Netherlands soon followed.

The importation of slaves into the United States was outlawed in 1807. In the same year, Britain used its naval power and its diplomatic muscle to outlaw trade in slaves by its citizens and to begin a campaign to stop the international trade in slaves. These efforts, however, were not successful until the 1860s because of the continued demand for plantation labor in the New World.

Because it took decades to end the trade in slaves, some historians doubt that the humanitarian impulse inspired the abolitionist movement. According to historian Walter Rodney, for example, Europe abolished the trans-Atlantic slave trade only because its profitability was undermined by the Industrial Revolution. Rodney argues that mass unemployment caused by the new industrial machinery, the need for new raw materials, and European competition for markets for finished goods are the real factors that brought an end to the trade in human cargo and the beginning of competition for colonial territories in Africa. Other scholars, however, disagree with Rodney, arguing that humanitarian concerns as well as social and economic factors were instrumental in ending the African slave trade.

Britain and the Gold Coast: The Early Years

By the early nineteenth century, the British, through conquest or purchase, had become masters of most of the forts along the coast. Two major factors laid the foundations of British rule and the eventual establishment of a colony on the Gold Coast: British reaction to the Asante wars and the resulting instability and disruption of trade, and Britain's increasing preoccupation with the suppression and elimination of the slave trade.

During most of the nineteenth century, Asante, the most powerful state of the Akan interior, sought to expand its rule and to promote and protect its trade. The first Asante invasion of the coastal regions took place in 1807; the Asante moved south again in 1811 and in 1814. These invasions, though not decisive, disrupted trade in such products as gold, timber, and palm oil, and threatened the security of the European forts. Local British, Dutch, and Danish authorities were all forced to come to terms with Asante, and in 1817 the African Company of Merchants signed a treaty of friendship that recognized Asante claims to sovereignty over large areas of the coast and its peoples.

The coastal people, primarily some of the Fante and the inhabitants of the new town of Accra, who were chiefly Ga, came to rely on British protection against Asante incursions, but the ability of the merchant companies to provide this security was limited. The British Crown dissolved the company in

1821, giving authority over British forts on the Gold Coast to Governor Charles MacCarthy, governor of Sierra Leone. The British forts and Sierra Leone remained under common administration for the first half of the century. MacCarthy's mandate was to impose peace and to end the slave trade. He sought to do this by encouraging the coastal peoples to oppose Kumasi rule and by closing the great roads to the coast. Incidents and sporadic warfare continued, however. MacCarthy was killed, and most of his force was wiped out in a battle with Asante forces in 1824. An Asante invasion of the coast in 1826 was defeated, nonetheless, by British and local forces, including the Fante and the people of Accra.

When the British government allowed control of the Gold Coast settlements to revert to the British African Company of Merchants in the late 1820s, relations with Asante were still problematic. From the Asante point of view, the British had failed to control the activities of their local coastal allies. Had this been done, Asante might not have found it necessary to attempt to impose peace on the coastal peoples. MacCarthy's encouragement of coastal opposition to Asante and the subsequent 1824 British military attack further indicated to Asante authorities that the Europeans, especially the British, did not respect Asante.

In 1830 a London committee of merchants chose Captain George Maclean to become president of a local council of merchants. Although his formal jurisdiction was limited, Maclean's achievements were substantial; for example, a peace treaty was arranged with Asante in 1831. Maclean also supervised the coastal people by holding regular court in Cape Coast, where he punished those found guilty of disturbing the peace. Between 1830 and 1843, while Maclean was in charge of affairs on the Gold Coast, no confrontations occurred with Asante, and the volume of trade reportedly increased threefold. Maclean's exercise of limited judicial power on the coast was so effective that a parliamentary committee recommended that the British government permanently administer its settlements and negotiate treaties with the coastal chiefs that would define Britain's relations with them. The government did so in 1843, the same year crown government was reinstated. Commander H. Worsley Hill was appointed first governor of the Gold Coast. Under Maclean's administration, several coastal tribes had submitted voluntarily to British protection. Hill proceeded to define the conditions and responsibilities of his jurisdiction over the protected areas. He negotiated a special treaty with a number of Fante and other local chiefs that became known as the Bond of 1844. This document obliged local leaders to submit serious crimes, such as murder and robbery, to British jurisdiction and laid the legal foundation for subsequent British colonization of the coastal area.

Additional coastal states as well as other states farther inland eventually signed the Bond, and British influence was accepted, strengthened, and expanded. Under the terms of the 1844 arrangement, the British gave the impression that they would protect the coastal areas; thus, an informal protectorate came into being. As responsibilities for defending local allies and managing the affairs of the coastal protectorate increased, the administration of the Gold Coast was separated from that of Sierra Leone in 1850.

At about the same time, growing acceptance of the advantages offered by the British presence led to the initiation of another important step. In April 1852, local chiefs and elders met at Cape Coast to consult with the governor on means of raising revenue. With the governor's approval, the council of chiefs constituted itself as a legislative assembly. In approving its resolutions, the governor indicated that the assembly of chiefs should become a permanent fixture of the protectorate's constitutional machinery, but the assembly was given no specific constitutional authority to pass laws or to levy taxes without the consent of the people.

In 1872 British influence over the Gold Coast increased further when Britain purchased Elmina Castle, the last of the Dutch forts along the coast. The Asante, who for years had considered the Dutch at Elmina as their allies, thereby lost their last trade outlet to the sea. To prevent this loss and to ensure that revenue received from that post continued, the Asante staged their last invasion of the coast in 1873. After early successes, they finally came up against well-trained British forces who compelled them to retreat beyond the Pra River. Later attempts to negotiate a settlement of the conflict with the British were rejected by the commander of their forces, Major General Sir Garnet Wolseley. To settle the Asante problem permanently, the British invaded Asante with a sizable military force. The attack, which was launched in January 1874 by 2,500 British soldiers and large numbers of African auxiliaries, resulted in the occupation and burning of Kumasi, the Asante capital.

The subsequent peace treaty required the Asante to renounce any claim to many southern territories. The Asante also had to keep the road to Kumasi open to trade. From this point on, Asante power steadily declined. The confederation slowly disintegrated as subject territories broke away and as protected regions defected to British rule. The warrior spirit of the nation was not entirely subdued, however, and enforcement of the treaty led to recurring difficulties and outbreaks of fighting. In 1896 the British dispatched another expedition that again occupied Kumasi and that forced Asante to become a protectorate of the British Crown. The position of *asantehene* was abolished, and the incumbent was exiled.

The core of the Asante federation accepted these terms grudgingly. In 1900 the Asante rebelled again but were defeated the next year, and in 1902 the British proclaimed Asante a colony under the jurisdiction of the governor of the Gold Coast. The annexation was made with misgivings and recriminations on both sides. With Asante subdued and annexed, British colonization of the region became a reality.

The Colonial Era: British Rule of the Gold Coast

Military confrontations between Asante and the Fante contributed to the growth of British influence on the Gold Coast. It was concern about Asante activities on the coast that had compelled the Fante states to sign the Bond of 1844. In theory, the bond allowed the British quite limited judicial powers—the trying of murder and robbery cases only. Also, the British could not acquire further judicial rights without the consent of the kings, chiefs, and people of the protectorate. In practice, however, British efforts to usurp more and more judicial authority were so successful that in the 1850s they considered establishing European courts in place of traditional African ones.

As a result of the exercise of ever-expanding judicial powers on the coast and also to ensure that the coastal peoples remained firmly under control, the British, following their defeat of Asante in 1874, proclaimed the former coastal protectorate a crown colony. The Gold Coast Colony, established on July 24, 1874, comprised the coastal areas and extended inland as far as the ill-defined borders of Asante.

The coastal peoples did not greet this move with enthusiasm. They were not consulted about this annexation, which arbitrarily set aside the Bond of 1844 and treated its signatories like conquered territories. The British, however, made no claim to any rights to the land, a circumstance that probably explains the absence of popular resistance. Shortly after declaring the coastal area a colony, the British moved the colonial capital from Cape Coast to the former Danish castle at Christiansborg in Accra.

The British sphere of influence was eventually extended to include Asante. Following the defeat of Asante in 1896, the British proclaimed a protectorate over the kingdom. Once the *asantehene* and his council had been exiled, the British appointed a resident commissioner to Asante, who was given both civil and criminal jurisdiction over the territories. Each Asante state was administered from Kumasi as a separate entity and was ultimately responsible to the governor of the Gold Coast. As noted above, Asante became a colony following its final defeat in 1901.

In the meantime, the British became interested in the broad areas north of Asante, known generally as the Northern Territories. This interest was prompted primarily by the need to forestall the French and the Germans, who had been making rapid advances in the surrounding areas. British officials had first penetrated the area in the 1880s, and after 1896 protection was extended to northern areas whose trade with the coast had been controlled by Asante. In 1898 and 1899, European colonial powers amicably demarcated the boundaries between the Northern Territories and the surrounding French and German colonies. The Northern Territories were proclaimed a British protectorate in 1902.

Like the Asante protectorate, the Northern Territories were placed under the authority of a resident commissioner who was responsible to the governor of the Gold Coast. The governor ruled both Asante and the Northern Territories by proclamations until 1946.

With the north under British control, the three territories of the Gold Coast—the Colony (the coastal regions), Asante, and the Northern Territories—became, for all practical purposes, a single political unit, or crown colony, known as "the dependency" or simply as the Gold Coast. The borders of present-day Ghana were realized in May 1956 when the people of the Volta region, known as British Mandated Togoland, voted in a plebiscite to become part of modern Ghana (see fig. 3).

Colonial Administration

Beginning in 1850, the coastal regions increasingly came

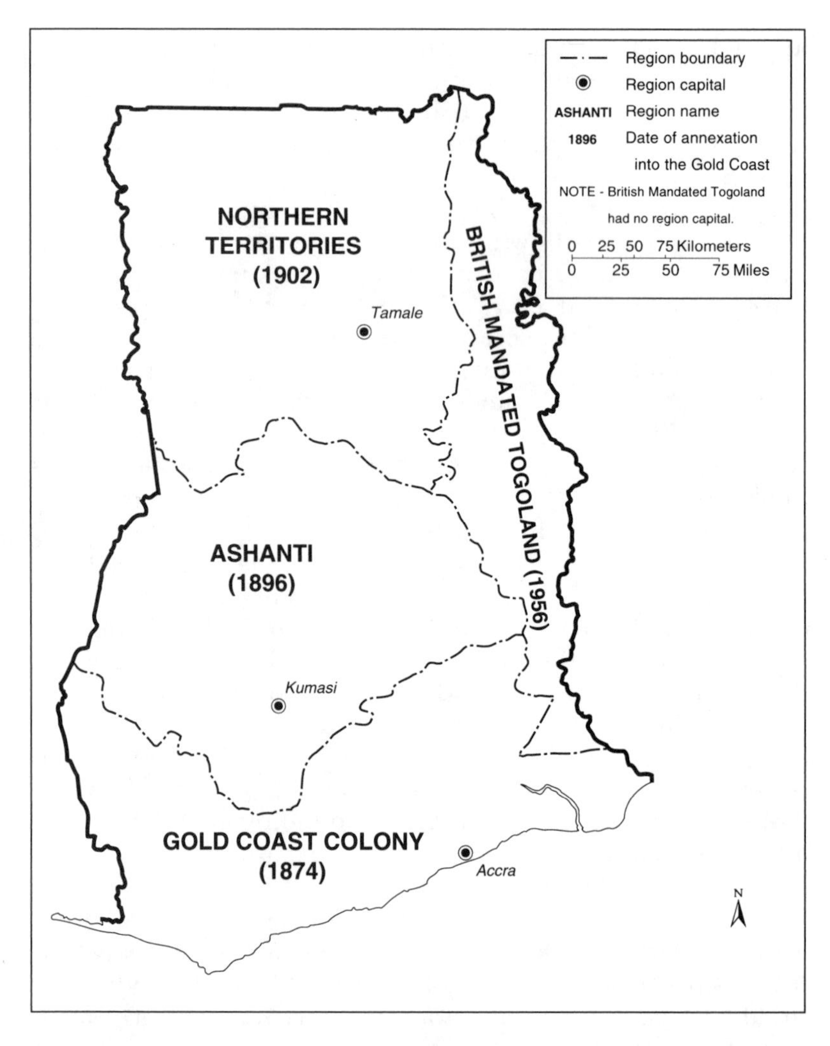

Source: Based on information from William Ernest Ward, *A History of Ghana*, London, 1958, 24.

Figure 3. Administrative Divisions of the Gold Coast, mid-1950s

under control of the governor of the British fortresses, who was assisted by the Executive Council and the Legislative Council. The Executive Council was a small advisory body of European officials that recommended laws and voted taxes, subject to the governor's approval. The Legislative Council included the members of the Executive Council and unofficial members initially chosen from British commercial interests. After 1900 three chiefs and three other Africans were added to the Legislative Council, these being chosen from the Europeanized communities of Accra, Cape Coast, and Sekondi. The inclusion of Africans from Asante and the Northern Territories did not take place until much later. Prior to 1925, all members of the Legislative Council were appointed by the governor. Official members always outnumbered unofficial members.

The gradual emergence of centralized colonial government brought about unified control over local services, although the actual administration of these services was still delegated to local authorities. Specific duties and responsibilities came to be clearly delineated, and the role of traditional states in local administration was also clarified.

The structure of local government had its roots in traditional patterns of government. Village councils of chiefs and elders were almost exclusively responsible for the immediate needs of individual localities, including traditional law and order and the general welfare. The councils, however, ruled by consent rather than by right. Chiefs were chosen by the ruling class of the society; a traditional leader continued to rule not only because he was the choice of what may be termed the nobility, but also because he was accepted by his people. The unseating or destooling of a chief by tribal elders was a fairly common practice if the chief failed to meet the desires or expectations of the community (see Traditional Patterns of Social Relations, ch. 2).

Traditional chiefs figured prominently in the system of indirect rule adopted by British authorities to administer their colonies in Africa. According to Frederick Lugard, architect of the policy, indirect rule was cost effective because it reduced the number of European officials in the field. By allowing local rulers to exercise direct administrative control over their people, opposition to European rule from the local population would be minimized. The chiefs, however, were to take instructions from their European supervisors. The plan, according to Lugard, had the further advantage of civilizing the natives because it exposed traditional rulers to the benefits of European political organization and values. This "civilizing" process notwithstanding, indirect rule had the ultimate advantage of guaranteeing the maintenance of law and order.

The application of indirect rule in the Gold Coast became essential, especially after Asante and the Northern Territories were brought under British rule. Before the effective colonization of these territories, the intention of the British was to use both force and agreements to control chiefs in Asante and the north. Once indirect rule was implemented, the chiefs became responsible to the colonial authorities who supported them. In many respects, therefore, the power of each chief was greatly enhanced. Although Lugard pointed to the civilizing influence of indirect rule, critics of the policy argued that the element of popular participation was removed from the traditional political system. Despite the theoretical argument in favor of decentralization, indirect rule in practice caused chiefs to look to Accra (the capital) rather than to their people for all decisions.

Many chiefs and elders came to regard themselves as a ruling aristocracy. Their councils were generally led by government commissioners, who often rewarded the chiefs with honors, decorations, and knighthood. Indirect rule tended to preserve traditional forms and sources of power, however, and it failed to provide meaningful opportunities for the growing number of educated young men anxious to find a niche in their country's development. Other groups were dissatisfied because there was not sufficient cooperation between the councils and the central government and because some felt that the local authorities were too dominated by the British district commissioners.

In 1925 provincial councils of chiefs were established in all three territories of the colony, partly to give the chiefs a colony-wide function. This move was followed in 1927 by the promulgation of the Native Administration Ordinance, which replaced an 1883 arrangement that had placed chiefs in the Gold Coast Colony under British supervision. The purpose was to clarify and to regulate the powers and areas of jurisdiction of chiefs and councils. Councils were given specific responsibilities over disputed elections and the unseating of chiefs; the procedure for the election of chiefs was set forth; and judicial powers were defined and delegated. Councils were entrusted with the role of defining customary law in their areas (the government had to approve their decisions), and the provincial councils were empowered to become tribunals to decide matters of customary law when the dispute lay between chiefs in different hierarchies. Until 1939, when the Native Treasuries Ordinance was passed, however, there was no provision for local budgets. In 1935 the Native Authorities Ordinance combined the central colonial government and the local authorities into a single governing system. New native authorities, appointed by the governor, were given wide powers of local government under the supervision of the central government's provincial commissioners, who assured that their policies would be those of the central government.

The provincial councils and moves to strengthen them were not popular. Even by British standards, the chiefs were not given enough power to be effective instruments of indirect rule. Some Ghanaians believed that the reforms, by increasing the power of the chiefs at the expense of local initiative, permitted the colonial government to avoid movement toward any form of popular participation in the colony's government.

Economic and Social Development

The years of British administration of the Gold Coast during the twentieth century were an era of significant progress in social, economic, and educational development. Transportation, for example, was greatly improved. The Sekondi-Tarkwa railroad, begun in 1898, was extended until it connected most of the important commercial centers of the south, and by 1937, there were 9,700 kilometers of roads. Telecommunication and postal services were initiated as well.

New crops were also introduced and gained widespread acceptance. Cacao trees, introduced in 1878, brought the first cash crop to the farmers of the interior; cocoa became the mainstay of the nation's economy in the 1920s when disease wiped out Brazil's trees. The production of cocoa was largely in the hands of Africans. The Cocoa Marketing Board was created in 1947 to assist farmers and to stabilize the production and sale of their crop. By the end of that decade, the Gold Coast was supplying more than half of the world's cocoa.

The colony's earnings increased further from the export of timber and gold. Gold, which initially brought Europeans to the Gold Coast, remained in the hands of Africans until the 1890s. Traditional techniques of panning and shaft mining, however, yielded only limited output. The development of modern modes of extracting minerals made gold mining an exclusively foreign-run enterprise. For example, Ashanti Goldfields Corporation, which was organized in 1897, gained a concession of about 160 square kilometers in which to prospect commercially for gold. Although certain tribal authorities profited greatly from the granting of mining concessions, it was the European mining companies and the colonial government that accumulated much of the wealth. Revenue from export of the colony's natural resources financed internal improvements in infrastructure and social services. The foundation of an educational system more advanced than any other in West Africa also resulted from mineral export revenue.

Many of the economic and social improvements in the Gold Coast in the early part of the twentieth century have been attributed to Frederick Gordon Guggisberg, governor from 1919 to 1927. Born in Toronto, Canada, Guggisberg joined the British army in 1889. During the first decade of the twentieth century, he worked as a surveyor in the British colonies of the Gold Coast and Nigeria, and later, during World War I, he served in France.

At the beginning of his governorship of the Gold Coast, Guggisberg presented a ten-year development program to the Legislative Council. He suggested first the improvement of transportation. Then, in order of priority, his prescribed improvements included water supply, drainage, hydroelectric projects, public buildings, town improvements, schools, hospitals, prisons, communication lines, and other services. Guggisberg also set a goal of filling half of the colony's technical positions with Africans as soon as they could be trained. His program has been described as the most ambitious ever proposed in West Africa up to that time. Another of the governor's programs led to the development of an artificial harbor at Takoradi, which then became Ghana's first port. Achimota College, which developed into one of the nation's finest secondary schools, was also a Guggisberg idea.

During the colonial years, the country's educational institutions improved markedly. From beginnings in missionary schools, the early part of the twentieth century saw significant advances in many fields, and, although the missions continued to participate, the government steadily increased its interest and support. In 1909 the government established a technical school and a teachers' training college at Accra; several other secondary schools were set up by the missions. The government steadily increased its financial backing for the growing number of both state and mission schools. In 1948 the country opened its first center of higher learning, the University College. It was through British-style education that a new Ghanaian elite gained the means and the desire to strive for independence.

The colony assisted Britain in both World War I and World War II. From 1914 to 1918, the Gold Coast Regiment served with distinction in battles against German forces in Cameroon

Asantehene Otumfuo Nana Opoku Ware II sitting in state to receive homage from his subjects
Courtesy Embassy of Ghana, Washington
The paramount chief of Nakong, Kasena people, far northern Ghana
Courtesy life in general *(Brook, Rose, and Cooper Le Van)*

and in the long East Africa campaign. In World War II, troops from the Gold Coast emerged with even greater prestige after outstanding service in such places as Ethiopia and Burma. In the ensuing years, however, postwar problems of inflation and instability severely hampered readjustment for returning veterans, who were in the forefront of growing discontent and unrest. Their war service and veterans' associations had broadened their horizons, making it difficult for them to return to the humble and circumscribed positions set aside for Africans by the colonial authorities.

The Growth of Nationalism and the End of Colonial Rule

As the country developed economically, the focus of government power gradually shifted from the hands of the governor and his officials into those of Ghanaians. The changes resulted from the gradual development of a strong spirit of nationalism and were to result eventually in independence. The development of national consciousness accelerated quickly after World War II, when, in addition to ex-servicemen, a substantial group of urban African workers and traders emerged to lend mass support to the aspirations of a small educated minority. Once the movement had begun, events moved rapidly—not always fast enough to satisfy the nationalist leaders, but still at a pace that surprised not only the colonial government but also many of the more conservative Africans.

Early Manifestations of Nationalism

As early as the latter part of the nineteenth century, a growing number of educated Africans found an arbitrary political system that placed almost all power in the hands of the governor through his appointment of council members increasingly unacceptable. In the 1890s, some members of the educated coastal elite organized themselves into the Aborigines' Rights Protection Society to protest a land bill that threatened traditional land tenure. This protest helped lay the foundation for political action that would ultimately lead to independence. In 1920 one of the African members of the Legislative Council, Joseph E. Casely-Hayford, convened the National Congress of British West Africa, which sent a delegation to London to urge the Colonial Office to consider the principle of elected representation. The group, which claimed to speak for all British

West African colonies, represented the first expression of political solidarity between intellectuals and nationalists of the area. Even though the delegation was not received in London (on the grounds that it represented only the interests of a small group of urbanized Africans), its actions aroused considerable support among the African elite at home.

Notwithstanding their call for elected representation as opposed to a system whereby the governor appointed council members, these nationalists insisted that they were loyal to the British Crown and that they merely sought an extension of British political and social practices to Africans. Notable leaders included Africanus Horton, Jr., J.M. Sarbah, and S.R.B. Attah-Ahoma. Such men gave the nationalist movement a distinctly elitist flavor that was to last until the late 1940s.

The constitution of 1925, promulgated by Guggisberg, created provincial councils of paramount chiefs for all but the northern provinces of the colony. These councils in turn elected six chiefs as unofficial members of the Legislative Council. Although the new constitution appeared to recognize African sentiments, Guggisberg was concerned primarily with protecting British interests. For example, he provided Africans with a limited voice in the central government; yet, by limiting nominations to chiefs, he drove a wedge between chiefs and their educated subjects. The intellectuals believed that the chiefs, in return for British support, had allowed the provincial councils to fall completely under control of the government. By the mid-1930s, however, a gradual rapprochement between chiefs and intellectuals had begun.

Agitation for more adequate representation continued. Newspapers owned and managed by Africans played a major part in provoking this discontent—six were being published in the 1930s. As a result of the call for broader representation, two more unofficial African members were added to the Executive Council in 1943. Changes in the Legislative Council, however, had to await a different political climate in London, which came about only with the postwar election of a British Labour Party government.

The new Gold Coast constitution of 1946 (also known as the Burns constitution after the governor of the time) was a bold document. For the first time, the concept of an official majority was abandoned. The Legislative Council was now composed of six ex-officio members, six nominated members, and eighteen elected members. The 1946 constitution also admitted representatives from Asante into the council for the first time. Even with a Labour Party government in power, however, the British continued to view the colonies as a source of raw materials that were needed to strengthen their crippled economy. Change that would place real power in African hands was not a priority among British leaders until after rioting and looting in Accra and other towns and cities in early 1948 over issues of pensions for ex-servicemen, the dominant role of foreigners in the economy, the shortage of housing, and other economic and political grievances.

With elected members in a decisive majority, Ghana had reached a level of political maturity unequaled anywhere in colonial Africa. The constitution did not, however, grant full self-government. Executive power remained in the hands of the governor, to whom the Legislative Council was responsible. Hence, the constitution, although greeted with enthusiasm as a significant milestone, soon encountered trouble. World War II had just ended, and many Gold Coast veterans who had served in British overseas expeditions returned to a country beset with shortages, inflation, unemployment, and black-market practices. These veterans, along with discontented urban elements, formed a nucleus of malcontents ripe for disruptive action. They were now joined by farmers, who resented drastic governmental measures that mandated the cutting down of diseased cacao trees in order to control an epidemic, and by many others who were unhappy that the end of the war had not been followed by economic improvements.

The Politics of the Independence Movements

Although political organizations had existed in the British colony, the United Gold Coast Convention (UGCC) was the first nationalist movement with the aim of self-government "in the shortest possible time." Founded in August 1947 by educated Africans such as J.B. Danquah, A.G. Grant, R.A. Awoonor-Williams, Edward Akufo Addo (all lawyers except for Grant, who was a wealthy businessman), and others, the leadership of the organization called for the replacement of chiefs on the Legislative Council with educated persons. For these political leaders, traditional governance, exercised largely via indirect rule, was identified with colonial interests and the past. They believed that it was their responsibility to lead their country into a new age. They also demanded that, given their education, the colonial administration should respect them and accord them positions of responsibility. As one writer on the period reported, "The symbols of progress, science, freedom, youth, all became cues which the new leadership evoked and reinforced." In particular, the UGCC leadership criticized the government for its failure to solve the problems of unemployment, inflation, and the disturbances that had come to characterize the society at the end of the war.

Their opposition to the colonial administration notwithstanding, UGCC members were conservative in the sense that their leadership did not seek drastic or revolutionary change. This was probably a result of their training in the British way of doing things. The gentlemanly manner in which politics were then conducted was to change after Kwame Nkrumah created his Convention People's Party (CPP) in June 1949.

Nkrumah was born at Nkroful in the Nzema area and educated in Catholic schools at Half Assini and Achimota. He received further training in the United States at Lincoln University and at the University of Pennsylvania. Later, in London, Nkrumah became active in the West African Students' Union and the Pan-African Congress. He was one of the few Africans who participated in the Manchester Congress of 1945 of the Pan-Africanist movement. During his time in Britain, Nkrumah came to know such outspoken anti-colonialists and intellectuals as the West Indian George Padmore and the African-American W.E.B. Du Bois. In 1947, when the UGCC was created in the Gold Coast to oppose colonial rule, Nkrumah was invited from London to become the movement's general secretary.

Nkrumah's tenure with the UGCC was a stormy one. In March 1948, he was arrested and detained with other leaders of the UGCC for political activism. Later, after the other members of the UGCC were invited to make recommendations to the Coussey Committee, which was advising the governor on the path to independence, Nkrumah broke with the UGCC and founded the CPP. Unlike the UGCC, which called for self-government "in the shortest possible time," Nkrumah and the CPP asked for "self-government now." The party leadership, made up of Nkrumah, Kojo Botsio, Komla A. Gbedemah, and a group of mostly young political professionals known as the "Verandah Boys," identified itself more with ordinary working people than with the UGCC and its intelligentsia.

Nkrumah's style and the promises he made appealed directly to the majority of workers, farmers, and youths who heard him; he seemed to be the national leader on whom they could focus their hopes. He also won the support of influential market women, who, through their domination of small-scale trade, served as effective channels of communication at the local level.

The majority of the politicized population, stirred in the postwar years by outspoken newspapers, was separated from both the tribal chiefs and the Anglophile elite nearly as much as from the British by economic, social, and educational factors. This majority consisted primarily of ex-servicemen, literate persons who had some primary schooling, journalists, and elementary school teachers, all of whom had developed a taste for populist conceptions of democracy. A growing number of uneducated but urbanized industrial workers also formed part of the support group. Nkrumah was able to appeal to them on their own terms. By June 1949, when the CPP was formed with the avowed purpose of seeking immediate self-governance, Nkrumah had a mass following.

The constitution of 1951 resulted from the report of the Coussey Committee, created because of disturbances in Accra and other cities in 1948. In addition to giving the Executive Council a large majority of African ministers, it created a Legislative Assembly, half the elected members of which were to come from the towns and rural districts and half from the traditional councils, including, for the first time, the Northern Territories. Although it was an enormous step forward, the new constitution still fell far short of the CPP's call for full self-government. Executive power remained in British hands, and the legislature was tailored to permit control by traditionalist interests.

With increasing popular backing, the CPP in early 1950 initiated a campaign of "positive action," intended to instigate widespread strikes and nonviolent resistance. When some violent disorders occurred, Nkrumah, along with his principal lieutenants, was promptly arrested and imprisoned for sedition. But this merely increased his prestige as leader and hero of the cause and gave him the status of martyr. In February 1951, the first elections were held for the Legislative Assembly under the new constitution. Nkrumah, still in jail, won a seat, and the CPP won an impressive victory with a two-thirds majority of the 104 seats.

The governor, Sir Charles Arden-Clarke, released Nkrumah and invited him to form a government as "leader of government business," a position similar to that of prime minister.

Nkrumah accepted. A major milestone had been passed on the road to independence and self-government. Nonetheless, although the CPP agreed to work within the new constitutional order, the structure of government that existed in 1951 was certainly not what the CPP preferred. The ministries of defense, external affairs, finance, and justice were still controlled by British officials who were not responsible to the legislature. Also, by providing for a sizable representation of traditional tribal chiefs in the Legislative Assembly, the constitution accentuated the cleavage between the modern political leaders and the traditional authorities of the councils of chiefs.

The start of Nkrumah's first term as "leader of government business" was marked by cordiality and cooperation with the British governor. During the next few years, the government was gradually transformed into a full parliamentary system. The changes were opposed by the more traditionalist African elements, particularly in Asante and the Northern Territories. This opposition, however, proved ineffective in the face of continuing and growing popular support for a single overriding concept—independence at an early date.

In 1952 the position of prime minister was created and the Executive Council became the cabinet. The prime minister was made responsible to the Legislative Assembly, which duly elected Nkrumah prime minister. The constitution of 1954 ended the election of assembly members by the tribal councils. The Legislative Assembly increased in size, and all members were chosen by direct election from equal, single-member constituencies. Only defense and foreign policy remained in the hands of the governor; the elected assembly was given control of virtually all internal affairs of the colony.

The CPP pursued a policy of political centralization, which encountered serious opposition. Shortly after the 1954 election, a new party, the Asante-based National Liberation Movement (NLM), was formed. The NLM advocated a federal form of government, with increased powers for the various regions. NLM leaders criticized the CPP for perceived dictatorial tendencies. The new party worked in cooperation with another regionalist group, the Northern People's Party. When these two regional parties walked out of discussions on a new constitution, the CPP feared that London might consider such disunity an indication that the colony was not yet ready for the next phase of self-government.

The British constitutional adviser, however, backed the CPP position. The governor dissolved the Legislative Assembly in order to test popular support for the CPP demand for immediate independence. The crown agreed to grant independence if so requested by a two-thirds majority of the new legislature. New elections were held in July 1956. In keenly contested elections, the CPP won 57 percent of the votes cast, but the fragmentation of the opposition gave the CPP every seat in the south as well as enough seats in Asante, the Northern Territories, and the Trans-Volta Region to hold a two-thirds majority of the 104 seats.

Prior to the July 1956 general elections in the Gold Coast, a plebiscite was conducted under United Nations (UN) auspices to decide the future disposition of British Togoland and French Togoland. The British trusteeship, the western portion of the former German colony, had been linked to the Gold Coast since 1919 and was represented in its parliament. The dominant ethnic group, the Ewe, were divided between the Gold Coast proper and the two Togos. A clear majority of British Togoland inhabitants voted in favor of union with their western neighbors, and the area was absorbed into the Gold Coast. There was, however, vocal opposition to the incorporation from some of the Ewe in southern British Togoland.

Independent Ghana

On August 3, 1956, the newly elected Legislative Assembly passed a motion authorizing the government to request independence within the British Commonwealth. The opposition did not attend the debate, and the vote was unanimous. The British government accepted this motion as clearly representing a reasonable majority. On March 6, 1957, the 113th anniversary of the Bond of 1844, the former British colony of the Gold Coast became the independent state of Ghana. The nation's Legislative Assembly became the National Assembly, and Nkrumah continued as prime minister. According to an independence constitution also drafted in 1957, Queen Elizabeth II was to be represented in the former colony by a governor general, and Sir Arden-Clarke was appointed to that position. This special relationship between the British Crown and Ghana would continue until 1960, when the position of governor general was abolished under terms of a new constitution that declared the nation a republic.

Ghana's monument to independence, Black Star Square, Accra
Courtesy James Sanders

The independence constitution of 1957 provided protection against easy amendment of a number of its clauses. It also granted a voice to chiefs and their tribal councils by providing for the creation of regional assemblies. No bill amending the entrenched clauses of the constitution or affecting the powers of the regional bodies or the privileges of the chiefs could become law except by a two-thirds vote of the National Assembly and by simple majority approval in two-thirds of the regional assemblies. When local CPP supporters gained control of enough regional assemblies, however, the Nkrumah government promptly secured passage of an act removing the special entrenchment protection clause in the constitution, a step that left the National Assembly with the power to effect any constitutional change the CPP deemed necessary.

Among the CPP's earliest acts was the outright abolition of regional assemblies. Another was the dilution of the clauses designed to ensure a nonpolitical and competitive civil service. This action allowed Nkrumah to appoint his followers to positions throughout the upper ranks of public employment. Thereafter, unfettered by constitutional restrictions and with an obedient party majority in the assembly, Nkrumah began his administration of the first independent African country south of the Sahara.

Nkrumah, Ghana, and Africa

Nkrumah has been described by author Peter Omari as a dictator who "made much of elections, when he was aware that they were not really free but rigged in his favor." According to Omari, the CPP administration of Ghana was one that manipulated the constitutional and electoral processes of democracy to justify Nkrumah's agenda. The extent to which the government would pursue that agenda constitutionally was demonstrated early in the administration's life when it succeeded in passing the Deportation Act of 1957, the same year that ethnic, religious, and regional parties were banned. The Deportation Act empowered the governor general and, therefore, subsequent heads of state, to expel persons whose presence in the country was deemed not in the interest of the public good. Although the act was to be applied only to non-Ghanaians, several people to whom it was later applied claimed to be citizens.

The Preventive Detention Act, passed in 1958, gave power to the prime minister to detain certain persons for up to five years without trial. Amended in 1959 and again in 1962, the act was seen by opponents of the CPP government as a flagrant restriction of individual freedom and human rights. Once it had been granted these legal powers, the CPP administration managed to silence its opponents. J.B. Danquah, a leading member of the UGCC, was detained until he died in prison in 1965. Kofi Abrefa Busia, leader of the opposition United Party (UP), formed by the NLM and other parties in response to Nkrumah's outlawing of so-called separatist parties in 1957, went into exile in London to escape detention, while other UP members still in the country joined the ruling party.

On July 1, 1960, Ghana became a republic, and Nkrumah won the presidential election that year. Shortly thereafter, Nkrumah was proclaimed president for life, and the CPP became the sole party of the state. Using the powers granted him by the party and the constitution, Nkrumah by 1961 had detained an estimated 400 to 2,000 of his opponents. Nkrumah's critics pointed to the rigid hold of the CPP over the nation's political system and to numerous cases of human rights abuses. Others, however, defended Nkrumah's agenda and policies.

Nkrumah discussed his political views in his numerous writings, especially in *Africa Must Unite* (1963) and in *Neo-Colonialism* (1965). These writings show the impact of his stay in Britain in the mid-1940s. The Pan-Africanist movement, which had held one of its annual conferences, attended by Nkrumah, at Manchester in 1945, was influenced by socialist ideologies. The movement sought unity among people of African descent and also improvement in the lives of workers, who, it was alleged, had been exploited by capitalist enterprises in Africa. Western countries with colonial histories were identified as the exploiters. According to the socialists, "oppressed" people ought to identify with the socialist countries and organizations that best represented their interests; however, all the dominant world powers in the immediate post-1945 period, except the Soviet Union and the United States, had colonial ties with Africa. Nkrumah asserted that even the United States, which had never colonized any part of Africa, was in an advantageous position to exploit independent Africa unless preventive efforts were taken.

According to Nkrumah, his government, which represented the first black African nation to win independence, had an important role to play in the struggle against capitalist interests on the continent. As he put it, "The independence of Ghana would be meaningless unless it was tied to the total liberation of Africa." It was important, then, he said, for Ghanaians to "seek first the political kingdom." Economic benefits associated with independence were to be enjoyed later, proponents of Nkrumah's position argued. But Nkrumah needed strategies to pursue his goals.

On the domestic front, Nkrumah believed that rapid modernization of industries and communications was necessary and that it could be achieved if the workforce were completely Africanized and educated. Even more important, however, Nkrumah believed that this domestic goal could be achieved faster if it were not hindered by reactionary politicians—elites in the opposition parties and traditional chiefs—who might compromise with Western imperialists. From such an ideological position, Nkrumah's supporters justified the Deportation Act of 1957; the Detention Acts of 1958, 1959, and 1962; parliamentary intimidation of CPP opponents; the appointment of Nkrumah as president for life; the recognition of his party as the sole political organization of the state; the creation of the Young Pioneer Movement for the ideological education of the nation's youth; and the party's control of the civil service. Government expenditures on road building projects, mass education of adults and children, and health services, as well as the construction of the Akosombo Dam, were all important if Ghana were to play its leading role in Africa's liberation from colonial and neo-colonial domination.

On the continental level, Nkrumah sought to unite Africa so it could defend its international economic interests and stand up against the political pressures from East and West that were a result of the Cold War. His dream for Africa was a continuation of the Pan-Africanist dream as expressed at the Manchester conference. The initial strategy was to encourage revolutionary political movements in Africa, beginning with a Ghana, Guinea, and Mali union, that would serve as the psychological and political impetus for the formation of a United States of Africa. Thus, when Nkrumah was criticized for paying little attention to Ghana or for wasting national resources in supporting external programs, he reversed the argument and accused his opponents of being short-sighted.

But the heavy financial burdens created by Nkrumah's development policies and Pan-Africanist adventures created new sources of opposition. With the presentation in July 1961 of the country's first austerity budget, Ghana's workers and farmers became aware of and critical of the cost to them of Nkrumah's programs. Their reaction set the model for the protests over taxes and benefits that were to dominate Ghanaian political crises for the next thirty years.

CPP backbenchers and UP representatives in the National Assembly sharply criticized the government's demand for increased taxes and, particularly, for a forced savings program. Urban workers began a protest strike, the most serious of a number of public outcries against government measures during 1961. Nkrumah's public demands for an end to corruption in the government and the party further undermined popular faith in the national government. A drop in the price paid to cocoa farmers by the government marketing board aroused resentment among a segment of the population that had always been Nkrumah's major opponent.

The Growth of Opposition to Nkrumah

Nkrumah's complete domination of political power had served to isolate lesser leaders, leaving each a real or imagined challenger to the ruler. After opposition parties were crushed, opponents came only from within the CPP hierarchy. Among its members was Tawia Adamafio, an Accra politician. Nkrumah had made him general secretary of the CPP for a brief time. Later, Adamafio was appointed minister of state for presidential affairs, the most important post in the president's staff at Flagstaff House, which gradually became the center for all decision making and much of the real administrative machinery for both the CPP and the government. The other leader with an apparently autonomous base was John Tettegah, leader of the Trade Union Congress. Neither, however, proved to have any power other than that granted to them by the president.

By 1961, however, the young and more radical members of the CPP leadership, led by Adamafio, had gained ascendancy over the original CPP leaders like Gbedemah. After a bomb attempt on Nkrumah's life in August 1962, Adamafio, Ako Adjei (then minister of foreign affairs), and Cofie Crabbe (all members of the CPP) were jailed under the Preventive Detention Act. The CPP newspapers charged them with complicity in the assassination attempt, offering as evidence only the fact that they had all chosen to ride in cars far behind the president's when the bomb was thrown.

For more than a year, the trial of the alleged plotters of the 1962 assassination attempt occupied center stage. The accused were brought to trial before the three-judge court for state security, headed by the chief justice, Sir Arku Korsah. When the court acquitted the accused, Nkrumah used his constitutional prerogative to dismiss Korsah. Nkrumah then obtained a vote from the parliament that allowed retrial of Adamafio and his associates. A new court, with a jury chosen by Nkrumah, found all the accused guilty and sentenced them to death. These sentences, however, were commuted to twenty years' imprisonment.

In early 1964, in order to prevent future challenges from the judiciary, Nkrumah obtained a constitutional amendment allowing him to dismiss any judge. At the same time, Ghana officially became a single-party state, and an act of parliament ensured that there would be only one candidate for president. Other parties having already been outlawed, no non-CPP candidates came forward to challenge the party slate in the general elections announced for June 1965. Nkrumah had been re-elected president of the country for less than a year when members of the National Liberation Council (NLC) overthrew the CPP government in a military coup on February 24, 1966. At the time, Nkrumah was in China. He took up asylum in Guinea, where he remained until he died in 1972.

The Fall of the Nkrumah Regime and Its Aftermath

Leaders of the 1966 military coup, including army officers Colonel E.K. Kotoka, Major A.A. Afrifa, Lieutenant General (retired) J.A. Ankra, and Police Inspector General J.W.K. Harlley, justified their takeover by charging that the CPP administration was abusive and corrupt. They were equally disturbed by Nkrumah's aggressive involvement in African politics and by his belief that Ghanaian troops could be sent anywhere in Africa to fight so-called liberation wars, even though they never did so. Above all, they pointed to the absence of democratic practices in the nation—a situation they claimed had affected the morale of the armed forces. According to Kotoka, the military coup of 1966 was a nationalist one because it liberated the nation from Nkrumah's dictatorship—a declaration that was supported by Alex Quaison-Sackey, Nkrumah's former minister of foreign affairs.

Despite the vast political changes brought about by the overthrow of Nkrumah, many problems remained. For example, the underlying ethnic and regional divisions within society had to be addressed. The apparent spirit of national unity that seemed to have developed during the Nkrumah years turned out to have resulted in part from his coercive powers as well as from his charisma. As a consequence, successive new leaders faced the problem of forging disparate personal, ethnic, and sectional interests into a real Ghanaian nation. The economic burdens, aggravated by what some described as past extravagance, would cripple each future government's ability to foster the rapid development needed to satisfy even minimal popular demands for a better life. The fear of a resurgence of an overly strong central authority would continue to dominate the constitutional agenda and to pervade the thinking of many educated, politically minded Ghanaians. Others, however, felt that a strong government was essential.

A considerable portion of the population had become convinced that effective, honest government was incompatible with competitive political parties. Many Ghanaians remained committed to nonpolitical leadership for the nation, even in the form of military rule. The problems of the Busia administration, the country's first elected government after Nkrumah's fall, illustrated the problems Ghana would continue to face.

The National Liberation Council and the Busia Years, 1966–71

The leaders of the coup that overthrew Nkrumah immediately opened the country's borders and its prison gates to allow the return from exile or release from preventive detention of all opponents of Nkrumah. The National Liberation Council (NLC), composed of four army officers and four police officers, assumed executive power. It appointed a cabinet of civil servants and promised to restore democratic government as quickly as possible. The ban on the formation of political parties remained in force until late 1968, but activity by individual figures began much earlier with the appointment of a succession of committees composed of civil servants and politicians as the first step in the return to civilian and representative rule.

These moves culminated in the appointment of a representative assembly to draft a constitution for the Second Republic of Ghana. Political party activity was allowed to commence with the opening of the assembly. By election time in August 1969, the first competitive nationwide political contest since 1956, five parties had been organized.

The major contenders were the Progress Party (PP), headed by Kofi A. Busia, and the National Alliance of Liberals (NAL), led by Komla A. Gbedemah. Critics associated these two leading parties with the political divisions of the early Nkrumah years. The PP found much of its support among the old opponents of Nkrumah's CPP—the educated middle class and traditionalists of Ashanti Region and the North. This link was strengthened by the fact that Busia had headed the NLM and its successor, the UP, before fleeing the country to oppose Nkrumah from exile. Similarly, the NAL was seen as the successor of the CPP's right wing, which Gbedemah had headed until he was ousted by Nkrumah in 1961.

The elections demonstrated an interesting voting pattern. For example, the PP carried all the seats among the Asante and the Brong. All seats in the northern regions of the country were closely contested. In the Volta Region, the PP won some Ewe seats, while the NAL won all seats in the non-Ewe northern section. Overall, the PP gained 59 percent of the popular vote and 74 percent of the seats in the National Assembly. The PP's victories demonstrated some support among nearly all ethnic groups. An estimated 60 percent of the electorate voted.

Immediately after the elections, Gbedemah was barred from taking his seat in the National Assembly by a Supreme Court decision involving those CPP members who had been accused of financial crimes. Gbedemah retired permanently from active participation in politics. The NAL, left without a strong leader, controlled thirty seats; in October 1970, it absorbed the members of three other minor parties in the assembly to form the Justice Party (JP) under the leadership of Joseph Appiah. The JP's combined strength constituted what amounted to a southern bloc with a solid constituency among most of the Ewe and the peoples of the coastal cities.

Busia, the PP leader in both parliament and the nation, became prime minister when the National Assembly met in September. An interim three-member presidential commission, composed of Major Afrifa, Police Inspector General Harlley of the NLC, and the chief of the defense staff, Major General A.K. Ocran, served in place of an elected president for the first year and a half of civilian rule. The commission dissolved itself in August 1970. Before stepping down, Afrifa criticized the constitution, particularly provisions that served more as a bar to the rise of a dictator than as a blueprint for an effective, decisive government. The electoral college chose as president Chief Justice Edward Akufo Addo, one of the leading nationalist politicians of the UGCC era and one of the judges dismissed by Nkrumah in 1964.

All attention, however, remained focused on Prime Minister Busia and his government. Much was expected of the Busia administration because its parliamentarians were considered intellectuals and, therefore, more perceptive in their evaluations of what needed to be done. Many Ghanaians hoped that their decisions would be in the general interest of the nation, as compared with those made by the Nkrumah administration, which were judged to satisfy narrow party interests and Nkrumah's personal agenda. The NLC had given assurances that there would be more democracy, more political maturity, and more freedom in Ghana because the politicians allowed to run in the 1969 elections were proponents of Western democracy. In fact, these were the same individuals who had suffered under the old regime and were, therefore, thought to understand the benefits of democracy.

Two early measures initiated by the Busia government were the expulsion of large numbers of noncitizens from the country and a companion measure to limit foreign involvement in small businesses. The moves were aimed at relieving the unemployment created by the country's precarious economic situation (see Historical Background, ch. 3). The policies were popular because they forced out of the retail sector of the economy those foreigners, especially Lebanese, Asians, and Nigerians, who were perceived as unfairly monopolizing trade to the disadvantage of Ghanaians. Many other Busia moves, however, were not popular. Busia's decision to introduce a loan program for university students, who had hitherto received free education, was challenged because it was interpreted as introducing a class system into the country's highest institutions of learning. Some observers even saw Busia's devaluation of the national currency and his encouragement of foreign investment in the industrial sector of the economy as conservative ideas that could undermine Ghana's sovereignty.

The opposition JP's basic policies did not differ significantly from those of the Busia administration. Still, the party attempted to stress the importance of the central government rather than that of limited private enterprise in economic development, and it continued to emphasize programs of primary interest to the urban work force. The ruling PP emphasized the need for development in rural areas, both to slow the movement of population to the cities and to redress regional imbalance in levels of development. The JP and a growing number of PP members favored suspension of payment on some foreign debts of the Nkrumah era. This attitude grew more popular as debt payments became more difficult to meet. Both parties favored the creation of a West African economic community or an economic union with neighboring West African states.

Despite broad popular support garnered at its inception and strong foreign connections, the Busia government fell victim to an army coup within twenty-seven months. Neither ethnic nor class differences played a role in the overthrow of the PP government. The crucial causes were the country's continuing economic difficulties, both those stemming from the high foreign debts incurred by Nkrumah and those resulting from internal problems. The PP government had inherited US$580 million in medium- and long-term debts, an amount equal to 25 percent of the gross domestic product (GDP—see Glossary) of 1969. By 1971 the US$580 million had been further inflated by US$72 million in accrued interest payments and US$296 million in short-term commercial credits. Within the country, an even larger internal debt fueled inflation.

Ghana's economy remained largely dependent upon the often difficult cultivation of and market for cocoa. Cocoa prices had always been volatile, but exports of this tropical crop normally provided about half of the country's foreign currency earnings. Beginning in the 1960s, however, a number of factors combined to limit severely this vital source of national income. These factors included foreign competition (particularly from neighboring Côte d'Ivoire), a lack of understanding of free-market forces (by the government in setting prices paid to farmers), accusations of bureaucratic incompetence in the Cocoa Marketing Board, and the smuggling of crops into Côte d'Ivoire. As a result, Ghana's income from cocoa exports continued to fall dramatically.

Austerity measures imposed by the Busia administration, although wise in the long run, alienated influential farmers, who until then had been PP supporters. These measures were part of Busia's economic structural adjustment efforts to put the country on a sounder financial base. The austerity programs had been recommended by the International Monetary Fund (IMF—see Glossary). The recovery measures also severely affected the middle class and the salaried work force, both of which faced wage freezes, tax increases, currency devaluations, and rising import prices. These measures precipitated protests from the Trade Union Congress. In response, the gov-

Kwame Nkrumah, prime minister and president, 1957–66
Courtesy Embassy of Ghana, Washington

Colonel Ignatius Kutu Acheampong, head of state and chairman of the National Redemption Council and Supreme Military Council, 1972–78
Courtesy Embassy of Ghana, Washington

ernment sent the army to occupy the trade union headquarters and to block strike actions—a situation that some perceived as negating the government's claim to be operating democratically.

The army troops and officers upon whom Busia relied for support were themselves affected, both in their personal lives and in the tightening of the defense budget, by these same austerity measures. As the leader of the anti-Busia coup declared on January 13, 1972, even those amenities enjoyed by the army during the Nkrumah regime were no longer available. Knowing that austerity had alienated the officers, the Busia government began to change the leadership of the army's combat elements. This, however, was the last straw. Lieutenant Colonel Ignatius Kutu Acheampong, temporarily commanding the First

Brigade around Accra, led a bloodless coup that ended the Second Republic.

The National Redemption Council Years, 1972–79

Despite its short existence, the Second Republic was significant in that the development problems the nation faced came clearly into focus. These included uneven distribution of investment funds and favoritism toward certain groups and regions. Furthermore, important questions about developmental priorities emerged. For example, was rural development more important than the needs of the urban population? Or, to what extent was the government to incur the cost of university education? And more important, was the public to be drawn into the debate about the nation's future? The impact of the fall of Ghana's Second Republic cast a shadow across the nation's political future because no clear answers to these problems emerged.

According to one writer, the overthrow of the PP government revealed that Ghana was no longer the pace-setter in Africa's search for workable political institutions. Both the radical left and the conservative right had failed. In opposing Nkrumah's one-party state, Busia allegedly argued that socialist rule in Ghana had led to unemployment and poverty for many while party officials grew richer at the expense of the masses. But in justifying the one-party state, Nkrumah pointed to the weaknesses of multiparty parliamentary democracy, a system that delayed decision-making processes and, therefore, the ability to take action to foster development. The fall of both the Nkrumah and the Busia regimes seemed to have confused many with regard to the political direction the nation needed to take. In other words, in the first few years after the Nkrumah administration, Ghanaians were unable to arrive at a consensus on the type of government suited to address their national problems.

It was this situation—the inability of the PP government to satisfy diverse interest groups—that ostensibly gave Acheampong an excuse for the January 13 takeover. Acheampong's National Redemption Council (NRC) claimed that it had to act to remove the ill effects of the currency devaluation of the previous government and thereby, at least in the short run, to improve living conditions for individual Ghanaians. Under the circumstances, the NRC was compelled to take immediate measures. Although committed to the reversal of the fiscal policies of the PP government, the NRC, by comparison, adopted policies that appeared painless and, therefore, popular. But unlike the coup leaders of the NLC, members of the NRC did not outline any plan for the return of the nation to democratic rule. Some observers accused the NRC of acting simply to rectify their own grievances.

To justify their takeover, coup leaders leveled charges of corruption against Busia and his ministers. In its first years, the NRC drew support from a public pleased by the reversal of Busia's austerity measures. The Ghanaian currency was revalued upward, and two moves were announced to lessen the burden of existing foreign debts: the repudiation of US$90 million of Nkrumah's debts to British companies, and the unilateral rescheduling of the rest of the country's debts for payment over fifty years. Later, the NRC nationalized all large foreign-owned companies. But these measures, while instantly popular in the streets, did nothing to solve the country's real problems. If anything, they aggravated the problem of capital flow.

Unlike the NLC of 1966, the NRC sought to create a truly military government; hence, in October 1975, the ruling council was reorganized into the Supreme Military Council (SMC), and its membership was restricted to a few senior military officers. The intent was to consolidate the military's hold over government administration and to address occasional disagreements, conflicts, and suspicions within the armed forces, which by now had emerged as the constituency of the military government. Little input from the civilian sector was allowed, and no offers were made to return any part of the government to civilian control during the SMC's first five years in power. SMC members believed that the country's problems were caused by a lack of organization, which could be remedied by applying military organization and thinking. This was the extent of the SMC philosophy. Officers were put in charge of all ministries and state enterprises; junior officers and sergeants were assigned leadership roles down to the local level in every government department and parastatal organization.

During the NRC's early years, these administrative changes led many Ghanaians to hope that the soldiers in command would improve the efficiency of the country's bloated bureaucracies. Acheampong's popularity continued into 1974 as the government successfully negotiated international loan agreements and rescheduled Ghana's debts. The government also provided price supports for basic food imports, while seeking to encourage Ghanaians to become self-reliant in agriculture and in the production of raw materials. In the Operation Feed Yourself program, all Ghanaians were encouraged to undertake some form of food production, with the goal of eventual food self-sufficiency for the country. The program enjoyed some initial success, but support for it gradually waned.

Whatever limited success the NRC had in these efforts, however, was overridden by other basic economic factors. Industry and transportation suffered greatly as world oil prices rose during and after 1974, and the lack of foreign exchange and credit left the country without fuel. Basic food production continued to decline even as the population grew, largely because of poor price management and urbanization. When world cocoa prices rose again in the late 1970s, Ghana was unable to take advantage of the price rise because of the low productivity of its old orchards. Moreover, because of the low prices paid to cocoa farmers, some growers along the nation's borders smuggled their produce to Togo or Côte d'Ivoire. Disillusionment with the government grew, particularly among the educated. Accusations of personal corruption among the rulers also began to surface.

The reorganization of the NRC into the SMC in 1975 may have been part of a face-saving attempt. Shortly after that time, the government sought to stifle opposition by issuing a decree forbidding the propagation of rumors and by banning a number of independent newspapers and detaining their journalists. Also, armed soldiers broke up student demonstrations, and the government repeatedly closed the universities, which had become important centers of opposition to NRC policies.

Despite these efforts, the SMC by 1977 found itself constrained by mounting nonviolent opposition. To be sure, discussions about the nation's political future and its relationship to the SMC had begun in earnest. Although the various opposition groups (university students, lawyers, and other organized civilian groups) called for a return to civilian constitutional rule, Acheampong and the SMC favored a union government—a mixture of elected civilian and appointed military leaders—but one in which party politics would be abolished. University students and many intellectuals criticized the union government idea, but others, such as Justice Gustav Koranteng-Addow, who chaired the seventeen-member ad hoc committee appointed by the government to work out details of the plan, defended it as the solution to the nation's political problems.

Supporters of the union government idea viewed multiparty political contests as the perpetrators of social tension and community conflict among classes, regions, and ethnic groups. Unionists argued that their plan had the potential to depoliticize public life and to allow the nation to concentrate its energies on economic problems.

A national referendum was held in March 1978 to allow the people to accept or reject the union government concept. A rejection of the union government meant a continuation of military rule. Given this choice, it was surprising that so narrow a margin voted in favor of union government. Opponents of the idea organized demonstrations against the government, arguing that the referendum vote had not been free or fair. The Acheampong government reacted by banning several organizations and by jailing as many as 300 of its opponents.

The agenda for change in the union government referendum called for the drafting of a new constitution by an SMC-appointed commission, the selection of a constituent assembly by November 1978, and general elections in June 1979. The ad hoc committee had recommended a nonparty election, an elected executive president, and a cabinet whose members would be drawn from outside a single-house National Assembly. The military council would then step down, although its members could run for office as individuals.

In July 1978, in a sudden move, the other SMC officers forced Acheampong to resign, replacing him with Lieutenant General Frederick W.K. Akuffo. The SMC apparently acted in response to continuing pressure to find a solution to the country's economic dilemma. Inflation was estimated to be as high as 300 percent that year. There were shortages of basic commodities, and cocoa production fell to half its 1964 peak. The council was also motivated by Acheampong's failure to dampen rising political pressure for changes. Akuffo, the new SMC chairman, promised publicly to hand over political power to a new government to be elected by July 1, 1979.

Despite Akuffo's assurances, opposition to the SMC persisted. The call for the formation of political parties intensified. In an effort to gain support in the face of continuing strikes over economic and political issues, the Akuffo government at length announced that the formation of political parties would be allowed after January 1979. Akuffo also granted amnesty to former members of both Nkrumah's CPP and Busia's PP, as well as to all those convicted of subversion under Acheampong.

The decree lifting the ban on party politics went into effect on January 1, 1979, as planned. The commission that had been working on a new constitution presented an approved draft and adjourned in May. All appeared set for a new attempt at constitutional government in July, when a group of young army officers overthrew the SMC government in June 1979.

Ghana and the Rawlings Era

On May 15, 1979, less than five weeks before constitutional elections were to be held, a group of junior officers led by Flight Lieutenant Jerry John Rawlings attempted a coup. Initially unsuccessful, the coup leaders were jailed and held for court-martial. On June 4, however, sympathetic military officers overthrew the Akuffo regime and released Rawlings and his cohorts from prison fourteen days before the scheduled election. Although the SMC's pledge to return political power to civilian hands addressed the concerns of those who wanted civilian government, the young officers who had staged the June 4 coup insisted that issues critical to the image of the army and important for the stability of national politics had been ignored. Naomi Chazan, a leading analyst of Ghanaian politics, aptly assessed the significance of the 1979 coup in the following statement:

> Unlike the initial SMC II [the Akuffo period, 1978–1979] rehabilitation effort which focused on the power elite, this second attempt at reconstruction from a situation of disintegration was propelled by growing alienation. It strove, by reforming the guidelines of public behavior, to define anew the state power structure and to revise its inherent social obligations. . . .
>
> In retrospect the most irreversible outcome of this phase was the systematic eradication of the SMC leadership. . . . [Their] executions signaled not only the termination of the already fallacious myth of the nonviolence of Ghanaian politics, but, more to the point, the deadly serious determination of the new government to wipe the political slate clean.

Rawlings and the young officers formed the Armed Forces Revolutionary Council (AFRC). The armed forces were purged of senior officers accused of corrupting the image of the military. In carrying out its goal, however, the AFRC was caught

A military shrine of an asafo *company, Fante people, coastal region*
Courtesy life in general *(Brook, Rose, and Cooper Le Van)*

between two groups with conflicting interests, Chazan observed. These included the "soldier-supporters of the AFRC who were happy to lash out at all manifestations of the old regimes; and the now organized political parties who decried the undue violence and advocated change with restraint."

Despite the coup and the subsequent executions of former heads of military governments (Afrifa of the NLC; Acheampong and some of his associates of the NRC; and Akuffo and leading members of the SMC), the planned elections took place, and Ghana had returned to constitutional rule by the end of September 1979. Before power was granted to the elected government, however, the AFRC sent the unambiguous message that "people dealing with the public, in whatever capacity, are subject to popular supervision, must abide by fundamental notions of probity, and have an obligation to put the good of the community above personal objective." The AFRC position was that the nation's political leaders, at least those from within the military, had not been accountable to the people. The administration of Hilla Limann, inaugurated on September 24, 1979, at the beginning of the Third Republic, was thus expected to measure up to the new standard advocated by the AFRC.

Limann's People's National Party (PNP) began the Third Republic with control of only seventy-one of the 140 legislative seats. The opposition Popular Front Party (PFP) won forty-two seats, while twenty-six elective positions were distributed among three lesser parties. The percentage of the electorate that voted had fallen to 40 percent. Unlike the country's previous elected leaders, Limann was a former diplomat and a noncharismatic figure with no personal following. As Limann himself observed, the ruling PNP included people of conflicting ideological orientations. They sometimes disagreed strongly among themselves on national policies. Many observers, therefore, wondered whether the new government was equal to the task confronting the state.

The most immediate threat to the Limann administration, however, was the AFRC, especially those officers who organized themselves into the "June 4 Movement" to monitor the civilian administration. In an effort to keep the AFRC from looking over its shoulder, the government ordered Rawlings and several other army and police officers associated with the AFRC into retirement; nevertheless, Rawlings and his associates remained a latent threat, particularly as the economy continued its decline. The first Limann budget, for fiscal year (FY—see Glossary) 1981, estimated the Ghanaian inflation rate at 70 percent for that year, with a budget deficit equal to 30 percent of the gross national product (GNP—see Glossary). The Trade Union Congress claimed that its workers were no longer earning enough to pay for food, much less anything else. A rash of strikes, many considered illegal by the government, resulted, each one lowering productivity and therefore national income. In September the government announced that all striking public workers would be dismissed. These factors rapidly eroded the limited support the Limann government enjoyed among civilians and soldiers. The government fell on December 31, 1981, in another Rawlings-led coup.

The Second Coming of Rawlings: The First Six Years, 1982–87

The new government that took power on December 31, 1981, was the eighth in the fifteen years since the fall of Nkrumah. Calling itself the Provisional National Defence Council (PNDC), its membership included Rawlings as chairman, Brigadier Joseph Nunoo-Mensah (whom Limann had dismissed as army commander), two other officers, and three civilians. Despite its military connections, the PNDC made clear that it was unlike other soldier-led governments. This was immediately proved by the appointment of fifteen civilians to cabinet positions.

In a radio broadcast on January 5, 1982, Rawlings presented a detailed statement explaining the factors that had necessitated termination of the Third Republic. The PNDC chairman assured the people that he had no intention of imposing himself on Ghanaians. Rather, he "wanted a chance for the people, farmers, workers, soldiers, the rich and the poor, to be part of the decision-making process." He described the two years since the AFRC had handed over power to a civilian government as a period of regression during which political parties attempted to divide the people in order to rule them. The ultimate purpose for the return of Rawlings was, therefore, to "restore human dignity to Ghanaians." In the chairman's words, the dedication of the PNDC to achieving its goals was different from any the country had ever known. It was for that reason that the takeover was not a military coup, but rather a "holy war" that would involve the people in the transformation of the socioeconomic structure of the society. The PNDC also served notice to friends and foes alike that any interference in the PNDC agenda would be "fiercely resisted."

Opposition to the PNDC administration developed nonetheless in different sectors of the political spectrum. The most obvious groups opposing the government were former PNP and PFP members. They argued that the Third Republic had not been given time to prove itself and that the PNDC administration was unconstitutional. Further opposition came from the Ghana Bar Association (GBA), which criticized the government's use of public tribunals in the administration of justice. Members of the Trade Union Congress were also angered when the PNDC ordered them to withdraw demands for increased wages. The National Union of Ghanaian Students (NUGS) went even further, calling on the government to hand over power to the attorney general, who would supervise new elections.

By the end of June 1982, an attempted coup had been discovered, and those implicated had been executed. Many who disagreed with the PNDC administration were driven into exile, where they began organizing their opposition. They accused the government of human rights abuses and political intimidation, which forced the country, especially the press, into a "culture of silence."

Meanwhile, the PNDC was subjected to the influence of contrasting political philosophies and goals. Although the revolutionary leaders agreed on the need for radical change, they differed on the means of achieving it. For example, John Ndebugre, secretary for agriculture in the PNDC government, who was later appointed northern regional secretary (governor), belonged to the radical Kwame Nkrumah Revolutionary Guards, an extreme left-wing organization that advocated a Marxist-Leninist course for the PNDC. He was detained and jailed for most of the latter part of the 1980s. Other members of the PNDC, including Kojo Tsikata, P.V. Obeng, and Kwesi Botchwey, were believed to be united only by their determination either to uplift the country from its desperate conditions or to protect themselves from vocal opposition.

In keeping with Rawlings's commitment to populism as a political principle, the PNDC began to form governing coalitions and institutions that would incorporate the populace at large into the machinery of the national government. Workers' Defence Committees (WDCs) People's Defence Committees (PDCs), Citizens' Vetting Committees (CVCs), Regional Defence Committees (RDCs), and National Defence Committees (NDCs) were all created to ensure that those at the bottom of society were given the opportunity to participate in the decision-making process. These committees were to be involved in community projects and community decisions, and individual members were expected to expose corruption and "anti-social activities." Public tribunals, which were established outside the normal legal system, were also created to try those accused of antigovernment acts. And a four-week workshop aimed at making these cadres morally and intellectually prepared for their part in the revolution was completed at the University of Ghana, Legon, in July and August 1983.

Various opposition groups criticized the PDCs and WDCs, however. The aggressiveness of certain WDCs, it was argued, interfered with management's ability to make the bold decisions needed for the recovery of the national economy. In response to such criticisms, the PNDC announced on December 1, 1984, the dissolution of all PDCs, WDCs, and NDCs, and their replacement with Committees for the Defence of the Revolution (CDRs). With regard to public boards and statutory corporations, excluding banks and financial institutions, Joint Consultative Committees (JCCs) that acted as advisory bodies to managing directors were created.

The public tribunals, however, despite their characterization as undemocratic by the GBA, were maintained. Although the tribunals had been established in 1982, the law providing for the creation of a National Public Tribunal to hear and determine appeals from, and decisions of, regional public tribunals was not passed until August 1984. Section 3 and Section 10 of the PNDC Establishment Proclamation limited public tribunals to cases of a political and an economic nature. The limitations placed on public tribunals by the government in 1984 may have been an attempt by the administration to redress certain weaknesses. The tribunals, however, were not abolished; rather, they were defended as "fundamental to a good legal system" that needed to be maintained in response to "growing legal consciousness on the part of the people."

At the time when the foundations of these sociopolitical institutions were being laid, the PNDC was also engaged in a debate about how to finance the reconstruction of the national economy. The country had indeed suffered from what some described as the excessive and unwise, if not foolish, expenditures of the Nkrumah regime. The degree of decline under the NRC and the SMC had also been devastating. By December 1981, when the PNDC came to power, the inflation rate topped 200 percent, while real GDP had declined by 3 percent per annum for seven years. Not only cocoa production but even diamonds and timber exports had dropped dramatically. Gold production had also fallen to half its preindependence level.

Ghana's sorry economic condition, according to the PNDC, had resulted in part from the absence of good political leadership. In fact, as early as the AFRC administration in 1979, Rawlings and his associates had accused three former military leaders (generals Afrifa, Acheampong, and Akuffo) of corruption and greed and of thereby contributing to the national crisis and had executed them on the basis of this accusation. In other words, the AFRC in 1979 attributed the national crisis to internal, primarily political, causes. The overthrow of the Limann administration by the PNDC in 1981 was an attempt to prevent another inept administration from aggravating an already bad economic situation. By implication, the way to resolve some of the problems was to stabilize the political situation and to improve the economic conditions of the nation radically.

At the end of its first year in power, the PNDC announced a four-year program of economic austerity and sacrifice that was to be the first phase of an Economic Recovery Program (ERP). If the economy were to improve significantly, there was need for a large injection of capital—a resource that could only be obtained from international financial institutions of the West. There were those on the PNDC's ideological left, however, who rejected consultation with such agencies because these institutions were blamed in part for the nation's predicament. Precisely because some members of the government also held such views, the PNDC secretary for finance and economic planning, Kwesi Botchwey, felt the need to justify World Bank (see Glossary) assistance to Ghana in 1983:

> It would be naive and unrealistic for certain sections of the Ghanaian society to think that the request for economic assistance from the World Bank and its affiliates means a sell-out of the aims and objectives of the Ghanaian revolution to the international community. . . . It does not make sense for the country to become a member of the bank and the IMF and continue to pay its dues only to decline to utilize the resources of these two institutions.

The PNDC recognized that it could not depend on friendly nations such as Libya to address the economic problems of Ghana. The magnitude of the crisis—made worse by widespread bush fires that devastated crop production in 1983–84 and by the return of more than one million Ghanaians who had been expelled from Nigeria in 1983, which had intensified the unemployment situation—called for monetary assistance from institutions with more resources.

Phase One of the ERP began in 1983. Its goal was economic stability. In broad terms, the government wanted to reduce inflation and to create confidence in the nation's ability to recover. By 1987 progress was clearly evident. The rate of inflation had dropped to 20 percent, and between 1983 and 1987, Ghana's economy reportedly grew at 6 percent per year. Official assistance from donor countries to Ghana's recovery program averaged US$430 million in 1987, more than double that of the preceding years. The PNDC administration also made a remarkable payment of more than US$500 million in loan arrears dating to before 1966. In recognition of these achievements, international agencies had pledged more than US$575 million to the country's future programs by May 1987. With these accomplishments in place, the PNDC inaugurated Phase Two of the ERP, which envisioned privatization of state-owned assets, currency devaluation, and increased savings and investment, and which was to continue until 1990.

Notwithstanding the successes of Phase One of the ERP, many problems remained, and both friends and foes of the PNDC were quick to point them out. One commentator noted the high rate of Ghanaian unemployment as a result of the belt-tightening policies of the PNDC. In the absence of employment or redeployment policies to redress such problems, he wrote, the effects of the austerity programs might create circumstances that could derail the PNDC recovery agenda.

Unemployment was only one aspect of the political problems facing the PNDC government; another was the size and breadth of the PNDC's political base. The PNDC initially espoused a populist program that appealed to a wide variety of rural and urban constituents. Even so, the PNDC was the object of significant criticism from various groups that in one way or another called for a return to constitutional government. Much of this criticism came from student organizations, the GBA, and opposition groups in self-imposed exile, who questioned the legitimacy of the military government and its declared intention of returning the country to constitutional rule. So vocal was the outcry against the PNDC that it appeared on the surface as if the PNDC enjoyed little support among those groups who had historically molded and influenced Ghanaian public opinion. At a time when difficult policies were being implemented, the PNDC could ill afford the continued alienation and opposition of such prominent critics.

By the mid-1980s, therefore, it had become essential that the PNDC demonstrate that it was actively considering steps toward constitutionalism and civilian rule. This was true notwithstanding the recognition of Rawlings as an honest leader and the perception that the situation he was trying to redress was not of his creation. To move in the desired direction, the PNDC needed to weaken the influence and credibility of all antagonistic groups while it created the necessary political structures that would bring more and more Ghanaians into the process of national reconstruction. The PNDC's solution to its dilemma was the proposal for district assemblies.

The District Assemblies

Although the National Commission for Democracy (NCD) had existed as an agency of the PNDC since 1982, it was not until September 1984 that Justice Daniel F. Annan, himself a member of the ruling council, was appointed chairman. The official inauguration of the NCD in January 1985 signaled PNDC determination to move the nation in a new political direction. According to its mandate, the NCD was to devise a viable democratic system, utilizing public discussions. Annan explained the necessity for the commission's work by arguing that the political party system of the past had lost track of the country's socio-economic development processes. There was the need, therefore, to search for a new political order that would be functionally democratic. Constitutional rules of the past, Annan continued, were not acceptable to the new revolutionary spirit, which saw the old political order as using the ballot box "merely to ensure that politicians got elected into power, after which communication between the electorate and their elected representative completely broke down."

After two years of deliberations and public hearings, the NCD recommended the formation of district assemblies as local governing institutions that would offer opportunities to the ordinary person to become involved in the political process. The PNDC scheduled elections of the proposed assemblies for the last quarter of 1988.

If, as Rawlings said, the PNDC revolution was a "holy war," then the proposed assemblies were part of a PNDC policy intended to annihilate enemy forces or, at least, to reduce them to impotence. The strategy was to deny the opposition a legitimate political forum within which it could articulate its objections to the government. It was for this reason, as much as it was for those stated by Annan, that a five-member District Assembly Committee was created in each of the nation's 110 administrative districts and was charged by the NCD with ensuring that all candidates followed electoral rules. The district committees were to disqualify automatically any candidate who had a record of criminal activity, insanity, or imprisonment involving fraud or electoral offenses in the past, especially after 1979. Also barred from elections were all professionals accused of fraud, dishonesty, and malpractice. The ban on political parties, instituted at the time of the Rawlings coup, was to continue.

By barring candidates associated with corruption and mismanagement of national resources from running for district assembly positions, the PNDC hoped to establish new values to govern political behavior in Ghana. To do so effectively, the government also made it illegal for candidates to mount cam-

Makola Market, the largest market in Accra
Courtesy life in general *(Brook, Rose, and Cooper Le Van)*

paign platforms other than the one defined by the NCD. Every person qualified to vote in the district could propose candidates or be nominated as a candidate. Candidates could not be nominated by organizations and associations but had to run for district office on the basis of personal qualifications and service to their communities.

Once in session, an assembly was to become the highest political authority in each district. Assembly members were to be responsible for deliberation, evaluation, coordination, and implementation of programs accepted as appropriate for the district's economic development; however, district assemblies were to be subject to the general guidance and direction of the central government. To ensure that district developments were in line with national policies, one-third of assembly members were to be traditional authorities (chiefs) or their representatives; these members were to be approved by the PNDC in consultation with the traditional authorities and other "productive economic groups in the district." In other words, a degree of autonomy may have been granted to the assemblies in the determination of programs most suited to the districts, but the PNDC left itself with the ultimate responsibility of making sure that such programs were in line with the national economic recovery program.

District assemblies as outlined in PNDC documents were widely discussed by friends and foes of the government. Some hailed the proposal as compatible with the goal of granting the people opportunities to manage their own affairs, but others (especially those of the political right) accused the government of masking its intention to remain in power. If the government's desire for democracy were genuine, a timetable for national elections should have been its priority rather than the preoccupation with local government, they argued. Some questioned the wisdom of incorporating traditional chiefs and the degree to which these traditional leaders would be committed to the district assembly idea, while others attacked the election guidelines as undemocratic and, therefore, as contributing to a culture of silence in Ghana. To such critics, the district assemblies were nothing but a move by the PNDC to consolidate its position.

Rawlings, however, responded to such criticism by restating the PNDC strategy and the rationale behind it:

> Steps towards more formal political participation are being taken through the district-level elections that we will be holding throughout the country as part of our decentralisation policy. As I said in my nationwide broadcast on December 31, if we are to see a sturdy tree of democracy grow, we need to learn from the past and nurture very carefully and deliberately political institutions that will become the pillars upon which the people's power will be erected. A new sense of responsibility must be created in each workplace, each village, each district; we already see elements of this in the work of the CDRs, the 31st December Women's Movement, the June 4 Movement, Town and Village Development Committees, and other organizations through which the voice of the people is being heard.

As for the categorization of certain PNDC policies as "leftist" and "rightist," Rawlings dismissed such allegations as "remarkably simplistic. . . . What is certain is that we are moving *forward*!" For the PNDC, therefore, the district elections constituted an obvious first step in a political process that was to culminate at the national level.

Rawlings's explanation notwithstanding, various opposition groups continued to describe the PNDC-proposed district assemblies as a mere public relations ploy designed to give political legitimacy to a government that had come to power by unconstitutional means. Longtime observers of the Ghanaian political scene, however, identified two major issues at stake in the conflict between the government and its critics: the means by which political stability was to be achieved, and the problem of attaining sustained economic growth. Both had preoccupied the country since the era of Nkrumah. The economic recovery programs implemented by the PNDC in 1983 and the proposal for district assemblies in 1987 were major elements in the government's strategy to address these fundamental and persistent problems. Both were very much part of the national debate in Ghana in the late 1980s.

* * *

Ghana, formerly the Gold Coast, was not a distinct entity until late in the nineteenth century. Its history before the arrival of the Europeans and even after the consolidation of British colonial rule must be studied as a part of the history of the portion of West Africa extending from Sierra Leone to Nigeria and northward into the Sahara. This is the region from which came the people and the social and political organizations that most influenced Ghanaians. *Peoples and Empires of West Africa, 1000–1800* by G.T. Stride and Caroline Ifeka gives a rich view of this period, with adequate attention to the future Ghana. So does the classic treatment by J.D. Fage in his *A History of West Africa: An Introductory Survey.* Robert Lystad's *The Ashanti* and Ivor Wilks's *Asante in the Nineteenth Century: The Structure and Evolution of a Political Order* both provide a comprehensive look at the history of the most influential of the purely Ghanaian kingdoms, without which an understanding of later Ghanaian history would be impossible. For the years of European commercial activities on the Guinea Coast, see Arnold Walter Lawrence's *Trade, Castles, and Forts of West Africa* and also his *Fortified Trade-posts: The English in West Africa, 1645–1822.* Other supplementary readings on the period can be found in works by Kwame Arhin, A. Adu Boahen, Nehemia Levtzion, Michael Crowder, and John K. Fynn.

Military readers may enjoy Paul Mmegha Mbaeyi's *British Military and Naval Forces in West African History, 1807–1874*, which provides an interesting view of the introductory years of colonial rule. The third part of William M. Hailey's *Native Administration in the British African Territories* provides exhaustive detail on the colonial period, while R.E. Wraith's *Guggisberg* is a fine description of an era when colonial policy could even have been defined as progressive. For information on the ending of British rule and the birth of nationalism, David E. Apter's *The Gold Coast in Transition* (revised and reprinted as *Ghana in Transition*) still provides an outstanding assessment. There are many books, polemic and scholarly, on the Nkrumah years. Peter T. Omari's *Kwame Nkrumah: Anatomy of an African Dictatorship* is most often cited. See also Bob Beck Fitch and Mary Oppenheimer's *Ghana: End of an Illusion.* Among the most valuable sources on what Ghana faced in the post-Nkrumah era are those by Deborah Pellow, Naomi Chazan, Maxwell Owusu, and Kwame Ninsin. (For further information and complete citations, see Bibliography.)

Chapter 2. The Society and Its Environment

An akuaba (fertility doll) (Asante)

GHANA, FORMERLY THE BRITISH colony of the Gold Coast, lies on the West African coast, just north of the equator. Its warm, humid climate is typical of the tropics. Ghana covers an area of approximately 239,000 square kilometers, much of it drained by the Volta River system. The population speaks languages that belong to the Kwa and Gur subfamilies of the Niger-Congo language group and is divided into more than 100 linguistic and cultural units. Ghana's population, as in most sub-Saharan African countries, consists of urban and rural workers, herders, traders, and fishermen. Matrilineal, patrilineal, and double-descent systems of social organization as well as villages and chiefdoms contribute to the national mosaic.

The precolonial social systems to which Ghanaians belonged consisted of both non-stratified and highly stratified societies. Virtually without exception, however, their organizing principles were based on locality, kinship/family, and clan structures. This is still true in the mid-1990s. Chiefs, who may be influential on the national level, were and still are selected from senior members of the lineages that are considered to have been among the founders of the community or ethnic group. Membership in a chiefly lineage carries some prestige.

Ghana's precolonial social order, in which kinship, lineage, and locality provided the framework of social, political, religious, and economic organization, has been undergoing profound change since before the colonial era. The modernization of Ghanaian economic, social, and political life intensified with independence in 1957. Fundamental to this change were improvements in communications and infrastructure, urbanization, the growth of the export and cash-crop economy, and the expansion of Western education. To accelerate the pace of modernization, the Education Act of 1960 made formal instruction both free and compulsory, but attitudes toward change varied from group to group. For example, in certain areas, especially in the north, compulsory education was not welcomed because it took children away from homes that depended on their labor in the fields. Although the benefits of education are understood today, the percentage of female enrollment in secondary and tertiary institutions of higher learning has remained disproportionately low in relation to the number of women in the general population.

As Ghana's population swelled from about 6.7 million in 1960 to 8.5 million in 1970 to an estimated 17.2 million in 1994, the central government found it increasingly difficult to bring about improvements in the standard of living at the same time that population growth threatened to outstrip food production and economic growth. The issue of effective family planning also required attention and resources, and the presence of acquired immune deficiency syndrome (AIDS) alarmed the medical community and the Ghanaian population alike. Although the ancestral extended family served as an effective mutual aid group in the rural areas, many village communities lacked modern amenities. In urban centers, housing shortages continued to be a major problem.Women's associations, such as the National Council on Women and Development, became a force for change, demanding educational and economic opportunities denied under indigenous and colonial rulers.

In the 1980s, the governing Provisional National Defence Council tried to address the nation's education problems by introducing a system that emphasized vocational and technical training for all students. A rural electrification program was also initiated. At the same time, village- and community-based primary care organizations enhanced child-care and nutritional programs aimed at illiterate mothers and those who held traditional notions about marital relations. Although it is difficult to evaluate the effectiveness of these programs in the short term, at least some major problems have been recognized and steps have been taken to deal with them. The success of such programs, however, depends on the extent to which indigenous and modern institutions and cultural values are balanced and, especially, on the manner in which conflict is resolved.

Physical Setting

Location and Size

Ghana, which lies in the center of the West African coast, shares borders with the three French-speaking nations of Côte d'Ivoire to the west, Togo to the east, and Burkina Faso (Burkina, formerly Upper Volta) to the north. To the south are the Gulf of Guinea and the Atlantic Ocean.

With a total area of 238,533 square kilometers, Ghana is about the size of Britain. Its southernmost coast at Cape Three Points is 4° 30' north of the equator. From here, the country extends inland for some 670 kilometers to about 11° north. The distance across the widest part, between longitude 1° 12' east and longitude 3° 15' west, measures about 560 kilometers. The Greenwich Meridian, which passes through London, also traverses the eastern part of Ghana at Tema.

Geographical Regions

Ghana is characterized in general by low physical relief. Indeed, the Precambrian rock system that underlies most of the nation has been worn down by erosion almost to a plain. The highest elevation in Ghana, Mount Afadjato in the Akwapim-Togo Ranges, rises only 880 meters above sea level.

There are, nonetheless, five distinct geographical regions. Low plains stretch across the southern part of the country. To their north lie three regions—the Ashanti Uplands, the Akwapim-Togo Ranges, and the Volta Basin. The fifth region, the high plains, occupies the northern and northwestern sector of the country (see fig. 4). Like most West African countries, Ghana has no natural harbors. Because strong surf pounds the shoreline, two artificial harbors were built at Takoradi and Tema (the latter completed in 1961) to accommodate Ghana's shipping needs.

The Low Plains

The low plains comprise the four subregions of the coastal savanna, the Volta Delta, the Accra Plains, and the Akan Lowlands. A narrow strip of grassy and scrubby coast runs from a point near Takoradi in the west to the Togo border in the east. This coastal savanna, only about eight kilometers in width at its western end, stretches eastward through the Accra Plains, where it widens to more than eighty kilometers, and terminates at the southeastern corner of the country at the lower end of the Akwapim-Togo Ranges.

Almost flat and featureless, the Accra Plains descend gradually to the gulf from a height of about 150 meters. The topography east of the city of Accra is marked by a succession of ridges and spoon-shaped valleys. The hills and slopes in this area are the favored lands for cultivation. Shifting cultivation is the usual agricultural practice because of the swampy nature of the very low-lying areas during the rainy seasons and the periodic blocking of the rivers at the coast by sandbars that form lagoons. A plan to irrigate higher elevations of the Accra Plains was announced in 1984. Should this plan come to reality, much of the area could be opened to large-scale cultivation.

To the west of Accra, the low plains contain wider valleys and rounded low hills, with occasional rocky headlands. In general, however, the land is flat and covered with grass and scrub. Dense groves of coconut palms front the coastline. Several commercial centers, including Winneba, Saltpond, and Cape Coast, are located here. Although Winneba has a small livestock industry and palm tree cultivation is expanding in the area away from the coast, the predominant occupation of the coastal inhabitants is fishing by dug-out canoe.

The Volta Delta, which forms a distinct subregion of the low plains, extends into the Gulf of Guinea in the extreme southeast. The delta's rock formation—consisting of thick layers of sandstone, some limestone, and silt deposits—is flat, featureless, and relatively young. As the delta grew outward over the centuries, sandbars developed across the mouths of the Volta and smaller rivers that empty into the gulf in the same area, forming numerous lagoons, some quite large, making road construction difficult. To avoid the lowest-lying areas, for example, the road between Accra and Keta makes an unusual detour inland just before reaching Ada and finally approaches Keta from the east along the narrow spit on which the town stands. This notwithstanding, road links with Keta continue to be a problem. By 1989 it was estimated that more than 3,000 houses in the town had been swallowed by flooding from the lagoon. In addition, about 1,500 other houses were destroyed by erosion caused by the powerful waves of the sea.

Ironically, it is this flat, silt-composed delta region with its abundance of water that supports shallot, corn, and cassava cultivation in the region. Moreover, the sandy soil of the delta gave rise to the copra industry. Salt-making, from the plentiful supply in the dried beds of the lagoons, provides additional employment. The main occupation of the delta people, however, continues to be fishing, an industry that supplies dried and salted fish to other parts of the country.

The largest part of the low plains is the Akan Lowlands. Some experts prefer to classify this region as a subdivision of the Ashanti Uplands because of the many characteristics they share. Unlike the uplands, however, the height of the Akan Lowlands is generally between sea level and 150 meters. Some

ranges and hills rise to about 300 meters, but few exceed 600 meters. The lowlands that lie to the south of the Ashanti Uplands receive the many rivers that make their way to the sea.

The Akan Lowlands contain the basins of the Densu River, the Pra River, the Ankobra River, and the Tano River, all of which play important roles in the economy of Ghana. The Densu River Basin, location of the important urban centers of Koforidua and Nsawam in the eastern lowlands, has an undulating topography. Many of the hills here have craggy summits, which give a striking appearance to the landscape. The upper section of the Pra River Basin, to the west of the Densu, is relatively flat; the topography of its lower reaches, however, resembles that of the Densu Basin and the area is a rich cocoa and food-producing region. The valley of the Birim River, one of the main tributaries of the Pra, is the country's most important diamond-producing area.

The Ankobra River Basin and the middle and lower basins of the Tano River to the west of the lowlands form the largest subdivision of the Akan Lowlands. Here annual rainfall between 1,500 and 2,150 millimeters helps assure a dense forest cover. In addition to timber, the area is rich in minerals. The Tarkwa goldfield, the diamond operations of the Bonsa Valley, and high-grade manganese deposits are all found in this area. The middle and lower Tano basins have been intensely explored for oil and natural gas since the mid-1980s. The lower basins of the Pra, Birim, Densu, and Ankobra rivers are also sites for palm tree cultivation.

Ashanti Uplands

Comprising the Southern Ashanti Uplands and the Kwahu Plateau, the Ashanti Uplands lie just north of the Akan Lowlands and stretch from the Côte d'Ivoire border in the west to the elevated edge of the Volta Basin in the east. Stretching in a northwest-to-southeast direction, the Kwahu Plateau extends 193 kilometers between Koforidua in the east and Wenchi in the northwest. The average elevation of the plateau is about 450 meters, rising to a maximum of 762 meters. The relatively cool temperatures of the plateau were attractive to Europeans, particularly missionaries, who founded many well-known schools and colleges in this region.

The plateau forms one of the important physical divides in Ghana. From its northeastern slopes, the Afram and Pru rivers flow into the Volta River, while from the opposite side, the Pra,

Birim, Ofin, Tano, and other rivers flow south toward the sea. The plateau also marks the northernmost limit of the forest zone. Although large areas of the forest cover have been destroyed through farming, enough deciduous forest remains to shade the headwaters of the rivers that flow from the plateau.

The Southern Ashanti Uplands, extending from the foot of the Kwahu Plateau in the north to the lowlands in the south, slope gently from an elevation of about 300 meters in the north to about 150 meters in the south. The region, however, contains several hills and ranges as well as several towns of historical and economic importance, including Kumasi, Ghana's second largest city and former capital of the Asante (also seen as Ashanti—see Glossary) empire (see The Precolonial Period, ch. 1). Obuasi and Konongo, two of the country's gold-mining centers, are also located here. The region is the country's chief producer of cocoa, and its tropical forests continue to be a vital source of timber for the lumber industry.

Akwapim-Togo Ranges

The Akwapim-Togo Ranges in the eastern part of the country consist of a generally rugged complex of folded strata, with many prominent heights composed of volcanic rock. The ranges begin west of Accra and continue in a northeasterly direction, finally crossing the frontier into Togo.

In their southeastern part, the ranges are bisected by a deep, narrow gorge cut by the Volta River. The head of this gorge is the site of the Akosombo Dam, which impounds the river to form Lake Volta. The ranges south of the gorge form the Akwapim section of the mountains. The average elevation in this section is about 450 meters, and the valleys are generally deep and relatively narrow. North of the gorge, for about eighty kilometers, the Togo section has broader valleys and low ridges. Beyond this point, the folding becomes more complex and heights increase greatly, with several peaks rising more than 610 meters above sea level. The country's highest point, Mount Afadjato, is located in this area.

The ranges are largely covered with deciduous forests, and their higher elevation provides a relatively cooler, pleasant climate. Small-scale subsistence farming is typical in the ranges. In addition to the cultivation of rice and other staples, coffee plantations are found in the Togo section of the ranges.

Volta Basin

Occupying the central part of Ghana, the Volta Basin covers about 45 percent of the nation's total land surface. Its northern section, which lies above the upper part of Lake Volta, rises to a height of 150 to 215 meters above sea level. Elevations of the Konkori Scarp to the west and the Gambaga Scarp to the north reach from 300 to 460 meters. To the south and the southwest, the basin is less than 300 meters. The Kwahu Plateau marks the southern end of the basin, although it forms a natural part of the Ashanti Uplands.

The basin is characterized by poor soil, generally of Voltaian sandstone. Annual rainfall averages between 1,000 and 1,140 millimeters. The most widespread vegetation type is savanna, the woodlands of which, depending on local soil and climatic conditions, may contain such trees as Red Ironwood and Shea.

The basin's population, principally made up of farmers, is low in density, especially in the central and northwestern areas, where tsetse flies are common. Archaeological finds indicate, however, that the region was once more heavily populated. Periodic burning evidently occurred over extensive areas for perhaps more than a millennium, exposing the soil to excessive drying and erosion, rendering the area less attractive to cultivators.

In contrast with the rest of the region are the Afram Plains, located in the southeastern corner of the basin. Here the terrain is low, averaging 60 to 150 meters in elevation, and annual rainfall is between 1,140 and about 1,400 millimeters. Near the Afram River, much of the surrounding countryside is flooded or swampy during the rainy seasons. With the construction of Lake Volta (8,515 hectares in surface area) in the mid-1960s, much of the Afram Plains was submerged. Despite the construction of roads to connect communities displaced by the lake, road transportation in the region remains poor. Renewed efforts to improve communications, to enhance agricultural production, and to improve standards of living began in earnest only in the mid-1980s.

The High Plains

The general terrain in the northern and northwestern part of Ghana outside the Volta Basin consists of a dissected plateau, which averages between 150 and 300 meters in elevation and, in some places, is even higher. Rainfall averages between 1,000 and 1,150 millimeters annually, although in the northwest it is closer to 1,350 millimeters. Soils in the high plains are more arable than those in the Volta Basin, and the population density is considerably higher. Grain and cattle production is the major economic activity in the high plains of the northern region. Since the mid-1980s, when former United States President Jimmy Carter's Global 2000 program (see Glossary) adopted Ghana as one of a select number of African countries whose local farmers were to be educated and financially supported to improve agricultural production, there has been a dramatic increase in grain production in northern Ghana. The virtual absence of tsetse flies in the region has led, moreover, to increased livestock raising as a major occupation in the north. In fact, the region is the country's largest producer of cattle.

Rivers and Lakes

Ghana is drained by a large number of streams and rivers. In addition, there are a number of coastal lagoons, the huge manmade Lake Volta, and Lake Bosumtwi, southeast of Kumasi, which has no outlet to the sea. In the wetter south and southwest areas of Ghana, the river and stream pattern is denser, but in the area north of the Kwahu Plateau, the pattern is much more open, making access to water more difficult. Several streams and rivers also dry up or experience reduced flow during the dry seasons of the year, while flooding during the rainy seasons is common.

The major drainage divide runs from the southwestern part of the Akwapim-Togo Ranges northwest through the Kwahu Plateau and then irregularly westward to the Côte d'Ivoire border. Almost all the rivers and streams north of this divide form part of the Volta system. Extending about 1,600 kilometers in length and draining an area of about 388,000 square kilometers, of which about 158,000 square kilometers lie within Ghana, the Volta and its tributaries, such as the Afram River and the Oti River, drain more than two-thirds of the country. To the south of the divide are several smaller, independent rivers. The most important of these are the Pra River, the Tano River, the Ankobra River, the Birim River, and the Densu River. With the exception of smaller streams that dry up in the dry seasons or rivers that empty into inland lakes, all the major rivers in the country flow into the Gulf of Guinea directly or serve as tributaries to other major rivers. The Ankobra and Tano are navigable for considerable distances in their lower reaches.

Navigation on the Volta River has changed significantly since 1964. Construction of the dam at Akosombo, about eighty kilometers upstream from the coast, created vast Lake Volta and the associated 768,000-kilowatt hydroelectric project. Arms of the lake extend into the lower-lying areas, forcing the relocation of 78,000 people to newly created townships on the lake's higher banks. The Black Volta River and the White Volta River flow separately into the lake. Before their confluence was submerged, the rivers came together in the middle of the country to form the main Volta River. The Oti River and the Daka River, the principal tributaries of the Volta in the eastern part of the country, and the Pru River, the Sene River, and the Afram River, major tributaries to the north of the Kawhu Plateau, also empty into flooded extensions of the lake in their river valleys. Lake Volta is a rich source of fish, and its potential as a source for irrigation is reflected in an agricultural mechanization agreement signed in the late 1980s to irrigate the Afram Plains. The lake is navigable from Akosombo through Yeji in the middle of the country; a twenty-four-meter pontoon was commissioned in 1989 to link the Afram Plains to the west of the lake with the lower Volta region to the east. Hydroelectricity generated from Akosombo supplies Ghana, Togo, and Benin.

On the other side of the Kwahu Plateau from Lake Volta are several river systems, including the Pra, Ankobra, Tano and Densu. The Pra is the easternmost and the largest of the three principal rivers that drain the area south of the Volta divide. Rising south of the Kwahu Plateau and flowing southward, the Pra enters the Gulf of Guinea east of Takoradi. In the early part of the twentieth century, the Pra was used extensively to float timber to the coast for export. This trade is now carried by road and rail transportation.

The Ankobra, which flows to the west of the Pra, has a relatively small drainage basin. It rises in the hilly region of Bibiani and flows in a southerly direction to enter the gulf just west of Axim. Small craft can navigate approximately eighty kilometers inland from its mouth. At one time, the Ankobra helped transport machinery to the gold-mining areas in the vicinity of Tarkwa. The Tano, which is the westernmost of the three rivers, rises near Techiman in the center of the country. It also flows in a southerly direction, but it empties into a lagoon in the southeastern corner of Côte d'Ivoire. Navigation by steam launch is possible on the southern sector of the Tano for about seventy kilometers.

A number of rivers are found to the east of the Pra. The two most important are the Densu and Ayensu, which are major sources of water for Accra and Winneba, respectively. The country has one large natural lake, Lake Bosumtwi, located about thirty-two kilometers southeast of Kumasi. It occupies the steep-sided caldera of a former volcano and has an area of about forty-seven square kilometers. A number of small streams flow into Lake Bosumtwi, but there is no drainage from it. In addition to providing an opportunity for fishing for local inhabitants, the lake serves as a tourist attraction.

Climate

The country's warm, humid climate has an annual mean temperature between 26°C and 29°C. Variations in the principal elements of temperature, rainfall, and humidity that govern the climate are influenced by the movement and interaction of the dry tropical continental air mass, or the harmattan, which blows from the northeast across the Sahara, and the opposing tropical maritime or moist equatorial system. The cycle of the seasons follows the apparent movement of the sun back and forth across the equator.

During summer in the northern hemisphere, a warm and moist maritime air mass intensifies and pushes northward across the country. A low-pressure belt, or intertropical front, in the airmass brings warm air, rain, and prevailing winds from the southwest. As the sun returns south across the equator, the dry, dusty, tropical continental front, or harmattan, prevails.

Climatic conditions across the country are hardly uniform. The Kwahu Plateau, which marks the northernmost extent of the forest area, also serves as an important climatic divide. To its north, two distinct seasons occur. The harmattan season, with its dry, hot days and relatively cool nights from November to late March or April, is followed by a wet period that reaches its peak in late August or September. To the south and southwest of the Kwahu Plateau, where the annual mean rainfall from north to south ranges from 1,250 millimeters to 2,150 millimeters, four separate seasons occur. Heavy rains fall from about April through late June. After a relatively short dry period in August, another rainy season begins in September and lasts through November, before the longer harmattan season sets in to complete the cycle.

The extent of drought and rainfall varies across the country. To the south of the Kwahu Plateau, the heaviest rains occur in the Axim area in the southwest corner of Ghana. Farther to the north, Kumasi receives an average annual rainfall of about 1,400 millimeters, while Tamale in the drier northern savanna receives rainfall of 1,000 millimeters per year. From Takoradi eastward to the Accra Plains, including the lower Volta region, rainfall averages only 750 millimeters to 1,000 millimeters a year.

Temperatures are usually high at all times of the year throughout the country. At higher elevations, temperatures are more comfortable. In the far north, temperature highs of 31°C are common. The southern part of the country is characterized by generally humid conditions. This is particularly so during the night, when 95 to 100 percent humidity is possible. Humid conditions also prevail in the northern section of the country during the rainy season. During the harmattan season, however, humidity drops as low as 25 percent in the north.

Population

Ghana's first postindependence population census in 1960 counted about 6.7 million inhabitants. By 1970 the national census registered 8.5 million people, about a 27 percent increase; the most recent official census in 1984 recorded a figure of 12.3 million—almost double the 1960 figure (see table 2, Appendix). The nation's population was estimated to have increased to about 15 million in 1990 and to an estimated 17.2 million in mid-1994. With an annual growth rate of 2.2 percent for the period between 1965 and 1980, a 3.4 percent growth rate for 1981 through 1989, and a 1992 growth rate of 3.2 percent, the country's population is projected to surpass 20 million by the year 2000 and 35 million by 2025.

Increasing population is reflected in other statistical representations as well. Between 1965 and 1989, a constant 45 percent of the nation's total female population was of childbearing age. The crude birth rate of 47 per 1,000 population recorded for 1965 dropped to 44 per 1,000 population in 1992. Also, the crude death rate of 18 per 1,000 population in 1965 fell to 13 per 1,000 population in 1992, while life expectancy rose from an average of forty-two years for men and forty-five years for women in 1970–75 to fifty-two and fifty-six years, respectively, in 1992. The 1965 infant mortality rate of 120 per 1,000 live births also improved to 86 per 1,000 live births in 1992. With the fertility rate averaging about seven children per adult female and expected to fall only to five children per adult female by the year 2000, the population projection of 35 million in 2025 becomes more credible. A number of factors, including improved vaccination against common diseases and nutritional education through village and community health-care systems, contributed to the expanding population. The rise in the nation's population generated a corresponding rise in the demand for schools, health facilities, and urban housing.

The gender ratio of the population, 97.3 males to 100 females, was reflected in the 1984 figures of 6,063,848 males to 6,232,233 females (see fig. 5). This was slightly below the 1970 figure of 98 males to 100 females, but a reversal of the 1960 ratio of 102.2 males to 100 females. The fall in the proportion of males to females may be partly attributed to the fact that men have left the country in pursuit of jobs.

Also significant in the 1984 census figures was the national age distribution. About 58 percent of Ghana's population in 1984 was either under the age of twenty or above sixty-five. Approximately 7 million people were represented in this category, about 4 million of them under the age of ten and, therefore, economically unproductive. The large population of young, economically unproductive individuals appeared to be growing rapidly. In the early 1990s, about half of Ghana's population was under age fifteen. If the under-twenty group and those above the age of sixty are regarded as a dependent group, the social, political, and economic implications for the 1990s and beyond are as grave for Ghana as they are for sub-Saharan Africa as a whole.

Population Distribution

Population density increased steadily from thirty-six per square kilometer in 1970 to fifty-two per square kilometer in 1984; in 1990 sixty-three persons per square kilometer was the estimate for Ghana's overall population density. These averages, naturally, did not reflect variations in population distribution. For example, while the Northern Region, one of ten administrative regions, showed a density of seventeen persons per square kilometer in 1984, in the same year Greater Accra Region recorded nine times the national average of fifty-two per square kilometer. As was the case in the 1960 and 1970 figures, the greatest concentration of population in 1984 was to the south of the Kwahu Plateau. The highest concentration of habitation continued to be within the Accra-Kumasi-Takoradi triangle, largely because of the economic productivity of the region. In fact, all of the country's mining centers, timber-producing deciduous forests, and cocoa-growing lands lie to the south of the Kwahu Plateau. The Accra-Kumasi-Takoradi triangle also is conveniently linked to the coast by rail and road systems—making this area an important magnet for investment and labor (see fig. 10).

By contrast, a large part of the Volta Basin is sparsely populated. The presence of tsetse flies, the relative infertility of the soil, and, above all, the scarcity of water in the area during the harmattan season affect habitation. The far north, on the other hand, is heavily populated. The eighty-seven persons per square kilometer recorded in the 1984 census for the Upper East Region, for example, was well above the national average. This density may be explained in part by the somewhat better soil found in some areas and the general absence of the tsetse fly; however, onchocerciasis, or river blindness, a fly-borne disease, is common in the north and has caused abandonment of some land. With the improvement of the water supply through well-drilling and the introduction of intensive agricultural extension services as part of the Global 2000 program since the mid-1980s, demographic figures for the far north could be markedly different by the next census.

Another factor affecting Ghana's demography is refugees. At the end of 1994, approximately 110,000 refugees resided in Ghana. About 90,000 were Togolese who had fled political violence in their homeland beginning in early 1993 (see Relations with Immediate African Neighbors, ch. 4). Most Togolese settled in the Volta region among their ethnic kinsmen. About 20,000 Liberians were also found in Ghana, having fled the civil war in their country (see International Security Concerns, ch. 5). Many were long-term residents. As a result of ethnic fighting in northeastern Ghana in early 1994, at least 20,000 Ghanaians out of an original group of 150,000 were still internally displaced at the end of the year. About 5,000 had taken up residence in Togo because of the strife.

Urban-Rural Disparities

Localities of 5,000 persons and above have been classified as urban since 1960. On this basis, the 1960 urban population totalled 1,551,174 persons, or 23.1 percent of total population. By 1970, the percentage of the country's population residing in urban centers had increased to 28 percent. That percentage

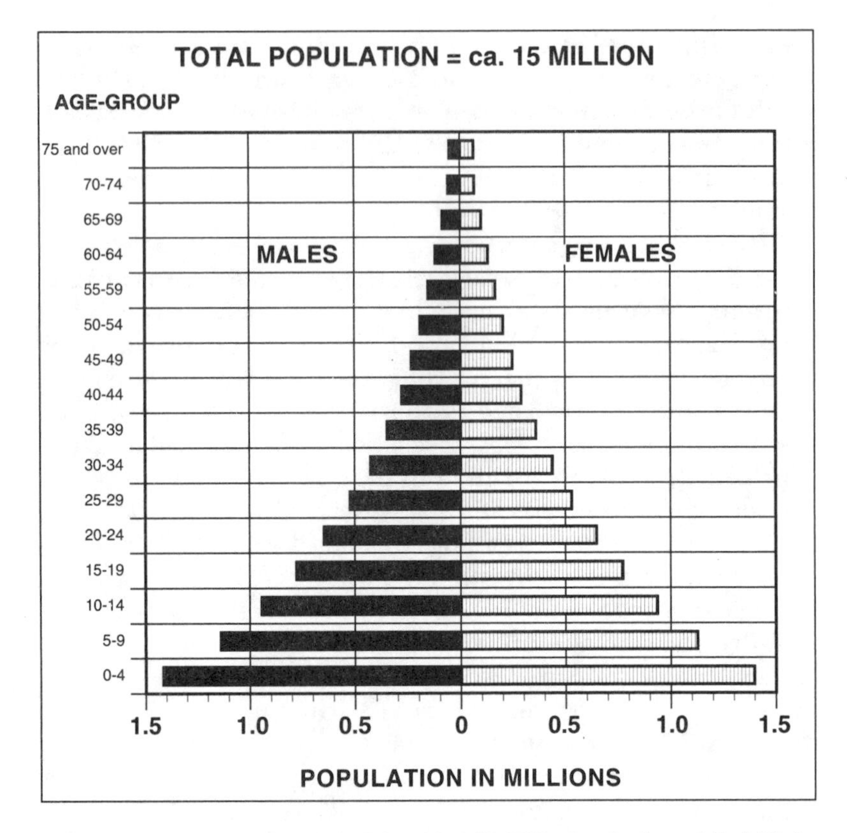

Source: Based on information from Eduard Bos, My T. Vu, Ann Levin, and Rudolfo A. Bulatao, *World Population Projections, 1992-93 Edition*, Baltimore, 1992, 238.

Figure 5. Estimated Population by Age and Gender, 1990

rose to 32 in 1984 and was estimated at 33 percent for 1992 (see table 3, Appendix).

Like the population density figures, the rate of urbanization varies from one administrative region to another. While the Greater Accra Region showed an 83-percent urban residency, the Ashanti Region matched the national average of 32 percent in 1984. The Upper West Region of the country recorded only 10 percent of its population in urban centers that year, which reflected internal migration to the south and the pattern of development that favored the south, with its minerals and forest resources, over the north. Urban areas in Ghana have customarily been supplied with more amenities than rural locations. Consequently, Kumasi, Accra, and many towns within the southern economic belt have attracted more people than the savanna regions of the north; only Tamale in the north has been an exception. The linkage of the national electricity grid to the northern areas of the country in the late 1980s may help to stabilize the north-to-south flow of internal migration.

The growth of urban population notwithstanding, Ghana continues to be a nation of rural communities. The 1984 enumeration showed that six of the country's ten regions had rural populations of 5 percent or more above the national average of 68 percent. Rural residency was estimated to be 67 percent of the population in 1992. These figures, though reflecting a trend toward urban residency, are not very different from the 1970s when about 72 percent of the nation's population lived in rural areas.

In an attempt to perpetuate this pattern of rural-urban residency and thereby to lessen the consequent socioeconomic impact on urban development, the "Rural Manifesto," which assessed the causes of rural underdevelopment, was introduced in April 1984. Development strategies were evaluated, and some were implemented to make rural residency more attractive. As a result, the Bank of Ghana established more than 120 rural banks to support rural entrepreneurs, and the rural electrification program was intensified in the late 1980s. The government, moreover, presented its plans for district assemblies as a component of its strategy for rural improvement through decentralized administration, a program designed to allow local people to become more involved in planning development programs to meet local needs (see District Assembly Elections, ch. 4).

Family Planning

A survey carried out between 1962 and 1964 in rural areas of the country and among the economically better-off urban population indicated the nature of the problem with population control in Ghana. The survey showed that rural families favored a total of seven or eight children and that the actual number of children in the better-off urban family ran between five and six. In neither case was there much interest in limiting the size of the family, although the urban group stated that it would recommend a maximum of three or four children to newly married couples.

The Ghanaian government has long shown an active interest in the population question. It was a cosponsor of a resolution on population growth and economic development in the 1962–63 session of the United Nations (UN) General Assembly and was the first sub-Saharan country to sign the "World Leaders' Declaration on Population" in 1967 that called attention to the population question. In 1969 it issued a general policy paper, "Population Planning for National Progress and Prosperity," that included provisions for family planning services. Subsequently, in 1969, it carried out a mass publicity and education campaign on family planning and during late 1970 sponsored an awareness week designed to encourage acceptance of family planning.

Some family planning services have been available since 1966, when the Planned Parenthood Association of Ghana was formed. In the early 1990s, branch offices of the organization were still functioning in regional capitals out of which field officers (usually women) organized community awareness campaigns. In addition to the obvious family planning activities, the Planned Parenthood Association and the United States government furnished technical and financial support to the government's effort to control population expansion. This support included aid for the demographic unit of the Sociology Department of the University of Ghana in the collection of data on attitudes toward population control and on family planning practices during the 1970s. The aid program also funded pilot projects that incorporated family planning education into basic health services and that provided training of medical and paramedical personnel.

Although many adult Ghanaians have at least some knowledge of family planning, data from the 1980s suggest almost no change in attitudes and practices from the 1960s. For example, most Ghanaian women still prefer large families and probably see their child-bearing abilities as a form of social and economic security (see The Position of Women, this ch.). In Africa, where the infant mortality rate is generally high, large families ensure that some children will survive. It is, therefore, not surprising that Ghana's population continues to grow rapidly in the 1990s.

In an effort to regulate the effects of rapid population growth, the government launched a substantial public education program for women in the late 1980s that continued into the 1990s. In numerous newspaper articles and at community health centers, the campaign stressed child nutrition and immunization and the spacing of births. Although family planning had been incorporated into basic women's health services, no attention was given to the role of men in family planning until the beginning of the 1990s when a campaign to control the spread of acquired immune deficiency syndrome (AIDS) addressed male promiscuity and the practice of polygamy (see Acquired Immune Deficiency Syndrome, this ch.). Because of government efforts and increased aid from the United States, some increase in the use of contraceptives and modern methods of birth control has occurred during the early 1990s. As is to be expected, family planning is more likely to be practiced among women who live in urban areas with greater access to family planning services and whose level of education is junior secondary school or above.

Ethnic Groups and Languages

In 1960 roughly 100 linguistic and cultural groups were recorded in Ghana. Although later censuses placed less emphasis on the ethnic and cultural composition of the population, differences, of course, existed and had not disappeared by the mid-1990s (see fig. 6). The major ethnic groups in Ghana include the Akan, Ewe, Mole-Dagbane, Guan, and Ga-Adangbe. The subdivisions of each group share a common cultural heritage, history, language, and origin. These shared attributes were among the variables that contributed to state formation in the precolonial period. Competition to acquire land for cultivation, to control trade routes, or to form alliances for protection also promoted group solidarity and state formation. The creation of the union that became the Asante confederacy in the late seventeenth century is a good example of such processes at work in Ghana's past (see The Precolonial Period, ch. 1).

Ethnic rivalries of the precolonial era, variance in the impact of colonialism upon different regions of the country, and the uneven distribution of social and economic amenities in postindependence Ghana have all contributed to present-day ethnic tensions. For example, in February 1994, more than 1,000 persons were killed and 150,000 displaced in the northeastern part of Ghana in fighting between Konkomba on one side and Nanumba, Dagomba, and Gonja on the other. The clashes resulted from long-standing grievances over land ownership and the prerogatives of chiefs. A military task force restored order, but a state of emergency in the region remained in force until mid-August.

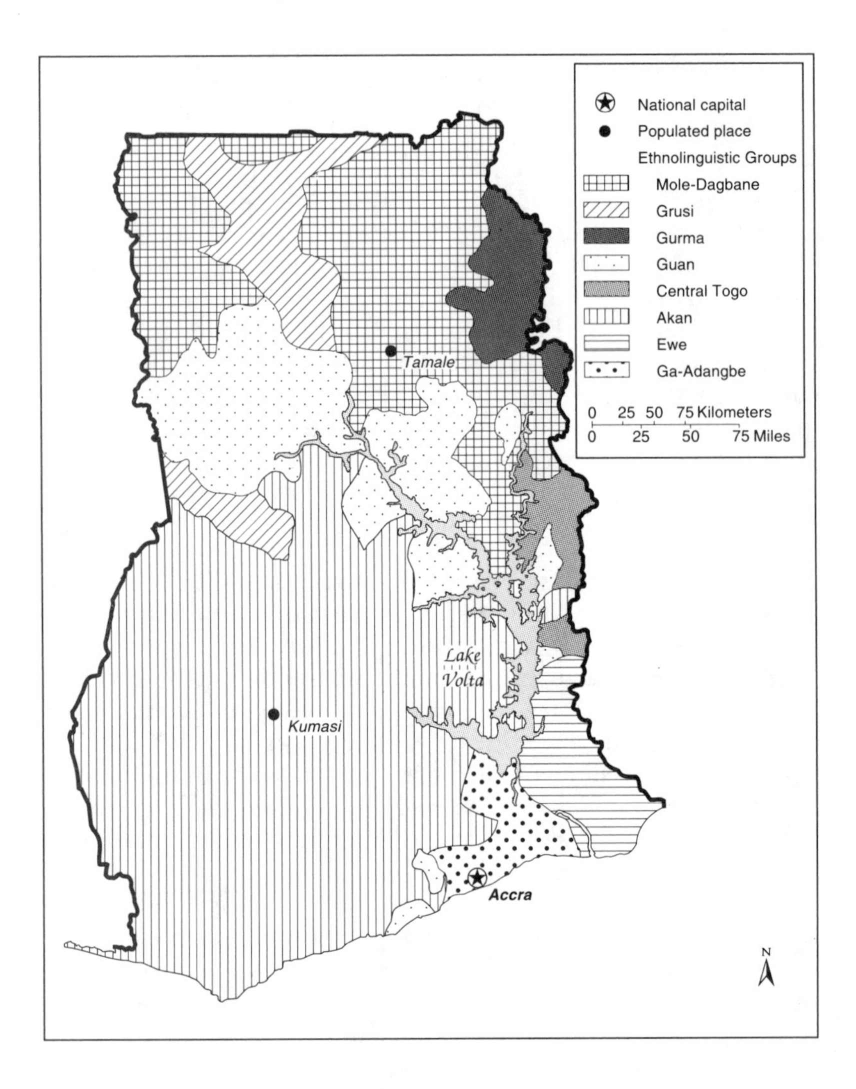

Figure 6. Principal Ethnolinguistic Groups

Although this violence was certainly evidence of ethnic tension in the country, most observers agreed that the case in point was exceptional. As one prolific writer on modern Ghana, Naomi Chazan, has aptly observed, undifferentiated recourse to ethnic categories has obscured the essential fluidity that lies at the core of shared ties in the country. Evidence of this fluidity lies in the heterogeneous nature of all administrative regions, in rural-urban migration that results in interethnic mixing, in the shared concerns of professionals and trade unionists that cut across ethnic lines, and in the multi-ethnic composition of secondary school and university classes. Ethnicity, nonetheless, continues to be one of the most potent factors affecting political behavior in Ghana. For this reason, ethnically based political parties are unconstitutional under the present Fourth Republic.

Despite the cultural differences among Ghana's various peoples, linguists have placed Ghanaian languages in one or the other of only two major linguistic subfamilies of the Niger-Congo language family, one of the large language groups in Africa. These are the Kwa and Gur groups, found to the south and north of the Volta River, respectively. The Kwa group, which comprises about 75 percent of the country's population, includes the Akan, Ga-Adangbe, and Ewe. The Akan are further divided into the Asante, Fante, Akwapim, Akyem, Akwamu, Ahanta, Bono, Nzema, Kwahu, and Safwi. The Ga-Adangbe people and language group include the Ga, Adangbe, Ada, and Krobo or Kloli. Even the Ewe, who constitute a single linguistic group, are divided into the Nkonya, Tafi, Logba, Sontrokofi, Lolobi, and Likpe. North of the Volta River are the three subdivisions of the Gur-speaking people. These are the Gurma, Grusi, and Mole-Dagbane. Like the Kwa subfamilies, further divisions exist within the principal Gur groups.

Any one group may be distinguished from others in the same linguistically defined category or subcategory, even when the members of the category are characterized by essentially the same social institutions. Each has a historical tradition of group identity, if nothing else, and, usually, of political autonomy. In some cases, however, what is considered a single unit for census and other purposes may have been divided into identifiable separate groups before and during much of the colonial period and, in some manner, may have continued to be separate after independence.

No part of Ghana, however, is ethnically homogeneous. Urban centers are the most ethnically mixed because of migration to towns and cities by those in search of employment. Rural areas, with the exception of cocoa-producing areas that have attracted migrant labor, tend to reflect more traditional population distributions. One overriding feature of the country's population is that groups to the south who are closer to the Atlantic coast have long been influenced by the money economy, Western education, and Christianity, whereas Gur-speakers to the north, who have been less exposed to those influences, have come under Islamic influence. These influences were not pervasive in the respective regions, however, nor were they wholly restricted to them.

Language Diversity

More than 100 languages and dialects are spoken in Ghana. In view of these linguistic and associated cultural differences, and, as a result of the country's colonial past, English has become Ghana's official language. It is used for all government affairs, large-scale business transactions, educational instruction, and in national radio and television broadcasts. In fact, the constitution of 1969 required that members of parliament speak, read, and understand English. In an effort to increase "grassroots participation" in government and to encourage non-English speakers to run for elective office, however, the 1992 Consultative Assembly on the Constitution recommended that the ability to communicate in English no longer be required of future members of parliament. In the mid-1980s, the Ministry of Education also encouraged teachers to use local languages for instruction during the first six years of formal education. These changes, however, have not lessened the importance of English in Ghanaian society.

Although Fante-Twi (a major Akan language), Ga, and Ewe are the most important Kwa languages spoken in the south, three subdivisions of the Gur branch—Mole-Dagbane, Grusi, and Gurma—dominate the northern region. Hausa, a language of northern Nigeria which spread throughout West Africa through trade, is also understood by some inhabitants in the northeastern part of the country. In northwestern Ghana, among the Dagari-speaking people and around frontier towns in western Brong-Ahafo, various dialects of the Mande language are spoken. Akan, Ewe, Ga, Nzema, Dagbane, and Hausa are the country's principal indigenous languages and are used in radio and television programming.

The literary tradition of northern Ghana has its roots in Islam, while the literature of the south was influenced by Christian missionaries. As a result of European influence, a number of Ghanaian groups have developed writing systems based on Latin script, and several indigenous languages have produced a rich body of literature. The principal written Ghanaian languages are the Twi dialects of Asante, Akwapim, and Fante. Other written languages are Nzema, Ewe, Dagbane, Ga, and

Kasena (a Grusi language). Most publications in the country, however, are written in English.

Major Ethnic Groups

On the basis of language and culture, historical geographers and cultural anthropologists classify the indigenous people of Ghana into five major groups. These are the Akan, the Ewe, the Guan, the Mole-Dagbane and related peoples of the north, and the Ga-Adangbe.

The Akan Group

The Akan people occupy practically the whole of Ghana south and west of the Black Volta River. Historical accounts suggest that Akan groups migrated from the north to occupy the forest and coastal areas of the south as early as the thirteenth century. Some of the Akan ended up in the eastern section of Côte d'Ivoire, where they created the Baule community.

When Europeans arrived at the coast in the fifteenth century, the Akan were established there. The typical political unit was the small state under the headship of an elder from one of the seven or eight clans (see Glossary) that composed Akan society. From these units emerged several powerful states, of which the oldest is thought to be Bono (also called Brong). As a result of military conquests and partial assimilation of weaker groups, well-known political entities, such as Akwamu, Asante (also seen as Ashanti—see Glossary), Akyem, Denkyira, and Fante emerged before the close of the seventeenth century. Asante, for example, continued to expand throughout the eighteenth century and survived as an imperial power until the end of the nineteenth century, when it succumbed to British rule (see The Precolonial Period, ch. 1).

The coastal Akan (Fante) were the first to have relations with Europeans. As a result of long association, these groups absorbed aspects of British culture and language. For example, it became customary among these people to accept British names as family names.

The primary form of Akan social organization is the extended family or the *abusua*—the basic unit in a society based on matriclans (see Glossary). Through the exogamous matriclan system, local identity and individual status, inheritance, succession to wealth and to political offices, and even basic relations within the village community are determined. Every lineage (see Glossary) is a corporate group with its own identity, group solidarity, exclusive property, and symbols. The ownership of a symbolic carved chair or stool, usually named after the female founder of the matriclan, became the means through which individuals traced their ancestry. These lineages have segmented into branches, each led by an elder, headman, or chief, but a branch, although it possesses a stool, is not an autonomous political or social unit. Possession of a ritually important stool is seen as vital, not only to the existence of each *abusua* but to the matriclan as a whole.

Despite the matrilineal focus of Akan societies, most traditional leadership positions are held by men. Male succession to inherited positions is, however, determined by relationship to mothers and sisters. Consequently, a man's valuable property is passed on not to his children, but to his brother or his sister's son. A man may also be expected to support the children of a maternal relative, whether deceased or alive, an expectation that may conflict with the interests of his own children. Matrilineal (see Glossary under "matrilineage") succession to property has been the cause of much litigation. There have been instances of wives and children turning to the courts for redress. In 1986 the government passed a number of laws that sought to bring the traditions of inheritance in line with changes that had occurred in the country. These laws, which included the Intestate Succession Law, the Customary Marriage and Divorce (Registration) Law, the Administration of Estate (Amendment) Law, and the Head of Family (Accountability) Law, recognized the nuclear family as the prime economic unit. Provision was made, however, for the identification of collective properties that belonged to the extended family.

Notwithstanding the 1986 legislation, the matriclan system of the Akan continued to be economically and politically important. Each lineage controlled the land farmed by its members, functioned as a religious unit in the veneration of its ancestors, supervised marriages, and settled internal disputes among its members (see Traditional Religion, this ch.). It was from the lineages and the associations they cultivated that the village, town, and even the state emerged. The Akan state, therefore, comprehended several kin-based units, one of which, usually the most prominent lineage, provided the paramount chief, who exercised at least some authority over incorporated groups. Every one of the incorporated groups, lineages, or territorial units had some autonomy under its own headman, chief, or elders. In any case, all chiefs were subject to removal from office if they acted in any manner that alienated a substantial number of people, especially influential ones.

The relative homogeneity of Akan cultures, languages, and authority structures has not led to political unity; the most important conflicts of the Akan in precolonial and colonial times, for example, were with other Akan groups. This is understandable if the state is seen as the arena of political life and as a set of institutions concerned with power, especially for internal regulation, and for the defense of its component members. The development of the Asante Empire, for example, was largely at the expense of the independence of the surrounding Akan, who were quick to reassert their autonomy, especially after 1896, when Asante was defeated and its king, the *asantehene* (king of Asante), was exiled to the Seychelles by the British. In the struggle for independence and in the period since then, political alignments have followed local interests rather than any conception of Akan ethnic unity.

The Ewe

The Ewe occupy southeastern Ghana and the southern parts of neighboring Togo and Benin. On the west, the Volta separates the Ewe from the Ga-Adangbe, Ga, and Akan. Subdivisions of the Ewe include the Anglo (Anlo), Bey (Be), and Gen on the coast, and the Peki, Ho, Kpando, Tori, and Ave in the interior. Oral tradition suggests that the Ewe immigrated into Ghana before the mid-fifteenth century. Although the Ewe have been described as a single language group, there is considerable dialectic variation. Some of these dialects are mutually intelligible, but only with difficulty.

Unlike the political and social organization of the Akan, where matrilineal rule prevails, the Ewe are essentially a patrilineal (see Glossary under "patrilineage") people. The founder of a community became the chief and was usually succeeded by his paternal relatives. The largest independent political unit was a chiefdom, the head of which was essentially a ceremonial figure who was assisted by a council of elders. Chiefdoms ranged in population from a few hundred people in one or two villages to several thousand in a chiefdom with a large number of villages and surrounding countryside. Unlike the Asante among the Akan, no Ewe chiefdom gained hegemonic power over its neighbor. The rise of Ewe nationalism in both Ghana and Togo was more of a reaction to the May 1956 plebiscite that partitioned Eweland between the Gold Coast and Togo than to any sense of overriding ethnic unity.

Substantial differences in local economies were characteristic of the Ewe. Most Ewe were farmers who kept some livestock, and there was some craft specialization. On the coast and immediately inland, fishing was important, and local variations in economic activities permitted a great deal of trade between one community and another, carried out chiefly by women.

The Guan

The Guan are believed to have begun to migrate from the Mossi region of modern Burkina around A.D. 1000. Moving gradually through the Volta valley in a southerly direction, they created settlements along the Black Volta, throughout the Afram Plains, in the Volta Gorge, and in the Akwapim Hills before moving farther south onto the coastal plains. Some scholars postulate that the wide distribution of the Guan suggests that they were the Neolithic population of the region. Later migrations by other groups such as the Akan, Ewe, and Ga-Adangbe into Guan-settled areas would then have led to the development of Guan-speaking enclaves along the Volta and within the coastal plains. The Guan have been heavily influenced by their neighbors. The Efutu, a subgroup of the Guan, for example, continue to speak Guan dialects, but have adopted (with modifications) the Fante version of some Akan institutions and the use of some Fante words in their rituals. As far as the other Guan subgroups are concerned, the Anum-Boso speak a local Ewe dialect, whereas the Larteh and Kyerepong have customs similar to Akwapim groups.

Constituting about a quarter of the Guan, the Gonja to the north have also been influenced by other groups. The Gonja are ruled by members of a dynasty, probably Mande in origin. The area is peopled by a variety of groups, some of which do not speak Guan. The ruling dynasty, however, does speak Guan, as do substantial numbers of commoners. Although neither the rulers nor most of the commoners are Muslims, a group of Muslims accompanied the Mande invaders and have since occupied a special position as scribes and traders.

The Gonja founded one of several northern kingdoms (see The Precolonial Period, ch. 1). In the eighteenth century, they, like their neighbors, were defeated by the expanding Asante Empire. Gonja became part of the British Northern Territories after the fall of Asante. Even though long-distance commerce

Fishermen offer their daily catch for sale on a beach near Accra
Courtesy James Sanders

led to the development of major markets, the Gonja continued to be subsistence farmers and migrant workers.

The Mole-Dagbane and Related Peoples of the North

Apart from the Guan-speaking Gonja, the Kyokosi or Chokosi (an Akan-speaking fragment), and the Mande-speaking Busanga in the northeasternmost part of Ghana, the ethnic groups to the north of the Black Volta speak Gur or Voltaic languages of the Niger-Congo language family. Three subgroups of Gur languages—the Mole-Dagbane (sometimes called Mossi-Grunshi), Gurma, and Grusi—are represented in this region. Of the three Gur subfamilies, Mole-Dagbane is by far the largest, being spoken by about 15 percent of the nation's population. Its speakers are culturally the most varied; they include the Nanumba, Dagomba, Mamprusi, Wala, Builsa, Frafra, Talensi, and Kusase.

For centuries, the area inhabited by the Gur has been the scene of movements of people engaged in conquest, expansion, and north-south and east-west trade. For this reason, a considerable degree of heterogeneity, particularly of political structure, developed here.

The structure of many small groups, varied as they are, suggests that most Gur-speakers once lived in small, autonomous communities and that the links among these communities were provided by kinship ties, which in their larger extensions cut across community boundaries, and by intermarriage. The salient figure was not political but ritual—it was the priest (*tendaana*; a Mole-Dagbane term) of the earth cult and shrine.

Although primarily a religious figure, the *tendaana*'s influence was keenly felt in kin-group and community decision making.

In some cases (for example, that of the Talensi), an independent community or chiefdom was aware that others like it shared the same culture and social structure, and there were occasional common rituals that brought independent communities together. In other cases (for example, the Dagaba), political and cultural boundaries were not sharp, and there was no sense that an ethnic group included some communities and excluded others, although shifting distinctions were made based on various cultural traits. In the case of the Dagaba, the most important or recurrent of these distinctions seemed to be, and in the mid-twentieth century continued to be, whether inheritance was exclusively determined in the patrilineal line or, at least in part, followed the matrilineal line.

In a few cases, some Mole-Dagbane people developed societies of larger scale under a ruling dynasty. These included the Dagomba, Mamprusi, and Gonja, who, like the Akan to the south, were known to have founded centralized states. Rulers of the centralized Mole-Dagbane societies were believed to be related to those of the Mossi kingdoms of Burkina and the smaller Nanumba kingdoms of Ghana. Historical research suggests that migrants imposed their rule on peoples already settled in the area. In some cases, these migrants extended their rule to other groups, at least for a time. Thus, many of the Gurma-speaking Konkomba were subject to Dagomba control. The ruling groups still maintain a clear sense of their own identity and some cultural and linguistic peculiarities, but in general they speak the local language.

The Ga-Adangbe

The Ga-Adangbe people inhabit the Accra Plains. The Adangbe are found to the east, the Ga groups to the west, of the Accra coastlands. Although both languages are derived from a common proto-Ga-Adangbe ancestral language, modern Ga and Adangbe are mutually unintelligible. The modern Adangbe include the people of Shai, La, Ningo, Kpone, Osudoku, Krobo, Gbugble, and Ada, who speak different dialects. The Ga also include the Ga-Mashie groups occupying neighborhoods in the central part of Accra, and other Ga-speakers who migrated from Akwamu, Anecho in Togo, Akwapim, and surrounding areas.

Debates persist about the origins of the Ga-Adangbe people. One school of thought suggests that the proto-Ga-Adangbe people came from somewhere east of the Accra plains, while another suggests a distant locale beyond the West African coast. In spite of such historical and linguistic theories, it is agreed that the people were settled in the plains by the thirteenth century. Both the Ga and the Adangbe were influenced by their neighbors. For example, both borrowed some of their vocabulary, especially words relating to economic activities and statecraft, from the Guan. The Ewe are also believed to have influenced the Adangbe.

Despite the archaeological evidence that proto-Ga-Adangbe speakers relied on millet and yam cultivation, the modern Ga reside in what used to be fishing communities. Today, such former Ga communities as Labadi and Old Accra are neighborhoods of the national capital of Accra. This explains why, in 1960, when the national enumeration figures showed the ethnic composition of the country's population, more than 75 percent of the Ga were described as living in urban centers. The presence of major industrial, commercial, and governmental institutions in the city, as well as increasing migration of other people into the area, has not prevented the Ga people from maintaining aspects of their traditional culture.

The Central Togo

The Central Togo groups are found to the north of Ewe country in the Akwapim-Togo Ranges. These groups are sometimes called the Togo remnants, on the assumption that they represent what is left of a once more widespread people who were absorbed either by the Akan or by the Ewe. Although some of the Central Togo groups are indigenous to the area, many are believed to have come to the mountain location for refuge from the numerous wars that were fought after the end of the seventeenth century by the Gonja, Asante, Dahomeans, and Akwamu. The refugees found protection and land and, therefore, settled in the ranges. Descent and inheritance seem to be patrilineal, and each group is autonomously organized under a chief.

The traditional mode of economic activity among the Central Togo people was the cultivation of rice, but today a substantial number of the people are engaged in cocoa farming. More than any Kwa or Gur group, the Central Togo people define themselves as Christian. A relatively high level of literacy and school attendance and a high proportion of professionals and technical workers characterize the Central Togo groups.

Social Organization and Social Change

The essential characteristic of the Ghanaian social system is its dual but interrelated nature. Even though the majority of the population still lives in rural areas and observes ancestral customs and practices, the process of modernization associated with urban life has, nonetheless, affected all Ghanaians' social behavior and values. Peoples, ideas, goods, and services flow constantly between urban and rural areas, blurring the distinction between so-called traditional and modern life. Relationships within traditional society are based on family membership, inherited status, and ancestral beliefs. In modern society, relationships are determined by achieved status, formalized education, membership in professional associations, and ethnic affiliation. Contemporary society, however, is grafted onto traditional roots, and although traditional social relationships have often been partially transformed to fit the needs of modern life, they continue to endure. The result is that, even those who live primarily in the modern urban setting are still bound to traditional society through the kinship system and are held to the responsibilities that such associations entail.

Traditional Patterns of Social Relations

The extended family system is the hub around which traditional social organization revolves. This unilineal descent group functions under customary law. It is a corporate group with definite identity and membership that controls property, the application of social sanctions, and the practice of religious rituals. Many local variations exist within the general framework of the lineage system. In some ethnic groups, the individual's loyalty to his or her lineage overrides all other loyalties; in other groups, a person marrying into the group, though never becoming a complete member of the spouse's lineage, adopts its interests.

Among the matrilineal Akan, members of the extended family include the man's mother, his maternal uncles and aunts, his sisters and their children, and his brothers. A man's children and those of his brothers belong to the families of their respective mothers. Family members may occupy one or several

An example of domestic architecture of the Kasena people at Nakong, far northern Ghana Courtesy life in general *(Brook, Rose, and Cooper Le Van)*

houses in the same village. The wife and her children traditionally reside at their maternal house where she prepares her food, usually the late evening meal, to be carried to her husband at his maternal house. Polygamy as a conjugal arrangement is on the decline for economic reasons; but where it has been practiced, visitation schedules with the husband were planned for the wives.

For the patrilineal and double-descent peoples of the north, the domestic group often consists of two or more brothers with their wives and children who usually occupy a single homestead with a separate room for each wife. Also, the largest household among the patrilineal Ewe includes some or all of the sons and grandsons of one male ancestor together with their wives, children, and unmarried sisters.

Irrespective of the composition of the family in either matrilineal or patrilineal societies, each family unit is usually headed by a senior male or headman who might either be the founding member of the family or have inherited that position. He acts in council with other significant members of the family in the management of the affairs of the unit. Elderly female members of matrilineal descent groups may be consulted in the decision-making process on issues affecting the family, but often the men wield more influence.

Family elders supervise the allocation of land and function as arbitrators in domestic quarrels; they also oversee naming ceremonies for infants, supervise marriages, and arrange funerals. As custodians of the political and spiritual authority of the unit, the headman and his elders ensure the security of the family. These obligations that bind the group together also grant its members the right of inheritance, the privilege to receive capital (either in the form of cattle or fishing nets) to begin new businesses, and the guarantee of a proper funeral and burial upon death. The extended family, therefore, functions as a mutual aid society in which each member has both the obligation to help others and the right to receive assistance from it in case of need.

To ensure that such obligations and privileges are properly carried out, the family also functions as a socializing agency. The moral and ethical instruction of children is the responsibility of the extended family. Traditional values may be transmitted to the young through proverbs, songs, stories, rituals, and initiations associated with rites of passage. Among the Krobo, Ga, and Akan, puberty rites for girls offer important occasions for instructing young adults. These methods of communication constitute the informal mode of education in the traditional society. It is, therefore, through the family that the individual acquires recognition and social status. As a result, the general society sees the individual's actions as reflecting the moral and ethical values of the family. Debts accrued by him are assumed by the family upon a member's death, and, therefore, his material gains are theirs to inherit.

Land is ordinarily the property of the lineage. Family land is thought of as belonging to the ancestors or local deities and is held in trust for them. As a result, such lands are administered by the lineage elders, worked by the members of the kinship group, and inherited only by members of that unit. Although sectors of such land may be leased to others for seasonal agricultural production, the land remains within the family and usually is not sold. However, it is not unusual for a man to set aside a portion of his acquired property as "reasonable gifts" for his children or wife, as has been the case, particularly, among matrilineal groups. For such gifts to be recognized, tradition requires that the presentation be made public during the lifetime of the donor, allowing the recipient to hold the public as witnesses should the gift be contested afterward, especially following the death of the donor.

A network of mutual obligations also joins families to chiefs and others in the general community. Traditional elders and chiefs act for the ancestors as custodians of the community. Thus, in both patrilineal and matrilineal societies, and from the small village to the large town, the position of the chief and that of the queen mother are recognized.

The chief embodies traditional authority. Chiefs are usually selected from the senior members of the lineage or several lineages that are considered to be among the founders of the community or ethnic group. Chiefs have extensive executive and judicial authority. Decisions on critical issues, such as those made by family elders, are based on wide discussions and consultations with adult representative groups of both sexes. Traditionally, legislation has not been a primary issue, for the rules of life are largely set by custom. Discussions are usually focused on the expediency of concrete actions within the framework of customary rules. Decisions, when taken by chiefs, are normally taken by chiefs-in-council and not by lone dictatorial fiat. The legitimacy of traditional authority, therefore, has usually been based on public consensus sanctioned by custom.

Although chiefs or other authority figures might come from designated families or clans, the interest of the common people is never ignored. Where the process of selecting as well as of advising chiefs is not given directly to the populace, it has often been vested in representatives of kin or local residence groups, elders, or other types of councils. Among the Akan, for example, the *asafo* (traditional men's associations, originally fighting companies—see Glossary) have played important roles as political action groups to protect the interests of the common people. The priests of some local shrines also acquired substantial authority that helped balance the powers of local chiefs. It was such checks and balances within the traditional scheme of authority relations, especially among the Akan, that led the British anthropologist, Robert S. Rattray, to refer to the traditional political structure as a "domestic democracy."

Social Change

Needless to say, contact with Europeans, Christians, and Muslims as well as colonialism greatly affected and modified indigenous customs, institutions, and values. A good example of this process is the office of local chief. British influence has been present for generations, and by the time of independence in 1957, the British had exercised substantial political authority over certain southern regions for more than a century. The office of the chief, traditionally used to manage the affairs of the village community and the ethnic group, was retained by the British as one of the most important agencies through which the populace received colonial instructions. As the architect of the British colonial policy of indirect rule, Frederick Lugard argued in his *Dual Mandate in British Tropical Africa* that the preservation of the office of the traditional chief was cost-effective because it presented the appearance of continuity in the changing political environment. As was the case in many British colonies in Africa, traditional chiefs in Ghana were allowed to hold court in matters relating to traditional customs. They also controlled some local lands for agricultural production, even when the timber and mineral resources were exploited by the colonial government.

Chiefs continued to be appointed by their own people during colonial times, but native administrators became increasingly accountable to the colonial government. Inevitably, the presence of other colonial agents, such as the small but effective colonial police and the resident commissioners, influenced the power of chiefs. Also, with the abolition of slavery, the imposition of colonial taxes, and the establishment of bureaucratic and judicial procedures, the social relationships that had existed in the precolonial period between chiefs and people were altered—at times radically and always permanently. Some individuals and groups lost power, while others gained influence as the British abolished some traditional functions and established new ones.

A combination of factors affected customary notions about the exercise of power—colonial rule, Christianity, the money economy, and Western-style education. Christian missionaries established the first Western schools (see Education, this ch.). Products of this formal school system became the new elite class of literate graduates who functioned as intermediaries between the indigenous people and the colonial power and, later, the world at large. Freed from lineage property as the sole means of attaining wealth and social status, the new elite developed new forms of social institutions and patterns of interaction. Such modes of behavior associated with modernization and urbanization and acquired through formal education and the formal market economy introduced certain value systems that were distinctly different from those within the traditional culture.

Of course, Western knowledge, technology, and organizations were not uniformly introduced throughout the country. They appeared first and in most concentrated form on the coast or in the Gold Coast Colony, where European influence was greatest and where many schools were established compared with Asante and other northern regions. Consequently, the coastal and southern peoples were the greatest beneficiaries of the new economic and social opportunities and, conversely, suffered the greatest social upheaval—especially in conflicts between the Western-educated Africans and their traditional chiefs. Traditional society adapted with particular swiftness to life in urban areas, in part because of the concentration of economic development and social infrastructure in such areas. The pace of change intensified in 1952 when Kwame Nkrumah, the first African-born prime minister of the Gold Coast, introduced the Accelerated Development Plan for Education (see The Education System, this ch.).

The impact of the urban region on rural, traditional life has been great. Migrations by Ghanaians from rural areas to urban centers either by those in search of work or for the pure enjoyment of urban conditions greatly increased after 1969 (see Population Distribution, this ch.). The result was a decline in rural agricultural productivity and an increased dependence on urban wage-earners by extended family relatives. What has been described as "rural dependency on the urban wage-earner" was acceptable to those within the traditional system, who saw the individual as socially important because he continued to function in a matrix of kin and personal relationships and obligations, because his social identity could not be separated from that of his lineage, and because the wealth or positions attained could be shared by, or would benefit, all members of the extended family. Such a position, however, contradicted the Western view of the individual as a free and separate social agent whose legal obligations were largely contractual rather than kin-based and whose relationships with other people depended on individual actions and interests. The very difficult economic conditions of the 1970s brought even more pressure to bear on the relationship between traditional and urban values; nonetheless, the modern and the traditional societies continued to exist side by side, and individuals continued to adapt themselves to the requirements of each.

Urban Society

In 1960, 23.1 percent of the population of Ghana resided in urban centers. The figure rose to 28 percent in 1970, 32 percent according to the 1984 census report, and an estimated 33 percent in 1994. The census figures show that while a majority of Ghanaians still live in rural areas, larger towns and cities continue to attract more immigrants than small ones. There is a high correlation between both the economic well-being of the individual and his or her educational level, and the tendency to migrate. A large number of migrants come from areas immediately adjacent to urban areas. Urban populations are therefore multiethnic in character. Even in this multiethnic urban environment, however, ethnic associations play important social roles—from the initial reception of new migrants to the burial of urban residents.

Formed by people from the same village, district, region, or ethnic background, ethnic associations in urban centers function like extended families in which membership entails obligations and benefits. Apart from the obvious assistance that such associations may render—such as introducing newcomers to the urban environment, organizing credit unions, or helping with weddings and funeral activities—associations may also contribute to the development of their home areas. For example, urban residents from towns and villages in the Kwahu Plateau area are known throughout Ghana for their mutual aid societies. Through their fund-raising activities, Kwahu associations have contributed to school building construction, rural electrification, and general beautification projects in their villages.

In urban centers, the degree of traditionalism or modernism demonstrated by an individual is determined to a large extent by the length of residency in an urban setting; by the level of education and, therefore, the degree of Westernization; by living habits; by the nature of work; and, in some measure, by religious affiliation. For analytic purposes, one scholar has divided Ghanaian urban residents, especially those in the upper ranks of urban society, into groups according to occupation. Within these groups are individuals who, on the basis of their education, professional standing, and participation in the urban milieu, are accorded high status. They include professionals in economics, politics, education, administration, medicine, law, and similar occupations who constitute the elite of their respective groupings.

View of central Accra along Kwame Nkrumah Avenue
Courtesy Embassy of Ghana, Washington
A main thoroughfare in Cape Coast
Courtesy James Sanders

Taken as a whole, however, such elites do not compose an upper class. The individuals who constitute the elites come from different social and ethnic backgrounds and base their power and social status on a variety of cultural values. Most of them continue to participate in some aspects of traditional society and socialize with members of their own or other lineage groups. Most important, they do not regard themselves as an elite group.

The working class constitutes the rank and file of the various trade union groups. The majority of them have completed the Middle School Leaving Certificate Examination. Some have secondary and technical educations. Unions have been politically active in the country since the 1960s. During the 1970s, members of the Trade Union Congress, the umbrella organization of workers, and the nation's university students joined together to call for political changes. In the 1980s, however, long-standing good relations with student organizations suffered when certain trade union groups attacked demonstrating university students. The primary function of the Trade Union Congress as a mutual aid group is to conduct negotiations with the government in an effort to improve the conditions and the wages of workers. Apart from such joint actions within the unions, the lives of working people in urban centers, like those of their elite counterparts, revolve around friends, family, and other mutual-aid networks.

Family life in more affluent urban areas approximates Western behavior in varying degrees. Decisions in the urban family are increasingly made by both parents, not just one. As children spend increasing amounts of time away from home, more of their values come from their peers and from adults who are not members of their lineage. Social activities organized by schools have become more important in the life of urban children and have reduced sibling interaction. As a result, a greater amount of socialization is taking place outside the kin group and immediate family. This contrasts with rural society in which family and lineage remain the most significant institutions.

As a result of weakening lineage ties in urban centers and of population movements that separate more and more individuals from kinsmen upon whom they would ordinarily depend for assistance, companionship, and entertainment, many urban residents have turned to voluntary-membership clubs and to organizations composed of people with shared interests rather than inherited links. Popular examples of such clubs are the Ghana Red Cross Society, the Accra Turf Club, and the Kristo Asafo (Christian Women's Club). Other organizations such as the Ghana Bar Association, the Registered Nurses Association, the Ghana Medical Association, and the Ghana National Association of Teachers address professional concerns.

The Position of Women

Women in premodern Ghanaian society were seen as bearers of children, retailers of fish, and farmers. Within the traditional sphere, the childbearing ability of women was explained as the means by which lineage ancestors were allowed to be reborn. Barrenness was, therefore, considered the greatest misfortune. In precolonial times, polygamy was encouraged, especially for wealthy men. Anthropologists have explained the practice as a traditional method for well-to-do men to procreate additional labor. In patrilineal societies, dowry received from marrying off daughters was also a traditional means for fathers to accumulate additional wealth. Given the male dominance in traditional society, some economic anthropologists have explained a female's ability to reproduce as the most important means by which women ensured social and economic security for themselves, especially if they bore male children.

In their *Seven Roles of Women: Impact of Education, Migration, and Employment on Ghanaian Mothers* (1987), Christine Oppong and Katherine Abu recorded field interviews in Ghana that confirmed this traditional view of procreation. Citing figures from the Ghana fertility survey of 1983, the authors concluded that about 60 percent of women in the country preferred to have large families of five or more children. A statistical table accompanying the research showed that the largest number of children per woman was found in the rural areas where the traditional concept of family was strongest. Uneducated urban women also had large families. On the average, urbanized, educated, and employed women had fewer children. On the whole, however, all the interviewed groups saw childbirth as an essential role for women in society, either for the benefits it bestows upon the mother or for the honor it brings to her family.The security that procreation provided was greater in the case of rural and uneducated women. By contrast, the number of children per mother declined for women with post-elementary education and outside employment. With a guaranteed income and little time at her disposal in her combined role as mother and employee, a woman's desire to procreate declined.

In rural areas of Ghana where non-commercial agricultural production was the main economic activity, women worked the land. Coastal women also sold fish caught by men. Many of the financial benefits that accrued to these women went into upkeep of the household, while those of the man were reinvested in an enterprise that was often perceived as belonging to his extended family. This traditional division of wealth placed women in positions subordinate to men. The persistence of such values in traditional Ghanaian society may explain some of the resistance to female education in the past.

In traditional society, marriage under customary law was often arranged or agreed upon by the fathers and other senior kinsmen of the prospective bride and bridegroom. This type of marriage served to link the two groups together in social relationships; hence, marriage within the ethnic group and in the immediate locality was encouraged. The age at which marriage was arranged varied among ethnic groups, but men generally married women somewhat younger than they were. Some of the marriages were even arranged by the families long before the girl attained nubility. In these matters, family considerations outweighed personal ones—a situation that further reinforced the subservient position of the wife.

The alienation of women from the acquisition of wealth, even in conjugal relationships, was strengthened by traditional living arrangements. Among matrilineal groups, such as the Akan, married women continued to reside at their maternal homes. Meals prepared by the wife would be carried to the husband at his maternal house. In polygamous situations, visitation schedules would be arranged. The separate living patterns reinforced the idea that each spouse is subject to the authority of a different household head, and because spouses are always members of different lineages, each is ultimately subject to the authority of the senior men of his or her lineage. The wife, as an outsider in the husband's family, would not inherit any of his property, other than that granted to her by her husband as gifts in token appreciation of years of devotion. The children from this matrilineal marriage would be expected to inherit from their mother's family (see Traditional Patterns of Social Relations, this ch.).

The Ewe and the Dagomba, on the other hand, inherit from fathers. In these patrilineal societies where the domestic group includes the man, his wife or wives, their children, and perhaps several dependent relatives, the wife is brought into closer proximity to the husband and his paternal family. Her male children also assure her of more direct access to wealth accumulated in the marriage with her husband.

The transition into the modern world has been slow for women. On the one hand, the high rate of female fertility in Ghana in the 1980s showed that women's primary role continued to be that of child-bearing. On the other hand, current research supported the view that, notwithstanding the Education Act of 1960, which expanded and required elementary education, some parents were reluctant to send their daughters to school because their labor was needed in the home and on farms. Resistance to female education also stemmed from the conviction that women would be supported by their husbands. In some circles, there was even the fear that a girl's marriage prospects dimmed when she became educated.

Where girls went to school, most of them did not continue after receiving the basic education certification. Others did not even complete the elementary level of education. At numerous workshops organized by the National Council on Women and Development (NCWD) between 1989 and 1990, the alarming drop-out rate among girls at the elementary school level caused great concern. For this reason, the council called upon the government to find ways to remedy the situation. The disparity between male and female education in Ghana was again reflected in the 1984 national census. Although the ratio of male to female registration in elementary schools was fifty-five to forty-five, the percentage of girls at the secondary school level dropped considerably, and only about 17 percent of registered students in the nation's universities in 1984 were female. According to United Nations Educational, Scientific, and Cultural Organization (UNESCO) figures published in 1991, the percentage of the female population registered at various levels of the nation's educational system in 1989 showed no improvement over those recorded in 1984 (see table 5, Appendix).

Despite what these figures might suggest, women have risen to positions of professional importance in Ghana. Early 1990s data showed that about 19 percent of the instructional staff at the nation's three universities in 1990 was female. Of the teaching staff in specialized and diploma-granting institutions, 20 percent was female; elsewhere, corresponding figures were 21 percent at the secondary school level, 23 percent at the middle school level, and as high as 42 percent at the primary school level. Women also dominated the secretarial and nursing professions in Ghana. When women were employed in the same line of work as men, they were paid equal wages, and they were granted maternity leave with pay.

For women of little or no education who lived in urban centers, commerce was the most common form of economic activity in the 1980s. At urban market centers throughout the country, women from the rural areas brought their goods to trade. Other women specialized in buying agricultural produce at discounted prices at the rural farms and selling it to retailers in the city. These economic activities were crucial in sustaining the general urban population. From the mid-1970s through the early 1980s, however, urban market women, especially those who specialized in trading manufactured goods, gained reputations for manipulating market conditions and were accused of exacerbating the country's already difficult economic situation. With the introduction of the Economic Recovery Program in 1983 and the consequent successes reported throughout that decade, these accusations began to subside (see Economic Recovery Program, ch. 3).

The overall impact of women on Ghanaian society cannot be overemphasized. The social and economic well-being of women, who as mothers, traders, farmers, and office workers compose slightly more than half of the nation's population, cannot be taken for granted. This was precisely the position taken by NCWD, which sponsored a number of studies on women's work, education, and training, and on family issues that are relevant in the design and execution of policies for the improvement of the condition of women. Among these considerations, the NCWD stressed family planning, child care, and female education as paramount.

Religion and Society

The religious composition of Ghana in the first postindependence population census of 1960 was 41 percent Christian, 38 percent traditionalist, 12 percent Muslim, and the rest (about 9 percent) no religious affiliation. A breakdown of the 1960 population according to Christian sects showed that 25 percent were Protestant (non-Pentecostal); 13 percent, Roman Catholic; 2 percent, Protestant (Pentecostal); and 1 percent, Inde-

Woman pounding cassava to make foo foo, *a starchy staple of the Ghanaian diet Courtesy* life in general *(Brook, Rose, and Cooper Le Van)*

pendent African Churches. The 1970 population census did not present figures on the religious composition of the nation.

The percentage of the general population considered to be Christian rose sharply to 62 percent according to a 1985 estimate. Whereas the Protestant (non-Pentecostal) sector remained at 25 percent, the percentage of Catholics increased to 15 percent. A larger rise, however, was recorded for Protestants (Pentecostals)—8 percent compared with their 2 percent representation in 1960. From being the smallest Christian sect, with a 1 percent representation among the general population in 1960, membership in the Independent African Churches rose the most—to about 14 percent by 1985. The 1985 estimate also showed that the Muslim population of Ghana rose to 15 percent. Conversely, the sector representing traditionalists and non-believers (38 and 9 percent, respectively, in 1960), saw dramatic declines by 1985—to 21 and about 1 percent, respectively. This shift, especially the increase in favor of the Independent African Churches, attests to the success of denominations that have adjusted their doctrines to suit local beliefs (see Syncretic Religions, this ch.).

Religious tolerance in Ghana is very high. The major Christian celebrations of Christmas and Easter are recognized as national holidays. In the past, vacation periods have been planned around these occasions, thus permitting both Christians and others living away from home to visit friends and family in the rural areas. Ramadan, the Islamic month of fasting, is observed by Muslims across the country. Important traditional occasions are celebrated by the respective ethnic groups. These festivals include the Adae, which occur fortnightly, and the annual Odwira festivals of the Akan. On these sacred occasions, the Akan ancestors are venerated. There are also the annual Homowo activities of the Ga-Adangbe, during which people return to their home towns to gather together, to greet new members of the family, and to remember the dead. The religious rituals associated with these festivities are strictly observed by the traditional elders of the respective ethic groups.

Christianity and Islam in Ghana

The presence of Christian missionaries on the coast of Ghana has been dated to the arrival of the Portuguese in the fifteenth century. It was the Basel/Presbyterian and Wesleyan/Methodist missionaries, however, who, in the nineteenth century, laid the foundation for the Christian church in Ghana. Beginning their conversions in the coastal area and among the Akwapim, these missionaries established schools as "nurseries of the church" in which an educated African class was trained. Almost all major secondary schools today, especially exclusively boys and girls schools, are mission- or church-related institutions. Although churches continue to influence the development of education in the country, church schools have been opened to all since the state assumed financial responsibility for formal instruction under the Education Act of 1960.

Various Christian denominations are well represented in Ghana. The Volta region has a high concentration of Evangelical Presbyterians. Many Akwapim are Presbyterians, and the Methodist denomination is strongly represented among the Fante. The Roman Catholic Church is fairly well represented in Central Region and Ashanti Region. Although no official figures exist to reflect regional distribution of the various denominations, it is generally agreed that the southern part of the nation is more Christian, while the north is more Islamic.

The unifying organization of Christians in the country is the Christian Council of Ghana, founded in 1929. Representing the Methodist, Anglican, Mennonite, Presbyterian, Evangelical Presbyterian, African Methodist Episcopal Zionist, Christian

Methodist, Evangelical Lutheran, F'Eden, and Baptist churches, and the Society of Friends, the council serves as the link with the World Council of Churches and other ecumenical bodies. The National Catholic Secretariat, established in 1960, also coordinates the different in-country dioceses. These Christian organizations, concerned primarily with the spiritual affairs of their congregations, have occasionally acted in circumstances described by the government as political. Such was the case in 1991 when both the Catholic Bishops Conference and the Christian Council of Ghana called on the military government of the Provisional National Defence Council (PNDC) to return the country to constitutional rule. The Roman Catholic newspaper, *The Standard*, was often critical of PNDC policies.

In the north, Islam predominates. Islam is based on what Muslims believe are the divine revelations received in seventh-century Arabia by the Prophet Muhammad. His life is recounted as the early history of the religion, beginning with his travels from the Arabian town of Mecca about A.D. 610. His condemnation of the polytheistic practices of the people of Mecca caused him to become an outcast. In A.D. 622 Muhammad was invited to the town of Yathrib, which became known as Medina (the city) through its association with him. The move, or hijra, known in the West as the hegira, marks the beginning of the Islamic Era and the Islamic calendar, as well as the inauguration of Islam as a powerful force in history. In Medina, Muhammad continued his preaching, ultimately defeated his detractors in battle, and consolidated his influence as both temporal and spiritual leader of most Arabs before his death in A.D. 632.

After Muhammad's death, his followers compiled those of his words that were regarded as coming directly from God into the Quran, the holy scripture of Islam. Other sayings and teachings as well as precedents of his behavior as recalled by those who knew him became the hadith ("sayings"). From these sources, the faithful constructed the Prophet's customary practice, or sunna, which they endeavor to emulate. The Quran, hadith, and sunna form a comprehensive guide to the spiritual, ethical, and social life of the faithful in most Muslim countries.

The God preached by Muhammad was previously known to his countrymen. Rather than introducing a new deity, Muhammad denied the existence of the pantheon of gods and spirits worshipped before his prophethood and declared the omnipotence of God, the unique creator. Muhammad is the "Seal of the Prophets," the last of the prophetic line. His revelations are said to complete for all time the series of revelations that were given earlier to Jews and Christians. Islam reveres as sacred only the message, not the Prophet. It accepts the concepts of guardian angels, the Day of Judgment, resurrection, and the eternal life of the soul.

The central requirement of Islam is submission to the will of God (Allah), and, accordingly, a Muslim is a person who has submitted his will to God. The most important demonstration of faith is the *shahada* (profession of faith), which states that "There is no God but God (Allah), and Muhammad is his prophet." *Salat* (daily prayer), *zakat* (almsgiving), *sawm* (fasting), and hajj (pilgrimage to Mecca) are also required of all Muslims.

The spread of Islam into West Africa, beginning with ancient Ghana in the ninth century, was mainly the result of the commercial activities of North African Muslims (see The Precolonial Period, ch. 1). The empires of both Mali and Songhai that followed ancient Ghana in the Western Sudan adopted the religion. Islam made its entry into the northern territories of modern Ghana around the fifteenth century. Mande or Wangara traders and clerics carried the religion into the area. The northeastern sector of the country was also influenced by Muslims who escaped the Hausa jihads of northern Nigeria in the early nineteenth century.

Most Ghanaian Muslims are Sunni, following the Maliki version of Islamic law. Sufism, involving the organization of mystical brotherhoods (*tariqa*) for the purification and spread of Islam, is not widespread in Ghana. The Tijaniyah and the Qadiriyah brotherhoods, however, are represented. The Ahmadiyah, a Shia (see Glossary) sect originating in nineteenth-century India, is the only non-Sunni order in the country.

Despite the spread of Islamism (popularly known as Islamic fundamentalism) in the Middle East, North Africa, and even in Nigeria since the mid-1970s, Ghanaian Muslims and Christians have had excellent relations. Guided by the authority of the Muslim Representative Council, religious, social, and economic matters affecting Muslims have often been redressed through negotiations. The Muslim Council has also been responsible for arranging pilgrimages to Mecca for believers who can afford the journey. In spite of these achievements, the council has not succeeded in taking initiatives for the upgrading of Islamic schools beyond the provision of basic Quranic instruction. This may explain the economic and technological gap between Muslims and non-Muslims. The Ghanaian Ahmadiyah Movement, which has established a number of vocational training centers, hospitals, and some secondary schools, is an exception.

Traditional Religion

Despite the presence of Islam and Christianity, traditional religions in Ghana have retained their influence because of their intimate relation to family loyalties and local mores. The traditional cosmology expresses belief in a supreme being (referred to by the Akan as Nyame and by the Ewe as Mawu). The supreme being is usually thought of as remote from daily religious life and is, therefore, not directly worshipped. There are also lesser gods that take "residency" in streams, rivers, trees, and mountains. These gods are generally perceived as intermediaries between the supreme being and society. Ancestors and numerous other spirits are also recognized as part of the cosmological order.

For all Ghanaian ethnic groups, the spirit world is considered to be as real as the world of the living. The dual worlds of the mundane and the sacred are linked by a network of mutual relationships and responsibilities. The action of the living, for example, can affect the gods or spirits of the departed, while the support of family or "tribal" ancestors ensures prosperity of the lineage or state. Neglect, it is believed, might spell doom.

Veneration of departed ancestors is a major characteristic of all traditional religions. The ancestors are believed to be the most immediate link with the spiritual world, and they are thought to be constantly near, observing every thought and action of the living. Some ancestors may even be reincarnated to replenish the lineage. Barrenness is, therefore, considered a great misfortune because it prevents ancestors from returning to life.

To ensure that a natural balance is maintained between the world of the sacred and that of the profane, the roles of the chief within the state, family elders in relation to the lineage, and the priest within society are crucial. The religious functions, especially of chiefs and lineage heads, are clearly demonstrated during such periods as the Odwira of the Akan, the Homowo of the Ga-Adangbe, or the Aboakyir of the Efutu (coastal Guan), when the people are organized in activities that renew and strengthen relations with their ancestors. Such activities include the making of sacrifices and the pouring of libations.

The religious activities of chiefs and lineage heads are generally limited to the more routine biweekly and annual festivities, but traditional priests—given their association with specific shrines—are regarded as specialized practitioners through whom the spirits of the gods may grant directions. Priests undergo vigorous training in the arts of medicine, divination, and other related disciplines and are, therefore, consulted on a more regular basis by the public. Because many diseases are believed to have spiritual causes, traditional priests sometimes act as doctors or herbalists. Shrine visitation is strongest among the uneducated and in rural communities. This fact, however, does not necessarily suggest that the educated Ghanaian has totally abandoned tradition; some educated and mission-trained individuals do consult traditional oracles in times of crisis.

Syncretic Religions

The rise of Apostolic or Pentecostal churches across the nation partly demonstrates the impact of social change and the eclectic nature of traditional cultures. These establishments, referred to by some as separatist or spiritual churches or cults, combine traditional beliefs in magic and divination with elements of Christianity. The major emphasis of the cults is on curative and preventive remedies, chants, and charms, such as "holy water," designed to ward off the power of witches and malevolent forces. Cults also offer social activities in addition to their religious and medical roles. Some have rival drum societies and singing groups that are highly popular among the young and women. To their adherents, these cults seem to offer a sense of security derived from belonging to a religious group that is new yet maintains the characteristics of traditional forms of occult consultation. The increasing popularity of these churches (Independent African and Pentecostal) is reflected in figures for membership, which rose from 1 and 2 percent, respectively, in 1960, to 14 and 8 percent, respectively, according to a 1985 estimate.

Although freedom of religion exists in Ghana, a Religious Bodies (Registration) Law 2989 was passed in June 1989 to regulate churches. By requiring certification of all Christian reli-

A tendaana, *or priest of the land, in front of his shrine in far northern Ghana (Talensi area)*
Courtesy life in general *(Brook, Rose, and Cooper Le Van)*

gious organizations operating in Ghana, the government reserved the right to inspect the functioning of these bodies and to order the auditing of their financial statements. The Ghana Council of Churches interpreted the Religious Bodies Law as contradicting the concept of religious freedom in the country. According to a government statement, however, the law was designed to protect the freedom and integrity of genuine religious organizations by exposing and eliminating groups established to take advantage of believers. The PNDC repealed the law in late 1992. Despite its provisions, all orthodox Christian denominations and many spiritual churches continued to operate in the country.

Health and Welfare

In precolonial Ghana, as in the rest of sub-Saharan Africa, traditional priests were important in providing treatment for the sick. The role of village priests in the medical sphere reflected the belief that unexplained illness, misfortune, and premature death were caused by supernatural agents. In the treatment of illness, therefore, the usual process was for the priest to use divination to determine the source of the malady and to suggest sacrifices to appease the causal agents before herbal medicine was prescribed for the patient. Since the introduction of Islam in Ghana in the fourteenth century, Muslim clerics have also been known to provide spiritual treatment and protection in the form of charms and amulets derived from Quranic beliefs.

The role of the village priests, who provided medical advice and sometimes treatment for the sick, has often been stressed over that of the herbalists, who served their communities solely as dispensers of medicinal herbs. Recent scholarship, however, has shown that villagers in the premodern era understood illness and misfortune to originate from both natural and supernatural sources. Even after a spiritually caused ailment was identified and the proper rituals performed, the final cure was usually via the application of medicinal herbs—a situation that made knowledge of the medicinal value of plants and herbs important. Herbal medicine was used in the treatment of diarrhea and stomach pains, for dressing wounds, as an antidote for poisons, and to stabilize pregnancies. Traditional healers continue to be relied upon, especially in the rural areas where modern health services are limited.

The medical value of traditional remedies varies. While the medicinal properties of herbs cannot be denied, in some cases herbs may be harmful and may result in severe infections or even death. It was for this reason that an association of traditional healers was formed in the 1960s with its headquarters at Nsawam in Greater Accra Region. The Traditional Healers' Association has tried to preserve the integrity of traditional medicinal practice. Its members have also attempted to assure the government, through the Ministry of Health, that the dispensation of herbal medicine has a role to play in modern medical practice in Ghana.

Western medicine was first introduced into the Gold Coast by Christian missionaries and missionary societies in the nineteenth century. Missionaries were almost the sole providers of modern medicine until after World War I. Important missionary medical facilities in Ghana today include Catholic-affiliated hospitals in Sunyani and Tamale, the Muslim Ahmadiyah facilities at Efiduasi-Asokori, and a Presbyterian hospital at Agogo in Eastern Region.

Attempts by the central government to expand Western medical care in the country were given serious consideration during the tenure of Frederick Gordon Guggisberg (1919–27) as governor of the Gold Coast. As part of his ten-year development program, Guggisberg proposed town improvements, improved water supply, and the construction of hospitals. It was during his era that Korle Bu, the first teaching hospital in the Gold Coast, was completed in 1925.

Since the end of World War II, the World Health Organization (WHO) and the United Nations Children's Fund (UNICEF) have provided financial and technical assistance for the elimination of diseases and the improvement of health standards. A shortage of medical specialists exists, however, and local facilities for training medical personnel need to be expanded and updated. As a consequence, many Ghanaians in the immediate post-World War II period continued to rely on traditional doctors and herbalists.

Despite efforts to improve medical conditions in the decades following World War II, the first postindependence census of 1960 did not provide data on the medical situation in Ghana. There was still no regular system for gathering medical statistics by the mid-1960s and no suggestion that one would be developed by 1970. During that period, available figures were gathered from scattered samplings and were collected on a haphazard basis or were the summation of hospital records and United Nations projections. Thus, only partial information about the total health situation was available. Records from the 1984 census and newspaper reports on seminars conducted on health-related issues, especially since the mid-1980s, now make it easier to evaluate national health.

Health Care

Ghana has the full range of diseases endemic to a sub-Saharan country. According to WHO, common diseases include cholera, typhoid, pulmonary tuberculosis, anthrax, pertussis, tetanus, chicken pox, yellow fever, measles, infectious hepatitis, trachoma, malaria, and schistosomiasis. Others are guinea worm or *dracunculiasis,* various kinds of dysentery, river blindness or onchocerciasis, several kinds of pneumonia, dehydration, venereal diseases, and poliomyelitis. According to a 1974 report, more than 75 percent of all preventable diseases at that time were waterborne. In addition, malnutrition and diseases acquired through insect bites continued to be common.

WHO lists malaria and measles as the leading causes of premature death in Ghana. Among children under five years of age, 70 percent of deaths are caused by infections compounded by malnutrition. Guinea worm reached epidemic proportions, especially in the northern part of the country, in 1988–89. Cerebral spinal meningitis also spread in the country and claimed a number of victims in the late 1980s. All these afflictions are either typical of tropical regions or common in developing countries.

To improve health conditions in Ghana, the Ministry of Health emphasized health services research in the 1970s. In addition, WHO and the government worked closely in the early 1980s to control schistosomiasis in man-made bodies of water. Efforts have been intensified since 1980 to improve the nation's sanitation facilities and access to safe water. The percentage of the national population that had access to safe water rose from 49.2 in 1980 to 57.2 percent in 1987. During that same period, the 25.6 percent of the population with access to sanitation services (public latrines, rubbish disposal, etc.) rose to 30.3 percent. According to WHO, however, many of the reported sanitation advances have been made in urban areas and not in rural communities where the majority of the population lives.

On the whole, however, Ghana's health conditions are improving. The result is reflected in the decline in infant mortality from 120 per 1,000 live births in 1965 to 86 per 1,000 live births in 1989, and a rate of overall life expectancy that increased from an average of forty-four years in 1970 to fifty-six years in 1993. To reduce the country's infant mortality rate further, the government initiated the Expanded Program on Immunization in February 1989 as part of a ten-year Health Action Plan to improve the delivery of health services. The government action was taken a step farther by the Greater Accra Municipal Council, which declared child immunization a prerequisite for admission to public schools.

Modern medical services in Ghana are provided by the central government, local institutions, Christian missions (private nonprofit agencies), and a relatively small number of private for-profit practitioners. According to the United Nations, about 60.2 percent of the country's total population in 1975 depended on government or quasi-government health centers for medical care. Of the available health facilities represented in the 1984 census, about 62.9 percent were still described as government and quasi-government institutions. Mission hospitals represented a large percentage of the remainder, while private hospitals constituted less than 2 percent of modern medical care facilities (see table 4, Appendix).

The medical system in Ghana comes under the jurisdiction of the Ministry of Health, which is also charged with the control of dangerous drugs, narcotics, scientific research, and the professional qualifications of medical personnel. Regional and district medical matters fall under the jurisdiction of trained medical superintendents. Members of the national Psychic and Healers' Association have also been recognized by the government since 1969. Over the years, all administrative branches of the Ministry of Health have worked closely with city, town, and village councils in educating the population in sanitation matters.

Many modern medical facilities exist in Ghana, but these are not evenly distributed across the country. Ministry of Health figures for 1990 showed that there were 18,477 hospital beds for the estimated national population of 15 million. World Bank (see Glossary) figures showed that in 1965 there was one physician to every 13,740 patients in Ghana. The ratio widened to one to 20,460 in 1989. In neighboring Togo, the doctor-to-patient ratio of one to 23,240 in 1965 improved to one to 8,700 in 1989; it was one to 29,530 in 1965 and one to 6,160 in 1989 for Nigeria, whereas in Burkina, the ratio of one to 73,960 in 1965 worsened to one to 265,250 in 1989. These figures show that while the doctor-patient ratio in Ghana gradually became less favorable, the ratio in neighboring countries, with the exception of Burkina, was rapidly improving.

The ratio of nurses to patients in Ghana (one to 3,730 in 1965), however, improved to one to 1,670 by 1989. Compared to Togo (one nurse to 4,990 patients in 1965 and one to 1,240 in 1989) and Burkina (one to 4,150 in 1965 and one to 1,680 in 1989), the rate of improvement in Ghana was slow. The improvement in Nigeria's nurse-to-patient ratio from one to 6,160 in 1965 to one to 1,900 in 1989 was exceptional. A rapidly growing Ghanaian population was not the only reason for unfavorable ratios of medical staff to patients; similar population growth was experienced in neighboring West African countries. Insofar as the Ghana Medical Association and the various nurses associations were concerned, better salaries and working conditions in Nigeria, for example, were significant variables in explaining the attraction of that country for Ghanaian physicians and other medical personnel. This attraction was especially true for male and, therefore, more mobile medical workers, as shown by the arguments of various health workers' associations in 1990 during demonstrations in support of claims for pay raises and improved working conditions.

Ghana adopted a number of policies to ensure an improved health sector. These included the introduction of minimum fees paid by patients to augment state funding for health services and a national insurance plan introduced in 1989. Also in 1989, the construction of additional health centers was intensified to expand primary health care to about 60 percent of the rural community. Hitherto, less than 40 percent of the rural population had access to primary health care, and fewer than half of Ghanaian children were immunized against various childhood diseases. The training of village health workers, community health workers, and traditional birth attendants was also intensified in the mid-1980s in order to create a pool of personnel to educate the population about preventive measures necessary for a healthy community.

Since 1986 efforts to improve health conditions in Ghana have been strengthened through the efforts of Global 2000 (see Glossary). Although primarily an agricultural program, Global 2000 has also provided basic health education, especially in the northern parts of the country where the spread of guinea worm reached epidemic proportions in 1989. Reports on the impact of Global 2000 on health have been positive in other ways as well. For example, participating farmers have significantly increased their agricultural output—a development that has contributed to a decline in malnutrition. Also, the number of cases of guinea worm had dropped significantly by early 1993.

Acquired Immune Deficiency Syndrome (AIDS)

In March 1986, the first case of acquired immune deficiency syndrome (AIDS) was reported in Ghana. In January 1991, a more detailed report on AIDS in Ghana appeared in which 107 human immunodeficiency virus (HIV) positive cases were said to have been recorded in 1987. Three hundred thirty-three people were identified as HIV positive by the end of March 1988, and there was a further increase to 2,744 by the end of April 1990. Of the April 1990 number, 1,226 were reported to have contracted AIDS. According to WHO annual reports, the disease continued to spread in the country. During 1991 the Komfo Anokye Teaching Hospital reported about fifty AIDS cases each month.

Although the reported figures were far below the number of known cases in East Africa and Central Africa, they were still alarming for a medical system already overburdened by traditional health problems. Seminars and conferences held to discuss the disease included the 1990 annual conference of the Ghana Academy of Arts and Sciences. The conference theme was the impact of international prostitution and the spread of AIDS. The Ministry of Health, with funding from WHO, had also set up surveillance systems to track the AIDS virus as part of its medium-term (1989–93) plan. According to the program, a countrywide sample of both high- and low-risk groups had been identified for testing at regular intervals to measure the prevalence of the disease. A thirty-member National Advisory Council on AIDS was established in late 1989 to advise the government on policy matters relating to the control and prevention of AIDS in the country. The Ministry of Health lacks adequately trained personnel and information management systems to combat the disease.

Because of the continued spread of infection and improved reporting, the country recorded 12,500 AIDS cases by the end of 1994, placing Ghana second only to neighboring Côte d'Ivoire, where more than 16,600 cases of AIDS were recorded, in the West Africa subregion. Of the Ghanaian AIDS cases, about 8,000 were people aged fifteen to forty-five; the remainder were mostly children aged five to ten. At the same time, Ghanaian health officials estimated the number of HIV positive cases at about 300,000. The incidence of HIV positive and AIDS cases was highest in Ashanti Region.

The most-affected age-group in Ghana is young working adults. Some 70 percent of the total infected population is female; on the basis of this finding, the Ministry of Health anticipates a significant increase in HIV-positive births in the future. Considering the gravity of the problem, in February 1994 the National Parliament recommended that a select committee on education and health be established to study and make recommendations for measures to control AIDS. In the meantime, radio, television, and billboard advertisements are being used as part of a national AIDS awareness program.

Social Welfare

In precolonial Ghanaian societies, it was normal for individuals to receive economic assistance from members of their extended families—including paternal and maternal uncles, aunts, grandparents, and cousins. The practice of expecting assistance from family members grew out of the understanding that the basis of family wealth derived from land and labor, both inherited from common ancestors. Even as individuals sought help from extended family members, they were in turn required to fulfill certain responsibilities, such as contributing labor when needed or participating in activities associated with rites of passage of family members. It is because of this mutual interdependence of the members of the family that anthropologist Robert S. Rattray defined the extended family in Ghana as the primary political unit. Today, the same system of welfare assistance prevails in rural areas, where more than two-thirds of the country's population resides.

Legislation for the provision of a modern national social security system went into effect in 1965. Further legislation was passed in 1970 to convert the system into a pension plan to provide for sickness, maternity, and work-related injury benefits. Government welfare programs at the time were the responsibility of the Department of Social Welfare under the Ministry of Labour and Social Welfare (now the Ministry of Mobilization and Social Welfare). As the national economy was reformed, the Workers' Compensation Act of 1986 was passed to guarantee wages to workers in the private sector while they were undergoing treatment for work-related injuries.

These plans, however, applied only to individuals employed in the formal sector of the economy. With about two-thirds of the country's population residing in rural areas, and with most urban residents engaged outside the formal economy, the traditional pattern of social security based on kin obligations still functions. In rural areas, individuals continue to turn to members of the extended family for financial aid and guidance, and the family is expected to provide for the welfare of every member. In villages, towns, and cities, this mutual assistance system operates within the larger kinship units of lineage and clan. In large urban areas, religious, social, and professionally based mutual assistance groups have become popular as a way to address professional and urban problems beyond the scope of the traditional kinship social security system (see Urban Society, this ch.).

According to a 1988 newspaper report, housing has become a major problem for city dwellers. The report indicated that former governments largely ignored the problem, thereby allowing the situation to reach an alarming state. The result is an acute shortage of affordable rental housing for urban workers and students, who have to pay exorbitant rents. This shortage in turn has resulted in working husbands' leaving their families in their home villages and returning only when their work schedules allow them time to visit.

The introduction of the "Rural Manifesto" of 1984 was an attempt by the PNDC administration to address a general development problem that included urban housing. According to the1984 plan, many services, such as the provision of pipe-borne water, banking facilities, and electricity, were to be introduced to the rural areas, thereby making such locations attractive to workers and others who might otherwise migrate to towns and cities. Because the implementation of these services, especially rural electrification, began in earnest only in the late 1980s, the plan's impact on rural-urban flow was as yet uncertain in the early 1990s.

Education

The dominant mode of transmitting knowledge in the precolonial societies of the Guinea Coast was through apprenticeship as smiths, drummers, or herbalists. By observing adult skills, or through proverbs, songs, and stories, children learned proper roles and behavior. Also, at various stages in life, especially during the puberty rites for young adults, intensive moral and ethical instruction from family or societal elders was given. The purpose of that "informal" education was to ensure that the individual was able to satisfy the basic traditional or communal needs, such as motherhood for women, and hunting, long-distance trading, or farming for men. It was also important that the religious sanctions associated with the various professions and stages in life be understood because the traditional society saw close relationships between religious and mundane activities.

Western-style education was introduced into the Gold Coast by missionaries as early as 1765. Many of these institutions, established by Presbyterian and Methodist missionaries, were located in the south of the country in what became the British Gold Coast Colony (see Christianity and Islam in Ghana, this ch.). In 1852 the British colonial government instituted a poll tax to raise money to support public schools, but the measure became unpopular and was abolished in 1861. Mission schools continued to spread, however, and by 1881 more than 139 had been established with an enrollment of about 5,000 students.

A board of education was set up in the 1880s to inspect schools and to standardize their management. Grants were established for private schools that met government standards, and the government devised regulations for the recognition of new schools. Primary education was emphasized until limited secondary education was introduced in the early 1900s.

After World War I, the development of education was given additional impetus under Governor Guggisberg. His education policies stressed the need for improved teacher training, equal education for girls, a greater emphasis on vocational training, and the establishment of secondary schools. In the governor's ten-year development plan, which was announced in 1919, education was given a special place, partly because of his goal of replacing Europeans with educated Africans in many administrative positions within the country. The policies were not fully implemented, especially at the secondary and vocational levels, but the Achimota School, a first-class secondary school designed to train Ghanaians for the lower levels of the civil service, was established in 1927. Although English remained the principal language of instruction in the school system, vernacular languages were also allowed in the primary schools, and the publication of textbooks in these languages began in earnest.

Stimulated by nationalist ideas of political and economic self-determination from the 1930s through the 1940s, popular demand for education reached such proportions that the combined efforts of the colonial government and the missions could not satisfy it. The result was the opening of hundreds of schools by local groups and individuals. The Convention People's Party (CPP) promise of free instruction during the 1951 election campaign was made in response to an increasing demand for education. Whereas some parents in the northern regions of the country resisted enrollment of their children, many in the south encouraged formal instruction because it was regarded as a virtual guarantee of acquiring white-collar jobs and wage-earning positions. Western education was accepted more readily in the southern sector of the country because Christian missionaries had been in that area longer than they had been in the north. The purpose of the CPP's free and compulsory education policy was to make formal education available to all at minimum cost.

In 1952 the CCP-led government drew up the Accelerated Development Plan for Education. The program, which became a reality in 1961, was designed to provide an education for

Korle Bu Hospital in Accra
Courtesy Embassy of Ghana, Washington
The University of Ghana at Legon
Courtesy Embassy of Ghana, Washington

every child aged six and above. To achieve this goal, the central government took responsibility for teacher training and funded schools through the Ministry of Education. Since this time, a considerable portion of the national budget has been spent on educating the population. Various attempts to shift the cost to students and parents, especially at the university level, have met great resistance.

The Education System

The country's education system at the beginning of the 1993–94 academic year comprised primary schools, junior secondary schools, senior secondary schools, polytechnic (technical and vocational) institutions, teacher training colleges, and university-level institutions.

In 1990–91, the latest year for which preliminary government statistics were available, 1.8 million pupils were attending more than 9,300 primary schools; 609,000 students were enrolled in about 5,200 junior secondary schools; and nearly 200,000 students were enrolled in some 250 senior secondary schools (see table 5, Appendix). In the mid-1980s, teachers on each of these levels numbered approximately 51,000, 25,000, and 8,800, respectively. In addition, 1989–90 enrollment in Ghana's approximately twenty-six polytechnic schools totalled almost 11,500 students; the teacher corps for these schools numbered 422. Education is free, although students have recently begun to pay textbook fees. The Education Act of 1960 foresaw universal education, but the constraints of economic underdevelopment meant that by the early 1990s this goal had not been realized. On the primary level, instruction is conducted in the local vernacular, although English is taught as a second language. Beyond primary school, however, English is the medium of instruction in an education system that owes much to British models.

Before the introduction of reforms in the mid-1980s, students at what was then the middle-school level took either the Middle School Leaving Certificate Examination and terminated their studies, or, at any time from seventh to tenth grade, the Common Entrance Examination, which admitted them to secondary or technical study. With the traditional six years of primary education, four years of middle schooling, and a seven-year secondary education (five years of preparation toward the Ordinary Level Certificate and two years of Advanced Level training) before entering degree-granting institutions, the average age of the first-year university student in Ghana was often about twenty-five.

Most students, however, did not continue formal instruction after the first ten years of education. Of the 145,400 students completing middle school in 1960, for example, only 14,000 sought secondary education. In 1970 only 9,300 of the more than 424,500 leaving middle school were admitted into secondary schools. Ministry of Education data for the 1984–85 academic year showed that of the 1.8 million students completing ten years of primary and middle schooling, only 125,600 continued into secondary schools, while fewer than 20,000 entered vocational and technical institutions. That same year, approximately 7,900 students were enrolled in the universities.

Although the government provides free tuition to all children of school age, and notwithstanding the fact that schools can be found all across the country, 1989–90 government statistics showed that more males continued to be enrolled in schools than females. In the first six grades of the educational system, only 45 percent of the students enrolled were female. The percentage of females in the school system decreased to 33 percent at the secondary school level, to 27 percent in polytechnical institutions, and to as low as 19 percent within the universities. Disparities in the male-female ratios found in the schools had not improved significantly by 1990–91. The emphasis on male education doubtless reflects traditional social values, which view the reproductive abilities of women as their primary role in life, while men are valued as breadwinners and, therefore, in need of education to compete in the contemporary economy (see The Position of Women, this ch.).

Despite a number of committee reports and proposals for educational reform, until mid-1980 the education system continued to place emphasis on traditional academic studies. Proponents of reform argued that the country's development needs required an education system that, beginning at the middle-school level, placed equal emphasis on training students in vocational and technical skills. It was further suggested that reforms could contribute to reducing the number of students who dropped out of school for lack of interest in traditional academic studies.

Partly as a result of earlier proposals for reform and partly in keeping with the government's economic reform program, fundamental change in the educational structure of the country was undertaken in the mid-1980s. The overall goals were to make curricula at all levels more relevant to the economic needs of the country, to reduce the length of pre-university instruction, and to improve the quality of teacher preparation. Increased enrollment in primary schools and a reduction in the rate of illiteracy were also to be pursued. The reforms were to be implemented in two phases: those for primary and middle schools were to be introduced in 1987–89, and those for secondary schools and the universities, in 1990–93.

The much-discussed changes in education became a reality in 1987 when all seventh-grade students, who otherwise would have entered the traditional first year of middle school, were instead admitted into new junior secondary schools (JSS) to begin a three-year combined training program in vocational, technical, and academic studies. The JSS system was a radical change in the structure of education in the country. It replaced the four-year middle school and the first three years of the traditional five-year secondary school system. After three years at the JSS, three years further training would be available in senior secondary schools (SSS), after which students could enter polytechnic institutions or the universities.

Pioneers in the JSS system sat for the first Basic Certificate of Education Examination in 1990. In this same year, seniors of the old middle-school system took the last Middle School Leaving Certificate Examination. Supporters of the JSS argued that the system would attract more students into technical, vocational, business, and agricultural institutions. It was also suggested that those students who did not gain admission into the SSS would be better equipped to enter the job market. Results of the first SSS certificate examination, announced in May 1994, however, showed that only 3.9 percent of students received passing marks. This poor showing was attributed to lack of textbooks, equipment, and trained teachers, and to inadequate time to prepare for the examination. Despite loud protests from students and parents, reform of the education system remained on course.

In addition to revamping middle-school education, changes were also introduced on all other educational levels. Fees for textbooks and supplies were instituted, primary curricula were revised, and food and housing subsidies were reduced or eliminated in secondary schools and the universities. In the early 1990s, however, the government appeared to be moving slowly in implementing further proposed reforms, such as new curricula in secondary schools and restructuring of the universities.

In the early 1990s, higher education was available at three institutions—the University of Ghana (located principally at Legon outside Accra), founded in 1948 as the University College of the Gold Coast; the University of Science and Technology at Kumasi, opened officially in 1952 as the Kumasi College of Technology; and the University of Cape Coast at Cape Coast, founded in 1961. In 1989–90 enrollment at all three institutions totalled 9,251, of whom 19 percent were female. In addition, large numbers of Ghanaians went abroad for university education, as they had in the past.

In anticipation that the new JSS and SSS structures would increase the number of students seeking advanced technical training, two more universities were proposed. The specialist institutions or colleges at Winneba, which offered post-secondary teacher training in such subjects as art, music, and physical education, were to be upgraded into an independent university college or were to be given associate relations with the University of Cape Coast. In September 1993, the University of Development Studies at Tamale opened. Designed initially to train agricultural specialists, it will eventually also offer degrees in health and development studies.

Problems in Education

At least two major educational issues faced Ghana in the early 1990s—the effort to shift part of the expense of education onto students, especially in the universities, and the future of the JSS innovation. Since the introduction of the Accelerated Development Plan for Education in 1952, the central government has shouldered much of the financial burden of education. In 1972, for example, about 20.1 percent of the total central government expenditure was spent on education. This figure rose to 25.7 percent in 1989. Compared with Nigeria, where only 4.5 percent and 2.8 percent of the total government expenditure was spent on education in 1972 and 1989, respectively, the Ghana figure was high even among its peers.

Efforts by the central government to shift the cost of education onto students, particularly at the university level, have been challenged. But despite the many demonstrations that were organized by the various student representative councils and the National Union of Ghanaian Students, the government resolved in the latter part of the 1980s to make university students pay for their boarding and lodging through loans. This policy, among others, was the cause of the unsettled relationship between university students and the government that characterized the early 1990s. In March 1993, an especially serious confrontation occurred in Accra between university students and police over the proposed charges. Such protests notwithstanding, the Ministry of Education proceeded with the changes for university funding on grounds that they were in line with the nation's Economic Recovery Program introduced in 1983 (see The Economic Recovery Program, ch. 3).

The introduction of the JSS system was also problematic. It had been agreed upon after the Dzobo Committee, chaired by N.K. Dzobo of the University of Cape Coast, reported in 1974 that the nation's educational establishment needed overhauling. In fact, this committee afforded education specialists and the public the opportunity to respond to a 1972 Ministry of Education proposal for the introduction of junior secondary schools. Despite the favorable evaluation of the Ministry of Education proposal by the Dzobo Committee, the proposed changes in the structure and content of primary and secondary education were never implemented, perhaps because of the difficult economic situation of the country in the mid-1970s.

When the JSS system was implemented in 1987, it was hailed by its supporters as the answer to the country's educational, social, and economic problems. Detractors, however, condemned it because of the limited time allowed for the development of necessary infrastructure, such as the provision of workshops, before the system went into effect. As a community-sponsored program, the JSS became a source of endless irritation to parents and guardians who had to contribute to building and equipping JSS workshops. There was also the concern that the JSS system would ultimately lead to an unfair distribution of educational resources because wealthier communities were likely to provide better facilities than those in poorer areas. Finally, it was argued that the JSS program did not challenge students enough because, unlike the former Middle School Leaving Certificate Examinations, all students writing the Basic Certificate of Education Examination conducted for the JSS received certificates of participation. The validity of these arguments, as well as the long-term impact of the new structure and content of education on the nation's development, remained to be demonstrated in the early 1990s.

Adult Education

A mass literacy campaign was started in 1951 as part of an overall community development program. The primary aim was to teach adults to read and write in their own languages as well as in English. Efforts continued during the 1950s and the 1960s, and in the 1970s an extensive literacy campaign was launched under the direction of the Ministry of Labor and Social Welfare using mass education teams. Literacy classes for adults were also conducted by local units of the Peoples' Education Association, a voluntary organization founded in 1949. This group, which included teachers, graduates, students, and interested persons, had branches throughout the country. Despite such organizational efforts, it was estimated by the United Nations in 1970 that about 70 percent of the nation's inhabitants above the age of fifteen (57 percent of males and 82 percent of females) were illiterate. The 1970 figure was a 5 percent improvement over an estimated 1960 adult literacy rate of 25 percent.

Responding to the continued high level of illiteracy in the country, the government established the Institute of Adult Education in 1970 at the University of Ghana. The Institute was to furnish resident tutorial staff drawn from universities, colleges, and secondary schools to teach a wide range of classes in different parts of the country. The Institute also organized an annual New Year School attended by leading educators, government officials, and numerous social welfare organizations. At such times, the achievements of the Institute as well as the future direction of adult education in Ghana were assessed.

During the 1989 New Year School held at the University of Ghana, for example, the relationship between adult education and economic development was emphasized in a speech read by Flight Lieutenant Jerry John Rawlings, the head of state. Also in 1989, reliable press reports held that the adult literacy rate in Ghana was about 40 percent of the total population; of the 60 percent of the population that was illiterate, 57 percent was female. Even though the 1989 figure was an improvement over that of 1970, the National Council on Women and Development still expressed concern and described the low percentage of literate adult females as alarming. The council attributed female illiteracy to high dropout rates in the elementary schools and called on the government to find ways to enforce compulsory education in the country (see The Position of Women, this ch.). Despite such calls for educational improvement, there was little reason to believe that the situation with respect to literacy had changed significantly by the mid-1990s.

As part of an effort to improve the overall awareness of women's education, various nursing and para-medical associations organized drama troupes as a means of instructing illiterate as well as rural women about the importance of nutrition, of child care, of family planning, and of sending their children to school. In the early 1990s, the impact of such activities on the nation's literacy rate could not yet be assessed.

* * *

Information on the geography of Ghana appears in a variety of sources. E.A. Boateng's *A Geography of Ghana*, published in 1966, is probably the most valuable. Basic archaeological data are in publications by Timothy F. Garrard, Kwaku Effah-Gyamfi, David Kiyaga-Mulindwa, Merrick Posnansky, Peter L. Shinnie, and L.B.Crossland. Kwamina Dickson's *A Historical Geography of Ghana* and James Anquandah's *Rediscovering Ghana's Past* are recommended as good reconstructions of Ghana's past.

Ethnographic information on the peoples of Ghana may be found in the works of Robert Sutherland Rattray, Kwabena J.H. Nketia, Kwesi Yanka, Kofi Abrefa Busia, Minion Morrison, Margaret J. Field, Jack Goody, and Marion Johnson. For more recent information, see M.E. Kropp Dakubu's *The Languages of Ghana.*

Much of the recent literature on Ghana describes changes in traditional society as it adjusts to the contemporary world. These often focus on the position of chiefs in relation to the modern state. Kofi Abrefa Busia's *The Position of the Chief in the Modern Political System of Ashanti*, A. Adu Boahen's *Ghana: Evolution and Change in the Nineteenth and Twentieth Centuries*, and Kwame Arhin's *Traditional Rule in Ghana: Past and Present* are among the most impressive. Also significant is Peter K. Sarpong's *Ghana in Retrospect: Some Aspects of Ghanaian Culture.* An extensive bibliography on the cultural environment of the country can be found in E.Y. Amedekey's *The Culture of Ghana: A Bibliography.*

Population figures on Ghana and other statistical information can be found in the *Quarterly Digest of Statistics* published by the Government of Ghana, Statistical Service. The same office also published the *Preliminary Report on the 1984 Census.* For complete bibliographical information on the country's census figures, see *Population of Ghana: An Annotated Bibliography,*

1980–1988, published by the Regional Institute for Population Studies at the University of Ghana. Excellent sources on women and on economic and social developments include the works of such scholars as Claire Robertson, Christine Oppong, Mason Oppenheim, and Gwendolyn Mikell. (For further information and complete citations, see Bibliography.)

Chapter 3. The Economy

Gold weight in the form of a striking scorpion (Asante)

GHANA'S ECONOMY HAS LEFT an indelible imprint on the country's social and political structures. Just as the presence of gold gave rise to the Asante confederacy and empire and attracted European traders and colonial rulers, so, too, were modern-day politicians moved to try to protect the country's wealth by establishing the first socialist regime in twentieth-century Africa. As the ambitious plans initiated by Ghana's first president, Kwame Nkrumah, unraveled in the late 1960s, however, military officers seized control of the country and promised to overturn what they perceived as a corrupt ruling class enriching itself from the nation's coffers. In the 1980s, military and civilian officials failed to revive the economy through stringent anti-corruption measures and embarked instead upon a restructuring of the economy.

The transformation of Ghana's economy undertaken in the 1980s was considered a test case for "structural adjustment" prescriptions advocated by international banking institutions. Faced with growing impoverishment in Africa as well as in much of the so-called developing world, the World Bank and the International Monetary Fund proposed radical programs to revive troubled economies and to restore their productivity. The government of Jerry John Rawlings turned to these agencies in 1983 and accepted their recommendations in exchange for assistance packages to ease Ghana's economic and social transformation. Foremost among the changes enacted in Ghana were the disengagement of the government from an active role in the economy and the encouragement of free-market forces to promote the efficient and productive development of local resources. The reformers cut government budgets, privatized state enterprises, devalued the currency, and rebuilt industrial infrastructure by means of assistance programs. As in other countries of Africa in the 1980s, government was identified as the problem, and free-market forces were seen as the solution.

By the 1990s, the effects of structural adjustment in Ghana were beginning to be assessed. According to the World Bank and other Western financial institutions, the economy had become much more stable, and production was on a more solid footing than it had been a decade earlier. Exports were up, government deficits had been reduced, and inflation was down. Many Ghanaians, however, questioned whether the structural adjustment benefited all Ghanaians or just a few sectors of the economy. Critics of the World Bank charged, moreover, that it concentrated on infrastructure such as airports, roads, and other macro-economic projects that did little to improve the lives of the average Ghanaian.

Under the sway of free-market forces, production had increased in Ghana's traditionally strong sectors, cocoa and gold, thereby reverting to the pre-independence economic structure; still, a more broadly based economy had not developed. In addition, substantial loans had been incurred by the government to promote those sectors—at the expense of current budget expenditures such as health and education—without a compensatory increase in government revenues. Ironically, the tax breaks prescribed to encourage these sectors worked against increased government revenues, so that by 1992 tax revenues began to drop. In addition, jobs not only had been cut from the once bloated public sector but also had not expanded in the more successful export sectors. Although the government claimed its finances were much healthier in the 1990s than in the 1980s, the long-term economic and social impact of structural adjustment was uncertain.

Relying heavily on the exploitation of some non-renewable and even endangered resources, Ghana's economy will have to expand to create a broader and better balanced economy. In addition to cocoa, Ghana's leading export commodities are gold, a non-renewable resource, and timber, the harvesting of which has included more than eighteen endangered species of trees and has led to alarming deforestation. Furthermore, Ghana's ocean waters are seriously overfished, leading the government to ban the catching of shellfish.

According to the government, Ghana's resources could be used to develop local manufacturing, the goal Nkrumah tried to reach through direct state intervention thirty years ago. Local manufacturing could create jobs, cut the import bill, and provide a more diversified economic base. The question for Ghana is whether free-market forces will be more successful in promoting healthy economic expansion than the failed policies of direct state intervention.

Historical Background

Endowed with gold and oil palms and situated between the trans-Saharan trade routes and the African coastline visited by successive European traders, the area known today as Ghana has been involved in all phases of Africa's economic development during the last thousand years. As the economic fortunes of African societies have waxed and waned, so, too, have Ghana's, leaving that country in the early 1990s in a state of arrested development, unable to make the "leap" to Africa's next, as yet uncertain, phase of economic evolution.

As early as the thirteenth century, present-day Ghana was drawn into long-distance trade, in large part because of its gold reserves. The trans-Saharan trade, one of the most wide-ranging trading networks of pre-modern times, involved an exchange of European, North African, and Saharan commodities for the products of the African savannas and forests, including gold, kola nuts, and slaves. Present-day Ghana, named the Gold Coast by European traders, was an important source of the gold traded across the Sahara. Centralized states such as Asante controlled prices by regulating production and marketing of this precious commodity (see The Pre-Colonial Period, ch. 1). As European navigational techniques improved in the fifteenth century, Portuguese and later Dutch and English traders tried to circumvent the Saharan trade by sailing directly to its southernmost source on the West African coast. In 1482 the Portuguese built a fortified trading post at Elmina and began purchasing gold, ivory, and pepper from African coastal merchants.

Although Africans for centuries had exported their raw materials—ivory, gold, kola nuts—in exchange for imports ranging from salt to foreign metals, the introduction of the Atlantic slave trade in the early sixteenth century changed the nature of African export production in fundamental ways (see Arrival of the Europeans, ch. 1). An increasing number of Ghanaians sought to enrich themselves by capturing fellow Africans in warfare and selling them to slave dealers from North America and South America. The slaves were transported to the coast and sold through African merchants, using the same routes and connections through which gold and ivory had formerly flowed. In return, Africans often received guns as payment, which could be used to capture more slaves and, more importantly, to gain and preserve political power.

An estimated ten million Africans, at least half a million from the Gold Coast, left the continent in this manner. Some economists have argued that the slave trade increased African economic resources and therefore did not necessarily impede development, but others, notably historian Walter Rodney, have argued that by removing the continent's most valuable resource—humans—the slave trade robbed Africa of unknown invention, innovation, and production. Rodney further argues that the slave trade fueled a process of underdevelopment, whereby African societies came to rely on the export of resources crucial to their own economic growth, thereby precluding local development of those resources. Although some scholars maintain that the subsequent economic history of this region supports Rodney's interpretation, no consensus exists on this point. Indeed, in recent years, some historians not only have rejected Rodney's interpretation but also have advanced the notion that it is the Africans themselves rather than an array of external forces that are to blame for the continent's economic plight.

When the slave trade ended in the early years of the nineteenth century, the local economy became the focus of the so-called legitimate trade, which the emerging industrial powers of Europe encouraged as a source of materials and markets to aid their own production and sales. The British, in particular, gained increasing control over the region throughout the nineteenth century and promoted the production of palm oil and timber as well as the continuation of gold production. In return, Africans were inundated with imports of consumer goods that, unlike the luxuries or locally unavailable imports of the trans-Saharan trade, quickly displaced African products, especially textiles.

In 1878 cacao trees were introduced from the Americas. Cocoa quickly became the colony's major export; Ghana produced more than half the global yield by the 1920s. African farmers used kinship networks like business corporations to spread cocoa cultivation throughout large areas of southern Ghana. Legitimate trade restored the overall productivity of Ghana's economy; however, the influx of European goods began to displace indigenous industries, and farmers focused more on cash crops than on essential food crops for local consumption.

When Ghana gained its independence from Britain in 1957, the economy appeared stable and prosperous. Ghana was the world's leading producer of cocoa, boasted a well-developed infrastructure to service trade, and enjoyed a relatively advanced education system. At independence, President Kwame Nkrumah sought to use the apparent stability of the

Ghanaian economy as a springboard for economic diversification and expansion. He began the process of moving Ghana from a primarily agricultural economy to a mixed agricultural-industrial one. Using cocoa revenues as security, Nkrumah took out loans to establish industries that would produce import substitutes as well as process many of Ghana's exports. Nkrumah's plans were ambitious and grounded in the desire to reduce Ghana's vulnerability to world trade. Unfortunately, the price of cocoa collapsed in the mid-1960s, destroying the fundamental stability of the economy and making it nearly impossible for Nkrumah to continue his plans. Pervasive corruption exacerbated these problems. In 1966 a group of military officers overthrew Nkrumah and inherited a nearly bankrupt country.

Since 1966 Ghana has been caught in a cycle of debt, weak commodity demand, and currency overvaluation, which has resulted in the decay of productive capacities and a crippling foreign debt. Once the price of cocoa fell in the mid-1960s, Ghana obtained less of the foreign currency necessary to repay loans, the value of which jumped almost ten times between 1960 and 1966. Some economists recommended that Ghana devalue its currency, the cedi (¢; for value of the cedi—see Glossary), to make its cocoa price more attractive on the world market, but devaluation would also have rendered loan repayment in United States dollars much more difficult. Moreover, such a devaluation would have increased the costs of imports, both for consumers and nascent industries.

Until the early 1980s, successive governments refused to devalue the currency (with the exception of the government of Kofi Abrefa Busia, which devalued the cedi in 1971 and was promptly overthrown). Cocoa prices languished, discouraging cocoa production altogether and leading to smuggling of existing cocoa crops to neighboring countries, where francs rather than cedis could be obtained in payment. As production and official exports collapsed, revenue necessary for the survival of the economy was obtained through the procurement of further loans, thereby intensifying a self-destructive cycle driven by debt and reliance on vulnerable world commodity markets.

By the early 1980s, Ghana's economy was in an advanced state of collapse. Per capita gross domestic product (GDP—see Glossary) showed negative growth throughout the 1960s and fell by 3.2 percent per year from 1970 to 1981. Most important was the decline in cocoa production, which fell by half between the mid-1960s and the late 1970s, drastically reducing Ghana's share of the world market from about one-third in the early 1970s to only one-eighth in 1982–83. At the same time, mineral production fell by 32 percent; gold production declined by 47 percent, diamonds by 67 percent, manganese by 43 percent, and bauxite by 46 percent. Inflation averaged more than 50 percent a year between 1976 and 1981, hitting 116.5 percent in 1981. Real minimum wages dropped from an index of 75 in 1975 to one of 15.4 in 1981. Tax revenue fell from 17 percent of GDP in 1973 to only 5 percent in 1983, and actual imports by volume in 1982 were only 43 percent of average 1975–76 levels. Productivity, the standard of living, and the government's resources had plummeted dramatically.

In 1981 a military government under the leadership of Flight Lieutenant Jerry John Rawlings came to power. Calling itself the Provisional National Defence Council (PNDC), the Rawlings regime initially blamed the nation's economic problems on the corruption of previous governments. Rawlings soon discovered, however, that Ghana's problems were the result of forces more complicated than economic abuse. Following a severe drought in 1983, the government accepted stringent International Monetary Fund (IMF—see Glossary) and World Bank (see Glossary) loan conditions and instituted the Economic Recovery Program (ERP).

Signaling a dramatic shift in policies, the ERP fundamentally changed the government's social, political, and economic orientation. Aimed primarily at enabling Ghana to repay its foreign debts, the ERP exemplified the structural adjustment policies formulated by international banking and donor institutions in the 1980s. The program emphasized the promotion of the export sector and an enforced fiscal stringency, which together aimed to eradicate budget deficits. The PNDC followed the ERP faithfully and gained the support of the international financial community. The effects of the ERP on the domestic economy, however, led to a lowered standard of living for most Ghanaians.

Overview of the Current Economy

In the early 1990s, Ghana's economic recovery still appeared uneven and was geared primarily to the export rather than domestic market. GDP had risen by an average of 5 percent per year since 1984, inflation had been reduced to about 20 percent, and export earnings had reached US$1 billion. Most production came from the export sector, and by the 1992–93 crop year, cocoa production surpassed 300,000 tons, placing Ghana third in the world. In 1990 exports of minerals—primarily gold but also diamonds, manganese, and bauxite—brought in US$234 million, an increase of 23.2 percent from the year before (see fig. 7). Nevertheless, salaries were low, and because the cost of public services continued to rise, Ghana's poor bore the brunt of the negative effects of the austerity program.

Despite devaluations by the Rawlings regime and rising exports, the government has been unable to fulfill a key stabilization goal of reducing the trade and current account deficits. To stimulate production in various sectors, the government has incurred loans to finance imports of necessary inputs such as machinery, fertilizer, and petroleum. As a result, the country's foreign debt exceeded US$4 billion in 1991. According to World Bank estimates, the country's debt continued to rise in 1992, and was equivalent to almost 63 percent of gross national product (GNP—see Glossary). In 1992 the debt service ratio (debt service as a proportion of exports) was 27 percent, an improvement over late 1980s levels, which averaged as high as 62.5 percent. To cover the deficits that result from loans and increased imports, the government came to rely on rising levels of foreign aid, with net aid disbursements increasing to an estimated US$550 million by 1990. Unfortunately, foreign investment, compared with aid, was weak except in the mining sector, and domestic savings were insufficient to finance the country's ambitious development projects.

Government policies have produced mixed results in terms of productivity and debt, and they have also incurred significant social costs through job elimination and reduced public expenditure policies. The government has addressed this problem by launching a special initiative to create 40,000 jobs providing services to the poorest groups. Spending on health and education also has increased as a proportion of GDP, but the central government believes that major poverty alleviation can come only with even faster and higher economic growth.

Structure of the Economy

Most government efforts to restore the productivity of the Ghanaian economy have been directed toward boosting the country's exports. These policies, however, have had numerous consequences. Following the initiation of the ERP in 1983 and the devastating drought of 1983, Ghana's GDP has registered

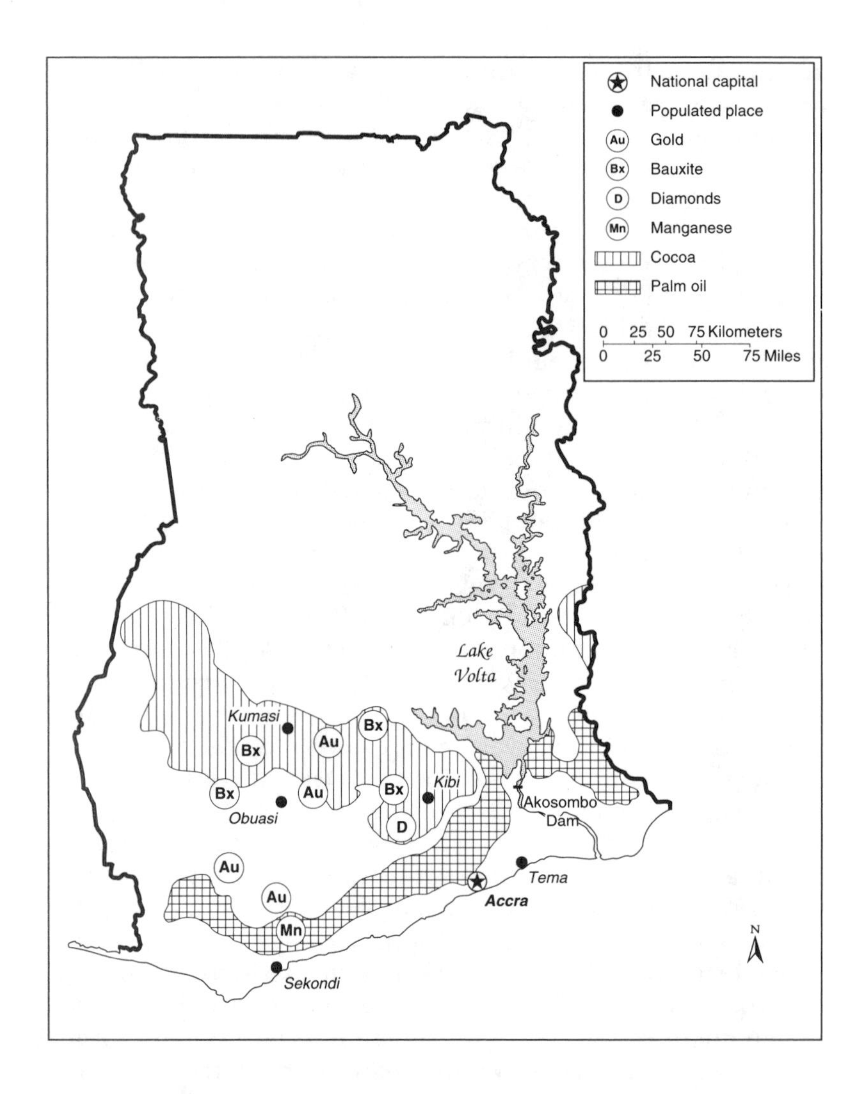

Figure 7. Economic Activity, 1994

steady growth, most of it attributable to the export sector, including cocoa and minerals and, to some extent, timber processing. The cost of this growth is apparent, however, in Ghana's growing external debts, which have financed rehabilitation of the export sector, and in the country's steady rate of inflation which has curbed consumer imports. The government has tried with limited success to avoid some of the country's historical pitfalls by broadening the range of both exports and trading partners. Nevertheless, prices for the goods that most Ghanaians purchase have been rising faster than the wages they receive for their work.

Gross Domestic Product

In current prices, Ghana's GDP rose from ¢511 billion in 1986 to ¢3 trillion in 1992. In constant 1987 prices, these GDP figures amounted to ¢713 billion (US$4.62 billion) in 1986 and ¢934 billion (US$6.06 billion) in 1992 (see table 6, Appendix).

During the 1980s, Ghana's economy registered strong growth of approximately 5 percent per year because of a reversal in the steadily declining production of the previous decade. Ghana's worst years were 1982 and 1983, when the country was hit with the worst drought in fifty years, bush fires that destroyed crops, and the lowest cocoa prices of the postwar period. Growth throughout the remainder of the decade reflected the pace of the economic recovery, but output remained weak in comparison with 1970 production levels. The same was true of consumption, minimum wages, and social services.

Growth fell off considerably in 1990 when another drought caused real GDP growth to decline by nearly two percentage points. Government estimates claimed that real GDP growth in 1993 was 6.1 percent, which reflected a recovery in cocoa output and an increase in gold production. At the same time, gross domestic fixed investment rose from 3.5 percent of the total in 1982 to 12.9 percent in 1992. The share of public consumption in GDP fell from a peak of 11.1 percent in 1986 to 9.9 percent in 1988, but appeared to have risen again to 13.3 percent in 1992.

Significant changes have taken place in the structure of GDP since the ERP began. Agriculture continues to be the bedrock of Ghana's economy, accounting for more than 48 percent of GDP in 1991. Agriculture's long-term importance has declined, however, in favor of that of industry, the contribution of which to GDP more than doubled from 1988 to 1991, when it constituted almost 16 percent of GDP, and in favor of services, the contribution of which was 35.3 percent in 1991. Notable changes have also occurred within the broader sectors: cocoa's share rose from 5.6 percent in 1983 to 9.5 percent in 1991; manufacturing's contribution increased from 3.9 percent to 8.7 percent; and construction output from 1.5 percent to 3.5 percent (see fig. 8; table 7, Appendix).

Debt and Inflation

ERP policies during the 1980s resulted in increased external debts as well as in relatively high inflation rates (see table 8, Appendix). Most ERP projects were funded by foreign loans, notably from the IMF. At the same time, the government repeatedly devalued the country's currency to raise producer prices for exports and to encourage production, but devaluation also led to price rises on all other goods as well. ERP attempts to promote production have, at least in the short term, resulted in higher debts and inflation.

World Bank figures show that Ghana's total external debt exceeded US$4 billion by 1991; this figure rose to nearly US$4.3 billion in 1992. The external deficit and requirements for repayments on principal were met through additional loans. The debt figures revealed a strong reliance on official creditors, who accounted for about 92 percent of public disbursed debt, and on concessional funding, which approached 60 percent of total external debt in 1992. In addition, Ghana began to borrow on international capital markets in 1991. Nevertheless, the country's debt service ratio fell at an annual average of 25 percent in 1991 and 1992, reflecting repayment of large IMF obligations and the ending of the government's use of IMF funding at the end of 1991. An additional factor was debt cancellation by a number of leading bilateral creditors totaling US$1.5 billion since 1989.

In the early 1990s, the government was unable to reduce high inflation significantly. Although down from the staggering levels of the early 1980s when inflation hit 123 percent because of drought, inflation in the following six years averaged almost 30 percent. Recovery in agricultural output in 1984 and 1985 helped shrink inflation rates, but a marginal decline in food production in 1986 was accompanied by an upward trend in inflation. For the next four years, ever higher food prices, driven by devaluation, contributed greatly to high inflation. By late 1994, the country's inflation rate stood at about 28 percent.

Trade

The promotion of Ghana's foreign trade has been central to all government plans to revive the economy since 1983. Under the ERP, export-producing industries received the most direct support; they also received the most indirect support through the improvement of their proximate infrastructure. By promoting exports, the government sought to obtain foreign exchange essential to repay debts and to ease the country's restrictions on imports. Imports, of course, are also necessary to upgrade many of the export industries hamstrung for lack of equipment.

Prior to 1983, economic conditions conspired to erode the terms of trade to such an extent that Ghanaians had reverted to smuggling goods across the borders as well as to trading on the black market on a significant scale. Ghanaians who had anything to sell could multiply their earnings by selling their goods in French-speaking countries, especially neighboring Côte d'Ivoire, and then changing the resultant francs into cedis at black-market rates. Smuggling cut down the amount of foreign exchange available for official transactions, leading to a reduction in imports, which hit manufacturing enterprises dependent on imported equipment and raw materials especially hard. As a result, many consumer goods were no longer available in Ghana, which further boosted smuggling across borders of those countries where such goods could be obtained. By 1982 the World Bank estimated that transactions on the parallel, or black, market constituted 32.4 percent of all domestic trade.

Since the start of the ERP in 1983, the government has introduced several policies to adjust the pattern of Ghana's trade structure. These include devaluing the currency as well as raising producer prices for crucial exports such as cocoa to offset the advantages of smuggling such goods across borders. In addition, the government introduced an interbank foreign exchange market to facilitate currency exchange. To ease the importation of essential capital goods, but not necessarily consumer goods, the government revised and reduced numerous import duties and trade taxes.

By the early 1990s, government efforts had resulted in the restoration of many of Ghana's historical trade relationships. Exports were again dominated by cocoa, which earned US$280 million in 1993. Other significant export commodities in 1993 were gold (US$416 million) and timber (US$140 million), followed by electricity, diamonds, and bauxite. Ghana's nontraditional exports, such as furniture, cola nuts, and pineapples, have also increased significantly. On the import side, fuel and energy, mainly oil, accounted for 16 percent of 1990 imports, followed by capital goods, 43 percent; intermediate goods, 28

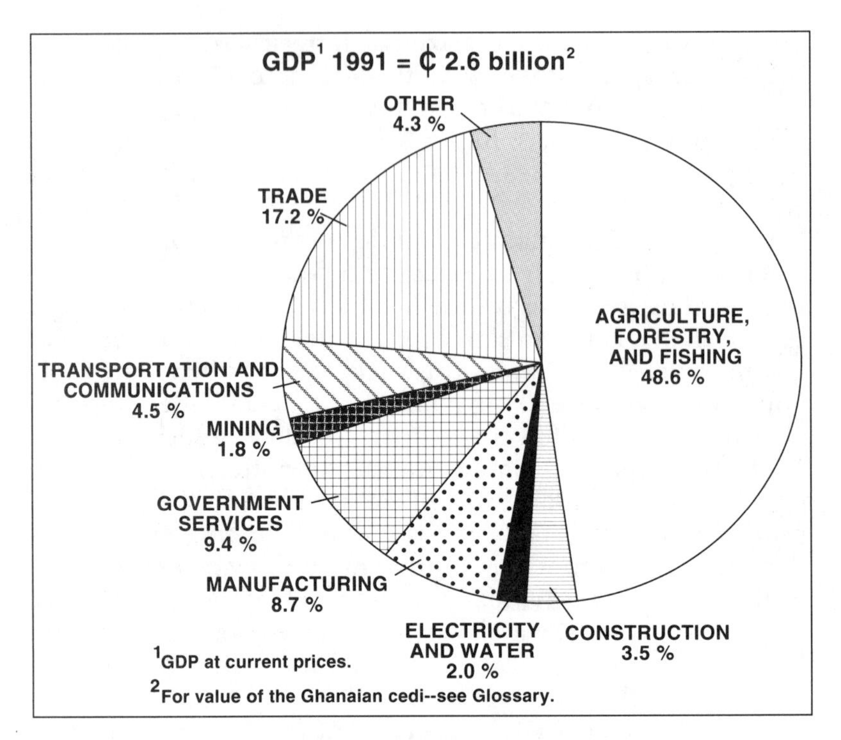

Source: Based on information from Economist Intelligence Unit, *Country Profile: Ghana, 1994–95*, London, 1994, 16.

Figure 8. Gross Domestic Product (GDP) by Sector, 1991

percent; and consumer goods, 10 percent, according to the World Bank.

In addition to supporting traditional export industries such as cocoa and gold, the government also attempted to diversify the content of Ghana's exports. To encourage nontraditional exports in the fishing and agriculture sectors, the government offered to refund 95 percent of import duties on goods destined for reexport and even to cancel sales taxes on manufactured goods sold abroad. In addition, the government devised a scale of tax rebates ranging from 20 percent to 50 percent determined by the volume of total production that was exported. These incentives generated considerable response. By 1988 more than 700 exporters were dealing in 123 export products, the major items being pineapples, marine and fish products (especially tuna), wood products, aluminum products, and salt. By 1990, the last year for which figures were available, the value of nontraditional exports had risen to US$62 million.

In 1992 the government's Ghana Export Promotion Council announced a plan to raise nontraditional exports to US$335 million by 1997 through increased market research, trade missions, trade fairs and exhibitions, and training. Among its most ambitious specific targets were increases in tuna and shrimp sales to US$45 million and US$32 million, respectively, by 1995, and increases in pineapple sales to US$12.5 million. In the manufacturing sector, wood products, aluminum goods, and processed rubber were targeted to yield US$44 million, US$42 million, and US$23 million, respectively. Earnings from salt were projected to rise to US$20 million.

In the early 1990s, Ghana continued to trade primarily with the European Community, particularly Britain and Germany. Britain continued to be the principal market for Ghanaian cocoa beans, absorbing approximately 50 percent of all cocoa beans exported. In 1992, Germany was the single most important destination of Ghana's exports, accounting for some 19 percent of all exports. Britain was next, accounting for about 12 percent, followed by the United States, 9 percent, and Japan, 5 percent. The same year, Britain supplied approximately 20 percent of Ghana's imports, followed by Nigeria, which provided 11 percent. The United States and Germany were third and fourth, respectively.

Ghana also belongs to the sixteen-member Economic Community of West African States (ECOWAS), founded in 1975 with headquarters in Abuja, Nigeria. ECOWAS is designed to promote the cultural, economic, and social development of its component states. To achieve these ends, ECOWAS seeks to foster regional cooperation in several areas, including removal of barriers to the movement of peoples and trade, harmonization of agricultural policies, improvements in infrastructure, and, as of 1991, renewed commitment to democratic political processes and non-aggression against member states.

Ghana also has a number of barter trade agreements with several East European countries, China, and Cuba. Under the agreements, imports of goods and services are paid for mainly by cocoa from Ghana. A major change occurred in 1991 when the German Democratic Republic (GDR, or East Germany) abrogated its barter trade agreement with Ghana following the union of the two Germanies. In spite of this, agreement was reached between the two countries to honor existing commitments. In late 1991, the Ghanaian government showed renewed interest in trade with the countries of Eastern Europe following the adoption of free-market systems in the wake of political upheavals in those countries. Ghanaian trade officials expect that the barter trade system will give way to open market operations.

Role of the Government

In the 1990s, the government continued to play a decisive role in the direction and pace of economic development in Ghana. Under the Economic Recovery Program initiated in 1983, the Rawlings government tried to shift the burden of economic growth from government to the private sector through a dual strategy of cutting government spending and promoting private production. In particular, the government tried to boost export production through currency devaluations, tax incentives, and government-funded development projects. At the same time, budget deficits were almost entirely wiped out. These measures caused drastic cutbacks in current government spending and widespread privatization, while the government incurred further loans (and thereby debt) to balance the country's budget.

The Economic Recovery Program

In 1983 the government launched the Economic Recovery Program (ERP) under the guidance of the World Bank and the IMF. The overriding purpose of the ERP was to reduce Ghana's debts and to improve its trading position in the global economy. The stated objectives of the program focused on restoring economic productivity at minimum cost to the government and included the following policies: lowering inflation through stringent fiscal, monetary, and trade policies; increasing the flow of foreign exchange into Ghana and directing it to priority sectors; restructuring the country's economic institutions; restoring production incentives; rehabilitating infrastructure to enhance conditions for the production and export of goods; and, finally, increasing the availability of essential consumer goods. In short, the government hoped to create an economic climate conducive to the generation of capital.

The ERP was carried out in roughly three phases. Beginning in 1983, the government focused on reducing its expenditures while creating incentives for private production. Initial expenditure cuts and improved tax collection brought the budget deficit down from 6.3 percent of GDP in 1982 to 0.1 percent by 1986, relieving government pressure on the banking system, while a series of cedi devaluations boosted export activity. During the second phase, which lasted from 1987 to 1989, the government moved to divest itself of many assets through privatization and to institute radical foreign exchange reforms to devalue the cedi further. Although privatization was sluggish, the hard-currency black market was nearly eliminated with the introduction of foreign exchange bureaus in 1988. In the ERP's third phase, the government intensified monetary reforms and reduced private corporate taxes to boost private-sector growth.

By the end of 1991, ERP efforts had improved the country's international financial reputation because of its ability to make loan repayments (although not wipe out foreign debt) and its first entry onto the international capital market in almost two decades. Critics maintained, however, that the ERP had failed to bring about a fundamental transformation of the economy, which still relied on income earned from cocoa and other agricultural commodities. Critics also contended that many Ghanaians had seen few, if any, benefits from the program.

In addition to its focus on stabilizing the country's financial structure, the ERP also aimed to promote production, especially in the export sectors. In 1986 the government began to rebuild infrastructure through a US$4.2 billion program, more than half of which was provided by external sources. This amount was divided roughly equally among infrastructure repair, energy imports (oil for machinery), and export industries. Increased imports financed by the IMF, the World Bank, and other sources made possible the rehabilitation and repair of some key parts of the infrastructure through the supply of spare parts and inputs for industry, mining, utilities, and agriculture.

Although the ERP was geared primarily toward restoring the country's international economic standing, it came under popular criticism inside Ghana for ignoring the plight of those not involved in the export sector. The overwhelming shift in resources was toward cocoa rehabilitation and other export sectors, not toward food production. Government employees, especially those in state enterprises, were actively targeted, and many lost their jobs. Farmers suffered as the percentage of the total budget devoted to agriculture fell from 10 percent in 1983 to 4.2 percent in 1986 and to 3.5 percent in 1988, excluding foreign aid projects. Although cocoa contributed less to Ghana's GDP than food crops, cocoa nonetheless received 9 percent of capital expenditures in the late 1980s; at the same time, it received roughly 67 percent of current agricultural expenditures because of its export value.

In response to criticism of such policies, the government initiated the US$85 million Program of Action to Mitigate the Social Costs of Adjustment (PAMSCAD). Beginning in 1988, the program sought to create 40,000 jobs over a two-year period. It was aimed at the poorest individuals, small-scale miners and artisans in particular, and communities were to be helped to implement labor-intensive self-help projects.

As part of PAMSCAD, ¢10 billion was slated in the 1993 budget for the rehabilitation and development of rural and urban social infrastructure. The new program, organized through PAMSCAD and the new district assemblies, was designed to focus on improving water supply, sanitation, primary education, and health care. An additional ¢51 billion was set aside for redeployment and end-of-service benefits for those who had lost their jobs in civil service and parastatal reorganizations.

In the early 1990s, the government was committed to continuing the policies of the ERP. New agreements were concluded with the World Bank to continue credit arrangements on condition that Ghana review and revise its various economic laws and regulations and support private-sector development. In particular, the government agreed to revise or to repeal existing laws and regulations affecting private investment that undermine the spirit of deregulation, economic liberalization, and exchange-rate reforms. The government also agreed to develop and to strengthen the institutional framework that would facilitate private investment. Key priorities for 1992 and afterward included giving new impetus to state enterprise reform, broadening the scope of banking-sector reforms, liberalizing the administrative framework, and strengthening public-sector management. Basic education and primary health-care services were to receive attention over the long term as well.

State Enterprises

State-owned enterprises in Ghana date to the colonial period and especially to the post-World War II era. For example, the British organized a number of public utilities, such as

Craftsmen making cane furniture in Accra
Courtesy James Sanders

water, electricity, postal and telegraph services, rail and road networks, and bus services. To foster exports of coffee, palm kernels, and cocoa, the Agricultural Produce Marketing Board was founded in 1949. In addition, the colonial government established the Industrial Development Corporation and the Agricultural Development Corporation to promote industries and agriculture. In the mid-1970s, the National Redemption Council under I. K. Acheampong also emphasized state enterprises. The Acheampong government established a number of new enterprises and partly or wholly nationalized a number of foreign-owned companies, including Ashanti Goldfields Corporation and Consolidated African Selection Trust. Intermittent efforts to improve performance and efficiency often led to the transferral of duties and functions to alternative state bodies but not to the wholesale privatization of ownership rights and assets.

By the 1980s, state enterprises were suffering along with most businesses in Ghana, but they were also held to blame for the economy's general condition. In particular, many were heavily subsidized and were draining much of the country's domestic loan capital. Under pressure from the World Bank and in accordance with the principles of the ERP, in 1984 the government began to sell state enterprises to private investors, and it initiated the State-Owned Enterprise Reform Program in 1988.

In 1984 there were 235 state enterprises in Ghana. The government announced that twenty-two sensitive enterprises would not be sold, including major utilities as well as transport, cocoa, and mining enterprises. In 1988 thirty-two were put up for sale, followed by a further forty-four in 1990 under what was termed the Divestiture Implementation Committee. By December 1990, thirty-four enterprises had been either partially or totally divested. Four were sold outright, a further eight were partially sold through share issues, and twenty-two were liquidated. Divestiture of fifteen additional enterprises was also underway, and by 1992 plans were afoot to privatize some of the nation's banks.

Joint ventures were set up for four enterprises, including two state mining companies, Prestea Goldfields and Ghana Consolidated Diamonds. In 1992 the Divestiture Implementation Committee considered resource-pooling programs to enable smaller domestic investors to buy up state enterprises. Such pooling would accelerate the program, but more importantly, it would enable the Provisional National Defence Council (PNDC) to deflect charges that it was auctioning off the nation's assets to foreigners.

The government also introduced a performance monitoring and evaluation system to improve state enterprise productivity and efficiency as well as to provide incentives for strong performers and disincentives for weak performers. By 1989 fifteen enterprises had responded positively, turning a combined pretax loss of ¢418 million from the previous year into pre-tax profits of ¢19 billion, following a 9 percent cut in costs and a 30 percent increase in sales. In early 1992, the chairman of the State Enterprises Commission announced that the government would pass legislation requiring state-owned enterprises to register as limited liability companies by 1993 to stimulate competition and to improve their performances.

Budgets

Major policies of the ERP and conditions of IMF funding were that the budget deficit be reduced and that resources be directed from current to capital spending. Consequently, the government achieved a budget surplus each year between 1986 and 1989 and simultaneously boosted the percentage of spending for development projects. During the mid-1980s, budget deficits as a percentage of GDP consistently declined, falling from 4.7 percent in 1982 to 2.7 percent in 1983 to 0.3 percent in 1987. To accomplish this, the government cut spending and reversed its budgetary priorities, raising capital investment at the expense of increased current consumption in order to promote future growth. The government allocated 62 percent of the budget to physical infrastructure and about 33 percent to the country's productive sector. At the same time, spending on social programs, including health, education, and welfare, declined drastically to between 4.7 and 5 percent. As a percentage of GDP, expenditures on health care fell from 1.2 percent in 1970 to 0.26 percent in 1980–83; during the same period, spending on education dropped from 3.9 percent to 0.85 percent.

The 1993 budget, consistent with ERP policies and objectives, aimed to stimulate private-sector growth through lowering taxes on commerce and corporations and by internally balancing accounts. The previous budget reduced the tax rate for commerce, printing, and publishing businesses from 50 percent to 35 percent, bringing these sectors into line with agriculture, manufacturing, real estate, construction, and services, the taxes on which were cut in 1991.

Relief for the financial sector was less generous. The tax rate was reduced from 50 percent to 45 percent to encourage more lending and better terms for borrowers and to reduce the 8 percent to 9 percent gap between deposit and lending rates of interest. The government also reduced the withholding tax on dividends from 15 percent to 10 percent, in line with 1991 cuts from 30 percent. The annual standard personal exemption for individual taxpayers was set at ¢150,000 (US$380), up from the previous ¢126,000. This figure reflected a 19 percent increase, 1 percent above Ghanaian inflation the previous year. The top marginal rate of tax was raised from 25 percent to 35 percent, payable on earnings over ¢14 million, compared with the previous level of ¢3 million. Finally, import taxes were reduced or abolished, including duties and sales taxes on all building materials. The super sales tax on luxury goods, introduced in 1990, was also abolished. A maximum rate of 10 percent was set on such imports.

Tax evasion and corruption, both of which are rampant throughout Ghana, severely affected the government's ability to collect taxes in all categories. In December 1993, the Ghanaian parliament passed the Serious Fraud Office Bill. This act empowered the Serious Fraud Office to investigate fraud and embezzlement crimes against the state. Despite this action, it is unlikely that the authorities will be able to stop tax evasion or other white-collar crimes anytime soon.

Reform of the tax base and prudent fiscal management contributed to budget surpluses and dramatically reduced government recourse to the banking sector. By the early 1990s, nonetheless, Ghana still relied heavily on external grants to achieve its twin goals of running balanced budgets and increasing necessary capital expenditures (see table 9, Appendix). Moreover, compared with the rest of sub-Saharan Africa, total government revenue as a proportion of GDP continued to be relatively low. It was less than 16 percent in 1990 (including grants), compared with an average of 19 percent for sub-Saharan Africa as a whole. In 1993 revenue raising efforts aimed to secure income equivalent to 22.2 percent of GDP.

By 1992 the government's financial position had weakened. From 1986 to 1991, government finances were in surplus. In 1992, however, tax receipts from all sources of revenue were below projected levels, and with national elections in view, the government relaxed its tight controls on spending. Despite inclusion of foreign funding as a source of revenue, the deficit for 1992 was estimated at ¢177 billion but fell to ¢119 billion in 1993. To rectify the situation, the government proposed to raise taxes on gasoline, kerosene, diesel fuel, and liquefied petroleum gas by as much as 60 percent.

Banking and Currency

Control of money-supply growth and liquidity management have been among the ERP's most difficult tasks, and expansion generally exceeded targets for most of the 1980s. The initial phase of monetary policy (1983–86) focused on reducing government borrowing from the domestic banking system and on using quantitative controls via credit ceilings. Although these succeeded in reducing domestic credit growth, larger than expected foreign earnings and the money market's inability to process them efficiently contributed to a rapid expansion in the broad money supply until the late 1980s.

The subsequent introduction of more dynamic monetary policies in 1989 involved a phase-in of indirect controls and market-based policy instruments. A further series of measures was introduced in 1990 to strengthen the responsiveness of interest rates to changes in liquidity conditions. There followed a phased increase in the Bank of Ghana's rediscount rate from 26 percent to 35 percent by mid-1991, the introduction of three- and five-year instruments later that year, and a widening of access to Bank of Ghana financial instruments in favor of the non-bank financial sector. The policies were quite effective. Money supply growth was brought convincingly under control in 1990 and 1991; however, a decline in interest rates and in monetary control, compounded by salary increases in the public sector, prompted monetary growth in 1992.

In January 1994, the Bank of Ghana relaxed its monetary policy. As a result, the government's 91-day treasury bill discount rate was lowered five percentage points to 27 percent. The interest rate equivalent of the discount rate fell from 34.78 percent to 28.95 percent. Savings deposit rates also fell in December 1993 from 17.5–22 percent to 15–22 percent. The wider range suggests competition for funds in the banking market. The range for longer-term money (two-year) declined from 22–32 percent to 25.2–28 percent.

Banking

Ghana has a well-developed banking system that was used extensively by previous governments to finance attempts to develop the local economy. By the late 1980s, the banks had suffered substantial losses from a number of bad loans in their portfolios. In addition, cedi depreciation had raised the banks' external liabilities. In order to strengthen the banking sector, the government in 1988 initiated comprehensive reforms. In particular, the amended banking law of August 1989 required banks to maintain a minimum capital base equivalent to 6 percent of net assets adjusted for risk and to establish uniform accounting and auditing standards. The law also introduced limits on risk exposure to single borrowers and sectors. These measures strengthened central bank supervision, improved the regulatory framework, and gradually improved resource mobilization and credit allocation.

Other efforts were made to ease the accumulated burden of bad loans on the banks in the late 1980s. In 1989 the Bank of Ghana issued temporary promissory notes to replace non-performing loans and other government-guaranteed obligations to state-owned enterprises as of the end of 1988 and on private-sector loans in1989. The latter were then replaced by interest-bearing bonds from the Bank of Ghana or were offset against debts to the bank. Effectively, the government stepped in and repaid the loans. By late 1989, some ¢62 billion worth of nonperforming assets had been offset or replaced by central bank bonds totaling about ¢47 billion.

In the early 1990s, the banking system included the central bank (the Bank of Ghana), three large commercial banks (Ghana Commercial Bank, Barclays Bank of Ghana, and Standard Chartered Bank of Ghana), and seven secondary banks. Three merchant banks specialized in corporate finance, advisory services, and money and capital market activities—Merchant Bank, Ecobank Ghana, and Continental Acceptances; the latter two were both established in 1990. These and the commercial banks placed short-term deposits with two discount houses set up to enhance the development of Ghana's domestic money market—Consolidated Discount House and Securities Discount House, established in November 1987 and June 1991, respectively. At the bottom of the tier were 100 rural banks, which accounted for only 5 percent of the banking system's total assets.

By the end of 1990, banks were able to meet the new capital adequacy requirements. In addition, the government announced the establishment of the First Finance Company in 1991 to help distressed but potentially viable companies to recapitalize. The company was established as part of the financial sector adjustment program in response to requests for easier access to credit for companies hit by ERP policies. The company was a joint venture between the Bank of Ghana and the Social Security and National Insurance Trust.

Despite offering some of the highest lending rates in West Africa, Ghana's banks enjoyed increased business in the early 1990s because of high deposit rates. The Bank of Ghana raised its rediscount rate in stages to around 35 percent by mid-1991, driving money market and commercial bank interest rates well above the rate of inflation, thus making real interest rates substantially positive. As inflation decelerated over the year, the rediscount rate was lowered in stages to 20 percent, bringing lending rates down accordingly.

At the same time, more money moved into the banking system in 1991 than in 1990; time and savings deposits grew by 45 percent to ¢94.6 billion, and demand deposits rose to ¢118.7 billion. Loans also rose, with banks' claims on the private sector up by 24.1 percent, to ¢117.4 billion. Banks' claims on the central government continued to shrink in 1991, falling to a mere

¢860 million from ¢2.95 billion in 1990, a reflection of continued budget surpluses. Claims on nonfinancial public enterprises rose by 12.6 percent to ¢27.1 billion.

Foreign bank accounts, which were frozen shortly after the PNDC came to power, have been permitted since mid-1985, in a move to increase local supplies of foreign exchange. Foreign currency accounts may be held in any of seven authorized banks, with interest exempt from Ghanaian tax and with transfers abroad free from foreign-exchange control restrictions. Foreign-exchange earnings from exports, however, are specifically excluded from these arrangements.

The Ghana Stock Exchange began operations in November 1990, with twelve companies considered to be the best performers in the country. Although there were stringent minimum investment criteria for registration on the exchange, the government hoped that share ownership would encourage the formation of new companies and would increase savings and investment. After only one month in operation, however, the exchange lost a major French affiliate, which reduced the starting market capitalization to about US$92.5 million.

By the end of 1990, the aggregate effect of price and volume movements had resulted in a further 10.8 percent decrease in market capitalization. Trading steadily increased, however, and by mid-July 1992, 2.8 million shares were being traded with a value of ¢233 million, up from 1.7 million shares with a value of ¢145 million in November 1991. The market continued to be small, listing only thirteen companies, more than half in retailing and brewing. In June 1993, Accra removed exchange control restrictions and gave permission to non-resident Ghanaians and foreigners to invest on the exchange without prior approval from the Bank of Ghana. In April 1994, the exchange received a considerable boost after the government sold part of its holdings in Ashanti Goldfields Corporation.

Currency

One of the most pressing economic problems faced by all postindependence Ghanaian governments was the overvaluation of the currency. In 1961 Ghana broke with the British pound sterling and pegged the value of the cedi to the United States dollar. As Ghana's terms of trade worsened in the 1960s, the real value of the cedi fell; however, successive governments feared either to float the cedi or to adjust its value, thereby raising the cost of imports and consumer prices. The overthrow of the Kofi A. Busia regime in 1971, following the introduction of a devaluation package, reinforced the unpopularity of such a move. The Acheampong government reversed course and revalued the cedi. It also increased the money supply to pay Ghana's debts, leading to a sharp divergence between the official and the real rates of exchange.

The overvalued cedi, on the one hand, and low, regulated prices for commodities, on the other, led to a robust smuggling industry and to an extensive black market in currency. It became common practice for Ghanaians, especially those living along the country's border, to smuggle Ghanaian produce such as cocoa and minerals into neighboring francophone countries. After selling on the local market, Ghanaians would then return home and trade their hard-currency Central African francs for cedis on the black market, making handsome profits. Smuggling and illegal currency operations had become so extensive by 1981 that the black-market rate for cedis was 9.6 times higher than the official rate, up from 1.3 in 1972. At the same time, reliable estimates placed transactions in the parallel economy at fully one-third of Ghana's GDP.

Fifteen months after the PNDC came to power, in April 1983, the government began efforts to devalue the cedi. Rawlings introduced a system of surcharges on imports and bonuses on exports that effectively devalued the currency because the surcharges on imports amounted to 750 percent of the amount being spent and the discounts on exports amounted to 990 percent. Further, an official devaluation began in October 1983 in which the exchange rate reached ¢90 to US$1 by March 1986. By 1993, ¢720 equaled US$1; by late 1994, ¢1,023 equaled US$1.

In September 1986, the government sought alternative methods for establishing the value of the cedi. At that time, the government relinquished its direct role in determining the exchange rate. The rate was instead determined at regular currency auctions under the pressure of market forces on the basis of a two-tier exchange-rate system, with one rate for essentials and another for non-essentials. In April 1987, the two auctions were unified. In subsequent reforms also designed to diminish smuggling and illegal currency dealings, private foreign-exchange bureaus were permitted to trade in foreign currencies beginning at the end of March 1988. By July 1989, there were 148 such bureaus operating, ninety-nine in Accra and thirty in Ashanti Region, with the remainder in other urban centers.

In 1987, US$207 million was allocated through the auction; and in 1988, US$267 million. By comparison, the foreign-exchange bureaus in the first year of operation, ending in March 1989, traded US$77 million worth of foreign currency, or about one-fourth the amount of foreign exchange allocated through the auction. Initially, prices at the auction and those at the foreign-exchange bureaus differed greatly. Efforts to reduce the difference, however, brought the gap from 29 percent in March 1988 to approximately 6 percent by February 1991. In early 1992, the auction was closed, although no official announcement was made. Purchasers were referred to the Bank of Ghana, which used an exchange rate determined largely on the basis of market forces.

The government also successfully slowed growth in the money supply. In the late 1980s, the average annual growth rate reached 61 percent. By 1990 it had dropped to 13.3 percent but then accelerated slightly to 16.7 percent, standing at ¢317 million the following year. In 1991 the Bank of Ghana introduced a ¢1,000 note, the highest denomination issued since independence in 1957. Previously, the highest denomination had been ¢500. A total of ¢50 billion of the new notes was printed.

Labor Force

Despite the revival of the export sector, most Ghanaians continued to find employment with the government or to rely on informal employment for their livelihood. An increasing number of Ghanaians also turned to smuggling or to crime to earn a living. Reductions in the number of government workers had not been offset by increased employment in the export sector by the early 1990s. At the same time, wages had not kept up with the cost of living. The government also sought to reform the education system, because increased education often led to better jobs and higher wages. However, because students were expected to bear an increasing portion of the cost of their education, it was unlikely that the poorest Ghanaians would be able to take full advantage of the school system.

National Requirements

Although the Ghanaian labor force grew throughout the

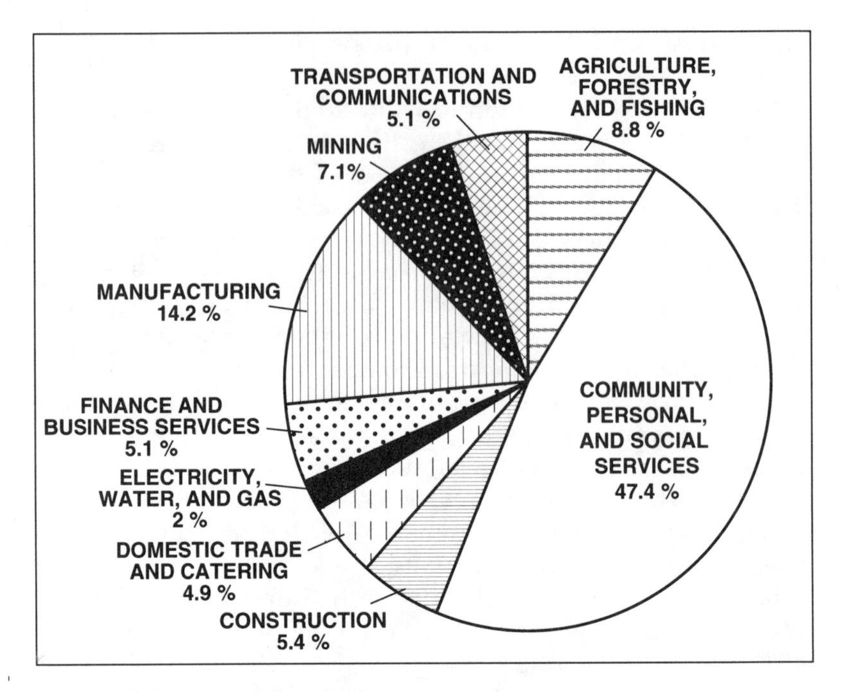

Source: Based on information from Ghana, Statistical Service, *Quarterly Digest of Statistics*, Accra, December 1991, Table 42.

Figure 9. Employment by Sector, 1988

1980s, the structure of employment remained relatively stable (see fig. 9). Between 1981 and 1988, the official number of workers grew by almost 100,000. Despite efforts under the ERP to stimulate private production, public-sector jobs still accounted for more than 80 percent of total employment over the decade. Employment in the public sector rose every year between 1981 and 1985 (from 175,700 to 397,100), but thereafter fell three years in a row, standing at 251,500 in 1988. By 1992 the number of public-sector workers had grown to an estimated 595,000, although some 55,000 had been declared redundant.

Considering the relative importance of public-sector employment, ERP policies to reduce the scope of state enterprises had a profound impact on patterns of unemployment. In the mid-1980s, cutbacks at the Ghana Cocoa Board (20,000 jobs), the Ghana National Trading Corporation (2,000 jobs), and the shipping enterprise, the Black Star Line (1,000 jobs), contributed to nearly 30,000 job losses in the parastatal sector alone by the end of 1986. The civil service lost an estimated 15,000 jobs in the same period. In 1990 fifteen of the remaining state-owned enterprises reduced their payrolls by about 13,000 employees; no figures were available for losses resulting from the liquidation of an additional twenty-two state enterprises that year.

Although ERP policies resulted in the loss of many jobs for Ghanaians, their implementation met relatively minor resistance from organized labor. The most serious challenge came in 1986 on the issue of income rather than that of layoffs. The unions threatened action in response to the government's decision (under pressure from the IMF) to abolish leave allowances, a crucial benefit that substantially supplemented low public-sector wages. In response, the government reversed its decision and revised the 1986 budget. After that, the government stepped up taxes on allowances and, in some cases, consolidated them into wages and salaries. Meanwhile, the unemployed continued to express concern over the slow materialization of end-of-service payments. In response, the 1992 budget contained proposals for packages comprising down payments, shares in profitable state-owned enterprises, and interest on deferred payments.

Income and Wages

During the 1980s, per capita income rose slightly but was overshadowed by the increased cost of living. Per capita income climbed from the decade low of US$340 in 1983 to US$400 by 1988 because of the devaluation of the cedi and rising producer prices. The same factors, however, worked to increase consumer prices four-fold from 1985 to 1988. This trend continued throughout the early 1990s as consumer prices rose from 393.2 in 1990 to 634.7 in 1993 based on a 1985 price index of 100.

Real wages and salaries are estimated to have fallen by an enormous 83 percent between 1975 and 1983 and to have continued to fall through 1989, forcing many workers to seek additional sources of income. The level of real wages reached in 1988 was less than half that attained in the mid-1970s; nevertheless, the government was committed under the ERP to holding down inflation and, hence, wages. In the 1990 budget, the government linked pay increases to productivity, inflation, and companies' ability to pay. With some exceptions, notably a one-time allowance for civil servants to compensate for increased fuel and transport costs in 1990, public-sector wages increased roughly in line with projected inflation in 1989, 1990, and 1991. In 1992, however, the government, which had scheduled elections late in the year, granted a salary increase to public-sector workers. Although no recent data were available for the private sector, wage increases under collective bargaining arrangements appeared to have been relatively modest.

Although increases in the minimum daily wage under the PNDC appear spectacular, they are linked to the steady devaluation of the cedi and have not overcome a constant erosion of worker purchasing power. Beginning in April 1984, the government increased the minimum daily wage to ¢35, then to ¢70 in January 1985, ¢90 in January 1986, and ¢122 in 1987. In March 1990, the minimum wage was raised to ¢218, and by August 1991, it had risen to ¢460, an increase of 111 percent as agreed to by the government, the Trade Union Congress, and the Ghana Employers Association.

In the face of popular elections and increasing strikes, the government agreed to massive pay raises at the end of 1992, including a 70 percent increase for nurses. Overall, civil service pay raises added more than ¢50 billion to the wage bill, reaching ¢175 billion in 1992, or 50 percent of government revenue. At the same time, the government moved to contain the wage bill by freezing staff recruitment in public-sector organizations as well as state salaries that exceeded those in the civil service.

Agriculture

Agriculture is Ghana's most important economic sector, employing more than half the population on a formal and informal basis and accounting for almost half of GDP and export earnings. The country produces a variety of crops in various climatic zones, which range from dry savanna to wet forest and which run in east-west bands across the country. Agricultural crops, including yams, grains, cocoa, oil palms, kola nuts, and timber, form the base of Ghana's economy.

Although Nkrumah attempted to use agricultural wealth as a springboard for the country's overall economic development, Ghanaian agricultural output has consistently fallen since the 1960s. Beginning with the drop in commodity prices in the late 1960s, farmers have been faced with fewer incentives to produce as well as with a general deterioration of necessary infrastructure and services. Farmers have also had to deal with increasingly expensive inputs, such as fertilizer, because of overvaluation of the cedi. Food production has fallen as well, with a decline in the food self-sufficiency ratio from 83 percent in 1961–66 to 71 percent in 1978–80, coupled with a four-fold increase in food imports in the decade prior to 1982. By 1983, when drought hit the region, food shortages were widespread, and export crop production reached an all-time low.

When the Rawlings government initiated the first phase of the ERP in 1984, agriculture was identified as the economic sector that could rescue Ghana from financial ruin. Accordingly, since that time, the government has invested significant funds in the rehabilitation of agriculture. Primarily through the use of loans and grants, the government has directed capital toward repairing and improving the transportation and distribution infrastructure serving export crops. In addition, specific projects aimed at increasing cocoa yields and at developing the timber industry have been initiated. Except for specific development programs, however, the government has tried to allow the free market to promote higher producer prices and to increase efficiency.

Although the government was criticized for focusing on exports rather than on food crops under the ERP, by the early 1990s the PNDC had begun to address the need to increase local production of food. In early 1991, the government announced that one goal of the Medium Term Agricultural Development Program 1991–2000 was to attain food self-sufficiency and security by the year 2000. To this end, the government sought to improve extension services for farmers and to improve crop-disease research. Despite the statements concerning the importance of food crops, however, the plan was still heavily oriented toward market production, improvement of Ghana's balance-of-payments position, and provision of materials for local industrial production. Furthermore, following World Bank guidelines, the government planned to rely more heavily on the private sector for needed services and to reduce the role of the public sector, a clear disadvantage for subsistence producers. In particular, industrial tree crops such as cocoa, coffee, and oil palm seedlings were singled out for assistance. Clearly, agricultural sectors that could not produce foreign-exchange earnings were assigned a lower priority under the ERP.

The government attempted to reduce its role in marketing and assistance to farmers in several ways. In particular, the Cocoa Marketing Board steadily relinquished its powers over pricing and marketing. The government, furthermore, established a new farmers' organization, the Ghana National Association of Farmers and Fishermen, in early 1991 to replace the Ghana Federation of Agricultural Cooperatives. The new organization was to be funded by the farmers themselves to operate as a cooperative venture at the district, regional, and national levels. Although the government argued that it did not want to be accused of manipulating farmers, the lack of government financial support again put subsistence producers at a disadvantage.

Cocoa

Cocoa production occurs in the forested areas of the country—Ashanti Region, Brong-Ahafo Region, Central Region, Eastern Region, Western Region, and Volta Region—where rainfall is 1,000–1,500 millimeters per year. The crop year begins in October, when purchases of the main crop begin, while the smaller mid-crop cycle starts in July. All cocoa, except that which is smuggled out of the country, is sold at fixed prices to the Cocoa Marketing Board. Although most cocoa production is carried out by peasant farmers on plots of less than three hectares, a small number of farmers appear to dominate the trade. Indeed, some studies show that about one-fourth of all cocoa farmers receive just over half of total cocoa income.

In 1979 the government initiated reform of the cocoa sector, focusing on the government's role in controlling the industry through the Cocoa Marketing Board. The board was dissolved and reconstituted as the Ghana Cocoa Board (Cocobod). In 1984 it underwent further institutional reform aimed at subjecting the cocoa sector to market forces. Cocobod's role was reduced, and 40 percent of its staff, or at least 35,000 employees, was dismissed. Furthermore, the government shifted responsibility for crop transport to the private sector. Subsidies for production inputs (fertilizers, insecticides, fungicides, and equipment) were removed, and there was a measure of privatization of the processing sector through at least one joint venture. In addition, a new payment system known as the Akuafo Check System was introduced in 1982 at the point of purchase of dried beans. Formerly, produce-buying clerks had often held back cash payments, abused funds, and paid farmers with false checks. Under the Akuafo system, a farmer was given a check signed by the produce clerk and the treasurer that he could cash at a bank of his choice. Plantation divestiture proceeded slowly, however, with only seven of fifty-two plantations sold by the end of 1990.

Although Ghana was the world's largest cocoa producer in the early 1960s, by the early 1980s Ghanaian production had dwindled almost to the point of insignificance. The drop from an average of more than 450,000 tons per year to a low of 159,000 tons in 1983–84 has been attributed to aging trees, widespread disease, bad weather, and low producer prices. In addition, bush fires in 1983 destroyed some 60,000 hectares of cocoa farms, so that the 1983–84 crop was barely 28 percent of the 557,000 tons recorded in 1964–65. Output then recovered to 228,000 tons in 1986–87. Revised figures show that production amounted to 301,000 tons in 1988–89, 293,000 tons in 1990–91, and 305,000 tons in 1992–93. After declining to 255,000 tons in 1993–94, the crop was projected to return to the 300,000 ton range in 1994–95.

In the early 1990s, Cocobod continued to liberalize and to privatize cocoa marketing. The board raised prices to producers and introduced a new system providing greater incentives for private traders. In particular, Cocobod agreed to pay traders a minimum producer price as well as an additional fee to cover the buyers' operating and transportation costs and to provide some profit. Cocobod still handled overseas shipment and export of cocoa to ensure quality control.

In addition to instituting marketing reforms, the government also attempted to restructure cocoa production. In 1983 farmers were provided with seedlings to replace trees lost in the drought and trees more than thirty years old (about one-fourth of the total number of trees in 1984). Until the early 1990s, an estimated 40 hectares continued to be added each year to the total area of 800,000 hectares under cocoa production. In addition, a major program to upgrade existing roads and to construct 3,000 kilometers of new feeder roads was launched to ease the transportation and sale of cocoa from some of the more neglected but very fertile growing areas on the border with Côte d'Ivoire. Furthermore, the government tried to increase Ghana's productivity from 300 kilograms per hectare to compete with Southeast Asian productivity of almost 1,000 kilograms per hectare. New emphasis was placed on extension services, drought and disease research, and the use of fertilizers and insecticides. The results of these measures were to be seen in rising cocoa production in the early 1990s.

Other Commercial Crops

The main industrial crops are oil palms, cotton, rubber, sugar cane, tobacco, and kenaf, which is used in the production of fiber bags. None is of strategic economic importance, and all, apart from oil palms, have suffered as a result of the country's economic difficulties. Despite claims that such crops could assist local industrialization efforts, the government has not focused the same attention on this sector as on export crops. For example, sugar cane output has diminished with the closure of the country's two sugar mills, which produced 237,000 tons per year in 1974–76, but only 110,000 tons in 1989.

The government has actually encouraged the export rather than the local processing of rubber, rehabilitating more than 3,000 hectares of plantations specifically for export production rather than revitalizing the local Bonsa Tire Company, which could produce only 400 tires per day in 1988 despite its installed capacity for 1,500 per day.

By the 1990s, the tobacco sector was expanding and moving toward higher export production. Ghana's dark-fired leaf probably grows too fast and requires too rich a soil to compete effectively with rival crops, but the potential for flue-cured and Burley varieties is good. Pricing difficulties had reduced tobacco production from 3,400 tons in the early 1970s to an estimated 1,433 tons in 1989. Output began to improve in 1990, however, reaching 2,080 tons.

The Leaf Development Company was established in 1988 to produce tobacco leaf for the local market and to lay the basis for a future export industry. In 1991 the company's first commercial crop amounted to 300 tons of flue-cured, 50 tons of Burley, and 50 tons of dark-fired tobacco (all green-leaf weights), of which 250 tons were exported, earning US$380,000. In 1991 Rothmans, the British tobacco company, acquired a 49.5 percent stake in the company and took over management of the Meridian Tobacco Company in partnership with the state-owned Social Security and National Insurance Trust. Another firm, the Pioneer Tobacco Company, announced a 92 percent increase in post-tax profits of more than ¢1 billion for 1991. The company declared dividends worth ¢360 million, double the amount paid out in 1990.

Cotton production expanded rapidly in the early and mid-1970s, reaching 24,000 tons in 1977, but it fell back to one-third of this figure in 1989. Since the reorganization of the

Felling timber. Forestry is one of Ghana's major industries and sources of exports.
Preparing a field for planting yams
Courtesy Embassy of Ghana, Washington

Ghana Cotton Development Board into the Ghana Cotton Company, cotton production has steadily increased from 4 percent of the country's national requirement to 50 percent in 1990. Between 1986 and 1989, Ghana saved US$6 million through local lint cotton production. The company expected that between 1991 and 1995, about 20,000 hectares of land would be put under cotton cultivation, enabling Ghana to produce 95 percent of the national requirement.

Food Crops and Livestock

The main food crops are corn, yams, cassava, and other root crops. Despite government efforts to encourage farmers to switch to production of staples, total food production fell by an average of 2.7 percent per year between 1971–73 and 1981–83. By 1983 Ghana was self-sufficient in only one staple food crop—plantains. Food imports rose from 43,000 tons in 1973 to 152,000 tons in 1981.

There were various reasons for this poor performance, including growing urbanization and a shift in consumer preference from starchy home-grown staples to rice and corn. However, farmers also suffered from shortages of production inputs, difficulties in transporting produce to market, and competition from imported foods that were underpriced because of the vastly overvalued cedi. Weather also played a major part, particularly in 1983, when drought cut cereal production from 518,000 tons in 1982 to only 450,000 tons at a time when an extra million people had to be fed after the expulsion of Ghanaians from Nigeria. Food imports in 1982–83 amounted to 115,000 tons (40 percent as food aid), with the 1983–84 shortfall estimated at 370,000 tons (of which food aid commitments covered 91,000 tons).

There was a spectacular improvement beginning in 1984, mainly because of recovery from the prior year's drought. By 1988 the agricultural sector had vastly expanded, with food crops responsible for the bulk of the increase. Drought conditions returned in 1990, bringing massive falls in the production of all food crops apart from rice, but better weather and improved production brought prices down in 1991.

In August 1990, the government moved to liberalize the agricultural sector, announcing the end of minimum crop prices. The measure's impact was difficult to gauge because higher production meant more food was available at better prices anyway. The government's medium-term plan, outlined in 1990, sought to raise average crop yields and to increase food security, with special attention to improved producer incentives and storage facilities.

Livestock production is severely limited by the incidence of the tsetse fly in Ghana's forested regions and by poor grazing vegetation elsewhere. It is of major importance only in the relatively arid north and has not been earmarked for special treatment in Ghana's recovery program. In 1989 there were an estimated 1.2 million cattle, 2.2 million sheep, 2 million goats, 550,000 pigs, and 8 million chickens in Ghana.

Forestry

Forests cover about one-third of Ghana's total area, with commercial forestry concentrated in the southern parts of the country. This sector accounted for 4.2 percent of GDP in 1990; timber was the country's third largest foreign-exchange earner. Since 1983 forestry has benefited from more than US$120 million in aid and commercial credits and has undergone substantial changes, resulting in doubled earnings between 1985 and 1990. In 1993 timber and wood products earnings totalled US$140 million against a targeted level of US$130 million. Between January and November 1994, exports amounted to 919,000 tons and earned US$212 million.

Until the 1980s, forestry production suffered because of the overvalued cedi and deterioration of the transportation infrastructure. Log production declined by 66 percent during 1970–81 and sawed timber by 47 percent. Exports fell from US$130 million in 1973 to US$15 million in 1983, and four nationalized firms went bankrupt during that period.

The forestry sector was given a large boost in 1986, mainly because of the World Bank's US$24 million timber rehabilitation credit, which financed imports of logging equipment. As a consequence, log production rose 65 percent in 1984–87, and export revenues rose 665 percent in 1983–88. Furthermore, the old Ghana Timber Marketing Board was disbanded and replaced by two bodies: the Timber Export Development Board, responsible for marketing and pricing; and the Forest Products Inspection Bureau, responsible for monitoring contracts, maintaining quality standards, grading products, and acting as a watchdog for illegal transactions. Some of the external financing underwrote these institutional changes, while much of the rest financed forestry management and research as well as equipment for logging, saw milling, and manufacturing.

The sector, however, faced several problems. The most important was severe deforestation. A century ago, Ghana's tropical hardwood forest extended from about the middle of the country southward to the sea. Moreover, nearly half the country was covered with forests, which included 680 species of trees and several varieties of mahoganies. Most of this wood has been cut. By the early 1990s, only about one-third of the country was still forested, and not all of this was of commercial value. This situation has forced the government to make difficult choices between desperately needed hard currency earnings and conservation. The Forest Resource Management Project, part of the ERP, was initiated in 1988, and in 1989 the government banned log exports of eighteen species. The government later extended the list and imposed high duties on other species, planning to phase out log and air-dried timber exports altogether by 1994.

Instead, the government hoped to increase sales of wood products to replace earnings from logs. Government figures showed that one cubic meter of lumber and plywood was worth more than twice as much as the same amount of logs; veneers earned five times as much; and other products, such as furniture and floorings, earned six times the price of an equivalent volume of logs. Improvements in the processing sector caused wood products (excluding lumber) to rise to about 20 percent of export earnings in 1991, accounting for 6.9 percent of volume exports. By comparison, wood products represented 11 percent of earnings and 5.5 percent of volume in 1985. The fall in the proportion of volume sales accounted for by logs was accompanied by a dramatic fall in their share in earnings, from 50–60 percent in the mid-1980s to 23 percent in 1990.

By the early 1990s, there were approximately 220 lumber processors in Ghana, but the industry operated under several constraints. Most overseas demand is for kiln-dried products, and Ghanaian manufacturers lack sufficient kilns to meet that demand. The cheap air-dried processing method is not satisfactory because air-dried wood tends to destabilize over time. Foreign investment incentives are not so attractive in this sector as in other sectors, for example, mining. Furthermore, infrastructure in the Western Region, where lumber processing is located, continues to be relatively neglected compared with mining and cocoa production regions. Other difficulties include lack of expertise at technological and managerial levels.

Scandals have been reported in Ghana's forestry industry since 1986, and they erupted again in early 1992. The most notable case involved African Timber and Plywood, once Ghana's largest exporter of round logs. In the mid-1980s, the government embarked on a US$36 million rehabilitation project to boost the company's production. In 1992 as much as US$2.3 million was alleged to have been siphoned off from the project through various malpractices, and a number of officials were arrested. Furthermore, the environmental group, Friends of the Earth, alleged that there had been additional thefts by numerous foreign companies totaling almost US$50 million in hard currency during the 1980s. In 1992 the government began investigating the activities of hundreds of companies, both foreign and local, that were alleged to have entered into a range of illegal dealings, including smuggling, fraudulent invoicing, violations of local currency regulations, corruption, bribery, and nonpayment of royalties. The corruption is so widespread, however, that it is unlikely that the Ghanaian authorities will stop timber-related crimes anytime soon.

Fishing

Fishing increased considerably in the late 1960s, from 105,100 tons of marine fish caught in 1967 to 230,100 tons in 1971. In 1982 the yield was 234,100 tons, composed of 199,100 tons of marine varieties and 35,000 tons of freshwater fish from Lake Volta. The industry was hit by fuel shortages, inadequate storage facilities, and the general economic difficulties of the 1970s and the 1980s. Nevertheless, by 1988 the fish catch was 302,900 tons; by 1991 it amounted to 289,675 tons, down from more than 319,000 tons in 1990.

Large-scale poaching by foreign vessels has severely depleted fish stocks in Ghana's 200-nautical-mile maritime Exclusive Economic Zone, causing major government concern. The most affected stocks are sea bottom-feeding fish. Tuna stocks reportedly remain unaffected. A 1992 Ministry of Food and Agriculture report recommended that the government accelerate mobilization of surveillance and enforcement units and step up regulation of trawler fleets. That same year, the government passed a fisheries law to curb overfishing and to help protect the marine environment. Fishermen were banned from catching specified shellfish, and all fishing vessel operators were required to obtain licenses. The law provided for a regulatory body—the Fisheries Monitoring, Control, Surveillance, and Enforcement Unit—as well as a fisheries advisory council. These organizations, however, both of which are underfunded and undermanned, are unlikely to stop illegal fishing activities anytime soon.

Mining and Petroleum Industries

Ghana's mineral sector had started to recover by the early 1990s after its severe decline throughout the 1970s. One indicator of the scale of decline was that by 1987, only four gold mines were operating in Ghana, compared with eighty in 1938. Throughout the 1970s, the output of gold, as well as bauxite, manganese, and diamonds, fell steadily. Foreign-exchange shortages inhibited mine maintenance, new exploration, and development investment. The overvalued cedi and spiraling inflation exacerbated mining companies' problems, as did smuggling and the deteriorating infrastructure. Energy supplies failed to meet the industry's growing needs; foreign-exchange shortages constrained oil imports, and domestically generated hydroelectricity was unable to make up the shortfall.

After 1983, however, the government implemented a series of measures to enhance the sector's appeal. In 1986 new mining legislation for the gold and diamond sectors replaced the previous complex and obsolete regulations, and a generous incentives system was established that allowed for external foreign-exchange retention accounts, capital allowances, and a flexible royalties payment system. Since 1986 the sector has benefited from a wave of fresh investment totaling US$540 million, and by the early 1990s mining was the country's second highest foreign-exchange earner.

Under legislation passed after 1983, the government liberalized and regularized the mining industry. For the first time, the government made small claim-holding feasible, with the result that individual miners sold increasing amounts of gold and diamonds to the state-operated Precious Minerals Marketing Corporation. In 1990 the company bought 490,000 carats of diamonds and 20,000 ounces of gold and earned a total of US$20.4 million through sales, 70 percent of it from diamond sales and 30 percent from gold bought from small-scale operators. Diamond output totaled 688,000 carats in 1991 and 694,000 carats in 1992, while gold production amounted to 843,000 fine ounces in 1991 and 1,004,000 fine ounces in 1992.

Furthermore, the government succeeded in attracting significant foreign investment into the sector and, by early 1991, had signed more than sixty mining licenses granting prospecting rights to international companies. To forestall domestic criticism of large-scale foreign control of the sector, the government announced in mid-1991 the establishment of a state-controlled holding company to buy shares in mines on behalf of foreign investors.

Gold

Ghana has produced and exported gold for centuries. In precolonial times, present-day Ghana was one source of the gold that reached Europe via trans-Saharan trade routes. In the fifteenth century, Portuguese sailors tried to locate and to control gold mining from the coast but soon turned to more easily obtained slaves for the Atlantic slave trade. Most gold mining before the mid-nineteenth century was alluvial, miners recovering the gold from streams. Modern gold mining that plumbs the rich ore deposits below the earth's surface began about 1860, when European concessionaires imported heavy machinery and began working in the western areas of present-day Ghana. The richest deposit, the Obuasi mine, was discovered by a group of Europeans who sold their rights to E.A. Cade, the founder of Ashanti Goldfields Corporation (AGC). Since the beginning of the twentieth century, modern mining in the Gold Coast has been pursued as a large-scale venture, necessitating significant capital investment from European investors.

Under British colonial rule, the government controlled gold mining to protect the profits of European companies. The colonial government also restricted possession of gold as well as of mercury, essential in recovering gold from the ore in which it is embedded. Following independence, foreign control of the sector was tempered by increasing government involvement under the Nkrumah regime; however, production began to decline in the late 1960s and did not recover for almost twenty years. In the mid-1960s, many mines began to hit poorer gold reefs. Despite the floating of the international gold price in the late 1960s, few investors were willing to invest, and the government failed to provide the capital necessary to expand production into new reefs. Of the two major gold mining enterprises, neither the State Gold Mining Corporation nor AGC (40 percent controlled by the government) expanded or even maintained production.

Under the ERP, the mining sector was targeted as a potential source of foreign exchange, and since 1984, the government has successfully encouraged the rejuvenation of gold mining. To offer incentives to the mining industry, the Minerals and Mining Law was passed in 1986. Among its provisions were generous capital allowances and reduced income taxes. The corporate tax rate was set at 45 percent, and mining companies could write off 75 percent of capital investment against taxes in the first year and 50 percent of the remainder thereafter. The government permitted companies to use offshore bank accounts for service of loans, dividend payments, and expatriate staff remuneration.

Companies are permitted to retain a minimum of 25 percent of gross foreign-exchange earnings from minerals sales in their accounts, a level that can be negotiated up to 45 percent. Reconnaissance licenses are issued for one-year renewable periods, prospecting licenses are valid for three years, and mining licenses are in force for up to thirty years. The government has the right to 10 percent participation in all prospecting and to extend its share if commercial quantities of a mineral are discovered. In response, between 1985 and 1990, eleven companies became active with foreign participation, representing investments totaling US$541 million. Since 1986 there has been a gradual recovery in overall production.

More than 90 percent of gold production in the early 1990s came from underground mines in western Ashanti Region, with the remainder coming from river beds in Ashanti Region and Central Region. AGC, the country's largest producer, mined 62,100 fine ounces in January 1992, the highest monthly production ever recorded since the company began operation in 1897. The company also lowered its costs in relation to production during the last quarter of 1991 from 0.26 percent in October to 0.24 percent in December. Production during the company's fiscal year of October 1990 to September 1991 was 569,475 fine ounces, 42 percent more than the previous year's figure of 400,757 fine ounces and the largest amount ever produced by the mine. The second largest amount produced was 533,000 fine ounces, produced in 1972.

AGC planned major expansions in the early 1990s funded by World Bank loans. In early 1991, the corporation announced the discovery of new reserves estimated at more than 8 million ounces, in addition to its known reserves of 22.3 million ounces. The new reserves include lower-grade and remnant

Production in a textile factory
Goldfields and processing plant at Obuasi, south of Kumasi
Courtesy Embassy of Ghana, Washington

ores that the corporation had been unwilling to mine because of high costs. AGC planned to lower costs through capital-intensive operations and a sharp reduction of labor costs. It also planned then to raise output from a projected 670,000 fine ounces for 1992 to more than 1 million fine ounces a year in 1995. The expansion was to be funded by an International Finance Corporation loan package totaling US$140 million. AGC was to put up the balance, estimated to exceed US$200 million.

AGC was not the only company to benefit from an upsurge in production. Despite its increased production, the company's overall share of the domestic gold market declined from 80 percent to 60 percent in the same period that other operators entered the industry. Provisional figures for 1991 showed that two new mines, Teberebie and Billiton Bogoso, produced 100,000 fine ounces each, while other companies, including State Gold Mining Corporation, Southern Cross Mining Company, Goldenrae, Bonte, and Okumpreko, were stepping up production.

Several other enterprises were on the drawing board or were about to open by mid-1992. The British company Cluff Resources had raised US$10.2 million to finance a new mine at Ayanfuri. The company had been involved in exploration since 1987 and planned to produce as much as 50,000 ounces of gold annually. A Canadian-Ghanaian joint-venture gold mine and associated processing facilities was commissioned in mid-1991 in Bogoso, western Ghana. Finally, in May 1992, a joint-venture company was created to prospect for gold in the Aowin Suamang district in Western Region. Shareholders in the new company included the Chinese government (32.68 percent), private investors in Hong Kong (32 percent), the Ghanaian government (10 percent), and private Ghanaian interests.

In 1992 Ghana's gold production surpassed 1 million fine ounces, up from 327,000 fine ounces in 1987. In March 1994, the Ghanaian government announced that it would sell half of its 55 percent stake in AGC for an estimated US$250 million, which would then be spent on development projects. The authorities also plan to use some of the capital from the stock sale to promote local business and to boost national reserves. The minister of mines and energy dispelled fears that the stock sale would result in foreign ownership of the country's gold mines by saying that the government would have final say in all major stock acquisitions.

Diamonds

The government also is trying to expand Ghana's diamond-mining industry, which has produced primarily industrial-grade gems from alluvial gravels since the 1920s. More than 11 million carats of proven and probable reserves are located about 110 kilometers northwest of Accra. The main producer is the state-owned Ghana Consolidated Diamonds (GCD), which operates in the Birim River Basin. In the 1960s, the company mined 2 million carats of diamonds a year, but annual production in 1991 amounted to only 146,000 carats. This downturn resulted from technical problems and GCD's weak financial position. Production from all mines came to 688,000 carats in 1991 and to 694,000 carats in 1992.

In the early 1990s, the government announced plans to privatize its diamond-mining operations and to expand production. At Accra's invitation, De Beers of South Africa agreed to undertake an eighteen-month feasibility study to determine the extent of the Birim River Basin diamond reserves. The survey was to cost US$1 million. A De Beers subsidiary will be the operator and manager of GCD, while Lazare Kaplan International, a New York-based diamond polishing and trading company, will produce and market the diamonds.

In 1989 the government established the Precious Minerals Marketing Corporation (PMMC) to purchase minerals from small producers in an effort to stem diamond smuggling. Estimates suggested that as much as 70 percent of Ghana's diamonds was being smuggled out of the country in the mid-1980s. In its first sixteen months of operation, the PMMC bought 382,423 carats of diamonds and 20,365 ounces of gold and sold 230,000 carats of diamonds worth US$8 million. The corporation also earned ¢130 million in 1991 on its jewelry operations, up 48 percent from the previous year, and it planned to establish joint marketing ventures with foreign firms to boost sales abroad. Nevertheless, because of new complaints over raw gem sales, the government in March 1992 ordered an investigation into the operations of the state agency and suspended its managing director.

Manganese

Ghana is one of the world's leading exporters of manganese; however, only 279,000 tons were produced in 1992, compared with the all-time high of 638,000 tons in 1974–75. Ghana has reserves exceeding 60 million tons, and considerable rehabilitation of the sector took place in the 1980s. Ghana National Manganese Corporation's mine and the surrounding infrastructure were repaired, helping to raise production from a low of 159,000 tons in 1983 to 284,000 tons in 1989 and 247,000 tons in 1990. The corporation earned US$20 million from its exports in 1991, up from US$11.6 million in 1989 and US$14.2 million in 1990. Approximately US$85 million was also invested by private investors at the newly explored Kwesikrom deposit.

Petroleum Exploration

Although commercial quantities of offshore oil reserves were discovered in the 1970s, by 1990 production was still negligible. In 1983 the government established the Ghana National Petroleum Corporation (GNPC) to promote exploration and production, and the company reached agreements with a number of foreign firms. The most important of these permitted US-based Amoco to prospect in ten offshore blocks between Ada and the western border with Togo. Petro Canada International has prospected in the Tano River Basin and Diamond Shamrock in the Keta Basin. In 1989 three companies, two American and one Dutch, spent US$30 million drilling wells in the Tano basin. On June 21, 1992, an offshore Tano basin well produced about 6,900 barrels of oil daily.

In the early 1990s, GNPC reviewed all earlier oil and gas discoveries to determine whether a predominantly local operation might make exploitation more commercially viable. GNPC wanted to set up a floating system for production, storage, offloading, processing, and gas-turbine electricity generation, hoping to produce 22 billion cubic feet per day, from which 135 megawatts of power could be generated and fed into the national and regional grid. GNPC also won a contract in 1992 with Angola's state oil company, Sonangol, that provides for drilling and, ultimately, production at two of Sonangol's offshore oil fields. GNPC will be paid with a share of the oil.

The country's refinery at Tema underwent the first phase of a major rehabilitation in 1989. The second phase began in April 1990 at an estimated cost of US$36 million. Once rehabilitation is completed, distribution of liquified petroleum gas will be improved, and the quantity supplied will rise from 28,000 to 34,000 barrels a day. Construction on the new Tema-Akosombo oil products pipeline, designed to improve the distribution system further, began in January 1992. The pipeline will carry refined products from Tema to Akosombo Port, where they will be transported across Lake Volta to northern regions. Distribution continues to be uneven, however. Other measures to improve the situation include a US$28 million project to set up a national network of storage depots in all regions.

The Tema Lube Oil Company commissioned its new oil blending plant, designed to produce 25,000 tons of oil per year, in 1992. The plant will satisfy all of Ghana's requirements for motor and gear lubricants and 60 percent of the country's need for industrial lubricants, or, in all, 90 percent of Ghana's demand for lubricant products. Shareholders include Mobil, Shell, and British Petroleum (together accounting for 48 percent of equity), GNPC, and the Social Security and National Insurance Trust.

Manufacturing and Tourism

Manufacturing

At independence in 1957, the Nkrumah government launched an industrialization drive that increased manufacturing's share of GDP from 10 percent in 1960 to 14 percent in 1970. This expansion resulted in the creation of a relatively wide range of industrial enterprises, the largest including the Volta Aluminum Company (Valco) smelter, saw mills and timber processing plants, cocoa processing plants, breweries, cement manufacturing, oil refining, textile manufacturing operations, and vehicle assembly plants. Many of these enterprises, however, survived only through protection. The overvalued cedi, shortages of hard-currency for raw materials and spare parts, and poor management in the state sector led to stagnation from 1970 to 1977 and then to decline from 1977 to 1982.

Thereafter, the manufacturing sector never fully recovered, and performance remained weak into the 1990s. Underutilization of industrial capacity, which had been endemic since the 1960s, increased alarmingly in the 1970s, with average capacity utilization in large- and medium-scale factories falling to 21 percent in 1982. Once the ERP began, the supply of foreign exchange for imported machinery and fuel substantially improved, and capacity utilization climbed steadily to about 40 percent in 1989. Nevertheless, by 1987 production from the manufacturing sector was 35 percent lower than in 1975 and 26 percent lower than in 1980.

Ghana's record with industrialization projects since independence is exemplified by its experience with aluminum, the country's most conspicuous effort to promote capital-intensive industry. This venture began in the mid-1960s with the construction of a 1,186-megawatt hydroelectric dam on the lower Volta River at Akosombo. Built with assistance from Britain, the United States, and the World Bank, the Akosombo Dam was the centerpiece of the Volta River Project (VRP), which the Nkrumah government envisioned as the key to developing an integrated aluminum industry based on the exploitation of Ghana's sizable bauxite reserves and its hydroelectric potential. Foreign capital for the construction of an aluminum smelter in Tema was obtained from US-based Kaiser Aluminum, which acquired a 90 percent share in Valco, and from US-based Reynolds Aluminum, which held a 10 percent share. Valco became the principal consumer of VRP hydroelectricity, using 60 percent of VRP-generated power and producing up to 200,000 tons of aluminum annually during the 1970s.

Changing global economic conditions and severe drought dramatically affected the Ghanaian aluminum industry during the 1980s. The discovery of vast bauxite reserves in Australia and Brazil created a global oversupply of the mineral and induced a prolonged recession in the aluminum trade. Under these conditions, Valco found it far more economical to import semi-processed alumina from Jamaica and South Korea than to rely on local supplies, despite the discovery in the early 1970s of sizable new deposits at Kibi. Valco's refusal to build an aluminum production facility brought Kaiser and Reynolds into bitter conflict with the government.

Severe drought compounded the effects of unfavorable market conditions by reducing the electricity generating capacity of the Akosombo Dam and by forcing a temporary shutdown of the smelter from 1983 to 1985. Aluminum production was slow to recover in the wake of the shutdown. In the early 1990s, aluminum production and exports continued to be negligible.

Drastic currency devaluation after 1983 made it exceptionally expensive to purchase inputs and difficult to obtain bank credit, which hurt businessmen in the manufacturing sector. Furthermore, the ERP's tight monetary policies created liquidity crises for manufacturers, while liberalization of trade meant that some enterprises could not compete with cheaper imports. These policies hurt industries beset by long recession, hyperinflation, outmoded equipment, weak demand, and requirements that they pay 100 percent advances for their own inputs. Local press reports have estimated the closure of at least 120 factories since 1988, mainly because of competitive imports. The garment, leather, electrical, electronics, and pharmaceuticals sectors have been particularly hard hit. In 1990, even the New Match Company, the only safety match company in the country, closed.

ERP strategies made it difficult for the government to assist local enterprises. Committed to privatization and the rule of free-market forces, the government was constrained from offering direct assistance or even from moderating some policies that had an obviously detrimental impact on local manufacturers. Nevertheless, the Rawlings government initiated programs to promote local manufacturing.

In 1986 the government established the Ghana Investment Center to assist in creating new enterprises. Between 1986 and 1990, the vast majority of projects approved—444 of 621—were in the manufacturing sector. Projected investment for the approved ventures was estimated at US$138 million in 1989 and at US$136 million in 1990. In the initial phase, timber was the leading sector, giving way in 1990 to chemicals. In 1991 the government established an office to deal with industrial distress in response to complaints that "unrestrained imports" of foreign products were undermining local enterprises. The 1992 budget included assistance for local industrialists; ¢2 billion was set aside as financial support for "deserving enterprises."

The dominant trends in manufacturing, nonetheless, were the involvement of foreign capital and the initiation of joint ventures. Significant new enterprises included a US$8 million Taiwanese-owned factory, capable of turning out ten tons of iron and steel products per hour, which began trials at Tema in 1989. Although approximately 500 projects had been approved since the investment code came into force in 1985, almost half had still not been launched by the end of 1989. Between 90 and 95 percent of the approved projects were joint ventures between foreign and local partners, 80 percent of which were in the wood industry. Restructuring of the sector was proceeding through divestiture, import liberalization, and promotion of small-scale industries.

Electric Power

In the early 1990s, Ghana's total generating capacity was about 1,187 megawatts, and annual production totalled approximately 6 million kilowatt hours. The main source of supply is the Volta River Authority with six 127-megawatt turbines. The authority's power plant at Akosombo provides the bulk of all electricity consumed in Ghana, some 60 percent of which is purchased by Valco for its smelter. The power plant also meets most of the energy needs of Togo and Benin, which amounted to an estimated equivalent of 180,000 tons of oil in 1991. The balance of Ghana's electricity is produced by diesel units owned by the Electricity Corporation of Ghana, by mining companies, and by a 160-megawatt hydroelectric plant at Kpong, about forty kilometers downstream from Akosombo. A third dam at Bui on the Black Volta River has been under study for some time, with the aim of increasing power supplies in northern Ghana or of selling power to Côte d'Ivoire and Burkina Faso (Burkina, formerly Upper Volta). There have been difficulties, however, in raising the funds needed for the 450-megawatt generating plant. Other sites with the potential for power generation, on the Pra River, the Tano River, the White Volta River, and the Ankobra River, would also require substantial investment.

Ghana has attempted to increase distribution of its electricity throughout the country. One program, funded by the World Bank's International Development Association, will provide reliable and widespread electricity in the urban and southern parts of the country. In addition, the extension of the national grid to the Northern Region was commissioned in 1989. The extension links northern Ghana to the power generated from the Akosombo Dam.

The second phase of the extension will connect major towns in Upper East Region with the regional capital, Bolgatanga, at a cost of US$100 million. The final phase will see exports of electricity across the northern border to Burkina. In early 1991, furthermore, the International Development Association announced a loan to the Electricity Corporation of Ghana to finance the supply and expansion of electricity networks in the northwestern areas of Accra. The corporation aims to extend the supply of electricity to all isolated centers where diesel is the main source of power.

Plans were also afoot to increase the supply of electricity by utilization of thermal energy. Construction was anticipated by

Hydroelectric sluices in the Akosombo Dam
Courtesy Embassy of Ghana, Washington

late 1994 on the country's first thermal power generating plant near Takoradi. Scheduled for completion in 1997, the plant will contribute 300 megawatts of electricity to the national grid.

Ghana has a National Nuclear Research Institute, which trains undergraduate and postgraduate students in the techniques of nuclear science application in such areas as agriculture, medicine, and research. In late 1994, work was nearing completion on a nuclear reactor at Kwabenyan, near Accra, to be used to aid research in these fields. In addition, a second nuclear physics center is to be established in Kumasi on the recommendation of the Ghana Atomic Energy Commission.

Tourism

Under Ghana's 1985 investment code, tourism is a priority sector with incentives and benefits for investors. The government hopes to triple its foreign exchange earnings from tourism under a five-year tourism plan, based on a projection that between 1991 and 1995, the number of tourists visiting Ghana every year will double from the 1991 base of 145,000. Jobs in the tourism industry are projected to reach 270,000, with more created in other sectors that derive business from the tourist trade. There are also incentives for star-rated hotels, approved tourist villages and beaches, and holiday recreational resorts. Investors are involved in the development of other tourist attractions, such as waterfalls, beaches, forts, castles, and historical sites, and even in specialized restaurants, tourist coaches, and buses. Incentives in this sector include tax and rate exemptions on building properties for three years in addition to investment and depreciation allowances.

Transportation and Telecommunications

Ghana's transportation and communications networks are centered in the southern regions, especially the areas in which gold, cocoa, and timber are produced. The northern and central areas are connected through a major road system; some areas, however, remain relatively isolated.

The deterioration of the country's transportation and communications networks has been blamed for impeding the distribution of economic inputs and food as well as the transport of crucial exports. Consequently, the first priority of the ERP was to repair physical infrastructure. Under the program's first phase (1983–86), the government allocated US$1.5 billion, or 36 percent of total investment, for that purpose and an additional US$222 million in 1987 for road and rail rehabilitation. In 1991 the Ghanaian government allocated 27 percent of its budget for various road schemes.

Foreign donor support helped to increase the number of new vehicle registrations from 8,000 in 1984 to almost 20,000 in 1989. The distribution of vehicles was skewed, however, because, by 1988, more than half of all vehicles were in Accra, which contained approximately 7 percent of the country's population. Furthermore, most new vehicles are intended for private use rather than for hauling goods and people, a reflection of income disparities. Transportation is especially difficult in eastern regions, near the coast, and in the vast, underdeveloped northern regions, where vehicles are scarce. At any one time, moreover, a large percentage of intercity buses and Accra city buses are out of service.

Roads and Railroads

Ghana contains about 32,250 kilometers of roads, of which about 12,000 kilometers are main roads. Approximately 6,000 kilometers are paved; the remainder are gravel, crushed stone, or graded earth. The country's rail network is 953 kilometers in length; all track is 1.067 meter (narrow) gauge and all but thirty-two kilometers are single track. The network connects Sekondi-Takoradi with Kumasi and Accra; branch lines run to Prestea, Awaso, Kade, Tema, and Shai Hills (see fig. 10). Poor rural infrastructure has been blamed for problems in agriculture, partly because transportation costs account for about 70 percent of the difference between farm prices and retail prices. Only about one-third of the feeder road network can carry vehicular traffic.

The government has no plans to extend the railway system beyond its limited coverage of the southwestern regions of the country. The western section of the rail system (Takoradi-Kumasi) was renovated under a US$240 million program, the bulk of which the World Bank financed. Figures indicate a downward trend in passenger traffic from a high of 389 per kilometer in 1988 to 277 per kilometer in 1990. Freight steadily increased throughout the 1980s from forty-four million tons per kilometer in 1984 to a decade high of 131 million tons per kilometer in 1989.

The government has instead focused on improvement of the road system. Since 1985 all trunk roads and about 2,900 kilometers of feeder roads as well as a number of bridges and drainage systems have been undergoing repairs. For example, 275 kilometers of the Accra-Kumasi road's northern section are slated to be repaved, but as of early 1994 only the 135 kilometers from Kumasi to Anyinam had been completed. In 1987 Japan offered US$80 million to rehabilitate the main road between Kumasi and Takoradi, which carries cocoa and timber exports; this project was well under way in 1993. By the early 1990s, a World Bank loan of US$22 million was funding the rehabilitation of three major roads in Accra in yet another effort to ease import and export traffic. The road between Tema and Akosombo, an important link in the transportation network between the Gulf of Guinea and Burkina, was also due for improvement.

Ports and Shipping

Ghana has two deep artificial harbors, one at Tema and the

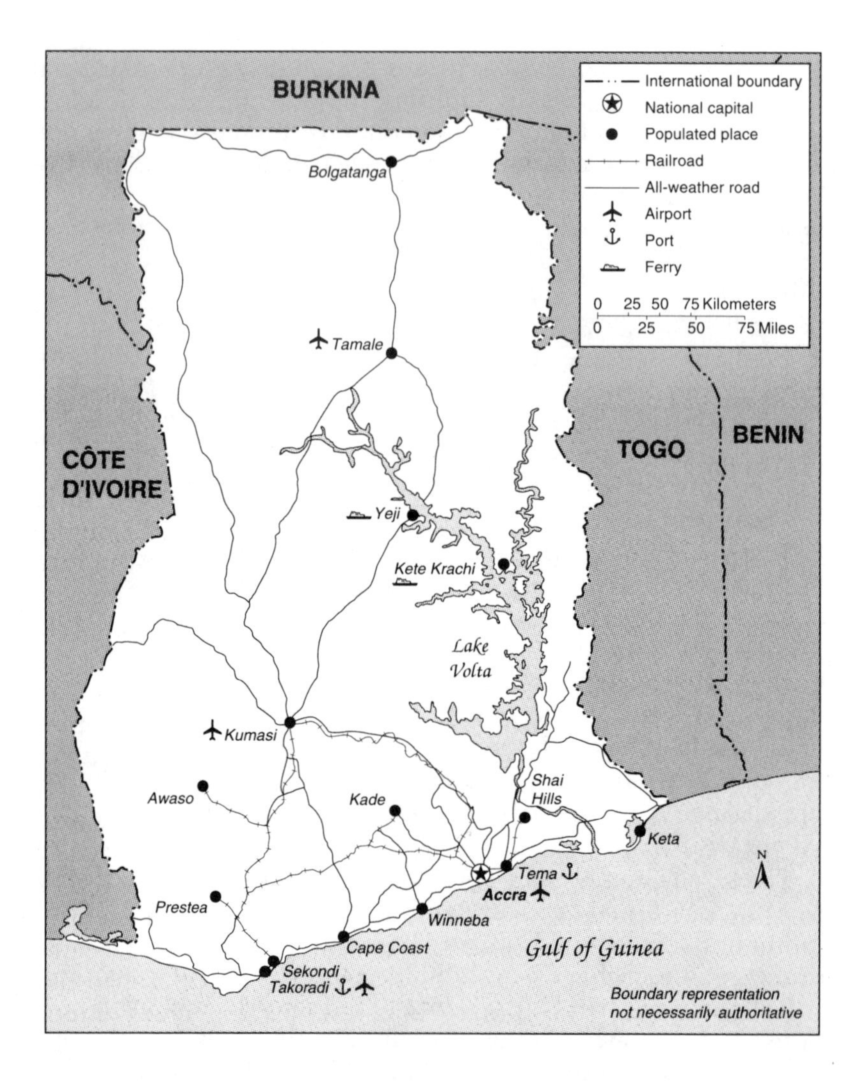

Figure 10. Transportation System, 1994

other at Takoradi. The first stage of the government's five-year plan to improve Ghana's physical infrastructure began with the expenditure of US$80 million to rehabilitate the port at Tema. As a result of the work, the port's capacity for handling dry tonnage rose by 50 percent to 2.7 million tons. Work planned at Takoradi should increase capacity by 128 percent to 1.6 million tons. The Volta River, the Ankobra River, and the Tano River provide 168 kilometers of perennial navigation for launches and lighters. Lake Volta provides 1,125 kilometers of arterial and feeder waterways. In addition, the government is developing new ports on Lake Volta to create an inland waterway network. Ghana's merchant marine service includes six ships (five cargo and one refrigerated).

Civil Aviation

On July 4, 1958, the Ghanaian government established Ghana Airways (GA) to replace the former African Airways Corporation. By the mid-1990s, GA operated international scheduled passenger and cargo service to numerous European, Middle Eastern, and African destinations, including London, Düsseldorf, Rome, Abidjan, Dakar, Lagos, Lomé, and Johannesburg. The airline also operates direct service to New York. The GA fleet includes two Fokker 28s, one McDonnell Douglas DC–10, and one McDonnell Douglas DC–9. Since the late 1980s, GA has received overhaul and maintenance service from, among others, Swissair, Field Aircraft Services, and Fokker Aviation. Historically, the airline has suffered from chronic financial problems and thus has had difficulties meeting its foreign debt obligations. Additionally, GA has been unable to purchase new aircraft to bolster its domestic and regional routes.

Ghana has eleven airports, six with hard surfaced runways. The most important are Kotoka International Airport at Accra and airports at Sekondi-Takoradi, Kumasi, and Tamale that serve domestic air traffic. In 1990 the government spent US$12 million to improve Accra's facilities. Workmen resurfaced the runway, upgraded the lighting system, and built a new freight terminal. Construction crews also extended and upgraded the terminal building at Kumasi. In early 1991, the government announced further plans to improve Accra's international airport. The main runway was upgraded, improvements were made in freight landing and infrastructure, and the terminal building and the airport's navigational aids were upgraded.

Telecommunications

Despite improvements carried out in the 1980s under the auspices of the Economic Community of West African States (ECOWAS), Ghana's telecommunications system continues to be one of the least developed in Africa. In 1994 the country counted about 50,000 telephones, or approximately 2.6 telephones per 1,000 people, one of the world's lowest figures. Telephone service is heavily concentrated in Accra, and even in the capital, only government offices, large commercial concerns, or wealthier households have telephone service. Domestic long-distance communications are carried over two radio-relay systems, one that extends east-west through the major coastal cities, and another that goes north from the capital to Burkina. International telecommunications, except to neighboring countries, are sent via a satellite ground station near Accra. This station, working with the International Telecommunications Satellite Organization (Intelsat) Atlantic Ocean Satellite, provides high-quality telephone, television, and data links to countries in Africa, Europe, and the Americas.

Broadcast service is typical of African countries. The country has four amplitude modulation (AM) radio stations and one frequency modulation (FM) radio station. Three shortwave transmitters provide countrywide service: two for domestic reception that broadcast in English and six local languages, and one international transmitter that broadcasts in English, French, and Hausa. There are four (eight translators) television stations. Television transmitters are located at or near Accra, Cape Coast, Kumasi, and Bolgatanga; eight low-power television repeaters are located in smaller cities. In 1993 the country had an estimated 4 million radio receivers and 250,000 television sets.

In 1992 the Ghanaian government approved the formation of a National Communications Commission. This organization undertakes numerous missions, including the promotion of research and development, improvement of communications, management of the radio frequency spectrum, and encouragement of private ownership in the telecommunications sector. Given Ghana's lack of resources and the difficulty of acquiring foreign aid, it is unlikely that the commission will make any significant improvements in the country's telecommunications system in the near future.

Foreign Investments and Assistance

Despite efforts to increase private capital participation in the Ghanaian economy, in the early 1990s foreign investments continued to be sparse, and the economy relied heavily on aid and loans. By 1991 the external debt exceeded US$4 billion, and it was nearly US$4.3 billion in 1992, an amount equal to the level of assistance provided by donors over the previous decade. The country continued to experience trade and service deficits even though exports increased.

Buses, such as this one at Navrongo in far northern Ghana, are a vital part of local transportation.
Courtesy life in general *(Brook, Rose, and Cooper Le Van)*
Traffic on the highway between Winneba and Accra
Courtesy James Sanders

Investment

Despite efforts to induce foreign investment in the economy, interest has been restricted primarily to the mining sector. Although at least eleven mining companies enjoyed some foreign participation by 1990, the government had succeeded in creating only two joint ventures in former state enterprises outside the mining industry.

In 1985 the government adopted an investment code to encourage foreign investment. It excluded the petroleum and mining sectors, for which the government introduced a separate code in 1986; and it offered special conditions for agriculture, manufacturing (for export, using local raw materials, and for the production of agricultural equipment, spare parts, and machine tools), construction, and tourism. Agricultural projects were given a 45 percent corporate income tax allowance, a 100 percent allowance on plant and equipment, and a 10 percent investment allowance. In manufacturing and construction, the investment allowance was 7.5 percent, with depreciation and capital allowances of 40 percent and 50 percent, respectively, the latter two halved in subsequent years. Finally, in tourism, the investment allowance was 7.5 percent, and the depreciation allowances were 50 percent for plant and 20 percent for buildings, which also were halved in subsequent years. In all cases, imports required for the projects were exempted from duties. Additional tax reductions were granted to projects located in Kumasi and Sekondi-Takoradi, while other areas (excluding Accra-Tema) were given even larger reductions.

Some activities (retail and wholesale trade, except where employed capital was over US$500,000; land transport; travel; advertising; estate agencies) were reserved for Ghanaian-owned firms. Foreign investors were required to supply a minimum of US$60,000 in the case of partnerships with Ghanaians, or US$100,000 in the case of fully owned enterprises. Only net foreign-exchange earning ventures were allowed to be fully owned by foreigners. The code guaranteed investments against nationalization, and where disputes needed arbitration, they were to be settled through existing international forums. Transfers abroad were allowed for dividend payments, debt servicing, charges for technology transfers, or liquidation of enterprises. Implementation of the code and processing of applications by potential investors were made the responsibilities of the Ghana Investment Center.

In mid-1993 Minister of Finance Kwesi Botchwey announced that a new investment code had been presented to Ghana's parliament. Under the new code, minimum foreign capital requirements for joint ventures will be dropped from US$60,000 to US$10,000, and the minimum for fully owned foreign enterprises will be reduced to US$50,000. Companies established solely for export will be exempt from the minimum capital requirement. The new code outlaws government expropriations and provides a five-year tax holiday for the agricultural and real estate sectors.

Foreign Assistance and Loans

Ghana's economic well-being and recovery program are closely tied to significant levels of foreign loans and assistance, especially from the World Bank and the International Monetary Fund. Altogether, between 1982 and 1990 foreign and multilateral donors disbursed a total of approximately US$3.5 billion in official development assistance; at the same time, the country's external debt reached US$3.5 billion. By 1991 the largest bilateral donors were Germany, the United States, Japan, and Canada, which together provided Ghana with US$656 million in development assistance. The largest multilateral donors in 1991 included the European Community, the IMF, and the International Development Association, which furnished almost US$435 million to Ghana.

In addition, the government obtained five IMF programs amounting to approximately US$1.6 billion: three standby loans, simultaneous Extended Fund Facility and Structural Adjustment Facility loans, and an Enhanced Structural Adjustment Facility loan in 1988. The government signed more than twenty policy-based program loans with the World Bank. The World Bank also sponsored six consultative group meetings; the first, held in November 1983, resulted in pledges of US$190 million. Between 1984 and 1991, almost US$3.5 billion more was raised at five additional meetings.

In 1991 Ghana successfully raised the country's first syndicated loan in almost twenty years in the amount of US$75 million. The loan's collateral was a proportion of the country's cocoa crop. Special arrangements were made to ensure that a specific amount of the crop was purchased using letters of credit. Then in March 1992, the IMF announced that following the expiration of Ghana's third and final arrangement under the Enhanced Structural Adjustment Facility, Ghana needed no further IMF financing. Even so, the Ghanaian government asked the IMF to monitor progress on the country's economic program and to continue policy dialogue.

In early 1994, Ghana accepted the obligations of Article VIII of the IMF's Articles of Agreement. According to the IMF, Ghana will no longer impose restrictions on payments and transfers for current international transactions or engage in discriminatory currency arrangements or multiple currency practice without IMF approval. Ghana's decision undoubtedly will enhance its image with foreign investors and bankers.

Balance of Trade and Payments

Despite efforts under the ERP to stabilize the country's balance of payments, Ghana's current account remained in deficit throughout the 1980s and into the early 1990s. Both trade and services deficits continued into the 1990s, given the country's dependence on concessional inflows and IMF funding. The current account deficit fell by US$91 million in 1986 from US$134 million in 1985, but it rose again by US$54 million in 1987. After another recovery in 1988, the deficit was back at US$99 million in 1989 and widened to US$228 million in 1990, US$253 million in 1991, and US$378 million in 1992. It was projected to fall to US$190 million in 1994 (see table 10, Appendix).

The government did succeed, however, in building up at least some external reserves. By the end of 1991, official foreign-exchange reserves totaled US$538 million, more than double the level at the end of 1990 and the highest amount for at least a decade. The increase resulted from the Bank of Ghana's attempt to boost reserves to cover more than four months' imports. For example, the government allowed exporting companies to retain some of their foreign-exchange earnings inside the country. For Ashanti Goldfields Corporation, the portion is 45 percent. Exporters of other products, except cocoa, may keep up to 35 percent of earnings in retention accounts, and the Ghana Cocoa Board may keep 10 percent. The retained export earnings can be used for the import of equipment, spare parts, and essential inputs as well as for meeting the exporters' external financial obligations. By late December 1991, foreign exchange reserves were sufficient to finance almost twenty weeks of imports. In 1992 foreign-exchange reserves dropped to US$291.6 million because the government had to use its reserves to cover current foreign obligations. By September 1993, the foreign-exchange reserve totalled US$276.9 million.

Foreign assets and liabilities of the Ghanaian banking system as a whole showed a positive trend. Compared with the first half of 1991, Ghana's assets with reporting banks rose by 14.7 percent to US$1 billion in the second half of the year. Assets at the end of 1991 were 12.7 percent higher than the US$923 million on hand at the end of 1990. Liabilities also rose significantly from US$368 million to US$437 million during the first half of 1991 and by 25.9 percent during the year as a whole. Overall, however, there was a positive net increase. Net assets stood at US$603 million at the end of 1991 as against US$539 million in June 1991 and US$576 million in December 1990.

Growth Trends and Potential

During the 1980s, the Ghanaian government successfully rehabilitated major economic sectors that had deteriorated since the 1960s. Throughout the decade, Ghana saw growth in GDP and the repair of some of its economic infrastructure. Through fiscal austerity, the government achieved balanced budgets at the same time that it invested in development projects. In particular, the export sector regained some strength by the early 1990s with a resurgence in cocoa, gold, and timber exports.

The cost of this growth, however, raised serious questions about the long-term viability of the government's programs. Growth has been possible only through foreign assistance and loans, which totaled US$7 billion by 1990. Although the government has been effective in directing these funds toward productive sectors, it has cut current spending on social services, which will require attention in the future. Currency devaluations, while helping exports, have increased both the cost of living and prices for imports. Most important, the government has emphasized export production, while subjecting import-substitution industries to stiff foreign competition and neglecting local crop production, leading to an increasing reliance on imports of goods and food. Thus, although exports have increased, they have been offset by rising imports, with the result that Ghanaians are increasingly subjected to higher prices.

The Economic Recovery Program has succeeded in allowing Ghana to regain its international credit standing and has curbed the worst excesses of economic protectionism. The country is in a position to exploit its considerable agricultural and mineral potential. At the same time, sustained long-term growth will require that attention be given to domestic industries and to consumption rather than exclusively to exports and the wealth generated thereby.

*   *   *

Sources on Ghana's economic past and present are relatively rich and varied because of the country's continuing prominence in discussions about economic development and structural adjustment programs on the African continent. For good historical studies, see Kwame Yeboah Daaku's *Trade and Politics on the Gold Coast, 1600–1720* and Edward Reynolds's *Trade and Economic Change on the Gold Coast, 1807–1874.* Polly Hill's study, *The Migrant Cocoa-Farmers of Southern Ghana: A Study in Rural Capitalism,* is a seminal examination of African economic initiative and enterprise during the colonial period. For the independence period, see Tony Killick's *Development Economics in Action: A Study of Economic Policies in Ghana,* Douglas Rimmer's *Staying Poor: Ghana's Political Economy, 1950–1990,* and Donald Rothchild's "Ghana and Structural Adjustment: An Overview." The multilateral assistance organizations have also published numerous studies of Ghana in light of its prominence as a showcase of structural adjustment policies. They include the Organisation for Economic Co-operation and Development study by Alan Roe and Hartmut Schneider, *Adjustment and Equity in Ghana,* the World Bank's *Ghana: 2000 and Beyond: Setting the Stage for Accelerated Growth and Poverty Reduction,* and the International Monetary Fund's *Ghana: Adjustment and Growth, 1983–91.* For statistics and current information, see *Ghana in Figures, Quarterly Digest of Statistics,* and *Statistical Newsletter,* all published by the Ghanaian government's Statistical Service, and the Economist Intelligence Unit's quarterly *Country Report: Ghana* and annual *Country Profile: Ghana.* Numerous periodicals contain much information about Ghana's economy, including *African Business, Africa Economic Digest,* and *Africa Research Bulletin.* (For further information and complete citations, see Bibliography.)

Chapter 4. Government and Politics

A wooden stool, decorated with silver, from the palace of the asantehene *in Kumasi; traditional symbol of authority (Asante)*

AFTER AN UNHAPPY SURVEY of the tragic history of liberal democracy in post-colonial Africa—a survey in which Ghana was certainly at the forefront—two astute observers of the African political scene asked, "If Western democracy . . . ended up looking like a sad cross between paternalism and corruption, what are the alternatives? What might an indigenous African form of democracy look like?" They claimed that the answer had to be sought in the ideas and forms of equality and participation found in the village council and similar institutions of community governance. Thus, according to them, a "greater reliance on modern variations of these forms might succeed where Western forms of democracy had failed."

Ideas similar to these helped inspire the 31st December 1981 Revolution in Ghana. The revolution set in motion a process of national democratic transformation linked to the unfulfilled democratic ideals and aspirations of the June 4, 1979, popular uprising led by Jerry John Rawlings, chairman of what became the Provisional National Defence Council (PNDC) after 1981. The PNDC leadership insisted that the revolution was not a carbon copy of any other revolution and that it was aimed at resolving Ghana's socio-economic problems, using Ghana's historical experiences and cultural traditions as a basis. Thus, the PNDC leadership effectively challenged the notion that the options for Ghana's evolving democratic institutions and popular grass-roots structures were limited to different versions of Marxism-Leninism, Western-style liberalism of the "left" or "right," or military rule, which had been practiced before the revolution and had not worked.

Accordingly, four major, related themes of PNDC rule remained relatively constant throughout the tumultuous transition to constitutional democracy, a movement that had widespread popular support. These were: a rejection of extreme ideological tendencies and of multiparty politics as practiced in Ghana since independence, which had been divisive, corrupt, and elitist; decentralization, aimed at the practical application of the ideas of mass participation going back to the early nationalist struggles against colonialism and at achieving a fundamental restructuring of the machinery of government; establishment of democratic structures and institutions at every level of society; and national unity and commitment to the ideals of

Pan-Africanism, nonalignment, and noninterference in the internal affairs of other countries.

What perhaps ultimately distinguished the PNDC period from others were, on the negative side, the extent of political violence, repression of political dissent, and widespread human rights violations, which especially characterized the early period of PNDC rule. On the positive side, the PNDC was noted for its extraordinary ability to put together a capable team with the political will and resourcefulness to pull the country out of its deepest economic crisis in living memory and to return the country to democracy in the face of persistent "counterrevolutionary" pressures, numerous coup attempts, and moves to destabilize the regime.

The PNDC government lasted for eleven turbulent years and survived presidential and parliamentary elections in 1992. In January 1993, Rawlings effected a relatively peaceful transition from military ruler to elected president of the Fourth Republic. His pledge of policy continuity has ensured that in many significant respects the PNDC remains in power, but there is an important difference. The present government was elected under a new democratic constitution that guarantees fundamental human rights, independence of the media, civil liberties, and the rule of law.

The Provisional National Defence Council

Within thirty-five years of Ghana's becoming a sovereign state, the country experienced, before its fourth return to multiparty democratic government in January 1993, nine different governments (three civilian and six military), including a Westminster-style parliamentary democracy, a socialist single-party republic, and several military regimes following coups in 1966, 1972, 1979, and 1981 (see Independent Ghana; The Fall of the Nkrumah Regime and Its Aftermath; and Ghana and the Rawlings Era, ch. 1; table 11, Appendix).

The national leadership of postcolonial Ghana inherited state machinery that had evolved under British rule and that emphasized strong centralization of power and top-down decision making. Kwame Nkrumah—prime minister, 1957–60; president, 1960–66—unsuccessfully attempted to create a socialist economy in the early 1960s, but his effort merely served to compound the inevitable problems and dangers of administrative centralization and state intervention in the economy. These problems, which survived Nkrumah, included political corruption, self-enrichment, misuse of power, lack of public accountability, and economic mismanagement, leading in turn to economic decline and stagnation and to the rapid erosion of political legitimacy and attendant coups d'état. Authoritarian or arbitrary styles of leadership that limited genuine democratic participation and public debate on policy as well as the lack of political vision of successive postcolonial regimes (with the exception of Nkrumah's) contributed greatly to political instability and to the rapid alternation of civilian and military rule.

One of the changes in government came on June 4, 1979, when a handful of junior officers seized power less than a month before scheduled elections. An Armed Forces Revolutionary Council (AFRC) was formed with the overriding objective of ridding Ghana of official corruption, indiscipline in public life, and economic mismanagement before handing over power to a civilian government. A relatively unknown twenty-nine-year-old air force flight lieutenant, Jerry John Rawlings, emerged as the leader of the AFRC. The so-called housecleaning exercise embarked upon by the AFRC was extended to a variety of civilian economic malpractices such as hoarding, profiteering, and black-marketing.

Parliamentary elections were duly held on June 18, 1979, as planned. A party of the Nkrumahist tradition, the People's National Party (PNP), won a majority of the parliamentary seats, and its leader, Hilla Limann, became president after a run-off election. On September 24, 1979, the AFRC handed over government to the PNP. At this time, Rawlings warned the PNP government that it was on probation and admonished the incoming officials to put the interest of the people first.

The PNP administration was short-lived. On December 31, 1981, Rawlings returned to office for the second time as head of the Provisional National Defence Council (PNDC). He insisted that the 31st December 1981 Revolution was necessitated, among other factors, by the failure of the PNP administration to provide effective leadership and by the virtual collapse of the national economy and of state services. Upon assuming power, Rawlings immediately declared a "holy war" aimed at restructuring national political institutions, establishing genuine democracy based on Ghanaian ideals and traditions, and rehabilitating the economy.

The Political Scene under the PNDC

For democracy to function effectively in Ghana, it was necessary to relate Western democratic processes to Ghanaian political traditions. Peter Du Sautoy, a former district commissioner, recalled his attempt to explain British democracy in the country before independence. His audience understood the process of election, but he was asked how one got rid of one's representative when he no longer seemed to be representative. Du Sautoy explained that one waited until the next election four or five years later. His Ghanaian audience felt that "this was most undemocratic—from time immemorial they had been able to get rid of their chiefs *at any time*, when, after mature consideration and discussion, they felt they no longer had confidence in them."

This observation clearly defines one enduring aspect of the relationship between politics and democracy as understood by the ordinary Ghanaian. It also highlights the significance of indigenous political ideology and attitudes that constitute the core elements of the contemporary Ghanaian political tradition. This political tradition, along with inherited colonial and Christian elements, informs and shapes the institutional pattern of political life. Its basic principles influence disputes and conflicts over the organization, distribution, maintenance, exercise, and transfer of power, and the allocation of economic resources in Ghanaian society.

The published speeches of Rawlings provide evidence of the effective use of symbols and principles drawn from ancestral religious beliefs, Christianity, and chieftaincy. Indeed, Rawlings insisted throughout PNDC rule that the revolution's main and long-term goal was to create a more just society in which the interests of the majority were not repressed in favor of those of a tiny minority and in which the productivity of all Ghanaians would increase. He saw participatory democracy as the best guarantee of such a society.

The PNDC leadership could scarcely avoid the ideological tension and strife generic to Ghanaian popular movements and mass-based political programs. Ironically, the ideological strife that haunted the PNDC leadership was similar to that which wrecked the PNP. In 1980 Limann, PNP leader and president of Ghana, had complained helplessly that the PNP as a mass party spanned the whole range of political ideas. He pointed out that party members included pragmatists, leftists, rightists, and centrists, and he stressed that no national party with a broad social base could escape this mix. The left wing of the PNP—for example, the Kwame Nkrumah Revolutionary Guards—was Limann's severest critic. Some of the leaders of the same left wing and similar organizations joined the PNDC and attempted unsuccessfully in the early years of the revolutionary period to transform what was clearly a nationalist, popular revolution in the direction of Marxism-Leninism (see The Second Coming of Rawlings: The First Six Years, 1982–87, ch. 1).

In the first year after the 1981 revolution, the PNDC regime established new political structures and legal institutions. The new administration rebuilt or reformed much of the pre-existing local, regional, and national administrative machinery of governance in accordance with the avowed goals of the revolution. During the following ten years, many of these new structures of governance and consultation were modified in response to the demands of efficiency, social and economic realities, and internal and external political pressures. A number of these institutional and structural changes were incorporated into the 1992 constitution of the Fourth Republic.

One such institution was the National Commission for Democracy (NCD), which evolved from the Electoral Commission of the Third Republic. In 1984 the NCD invited the public to submit proposals on the future form of democratic government for the country. In addition, public meetings were held to discuss ways to realize true democracy in Ghana. As a result of these and other efforts, the NCD published its "Blue Book" on the creation of district political authority and on holding elections. These efforts culminated in the district elections of 1988 and the subsequent establishment of 110 district assemblies. In July 1990, the NCD initiated more public debates on the future political system of the country. This marked a significant step in the transition to democracy, which ended with the presidential and parliamentary elections in November and December 1992.

By the late 1980s, the PNDC comprised nine members, the most important being Rawlings, the chairman. It was the highest legislative and administrative body of the state. Below the PNDC was the Committee of Secretaries (cabinet), made up of nineteen secretaries (ministers) who met on a weekly basis under the chairmanship of a PNDC member (see fig. 11). The most prominent of the secretaries were those in charge of finance and economic planning, foreign affairs, education and

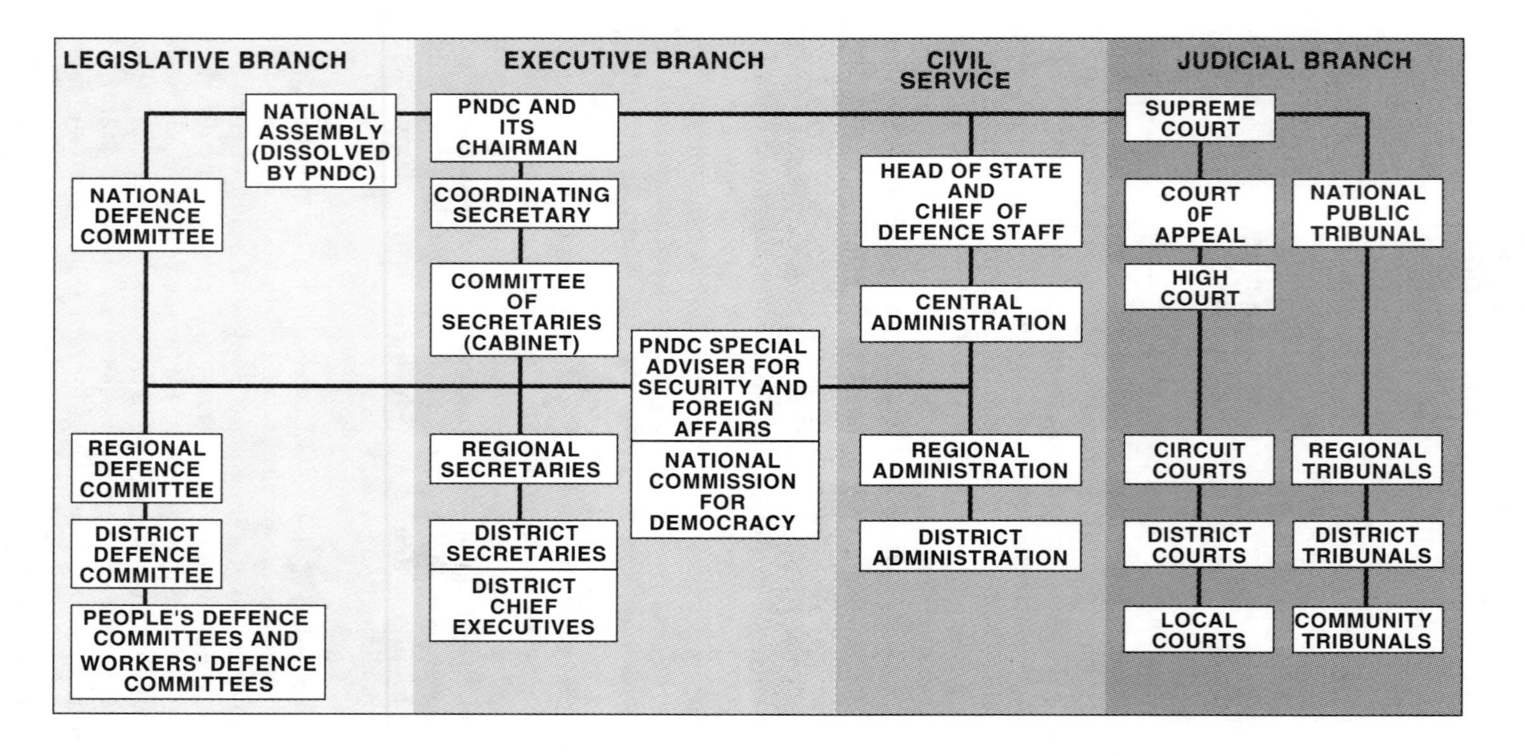

Figure 11. Structure of Provisional National Defence Council (PNDC), 1982–88

culture, local government and rural development, agriculture, health, mobilization and productivity, and chieftaincy affairs.

Revolutionary Organs

To lay the foundation for true democracy in Ghana, the PNDC created a controversial countrywide network of People's Defence Committees (PDCs) and Workers' Defence Committees (WDCs), reorganized and renamed in late 1984 as Committees for the Defence of the Revolution (CDRs). Established in villages, urban communities, and workplaces, the CDRs were intended to be organs of popular power and political initiative. Forces' Defence Committees were established in the armed forces and the police service.

The most important aspect of the reorganization of the PDCs and the WDCs from the standpoint of the political and socioeconomic functions of the CDRs was the opening up of membership to all Ghanaians. This decision reversed the earlier exclusion from PDC/WDC membership of elite groups, such as chiefs and so-called exploiting classes. The change returned the revolution to its original objective of involving all Ghanaians in decision making and opened up possibilities for genuine national reconciliation. According to official directives, the principal functions of the CDRs were to ensure democratic participation in decision making in all communities and workplaces; to guard against corruption, abuse of power, sabotage, and social injustice; and to promote sustained national productivity by focusing efforts on the productive sectors of the economy.

The other mass organizations of the revolution were the National Mobilisation Program, the 31st December Women's Movement, the Civil Defence Organisation (the militia), the National Youth Organising Commission, and the June Fourth Movement. The National Mobilisation Program started as an emergency program to receive and resettle Ghanaian returnees from Nigeria in 1983. It soon developed into a cooperative movement engaged in a variety of economic and community development projects throughout Ghana. The 31st December Women's Movement aimed to bring about the political, social, and economic emancipation of Ghanaian women, especially rural women.

The Civil Defence Organisation, popularly known as the militia, was set up as a paramilitary institution to assist other state organizations in national emergencies such as invasions, bush fires, and floods. Members received special training in combat readiness to defend the nation against internal and external aggression and economic sabotage. The militia, in addition to combating crime in local communities, engaged in voluntary social and economic activities to help promote community development. In this effort, it was often assisted by the National Youth Organising Commission, created in 1982 as part of the PNDC's efforts to establish a youth movement to carry out the objectives of the 31st December 1981 Revolution.

The June Fourth Movement was a militant mass revolutionary movement dedicated to keeping alive the ideals of the June 4, 1979, uprising that Rawlings had led. It sought to arouse the population at large to assist in establishing so-called people's power within the avowed objectives of the revolutionary process. On a practical level, it worked with the militia and the National Youth Organising Commission in various community development projects.

Participatory opportunities of the ordinary Ghanaian citizen were significantly expanded through membership in revolutionary organs. Before the establishment of the district assemblies in 1989, the PNDC government was thus able to reach the rural population and to broaden its base of support by direct consultation. This was achieved through chiefs, the CDRs, and other national bodies such as the Democratic Youth League of Ghana, which in 1988 claimed a nationwide membership of more than 100,000. Other such groups included farmers' organizations, market women's associations, trade union groups, students' organizations, and religious and other bodies. The PNDC's political opposition, however, hotly contested the democratic nature of such organs and saw them as nothing but state-sponsored vigilantes engaged in intimidation and human rights abuses.

The Transition from Military Rule to Democratic Government

Political Ferment under the PNDC

As the country prepared to move toward constitutional rule in the late 1980s, the major concern of Ghanaians was how to ensure a relatively smooth and peaceful democratic transition. This concern was shared by the opposition, the activities of which were under constant surveillance by the national security agencies, and by the ruling PNDC, under pressure to present a clear, firm timetable and program for a return to constitutional government.

The transition process had unsavory features that many Ghanaians believed could lead to an outbreak of violence. Intense mutual suspicion and antipathy existed between the PNDC leadership and the opposition going back to the June 4, 1979, uprising and the draconian measures taken by the AFRC. On one side, Rawlings and the PNDC saw the opposition leaders not as individuals genuinely interested in real democracy but as elitist, corrupt, and self-seeking "big men" who had vowed to fight to the bitter end to reverse the gains of the revolution and to restore the old system of corruption and exploitation.

On the other side, the opposition viewed Rawlings and his Ewe ethnic henchmen, notably Kojo Tsikata, his chief of security, as a bloodthirsty group with the worst human rights record in postcolonial Ghanaian history and one that was determined to retain power by any means. Many opposition leaders could not forgive Rawlings for the loss of lives, power, and property, and for the incarcerations inflicted on friends and relatives, if not on themselves, by the PNDC regime. The once respectable professional elite of comfortable lawyers, doctors, university professors, businessmen, and politicians in exile abroad could not hide their outrage at Ghana's being ruled by, in their view, a young, inexperienced, half-educated military upstart.

It is against this background of intense mutual hostility and distrust and vicious political rivalry that the evolution of the democratic transition between 1988 and the inauguration of the Fourth Republic in January 1993 should be assessed and understood. This long transition process was characterized by two related struggles: the struggle for recovery from decades of economic decline and for better living standards for the average Ghanaian; and the struggle for "true democracy," the meaning of which was hotly debated and gradually shifted, especially after 1988. These national struggles led to the reconstitution of old political alliances and to the emergence of new political groupings.

That it took the PNDC more than ten years to lift the ban imposed on political parties at the inception of PNDC rule not only demonstrated the PNDC's control over the pace and direction of political change but also confirmed the shallowness of the political soil in which the party system was rooted. Party activity had been banned under all of the military governments that had dominated nearly twenty out of the thirty-five years of Ghana's postcolonial existence. Even during periods of civilian administration, party organization had been largely urban centered and rudimentary. It had depended far more on personal alliances and on ethnic and local ties, as well as on patron-client relationships, than on nationally institutionalized structures. Party politics had tended to generate corruption and factionalism. The party system, therefore, never had any real hold on the consciousness of the average Ghanaian, especially the rural Ghanaian.

All the same, three major electoral political traditions have emerged in Ghana since the 1950s, namely, the Nkrumahist tradition, the Danquah-Busiaist tradition, and the more recent Rawlingsist tradition. These traditions are identified with their founders—each a commanding political figure—and are not necessarily mutually exclusive. In political terms, the Nkrumahists are generally considered "leftist" and "progressive," the Danquah-Busiaists more "rightist" and more "conservative," and the Rawlingsists "populist" and "progressive." In practice, however, the traditions are less distinguishable by ideological orientation than by dominant personalities and ethnic origins.

Against this background, the opposition call for multiparty democracy had to overcome great odds, not least of which was the intense prejudice of the chairman of the PNDC against political parties. Rawlings strongly believed that party politics had hitherto produced two forms of abuse of power—the "corrupt dictatorship" of the Kofi Abrefa Busia regime (1969–72) and the "arrogant dictatorship" of the Nkrumah (1957–66) and Limann (1979–81) governments. Nonpartisan, honest, and accountable government would provide an effective antidote to these abuses, he argued. Indeed, Rawlings appeared to have an almost fanatical belief that corruption was at the root of nearly all of Ghana's problems and that, if only it could be stamped out, the country would return to its former prosperity.

In reaction to Rawlings's position, opposition groups, such as the London-based Ghana Democratic Movement and the Campaign for Democracy in Ghana, and individuals within and outside Ghana committed to multiparty democracy, grew increasingly desperate as they focused on the single aim of overthrowing the PNDC regime. Between 1983 and 1986, at least a dozen coup plots were uncovered by an efficient and much-feared state security system (see The 1981 Coup and the Second Rawlings Government, ch. 5). At the same time, vigorous debates occurred within the PNDC, radical organizations, and trade unions over the direction of economic policy, the content and form of true democracy, and the desirability of accepting International Monetary Fund (IMF—see Glossary) support for Ghana's Economic Recovery Program (ERP) (see The Economic Recovery Program, ch. 3).

Urban workers and students especially exhibited growing frustration at their inability to influence policy or to express dissent through readily available channels. Many urban workers felt the CDRs did not effectively represent the opinions of workers in the way that the PDCs and the WDCs had done before their reorganization. In general, public criticism of government policy was discouraged. In the face of repeated coup plots and destabilization attempts, which lasted throughout the PNDC period, the regime was eager to retain tight control of the political situation, and an independent press had difficulty surviving. All the same, the PNDC was clearly aware of the urgent need for the government to provide genuine democratic channels and institutions to enable workers, students, professional bodies, and other interest groups to express dissent and to provide constructive criticism of government policy. There was, therefore, a concerted effort to transform the CDRs and other revolutionary organs into real instruments of grass-roots democracy. The implementation of the government decentralization program and the establishment of district assemblies were likewise aimed at furthering the process of genuine popular democratization.

Interest Groups and National Politics

Among the politically active and influential organizations and interest groups are the Trade Union Congress (TUC), the Ghana Bar Association (GBA), the Christian Council of Ghana (CCG), the Catholic Bishops Conference (CBC), the Ghana Journalists Association, the National Union of Ghanaian Students (NUGS), the regional houses of chiefs, and the National House of Chiefs. Because political parties in Ghana have been weak and the national political system itself has been unstable, the enduring nature of some of these firmly established interest groups has often substituted for political stability. As a result of their stabilizing and quasi-political institutional role, interest groups such as the CBC, the CCG, and the GBA have exerted enormous influence on national policy. The relationship between incumbent governments and these powerful interest groups has never been easy, however; the government has invariably tried to co-opt or to control, if not to intimidate, the leadership of these urban-based organizations.

Of all politically active organizations, the TUC has always had the largest following, with a total membership in the early 1990s of more than 500,000. This figure includes workers and salaried employees in the public and the private sectors who are members of the seventeen unions that are affiliated with the TUC. Since independence, successive governments have made repeated attempts to control it. Rawlings enjoyed the support of the TUC during the first two years of PNDC rule, but the stringent austerity measures introduced in the ERP in 1983 led to discontent among union members adversely affected by devaluation, wage restraints, and lay-offs. By 1985 the original support enjoyed by the PNDC in labor circles had all but disappeared. The PNDC worked hard to regain union support, however, and the National Democratic Congress government of the Fourth Republic has continued to woo the unions through tripartite consultations involving itself, the TUC, and employers.

From the inception to the end of PNDC rule in 1992, the CCG, the CBC, the GBA, NUGS, and the National House of Chiefs played prominent roles in the transition to democracy. These organizations took the provisional nature of the PNDC regime quite literally, calling for a quick return to democratic national government. Although NUGS and the GBA consistently demanded a return to multiparty democracy, the CCG, the CBC, and the national and regional houses of chiefs favored a nonpartisan national government. While the NUGS and GBA leadership used methods that frequently provoked confrontation with the PNDC, the CBC and the national and regional houses of chiefs preferred a more conciliatory method of political change, emphasizing national unity.

The CCG, the CBC, and the national and regional houses of chiefs function openly as independent national lobbies to promote common rather than special interests. They insist on negotiation and mediation in the management of national disputes, and they advocate policy alternatives that stress the long-term needs of society. In the past, they have taken bold initiatives to attain the abrogation of state measures and legislation that violate human rights or that threaten law and order. All three bodies share a commitment to democracy, the rule of law, and the creation of political institutions that reflect Ghanaian cultural traditions.

The GBA, like the other professional associations in Ghana, is concerned with maintaining the dignity of the legal profession through a code of professional ethics and with promoting further learning and research in the profession. The main objectives of the GBA according to its constitution include the defense of freedom and justice, the maintenance of judicial independence, and the protection of human rights and fundamental freedoms as defined under the United Nations Universal Declaration of Human Rights and Fundamental Freedoms. These objectives, by definition, have inevitably pitted the GBA against both military regimes and one-party governments, which on their part have considered the GBA at best a necessary evil.

NUGS and its national executive, representing the more than 8,000 students of Ghana's three universities in Accra-Legon, Kumasi, and Cape Coast, are among the most vocal and articulate pressure groups in Ghana. By reason of their higher education in a largely illiterate society, students have often been in a position to agitate for far-reaching political, economic, and social change. Indeed, students have been in the forefront of political activism in Ghana since independence. NUGS was most vocal in its support of Rawlings and the PNDC in 1982, but this changed as the PNDC adopted policies that NUGS considered to be against the welfare of students in particular and of Ghanaians in general.

The CCG, another vocal and influential interest group, was founded in 1929. The CCG's principal function is advisory; it acts through consultation among its member churches. The CCG operates through several committees, including education, social action (national affairs), and literacy campaigns. The CCG is a member of the World Council of Churches and other ecumenical bodies, and it is a strong advocate of human rights.

The CBC, the highest local unifying authority of the Roman Catholic Church in Ghana, dates to 1950, although the church itself has been in Ghana since the fifteenth century. The CBC has established a Joint Social Action Committee for cooperation between it and the CCG.

The National House of Chiefs and the ten regional houses of chiefs represent more than 32,000 recognized traditional rulers who exercise considerable influence throughout Ghana, especially in the countryside. As trustees of communal lands and natural resources, chiefs are often the pivot around which local socio-economic development revolves. The 1992 constitution, like all previous constitutions, guarantees the institution of chieftaincy together with its traditional councils as established by customary law and usage. To preserve their role as symbols of national unity, however, chiefs are forbidden from active participation in party politics.

District Assembly Elections

The main political preoccupations of the PNDC and the Ghanaian public in 1988 were the implementation of the government's decentralization program and the elections to the new District Assemblies (DAs). In a speech commemorating his fifth year in power in January 1987, Rawlings had announced proposals for the decentralization of government. These had included promises of elections for DAs and a national debate on the ERP. The debate on the ERP never materialized, but debates on the elections and the DAs did.

Among the radical changes introduced in local government elections were provisions that no cash deposits were required of candidates for district-level elections and that illiteracy in English was no longer a disqualification. To accommodate non-English speakers in the DAs and to make assembly debates accessible to the majority of constituents, local languages could be used in the DAs. The elections were to be nonpartisan: the ban on political parties was not lifted. Implementation of the decentralization program and preparation for the district elections did not completely silence the opposition, nor did it remove the sources of public discontent and disaffection toward the government within some sections of the Ghanaian population.

In 1988 there was no indication of what political structures and institutions would be established above the DAs at regional and national levels. Nor was it clear whether creation of the DAs was intended to broaden the civilian support base of the PNDC, thereby legitimizing and perpetuating PNDC rule indefinitely. Some felt that the word "provisional" in the regime's name sounded a bit hollow after five years in power. Indeed, many read the proposed district elections as a strategy similar to the union government proposal in 1978 that had not been implemented because of its widespread unpopularity (see The National Redemption Council Years, 1972–79, ch. 1).

In February 1988, Adu Boahen, a retired history professor and later a presidential candidate and Rawlings's main chal-

Sessional Meeting of a House of Chiefs
Courtesy Embassy of Ghana, Washington

lenger, delivered three lectures in which he severely criticized military rule in Ghana and the PNDC regime in particular as the causes of political instability. He affirmed that the AFRC led by Rawlings in 1979 was completely unnecessary. He attacked the alleged domination of the PNDC regime and of major national institutions by the Ewe and called for an interim coalition government within a year and for a return to multiparty democracy by 1992. The state-owned national media attacked Boahen's criticism of the PNDC but did not report the original text of the lectures.

For the DA elections, the country was divided into three zones by region. Zone one consisted of Western Region, Central Region, Ashanti Region, and Eastern Region; zone two, of Upper East Region, Upper West Region, and Northern Region; and zone three, of Greater Accra Region, Volta Region, and

Brong-Ahafo Region (see fig. 1). The first round of the nonpartisan elections took place on December 6, 1988, in zone one of the country, with polling in zones two and three following on January 31 and February 28, 1989, respectively (see table 12, Appendix). District election committees disqualified several candidates in a number of districts for various offenses, including nonpayment of taxes, refusal to participate in communal labor, and shirking other civic responsibilities. With an estimated average turnout rate of about 60 percent of registered voters (some rural districts had a 90 percent turnout), the highest for any election in two decades, most Ghanaians saw this first step toward the establishment of national democratic institutions as quite successful. The opposition, although critical of the composition of the DAs, accepted the assemblies in principle.

The DAs gave new momentum to the exercise of grass-roots democracy as well as to local determination of and implementation of development projects. The principle of nonpartisan, decentralized political structure proved popular. By-laws passed by the DAs had to be deposited with the PNDC secretariat immediately after their passage. If within twenty-one days the PNDC raised no objection to them, they automatically became law.

Some elected representatives, a majority of whom were farmers and school teachers, resented the fact that PNDC appointees, mostly chiefs and professionals who constituted one-third of the memberships of the DAs, often sought to dominate the proceedings. Also, most of the districts and their people were poor, and the DAs' quick resort to taxes and numerous levies to raise much-needed revenue proved burdensome and unpopular. In some parts of the country, for example Cape Coast and Accra, there were protests and tax revolts. In August 1989, regional coordinating councils were formed in all ten regions to streamline the work of the DAs and to coordinate district policies and projects. The PNDC made it clear that DAs had no power to collect or to levy income taxes.

Charting the Political Transition

The inauguration of the DAs removed some of the political pressures on the PNDC, but political ferment continued in some sectors of the population. So, too, did the arrest and detention of leading opponents of the PNDC regime. The most publicized of the latter was the arrest and detention in

September 1989 of Major Courage Quarshigah, ex-commandant of the Ghana Military Academy and a former close ally of Rawlings. He was accused of leading an attempted coup and of an alleged plot to assassinate Rawlings (see The 1981 Coup and the Second Rawlings Government, ch. 5).

A new phase of the political struggle of the opposition against the PNDC opened in January 1990 when the GBA called on the PNDC to initiate immediately a referendum that would permit the Ghanaian people to determine openly the form of constitutional government they wished for themselves. In his end-of-year message in 1989, Rawlings had promised that the government would strengthen participatory democracy at the grass-roots level. He also proposed that the NCD initiate nationwide consultations with various groups to determine the country's economic and political future. These consultations consisted of a series of seminars, in all ten regional capitals, that ran from July 5 to November 9, 1990, at which the public was invited to express its views.

Meanwhile, the CBC issued a communiqué calling for a national debate on Ghana's political future. On July 24, the Kwame Nkrumah Revolutionary Guards (KNRG) issued a statement calling for a return to multiparty democracy, for the lifting of the ban on political parties, and for the creation of a constituent assembly to draft a new constitution to be approved by a national referendum. On August 1, the KNRG, other opposition organizations, and some prominent Ghanaians formed the Movement for Freedom and Justice (MFJ). Adu Boahen was named interim chairman. The MFJ identified the restoration of multiparty democracy and the rule of law in Ghana as its main objectives. Its leaders immediately complained about harassment by the security agencies and about denial of permits to hold public rallies by the police.

Debate about the country's political future dominated 1991. In his broadcast to the nation on New Year's Day, Rawlings outlined steps toward the next stages in the country's political evolution, which included issuance of an NCD report on what form of democracy Ghanaians preferred. The PNDC made it clear that it did not favor multiparty democracy, although its spokesmen indicated that the PNDC had an open mind on the matter. The MFJ immediately called for a constituent assembly, where all parties, including the PNDC, would submit proposals for Ghana's constitutional future. Meanwhile, the PNDC unveiled a statue of J.B. Danquah, Nkrumah's political opponent, after an announcement in 1990 that it would build a statue and a memorial park for Nkrumah. This was a clear attempt to placate and to woo both the Ghanaian "political right" and Nkrumahists of the "left" simultaneously.

In late March, the NCD presented its findings on "true democracy" to the PNDC. After receiving the NCD report, the PNDC announced in May that it accepted the principle of a multiparty system. In its response to the NCD report, the PNDC pledged to set up a committee of constitutional experts that would formulate the draft constitutional proposals to be placed before a national consultative assembly. The committee came into being in May. A 258-member National Consultative Assembly was elected in June with the task of preparing a draft constitution for submission to the PNDC not later than December 31, 1991. The PNDC was then to submit the draft constitution to a national referendum, after which, if approved, it was to enter into force on a date set by the PNDC.

In August Rawlings announced that presidential and parliamentary elections would be held before the end of 1992 and that international observers would be allowed. By the end of 1991, however, the PNDC had not announced when the ban on political parties would be lifted, although many individuals and organizations, such as the Kwame Nkrumah Welfare Society, the Friends of Busia and Danquah, and the Eagle Club, had formed or reemerged and were active as parties in all but name. Despite persistent acrimony surrounding the management and control of the transition process, the PNDC appointed an independent Interim National Electoral Commission in February 1992. The commission was responsible for the register of voters, the conduct of fair elections, and the review of boundaries of administrative and electoral areas.

In a nationwide radio and television broadcast on March 5 marking the thirty-fifth anniversary of Ghana's independence, Rawlings officially announced the following timetable for the return to constitutional government: presentation of the draft constitution to the PNDC by the end of March 1992; a referendum on the draft constitution on April 28, 1992; lifting of the ban on political parties on May 18, 1992; presidential elections on November 3, 1992; parliamentary elections on December 8, 1992; and the inauguration of the Fourth Republic on January 7, 1993.

The PNDC saw the constitutional referendum as an essential exercise that would educate ordinary Ghanaians about the draft constitution and that would create a national consensus. The PNDC opposition urged its supporters and all Ghanaians to support the draft constitution by voting for it. In the April 1992 national referendum, the draft constitution was overwhelmingly approved by about 92 percent of voters. Although the turnout was lower than expected (43.7 percent of registered voters), it was higher than that of the 1978 referendum (40.3 percent) and that of the 1979 parliamentary elections (35.2 percent). The new constitution provided that a referendum should have a turnout of at least 35 percent, with at least 70 percent in favor, in order to be valid.

After the lifting of the ban on party politics in May, several rival splinter groups or offshoots of earlier organizations, notably the so-called Nkrumahists and Danquah-Busiaists, as well as new groups, lost no time in declaring their intention to register as political parties and to campaign for public support. In June the Washington-based International Foundation for Electoral Systems, which had sent a team to Ghana to observe the April referendum, issued a report recommending re-registration of voters as quickly as possible if Ghana were to have truly competitive presidential and parliamentary elections. The foundation claimed that the total number of registered voters—8.4 million—was improbable. Given an estimated national population of about 16 million—of whom about half were under age fifteen—the Foundation concluded that with a voting age of eighteen, the total registrable population ought not to be above 7.75 million.

This discovery fueled a persistent opposition demand to reopen the voters register, but constraints of time, technology, and money made such an effort impossible. Instead, the Interim National Electoral Commission embarked on a "voters register cleansing." Only about 180,000 names were removed from the referendum register, however, leaving the total registered voters at 8.23 million, a statistical impossibility, the opposition insisted. Estimates put the actual number of registered voters at about 6.2 million, making the 3.69 million turn-out at the referendum an adjusted 59.5 percent.

Presidential Elections

Despite protests and demands for a new voters register, which had not been met when nominations for presidential candidates for the November 3 elections closed on September 29, 1992, five presidential candidates representing five political parties filed their nomination papers. Apart from Rawlings, who after months of uncertainty decided to run as a candidate for the National Democratic Congress (NDC), the other four presidential candidates were Adu Boahen of the New Patriotic Party (NPP); Hilla Limann, former president of Ghana, of the People's National Convention (PNC); Kwabena Darko, a multimillionaire businessman, of the National Independence Party (NIP); and Lieutenant General (retired) Emmanuel Erskine, of the People's Heritage Party (PHP). The PNC, the NIP, and the PHP were all Nkrumahists. A much-discussed alliance among these fractious and disorganized parties did not materialize, even though just before the elections there was talk of a possible grand anti-Rawlings coalition.

The real issue of the 1992 presidential election was whether Rawlings would succeed in holding on to power as a democratically elected head of state after nearly eleven years as an unelected one. The slogan of the NDC was "continuity," meaning the continuity of PNDC policies. In fact, to many Ghanaians, the NDC party was the same as the PNDC without the initial "P." The opposition, by contrast, could not articulate a clear, consistent, and convincing alternative program.

The most serious challenge to Rawlings came from Boahen, who had significant support among the urban middle classes and among his ethnic kin in Ashanti Region. The inevitable split of the Nkrumahist vote weakened the chances of each of the three Nkrumahist candidates. Darko was hardly known outside Kumasi and Accra, and Limann was popularly seen as a weak and dull leader. Erskine was hardly a household word, even in his home area of Central Region. The presidential election was not fought over ideology or clearly presented political programs, but rather over personalities, over Rawlings's human rights record, and over allegations that he had been in power for too long.

After elections in 200 constituencies (sixty new electoral constituencies had been added to the old 140) on November 3, 1992, Rawlings won a convincing majority over all his opponents combined. The margin of victory surprised not only Rawlings, but his political rivals as well. The hoped-for run-off election did not materialize because Rawlings had gained an outright majority of almost 60 percent of the nearly 4 million votes cast.

Rawlings won resoundingly in regions where his opponents, especially Boahen, had been expected to carry the day. Boahen

Campaign billboards erected for the national elections of late 1992. Such billboards appeared throughout Ghana, an indication of the competitive nature of the elections.
Courtesy James Sanders

received 30.4 percent of the total votes; Limann, 6.7 percent; Darko, 2.8 percent; Erskine, 1.7 percent; and Rawlings, 58.3 percent. Rawlings even won 62 percent of the vote in Brong-Ahafo Region, which was considered a stronghold of the Danquah-Busiaist political tradition. He also won in Greater Accra Region, where NUGS, the GBA, the TUC, and the middle-class opposition had been unsparing in their anti-PNDC attacks. Boahen received a majority vote in his NPP heartland, Ashanti Region, and in Eastern Region where he was born.

A public opinion poll conducted in late 1990 and early 1991 in Accra, Kumasi, and Sekondi-Takoradi indicated some of the reasons for Rawlings's victory. The poll suggested that, in spite of the PNDC's record of human rights abuses and the negative impact of the ERP, the PNDC was more popular in urban areas than had been thought. The PNDC was perceived as having done much to rehabilitate the country's infrastructure, to instill national pride, and to improve the efficiency and honesty of government spending. Although many of the respondents felt that their standard of living had worsened since the PNDC came to power and since the implementation of the Structural Adjustment Program, a significant number also indicated that they and the country would have been worse off without the ERP. Although many considered the PNDC too authoritarian, Rawlings personally continued to be very popular and received much of the credit for the PNDC's successes, while the PNDC as a whole was blamed for its more negative characteristics.

The shock of the NPP's electoral defeat led immediately to disturbances in some regional capitals. A curfew was imposed in Kumasi, but in most of the country, the results were accepted without incident. The opposition parties, however, immediately protested, crying fraud as well as rigging of the ballot and asking the interim electoral commission not to declare a winner until allegations of irregularities had been investigated. On November 10, however, the commission formally declared Rawlings the winner.

Meanwhile, the opposition parties had announced their intention to boycott the parliamentary elections rescheduled from December 8 to December 29, following an appeal to the interim electoral commission. Efforts to get the opposition to reconsider its boycott proved unsuccessful, even after the National House of Chiefs announced in late November that it felt the presidential election had been fair and free. Many

European ambassadors in Accra likewise announced that they had no difficulty recognizing Rawlings's victory. International election monitoring teams from the Organization of African Unity, the Commonwealth of Nations, and the Carter Center in the United States also endorsed the results of the presidential election, although with reservations in some cases.

Parliamentary Elections

The PNDC indicated that it intended to proceed with parliamentary elections with or without the opposition parties. In a gesture to its opponents, however, the PNDC extended the deadline for all parties to register independent candidates, but opposition party officials threatened to deal severely with any party member who ran as an independent candidate. Amid sporadic political violence—some of it linked to the opposition, arrests of members of opposition groups by state security officers, and accusations of PNDC intimidation and harassment by the four opposition parties boycotting the elections—parliamentary elections were held on December 29, 1992, without the participation of the opposition parties.

Ironically, in boycotting the parliamentary elections, the opposition offered the PNDC the continuity it had been vigorously campaigning for and undermined any possibility of multiparty parliamentary democracy in the first term of the Fourth Republic. At the close of nominations for the elections on December 1, the NDC was unopposed in fifteen of the 200 constituencies. Only five candidates from the four main opposition parties had registered. According to the Interim National Electoral Commission, of the 7.3 million registered voters, more than 2 million voted on election day. The supporters of the four opposition parties stayed away, as did many NDC supporters, who felt that an NDC landslide victory was a foregone conclusion. The number of registered voters excluded twenty-three constituencies where the candidates were elected unopposed, so the turnout represented 29 percent of voters in 177 constituencies. The NDC swept the board, winning 189 of the 200 parliamentary seats, including the twenty-three who were elected unopposed. Two other parties allied with the NDC in what was called the Progressive Alliance—the National Convention Party and the Every Ghanaian Living Everywhere Party—won eight seats and one seat, respectively. The remaining two seats were captured by two independent women candidates, part of a group of sixteen women elected to parliament, the largest number ever in Ghana.

In the presidential election, almost 4 million out of 8.3 million registered voters had cast their votes in all 200 constituencies combined, for a turnout of 48 percent. The total votes cast in the parliamentary elections represented 51.5 percent of the votes cast in the presidential election. The opposition parties were quick to ascribe the low turnout to the effectiveness of their boycott. But the low turnout was also explained in part by the absence of real issues and the fact that many people chose to stay at home over the Christmas holidays.

Rawlings and the NDC won the elections because the opposition was divided for the most part and failed to present a credible alternative to the PNDC. The programs on which the opposition campaigned did not differ substantially from those the PNDC had been implementing since 1983. The opposition parties, for example, advocated a free enterprise economy, political decentralization, rural development, and liberal democracy—measures already on the PNDC agenda.

When external pressures in line with political reforms elsewhere on the continent persuaded Rawlings to return to multiparty democracy at the national level, he could do so without taint of corruption. Despite widespread human rights abuses in the early years of the revolution, he had demonstrated genuine concern for the well-being of the people of Ghana.

Rawlings also won because, as head of state for more than a decade, his name had become a household word, and he was able to exploit the advantages of incumbency. He had won favor with a wide range of interest groups, influential chiefs, and local leaders. Rawlings had behind him a well-established nationwide network of CDRs, the 31st December Women's Movement, other so-called revolutionary organs, and dedicated district secretaries and chiefs for the propagation of his message. All these bodies and groups had been active long before the fractious political parties, the rival leaders of which were hardly known beyond the major cities, had struggled into existence. Finally, Rawlings won because of widespread belief in his personal sincerity and integrity.

The Fourth Republic

The 1992 Constitution

The 1992 Constitution of the Republic of Ghana that came

into effect on January 7, 1993, provides the basic charter for the country's fourth attempt at republican democratic government since independence in 1957. It declares Ghana to be a unitary republic with sovereignty residing in the Ghanaian people. Drawn up with the intent of preventing future coups, dictatorial government, and one-party states, it is designed to foster tolerance and the concept of power-sharing. The document reflects the lessons drawn from the abrogated constitutions of 1957, 1960, 1969, and 1979, and it incorporates provisions and institutions drawn from British and United States constitutional models.

The 1992 constitution, as the supreme law of the land, provides for the sharing of powers among a president, a parliament, a cabinet, a Council of State, and an independent judiciary (see fig. 12). Through its system of checks and balances, it avoids bestowing preponderant power on any specific branch of government. Executive authority is shared by the president, the twenty-five-member Council of State, and numerous advisory bodies, including the National Security Council. The president is head of state, head of government, and commander in chief of the armed forces of Ghana. He also appoints the vice president.

Legislative functions are vested in the National Parliament, which consists of a unicameral 200-member body plus the president. To become law, legislation must have the assent of the president, who has a qualified veto over all bills except those to which a vote of urgency is attached. Members of parliament are popularly elected by universal adult suffrage for terms of four years, except in war time, when terms may be extended for not more than twelve months at a time beyond the four years.

The structure and the power of the judiciary are independent of the two other branches of government. The Supreme Court has broad powers of judicial review. It is authorized by the constitution to rule on the constitutionality of any legislative or executive action at the request of any aggrieved citizen. The hierarchy of courts derives largely from British juridical forms. The hierarchy, called the Superior Court of Judicature, is composed of the Supreme Court of Ghana, the Court of Appeal (Appellate Court), the High Court of Justice, regional tribunals, and such lower courts or tribunals as parliament may establish. The courts have jurisdiction over all civil and criminal matters.

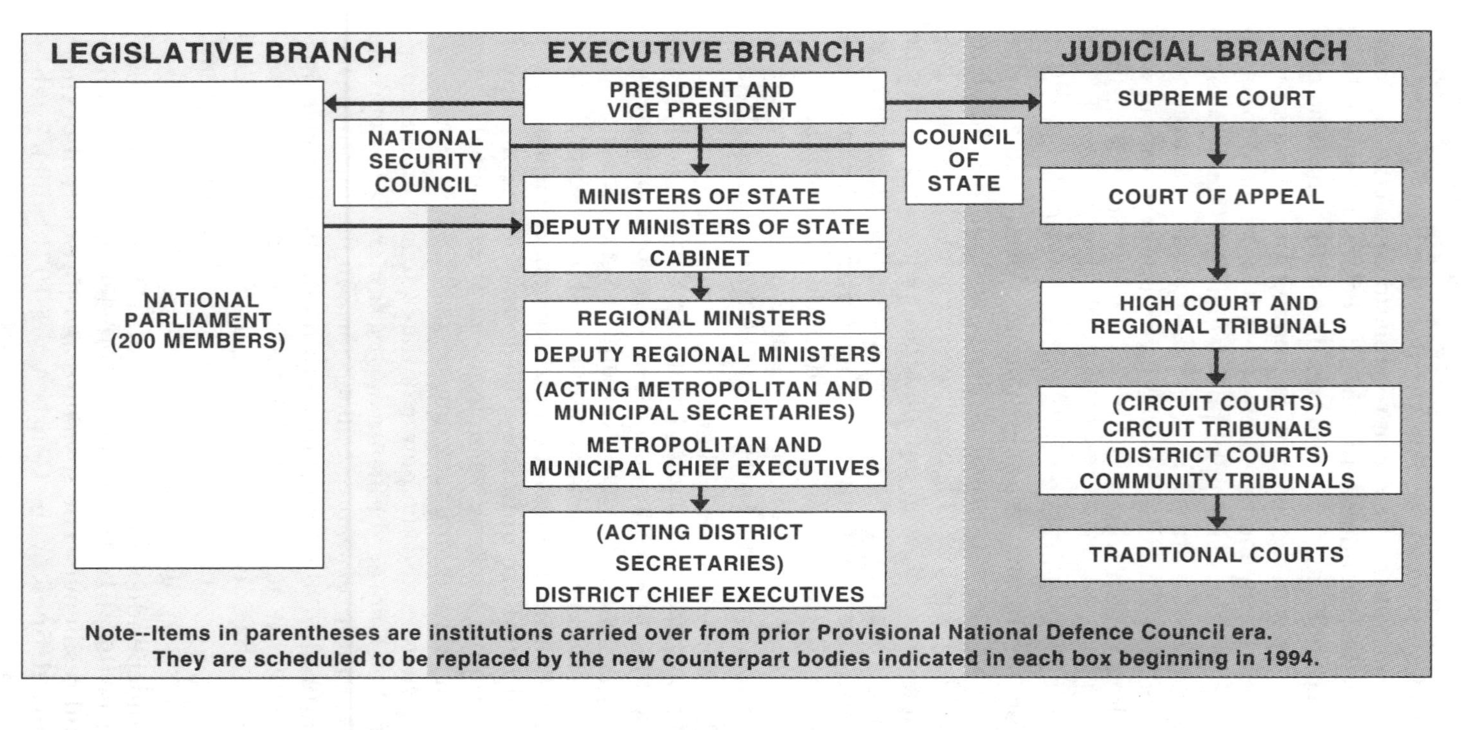

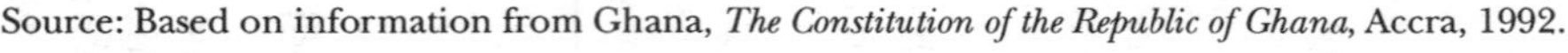
Source: Based on information from Ghana, *The Constitution of the Republic of Ghana*, Accra, 1992.

Figure 12. Structure of Government of the Fourth Republic, 1994

The legal system is based on the constitution, Ghanaian common law, statutory enactments of parliament, and assimilated rules of customary (traditional) law. The 1992 constitution, like previous constitutions, guarantees the institution of chieftaincy together with its traditional councils as established by customary law and usage. The National House of Chiefs, without executive or legislative power, advises on all matters affecting the country's chieftaincy and customary law.

The 1992 constitution contains the most explicit and comprehensive provisions in Ghana's postcolonial constitutional history regarding the system of local government as a decentralized form of national administration. These provisions were inspired to a large extent by current law and by the practice of local government under the PNDC. Another constitutional innovation is the enshrinement of fundamental human rights and freedoms enforceable by the courts. These rights include cultural rights, women's rights, children's rights, the rights of disabled persons, and the rights of the ill. The constitution also guarantees the freedom and independence of the media and makes any form of censorship unconstitutional. In addition, the constitution protects each Ghanaian's right to be represented by legitimately elected public officials by providing for partisan national elections and non-partisan district elections.

Every citizen of Ghana eighteen years of age or above and of sound mind has the right to vote. The right to form political parties is guaranteed—an especially important provision in light of the checkered history of political parties in postcolonial Ghana. Political parties must have a national character and membership and are not to be based on ethnic, religious, regional, or other sectional divisions.

Finally, highly controversial provisions of the constitution indemnify members and appointees of the PNDC from liability for any official act or omission during the eleven years of PNDC rule. These provisions seem designed to prevent the real possibility of retribution, should a new government hostile to the PNDC replace it, and to foster a climate of peace and reconciliation.

The Judiciary

Since independence in 1957, the court system, headed by the chief justice, has demonstrated extraordinary independence and resilience. The structure and jurisdiction of the courts were defined by the Courts Act of 1971, which established the Supreme Court of Ghana (or simply the Supreme Court), the Court of Appeal (Appellate Court) with two divisions (ordinary bench and full bench), and the High Court of Justice (or simply the High Court), a court with both appellate and original jurisdiction. The act also established the so-called inferior and traditional courts, which, along with the above courts, constituted the judiciary of Ghana according to the 1960, 1979, and 1992 constitutions.

Until mid-1993, the inferior courts in descending order of importance were the circuit courts, the district courts (magistrate courts) grades I and II, and juvenile courts. Such courts existed mostly in cities and large urban centers. In mid-1993, however, Parliament created a new system of lower courts, consisting of circuit tribunals and community tribunals in place of the former circuit courts and district (magistrate) courts (see Developing Democratic Institutions, this ch.). The traditional courts are the National House of Chiefs, the regional houses of chiefs, and traditional councils. The traditional courts are constituted by the judicial committees of the various houses and councils. All courts, both superior and inferior, with the exception of the traditional courts, are vested with jurisdiction in civil and criminal matters. The traditional courts have exclusive power to adjudicate any case or matter affecting chieftaincy as defined by the Chieftaincy Act of 1971.

Judicial appointments are made by the chief justice on the advice of the independent Judicial Council of Ghana and are subject to government approval. The PNDC Establishment Proclamation abolished the Judicial Council, but it was reestablished by the 1992 constitution.

Ghana also has quasi-judicial agencies and institutions. Examples of these are the Reconciliation Committee of the Department of Social Welfare and Community Development, provision for private hearings at home, and the use of various spiritual agencies, such as shrines, churches, Muslim *malams*, and specialists in the manipulation of supernatural powers to whom many ordinary people resort.

Noteworthy for both the colonial and the postcolonial periods up to the present are the special courts, public tribunals, politico-military bodies such as *asafo* companies (see Glossary), and vigilante groups. These bodies exercise quasi-judicial, extra-judicial, and law enforcement functions that often complement, and in some cases attempt to supplant, the functions of the regular or traditional courts.

Of these special courts, the former public tribunals deserve special mention. Following the 1981 revolution, the PNDC established a number of judicial institutions intended to check abuse and corruption within the regular courts. These special courts, called people's courts or public tribunals, were established in August 1982 as a separate system for administering justice alongside the country's regular courts. Their purpose was to regulate the administration of justice to prevent frivolous abuse of court powers and to obtain the truth by concentrating on the facts of the case rather than on questions of law.

The public tribunals, which consisted of the National Public Tribunal, regional public tribunals, and district and community public tribunals, were an attempt to "democratize" the administration of justice by making it possible for the public at large to participate actively in judicial decision making. They were also meant to correct perceived deficiencies of the regular courts, to enhance the general accessibility of law to the common people, to promote social justice, and to provide institutional safeguards that would secure public accountability. The right of appeal against the verdict of the tribunals was not originally provided for until public outcry led to the introduction of appeals procedures in 1984.

Under the PNDC, the public tribunals exercised only criminal jurisdiction. They dealt with three categories of offenses against the state: criminal offenses referred to them by the PNDC government, certain offenses under the country's Criminal Code, and offenses listed in the Public Tribunals Law of 1984. Proceedings of the tribunals were generally public and swift; sentences were frequently harsh and included death by firing squad. Under the Public Tribunals Law of 1984, without prejudice to the appellate system set out in the law itself, no court or other tribunal could question any decision, order, or proceeding of a public tribunal.

The creation of public tribunals and the PNDC's violent attack on lawyers set the PNDC on a collision course with the Ghana Bar Association, which forbade its members to sit on public tribunals. Many of the rulings of the public tribunals were cited by Amnesty International and other human rights organizations as violations of such rights as freedom of the press and habeas corpus (see Human Rights, ch. 5). Under the Fourth Republic, the public tribunals were incorporated into the existing court hierarchy (see Developing Democratic Institutions, this ch.).

The Civil Service

The civil service, an integral part of the executive branch of government, is a major component of the public services of Ghana, which come under supervision of the Public Services Commission. Ghana's civil service is organized along British lines and constitutes one of the most enduring legacies of British colonial rule. The 1992 constitution provides that the president, acting in accordance with the advice of the Public Services Commission, appoint a public officer to head the civil service.

The civil service is Ghana's single largest employer, and its union is large and strong. It recruits graduates of Ghana's three universities and other educational institutions through a system of competitive examinations. Staffing of the civil and the public services with competent personnel is the principal function of the Public Services Commission, which serves as the government's central personnel agency.

The Office of the Head of Civil Service includes a large team of administrators, executive and management analysts, and other technical experts. These officials supervise a hierarchy of graded personnel working in such areas as health, agriculture, transportation and communications, and local government. Working in cooperation with them are other state bodies such as the Chieftaincy Secretariat, Audit Service, Public Services Commission, and Ghana Cocoa Board. Since the launching in 1983 of the ERP, an austere economic program that the NDC government of the Fourth Republic continues to implement, the civil service has been cut drastically. Despite the retrenchment, civil servants have not engaged in organized protests or strikes, although they have threatened to do so.

The Media

The Ghanaian government owns the only two major daily newspapers, the *Daily Graphic* (known as the *People's Daily Graphic* under the PNDC) and the *Ghanaian Times*, with 1994 daily circulations of 80,000–100,000 and 60,000–70,000, respectively (circulation varies according to the availability of newsprint). The other daily, *The Pioneer*, established in 1930, is an independent paper with a circulation of about 30,000. There are also a number of weekly newspapers with substantial circulations, including the independents, the *Christian Messenger* and the *Standard*, and the state-owned *Sunday Mirror* and *Weekly*

Spectator, the latter two with 1994 circulations of 85,000 and about 90,000, respectively. A number of state-owned and independent periodicals appear in English and in African languages.

The 1979 constitution, which the PNDC suspended after taking power, was the first to give special attention to Ghana's mass media. It prohibited press licensing, outlawed censorship, and guaranteed freedom of expression and equal access to the state-owned media. The constitution also provided for the establishment of an independent press commission, the responsibilities of which included appointing chief executives and boards of directors for the state-owned media, preserving press freedom, and maintaining the highest professional standards.

Under the PNDC, self-censorship was the rule in the media. The government considered it the responsibility of the state-owned media, if not the media in general, to project a good image of the government and to defend government programs and policies. To ensure compliance with this policy, the PNDC hired and dismissed editorial staff and other media personnel of government-owned publications. The Ghana Journalists Association, which acted as a pressure group for the advancement of the professional interests of journalists, had little real influence. The Newspaper Licensing Law, reintroduced by the PNDC in 1983, discouraged or inhibited the establishment and the freedom of private media.

The state-owned media and some of the privately owned local newspapers attacked Ghanaian journalists who worked or wrote for the foreign press, accusing them of supporting or collaborating with organizations opposed to the PNDC. With the suspension of the 1979 constitution, such rights as freedom of the press, freedom of assembly, and freedom of association were not guaranteed but were merely granted at the discretion of the PNDC; however, numerous professional and civic organizations and independent newspapers that were non-political were allowed to exist and to operate freely.

The Committee of Experts (Constitution) Law of May 1991, which established the Committee of Experts to draw up proposals for a draft constitution, required that the proposals should assure the freedom and the independence of the media. Accordingly, the 1992 constitution guarantees fundamental human rights and civil liberties, including the freedom and the independence of the media. To protect the independence of the media, the National Media Commission was created in 1993 in accordance with a constitutional provision. The commission, an independent body, is charged with ensuring that all types of media, private as well as state-owned, are free of government control and interference. Under the Fourth Republic, the press has begun to enjoy a significant degree of toleration and freedom of expression.

Regional and Local Government

Before the changes in regional and local administration under the PNDC, Ghana had a highly centralized government structure in which local people and communities were little involved in decision making. Local government services were poor and depended largely on funds and personnel provided by the national government in Accra. Since the 31st December 1981 Revolution, however, local government has increasingly benefited from the decentralization of government ministries and from the establishment of district assemblies in 1989.

Ghana is divided into ten administrative regions, each headed by a regional secretary. The ten regions and their regional capitals are: Greater Accra Region (Accra), Eastern Region (Koforidua), Central Region (Cape Coast), Western Region (Sekondi-Takoradi), Volta Region (Ho), Ashanti Region (Kumasi), Brong-Ahafo Region (Sunyani), Northern Region (Tamale), Upper East Region (Bolgatanga), and Upper West Region (Wa) (see fig. 1). After taking power, the PNDC launched a decentralization plan in December 1982 designed to restructure government machinery to promote democracy and greater efficiency. The plan proposed a three-tier system of local government to replace the four-tier system established in 1978.

This early decentralization plan, however, was not implemented. Instead, interim management committees were organized to manage the affairs of the district councils. PNDC district secretaries were appointed chairmen of their respective district councils and were responsible for day-to-day administration. Membership of the interim management committees normally consisted of respected citizens of the district, such as chiefs, headmasters, retired administrators, and teachers. At the lowest levels, local government remained in the hands of village, town, or area development committees; People's Defence Committees; and chiefs and their traditional councils, who still wielded considerable influence in most rural areas.

On July 1, 1987, the PNDC launched a three-tier system of local government. The principal innovations of the new system included creating 110 administrative districts to replace the sixty-five districts that had existed before and changing the name District Council to District Assembly. The District Assembly was to be the highest political and administrative authority in each district, with deliberative, executive, and legislative powers; it was responsible for creating the two lower-level tiers, town or area councils and unit committees, within its jurisdiction (see fig. 13).

The membership of the District Assembly included a district secretary appointed by the PNDC. Two-thirds of the members were directly elected by universal adult suffrage on a non-partisan basis; the other third were appointed by the PNDC from the district in consultation with traditional authorities and various associations. Appointed members held office for a maximum of two consecutive terms, that is six years. Elections to the District Assembly were to be held every three years (the 1992 constitution provides for a four-year term and reduces the number of appointed members from one-third to no more than thirty percent of the total membership). The District Assembly was made responsible for the overall development of the district.

A 1990 law ensures that people at the grass-roots level have the opportunity to help make decisions that affect them regardless of their education or socio-economic backgrounds, as long as they are eighteen years or older and are customarily residents of the district. Finally, in each of the ten regions, a Regional Coordinating Council was established consisting of the regional secretary, the deputies of the regional secretaries acting as ex-officio members, all district secretaries in the region, and all presiding members of the district assemblies in the region. The 1992 constitution added at least two chiefs to the membership of each council. The functions of the council include the formulation and the coordination of programs through consultation with district assemblies in the region. The council is responsible for harmonizing these programs with national development policies and priorities, and for monitoring, implementing, and evaluating programs and projects within the region.

A local government law passed in 1991 created thirteen submetropolitan district councils and fifty-eight town or area councils under three metropolitan assemblies; 108 zonal councils

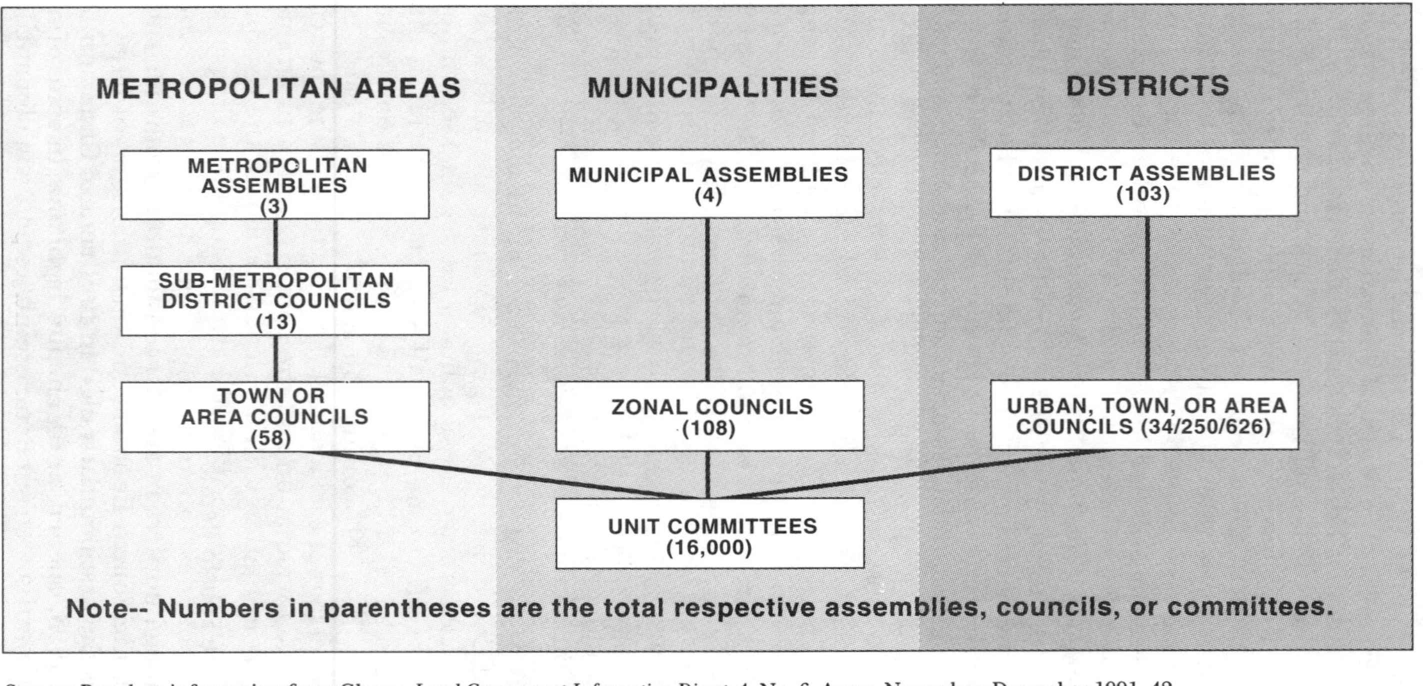

Source: Based on information from Ghana, *Local Government Information Digest*, 4, No. 6, Accra, November–December 1991, 42.

Figure 13. Structure of Local Government, 1994

under four municipal assemblies; and thirty-four urban, 250 town, and 626 area councils under 103 district assemblies. (District assemblies, of which there are 110, are designated metropolitan and municipal assemblies in metropolitan centers and major cities.) In addition, 16,000 unit committees were established under metropolitan, municipal, and district assemblies throughout the country. No Urban Council, Zonal Council, Town Council, or Unit Committee has the power to levy any taxes without the approval of the relevant assembly.

The functions of urban, zonal, and town councils include assuming the functions of the former town and village development committees and assisting any person authorized by the assembly to collect revenues due the assembly. In addition, the councils organize annual congresses of the people within their respective jurisdictions to discuss economic development and to raise contributions to fund such development. Membership in urban, zonal, or town councils and in unit committees consists of both elected and appointed people from within the respective jurisdiction.

Each of the ten regions is administered from the regional headquarters or capital by a regional secretary, who is the regional political and administrative head. The regional secretary is supported by metropolitan and municipal secretaries and their metropolitan and municipal assemblies as well as by district secretaries and the district assemblies they head. At the regional headquarters, the regional secretary is assisted by a Regional Consultative Council and a Regional Coordinating Council, both chaired by the regional secretary. The number of administrative districts within regions varies—Ashanti Region having the most—eighteen—and Greater Accra Region and Upper West Region, the fewest—five. The establishment of a district assembly in each region ensured that, with the local people in control of their own affairs, no part of the country would be neglected.

Political Dynamics under the Fourth Republic

Launching the Fourth Republic

The coming into force of the new constitution with the inauguration of the Fourth Republic and the installation of Jerry Rawlings as the first popularly elected president of Ghana on January 7, 1993, opened a new chapter in Ghana. In spite of the heat of partisan politics, the country's political climate remained encouragingly peaceful on the whole. There were clear indications that both the ruling National Democratic Congress (NDC) and opposition parties and groups as well as the general public were committed to making constitutional democracy work.

The new government faced several challenges in early 1993. One of the most serious, of course, was the problem of persistent and widespread economic hardship. Another was the institutionalization of democratic practice and constitutionalism in a de facto single-party parliament that resulted from the opposition boycott of parliamentary elections. In boycotting the elections, the main opposition parties, who together received about 40 percent of the total vote in the presidential election, denied themselves not only potential cabinet appointments but also any direct representation in parliament and any opportunity for real power-sharing.

This was regrettable, because throughout Ghana's postindependence history, the legislature has been the weakest of the three branches of government. Without sitting in parliament, the opposition could hardly constitute an effective shadow cabinet or function as a credible government-in-waiting. The creation of a new voters register and a national individual identification system as called for by the opposition, which Rawlings publicly acknowledged as necessary, would also help build a more effective and durable multiparty democracy. A step in this direction came in early 1994 when the National Electoral Commission, created in 1993, set up the Inter-Party Advisory Committee to advise it on electoral issues. This gesture has helped dispel the opposition's view that the electoral commission is a pro-government body.

Since the 1992 elections, the opposition parties, notably the NPP led by Adu Boahen, have sought to prove their commitment to constitutionalism by organizing public rallies, peaceful demonstrations, and press conferences. They have been aided by the emergence of a vigorous private press and by state-controlled media that have sought to report the views of opposition groups. The opposition also has chosen to go to court against alleged breaches of the constitution rather than to resort to confrontation and violence. Indeed, the NPP has urged its supporters to familiarize themselves with their constitutional rights, to criticize the government when it is wrong, and, whenever necessary, to resort to the courts and not to violence.

Such tactics on the part of the opposition are consistent with the principal concerns raised by Rawlings at the inauguration of the Fourth Republic. In his presidential address, Rawlings called for consultation and cooperation with all political groups in the country. He said that the NDC government would continue to reach out to the opposition parties that had boycotted the elections because it was the government's aim to establish a culture of tolerance, consultation, and consensus-building based on mutual respect.

In his address, Rawlings also indicated the basic orientation of his government. He emphasized that the condition of the national economy "must be the foundation of Ghana's democratic aspirations and remained the government's greatest challenge." He noted that his government was determined to continue the Economic Recovery Program (ERP) and that the new constitutional order could not be divorced from the changes brought about by the 31st December 1981 Revolution. In addition, he remarked that he bore no personal grudge against any person or any group (having in mind the pre- and postpresidential election disturbances and violence) and invited others to adopt the same attitude.

Rawlings assured the armed forces that they would remain actively involved in all national endeavors and also indicated that Ghana's role in world affairs would not change. The continuity in domestic, economic, and foreign policy that Rawlings stressed is reflected in the government's ministerial and other appointments. For example, at the end of May 1993, twenty-one of thirty-five ministers had been secretaries under the former PNDC government; many of them held the same portfolios that they had previously held.

Despite some positive steps toward national reconciliation, part of the opposition continued to distrust the new administration. In the view of these critics, the PNDC was still in power, and, accordingly, they referred to the new administration as "P/NDC" or "(P)NDC." Some members of the opposition also saw the new parliament as merely a rubber-stamp of the ruling NDC administration. The reappointment of numerous PNDC secretaries to the new NDC administration as well as the NDC pledge of continuity in economic and social policy confirmed the worst fears of the opposition. The same could be said of a presidential order in January 1993 to the effect that persons who had been in office as PNDC secretaries for ministries, regions, or districts should continue in their offices to avoid the breakdown of the machinery of government. As the opposition was quick to point out, the presidential order technically violated the constitution; however, given the extenuating circumstances created by the postponement of the parliamentary elections, the order was probably unavoidable.

Developing Democratic Institutions

The growing importance of the legislative arm of the government in national affairs was reflected in several developments. At the state opening of parliament on April 29, 1993, President Rawlings gave an address in which he emphasized that the contributions of all citizens are necessary in order to achieve the national goals of economic development and social justice. He reminded Ghanaians that the proper forum for political debate under constitutional rule is parliament and called upon the leaders of the parties in his ruling Progressive Alliance (the NDC, the National Convention Party (NCP), and the Every Ghanaian Living Everywhere Party) to welcome serious dialogue with the opposition outside parliament. Such a move would enable the opposition parties that had boycotted the parliamentary elections to contribute to national political debate. The NPP made its views on national policy heard through invited participation in parliamentary committees, thus attempting to influence debates and particular legislation.

The executive and the legislative branches worked to ensure passage of nine measures that would establish certain major state institutions by the July 7, 1993, deadline stipulated in the constitution. The institutions created were the National Commission on Civic Education, the National Electoral Commission, the District Assemblies Common Fund, the Commission on Human Rights and Administrative Justice, the Minerals Commission, the Forestry Commission, the Fisheries Commission, the National Council for Higher Education, and the National Media Commission.

The Courts Act of July 6, 1993, incorporated the public tribunals created under the PNDC into the established court system. It defined the jurisdiction of regional tribunals and established lower courts—circuit tribunals and community tribunals—to replace the circuit courts and the district (magistrate) courts. It also established the National House of Chiefs, the regional houses of chiefs, and traditional councils, and it provided that parliament could create other tribunals as the need arose. The tribunals are empowered to try criminal and civil cases. Throughout 1993 and 1994, however, the Judicial Council of Ghana was working to amend the Courts Act to allow the pre-existing circuit and district courts to hear cases meant for circuit and community tribunals until such time as the new tribunals become fully operational. The establishment of the lower tribunals has been delayed because of lack of staff and of suitable court buildings in all 110 districts, most of which are poor and rural.

Parliament also passed the controversial Serious Fraud Office Bill. This bill established a Serious Fraud Office as a specialized agency of the state to monitor, investigate, and, on the authority of the attorney general, prosecute fraud and serious economic crimes. According to the bill's proponents, complex fraud and economic crimes were being committed that posed a direct threat to national security and that were possibly linked to illegal drug trafficking, but they could not be adequately investigated and prosecuted under existing law.

Critics of the bill, which included the Ghana Bar Association, saw it as an attempt on the part of the ruling NDC to destroy the NPP, which considers itself the party of business. They also viewed it as containing provisions conflicting directly with constitutionally guaranteed fundamental rights to liberty and property. Under the bill's provisions, anyone can be investigated for fraud except the president, in whose case the constitution provides elaborate procedures for impeachment in case of abuse of power and trust.

Parliament's success can be attributed to the leaders of the opposition and the ruling Progressive Alliance, who chose to settle their differences through dialogue and constitutional means rather than through confrontation. The same tendency to operate within the framework of the new constitution applies to the judicial realm as well, where the opposition, especially the NPP, declared itself the principal watchdog and custodian of civil liberties and of the 1992 constitution. This task is consistent with the leading role played by the opposition in the demand for a return to constitutional rule during the PNDC era.

On July 22, 1993, a week after celebrating its first anniversary, the NPP won three major and surprising victories in the Supreme Court. The court, which the opposition believed to be under the control of the executive, upheld two suits intended to nullify certain existing laws and decrees that the NPP claimed conflicted with the 1992 constitution. In the first suit, the court ordered the Ghana Broadcasting Corporation to grant the NPP "fair and equal access to its facilities within two weeks" to enable the party to articulate its views on the 1993 budget in the same manner as the ruling NDC.

In the second judgment, the court ruled that certain sections of Public Order Decree 1972 were inconsistent with the 1992 constitution, which grants the individual the right to demonstrate or to take part in a procession without necessarily obtaining a permit from the police. The NPP had challenged as unconstitutional the arrest and subsequent prosecution of some of its members for demonstrating against the 1993 budget on February 15, 1993. On that day, the Accra police had assaulted the demonstrators, severely injuring many of them. The verdict in the NPP suit also applied to the shooting attack on university students by commandos on March 22–23. The students were protesting the government's refusal to meet their demand for an increase in student loans from 90,000 to 200,000 cedis (for value of the Ghanaian cedi—see Glossary) because of a rise in the cost of living. A third suit, which concerned police powers with respect to public assemblies, did not go forward because the law had been repealed.

Two months later, the NPP scored another victory in the Supreme Court when the party sought a declaration to stop the election of district chief executives (DCEs) ahead of anticipated District Assembly elections. The NPP noted that the election of DCEs by sitting district assemblies that had only a few months' remaining tenure in office would infringe the letter and the intent of the constitution, which requires that newly elected assemblies, not outgoing assemblies, elect DCEs. The court granted the NPP's application for an interim injunction and ordered the suspension of DCE elections until the court could examine the constitutionality of the elections process. Candidates for election as DCEs had been nominated by President Rawlings. Within a few days, an announcement was made that Rawlings had only appointed acting district secretaries, not DCEs, for all 110 district assemblies; the president's appointees, however, appeared to be mostly the same individuals nominated as DCEs. The opposition then took this matter to the Supreme Court on a charge of unconstitutionality, but the court upheld Rawlings's action in May 1994.

To crown the constitutional victories of the NPP, the Supreme Court ruled at the end of 1993 that December 31, marking the 31st December 1981 Revolution, should no longer

Jerry John Rawlings being sworn in as president of the Fourth Republic of Ghana, January 1993
Courtesy Embassy of Ghana, Washington

be celebrated as a public holiday. The NPP had been particularly outraged when newly elected President Rawlings declared that any interpretation of the 1992 constitution would be subject to the spirit of the June 4, 1979, uprising and the 31st December 1981 Revolution. For the opposition, these events had ushered in the most repressive and bloody decade in the country's postcolonial history, and they had no place in the new democratic constitutional order.

The NPP, after documenting alleged irregularities of the November 1992 presidential elections, consolidated its position as the main opposition party in the country. It presented itself as the "constitutional" party, the objectives of which are to ensure that constitutional rule is established in Ghana and that the private sector becomes the engine of growth and development. Furthermore, at a widely reported press conference in

July 1993 marking the first anniversary of the NPP, the party's chairman proclaimed his party's readiness to "do business" with the NDC government.

Doing business with the government did not mean, as many NPP members had feared, that some members of the NPP executive would take posts in the NDC administration. It meant talking face-to-face with the president, the legislature, and the judiciary as well as with independent institutions of state. These dealings were intended to enhance the constitutional rights of all Ghanaians and to ensure respect for human rights and proper management of the economy.

The new NPP policy—that of promoting dialogue between the NPP and the government, which began in November 1993—contributed to a reduction of political tension in the country. Unlike some of its West African neighbors that are haunted by political uncertainty and torn by war and civil strife, Ghana continued to enjoy relative peace and political stability. This was true despite the flare-up of interethnic violence and killing in the northern region between the Konkomba and the Nanumba in early 1994, leading to the declaration of a brief state of emergency in the region.

The minor opposition parties of the Nkrumahist tradition, which had boycotted dialogue with the NDC government, also managed after a long period of internal bickering to put their houses in order in anticipation of the 1996 presidential and parliamentary elections. The parties subscribing to the ideals of Nkrumah's Convention People's Party, with the exception of the People's National Convention led by former president Limann, united to form the new People's Convention Party, receiving a certificate of registration in January 1994.

One of the major concerns of the NPP and other opposition parties was the existence in the Fourth Republic of paramilitary groups and revolutionary organs, such as CDRs, which had not been disbanded. In August 1993, all CDRs were put into a new organization known as the Association of Committees for the Defence of the Revolution. This new association was to continue mobilizing the populace for community development and local initiatives within the framework of the 1992 constitution.

The NPP persisted in its demands for a new voters register and for national identity cards to ensure free and fair elections in 1996. When President Rawlings suggested that it was cheaper to revise the voters register than to issue national identity cards, the cost of which would be prohibitive for the government, the NPP threatened to boycott the 1996 elections unless both electoral demands were met. The potential boycott was seemingly averted in February 1994 when the United States pledged to fund the printing of identity cards for voters in the 1996 elections.

The following August, the chairman of the National Electoral Commission promised that the commission would take appropriate steps to ensure that the presidential and parliamentary elections in 1996 would be free and fair. These steps were to include the training of some 80,000 party agents as observers. The National Electoral Commission later indicated that identification cards would be issued to voters during registration for a new and revised electoral roll in September 1995. The Commission also favored holding the elections on the same day and felt that Ghanaians living abroad should have the right to vote. Eventually the NDC government promised to ensure that the 1996 elections would be free and fair and that international observers would be allowed.

Meanwhile, on March 22, 1994, the first nonpartisan district-level elections to be conducted under the Fourth Republic were successfully held in all but thirteen districts, mostly in the north, where polling was postponed because of interethnic conflicts. About 10,880 candidates, 383 of them women, competed for 4,282 seats in ninety-seven district, municipal, and metropolitan assemblies. The new district assemblies were inaugurated in June 1994, marking another step in the establishment of a democratic system of local government.

By mid-1994, there was general agreement that the government's human rights record had improved considerably. The improvement resulted in part from the activities of the many human rights groups being established in the country. The Ghana Committee on Human and People's Rights, founded by a group of dedicated lawyers, trade unionists, and journalists and inaugurated in January 1991, was perhaps the most prominent of these. Another was the Commission on Human Rights and Administrative Justice, a government body established in 1993 designed to deal with human rights issues and violations (see Human Rights, ch. 5).

Foreign Relations

Guiding Principles and Objectives

Ghana's foreign policy since independence has been characterized by a commitment to the principles and ideals of nonalignment and Pan-Africanism as first enunciated by Kwame Nkrumah in the early 1960s. For Nkrumah, nonalignment meant complete independence from the policies and alliances of both East and West and support for a worldwide union of so-called nonaligned nations as a counter to both East and West power blocs. Pan-Africanism, by contrast, was a specifically African policy that envisioned the liberation of African peoples from Western colonialism and the eventual economic and political unity of the African continent (see The Organization of African Unity and the Rest of Africa, this ch.).

The PNDC, like most of its predecessors, made serious and consistent attempts at the practical application of these ideals and principles, and its successor, the NDC government, promises to follow in the PNDC's footsteps. Under the NDC, Ghana remains committed to the principle of nonalignment in world politics. Ghana is also opposed to interference in the internal affairs of both small and large countries. This is a departure from Nkrumah's foreign policy approach; Nkrumah was frequently accused of subverting African regimes, such as Togo and Côte d'Ivoire, which he considered ideologically conservative. The NDC government, like the PNDC before it, believes in the principle of self-determination, including the right to political independence and the right of people to pursue their economic and social development free from external interference. Another feature of NDC rule carried over from the PNDC era is faithfulness to what a leading scholar of Africa has called "one of the most successful neoclassical economic reform efforts supported by the IMF and the World Bank."

The broad objectives of Ghana's foreign policy thus include maintaining friendly relations and cooperation with all countries that desire such cooperation, irrespective of ideological considerations, on the basis of mutual respect and noninterference in each other's internal affairs. Africa and its liberation and unity are naturally the cornerstones of Ghana's foreign policy. Because Ghana was a founding member of the Organization of African Unity (OAU), NDC policy is to adhere faithfully to the OAU Charter.

Another important principle of Ghana's foreign policy involves the closest possible cooperation with neighboring countries with which the people of Ghana share cultural history, ties of blood, and economics. The results have included various bilateral trade and economic agreements and permanent joint commissions involving Ghana and its immediate neighbors, sometimes in the face of latent ideological and political differences and mutual suspicion, as well as numerous reciprocal state visits by high-ranking officials. These measures have contributed significantly to subregional cooperation, development, and the reduction of tension.

As an example of Ghana's interest in regional cooperation, the country enthusiastically endorsed formation of the Economic Community of West African States (ECOWAS) in 1975. This organization was created specifically to foster intraregional economic and political cooperation (see Trade, ch. 3). It has served as a useful vehicle for contacts with neighboring West African governments and for channeling increased Ghanaian exports to regional markets. Since 1990 ECOWAS has been engaged in a peacekeeping mission in Liberia to which Ghana has contributed a large contingent of troops. Ghana has participated in other international peacekeeping efforts as well, sending soldiers to operations of the United Nations (UN) in Cambodia in 1992–93 and Rwanda in 1993–94 (see International Security Concerns, ch. 5).

In August 1994, Rawlings became ECOWAS chairman, a post that had eluded him since the PNDC came to power. He immediately undertook several initiatives to reduce tensions and conflict in West Africa. Notable among them was the Akosombo Accord of September 12, 1994, designed to end civil war in Liberia.

Relations with Immediate African Neighbors

The NDC government continues to work to improve and to strengthen relations with all of its neighbors, especially Togo, Côte d'Ivoire, Nigeria, and Burkina Faso (Burkina, formerly Upper Volta). In the early days of PNDC rule, relations with Togo, Côte d'Ivoire, and Nigeria were particularly cool and even antagonistic. By 1994 Ghana's relations with its West African neighbors, especially Côte d'Ivoire and Togo, had improved significantly.

Togo and Côte d'Ivoire

In the early 1980s, Côte d'Ivoire and Togo worried that "the Rawlings fever," the "revolution," might prove contagious. Both countries were headed by long-lived conservative governments faced with potentially dangerous internal and external opposition. The strains in relations among Ghana, Togo, and Côte d'Ivoire have a long history; in Togo's case, they go back to pre-independence days.

After 1918, following the defeat of Germany, the League of Nations divided the German colony of Togoland from north to south, a decision that divided the Ewe people among the Gold Coast, British Togoland, and French Togoland. After 1945, the UN took over the Togoland mandates. During the 1950s, when the independence of Ghana was in sight, demands grew for a separate Ewe state, an idea that Kwame Nkrumah, leader of the Gold Coast independence movement, opposed. Following a UN plebiscite in May 1956, in which a majority of the Ewe voted for union with Ghana, British Togoland became part of the Gold Coast. After Togolese independence in 1960, relations between Togo and Ghana deteriorated, aggravated by political differences and incidents such as smuggling across their common border. At times, relations have verged on open aggression.

During the mid-1970s, Togolese President General Gnassingbe Eyadema for a time revived the claim to a part or all of former British Togoland. Two leading Ewe members from the Volta Region sent a petition to the UN in 1974. By 1976 a Togoland Liberation Movement and a National Liberation Movement for Western Togoland existed and were agitating for separation from Ghana. The Eyadema government publicly backed their demands, although it subsequently agreed to cooperate with the Ghanaian government against the separatist movements and against smuggling. A factor influencing Eyadema's cooperative attitude was doubtless Togo's dependence upon electricity from Ghana's Akosombo Dam.

A consistent preoccupation of Ghana, Togo, and Côte d'Ivoire is that of national security. The PNDC regime repeatedly accused both Togo and Côte d'Ivoire of harboring armed Ghanaian dissidents who planned to overthrow or to destabilize the PNDC. The PNDC also accused both countries of encouraging the smuggling of Ghanaian products and currencies across their borders, thus undermining Ghana's political and economic stability at a time when Ghana was experiencing a deep economic crisis.

In June 1983, when the PNDC was barely eighteen months old, groups opposed to the PNDC made a major attempt to overthrow it. Most of the rebels reportedly came from Togo. In August 1985, Togo in turn accused Ghana of complicity in a series of bomb explosions in Lomé, the Togolese capital. In

July 1988, an estimated 124 Ghanaians were expelled from Togo. Nevertheless, relations subsequently improved significantly, leading in 1991 to the reactivation of several bilateral agreements.

Greatly improved relations between Ghana and Togo, especially after October 1990 when opposition pressure forced Eyadema to agree to a transition to multiparty democracy, however, could hardly disguise the persistence of old mutual fears about threats to internal security. For instance, less than three weeks after Ghana's Fourth Republic was inaugurated, an immense refugee problem was created in Ghana. Following random attacks and killings of civilians in Lomé by Eyadema's army on January 26, 1993, hundreds of thousands of terrorized Togolese began fleeing into Ghana. At the end of January, Ghanaian troops were placed on high alert on the Ghana-Togo border, although Obed Asamoah, the Ghanaian minister of foreign affairs, assured all concerned that there was no conflict between Ghana and Togo.

Sporadic shooting incidents in the spring continued to produce a regular flow of refugees into Ghana. By May, following Togo's partial closure of the border, all persons living in Togo, including diplomats, had to obtain a special permit from the Togolese interior ministry to travel to Ghana by road. Travelers from Ghana were allowed into Togo but were not permitted to return. By early June, half of Lomé's 600,000 residents were estimated to have fled to neighboring Ghana and Benin.

At the beginning of 1994, relations between Ghana and Togo became even worse. On January 6, a commando attack occurred in Lomé, which Togolese authorities described as an attempt to overthrow Eyadema. The Togolese government accused Ghana of direct or indirect involvement and arrested Ghana's chargé d'affaires in Lomé. Togolese troops then bombarded a border post, killing twelve Ghanaians. Camps for Togolese refugees in Ghana also were reportedly bombarded. The Ghanaian government announced that it would press Togo to compensate the families of those killed. By mid-year, however, relations had improved markedly. In August Togo supported the nomination of Rawlings for the post of ECOWAS chairman. Thereafter, a joint commission was set up to examine border problems, in mid-November a Ghanaian ambassador took up residence in Togo for the first time since the early 1980s, and Togo was considering the reopening of its border with Ghana.

Ghana-Côte d'Ivoire relations suffered from the same ups and downs that characterized Ghana-Togo relations. In early 1984, the PNDC government complained that Côte d'Ivoire was allowing Ghanaian dissidents to use its territory as a base from which to carry out acts of sabotage against Ghana. Ghana also accused Côte d'Ivoire of granting asylum to political agitators wanted for crimes in Ghana. Relations between Ghana and Côte d'Ivoire improved significantly, however, after 1988. In 1989, after fifteen years without progress, the Ghana-Côte d'Ivoire border redemarcation commission finally agreed on the definition of the 640-kilometer border between the two countries. The PNDC thereafter worked to improve the transportation and communication links with both Côte d'Ivoire and Togo, despite problems with both countries.

By 1992 Ghana's relations with Côte d'Ivoire were relatively good. Hopes for lasting improvement, however, were quickly dashed following a series of violent incidents in late 1993 and early 1994. The incidents began on November 1, 1993, with the return of sports fans to Côte d'Ivoire following a championship soccer match in Kumasi, Ghana, that had resulted in the elimination of Côte d'Ivoire from competition. Ghanaian immigrants in Côte d'Ivoire were violently attacked, and as many as forty or more Ghanaians were killed.

Thereafter, scores of other Ghanaians lost their property as they fled for their lives. Some 1,000 homes and businesses were looted. More than 10,000 Ghanaians out of the approximately 1 million living in Côte d'Ivoire were immediately evacuated by the Ghanaian government, and more than 30,000 Ghanaians were reported to have sought refuge in the Ghanaian and other friendly embassies. A twenty-member joint commission (ten from each country) was established to investigate the attacks, to recommend compensation for victims, and to find ways of avoiding similar incidents in the future. In October 1994, the two nations resumed soccer matches after a Togolese delegation helped smooth relations between them.

Burkina

With the coming to power of Thomas Sankara in Burkina in 1983, relations between Ghana and Burkina became both warm and close. Indeed, Rawlings and Sankara began discussions about uniting Ghana and Burkina in the manner of the defunct Ghana-Guinea-Mali Union, which Nkrumah had sought unsuccessfully to promote as a foundation for his

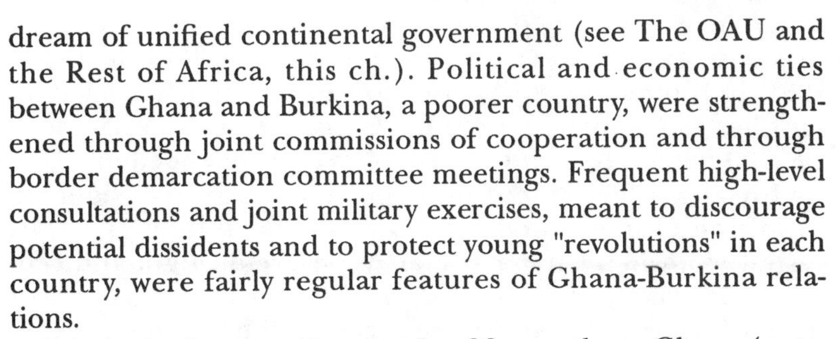

Jerry John Rawlings, president of the Fourth Republic of Ghana
Courtesy Embassy of Ghana, Washington

dream of unified continental government (see The OAU and the Rest of Africa, this ch.). Political and economic ties between Ghana and Burkina, a poorer country, were strengthened through joint commissions of cooperation and through border demarcation committee meetings. Frequent high-level consultations and joint military exercises, meant to discourage potential dissidents and to protect young "revolutions" in each country, were fairly regular features of Ghana-Burkina relations.

Ethnic ties between the people of far northern Ghana (notably the Mossi) and Burkina, divided by artificial borders inherited from colonial rule, grew stronger as easy border crossings and the free exchange of goods and services contributed to marked improvements in the material and the social welfare of peoples on both sides of the border. The PNDC, for example, established road, air, and telecommunications links between Ghana and Burkina.

Ghana's warm relations with Burkina received a serious but temporary setback with the assassination of Sankara in October 1987. His successor, Blaise Campaore, was widely believed to have been responsible for the assassination. As a result, relations between Ghana and Burkina cooled. Rawlings and Campaore met briefly for the first time in early 1988 in Tamale, the capital of Ghana's Northern Region, to discuss Ghana-Burkina relations.

The outbreak of civil war in Liberia in 1989 found the two countries on opposite sides of the conflict (see International Security Concerns, ch. 5). Ghana, at great financial and human cost, immediately repatriated about 10,000 Ghanaians living in Liberia and, beginning in mid-1990, contributed a contingent to a multinational peacekeeping force second in size only to one sent by Nigeria. From 1990 to 1993, Campaore's role in the Liberian conflict was at odds with an ECOWAS peace initiative spearheaded by Ghana and Nigeria, because Burkina was believed to be supplying arms to rebel leader Charles Taylor, long regarded as the main obstacle to peace. In 1994 relations between Burkina and Ghana showed signs of warming at a time when Campaore appeared to be reassessing his policies in Liberia and toward Ghana and Nigeria.

Nigeria

Ghana's relations with Nigeria, West Africa's leading country, began on a sour note in the early period of PNDC rule. Tension rose immediately after the PNDC deposed Limann in 1981. In protest, Nigeria refused to continue much-needed oil supplies to Ghana. At the time, Ghana owed Nigeria about US$150 million for crude oil supplies and depended on Nigeria for about 90 percent of its petroleum needs. Nigeria's expulsion of more then 1 million Ghanaian immigrants in early 1983, when Ghana was facing severe drought and economic problems, and of another 300,000 in early 1985 on short notice, further strained relations between the two countries.

In April 1988, a joint commission for cooperation was established between Ghana and Nigeria. A bloodless coup in August 1985 had brought Major General Ibrahim Babangida to power in Nigeria, and Rawlings took advantage of the change of administration to pay an official visit. The two leaders discussed a wide range of issues focusing on peace and prosperity within West Africa, bilateral trade, and the transition to democracy in both countries. In early January 1989, Babangida reciprocated with an official visit to Ghana, which the PNDC hailed as a watershed in Ghana-Nigeria relations.

Subsequent setbacks that Babangida initiated in the democratic transition process in Nigeria clearly disappointed Accra. Nonetheless, the political crisis that followed Babangida's annulment of the results of the June 1993 Nigerian presidential election and Babangida's resignation from the army and presidency two months later did not significantly alter the existing close relations between Ghana and Nigeria, two of the most important members of ECOWAS and the Commonwealth of Nations. After the takeover in November 1993 by General Sani Abacha as the new Nigerian head of state, Ghana and Nigeria continued to consult on economic, political, and security issues affecting the two countries and West Africa as a whole. Between early August 1994, when Rawlings became ECOWAS chairman, and the end of the following October, the Ghanaian president visited Nigeria three times to discuss the peace process in Liberia and measures to restore democracy in that country.

The Organization of African Unity and the Rest of Africa

Beginning with the independence of Ghana in 1957 under Kwame Nkrumah, Pan-Africanism, as a movement uniting all peoples of the African continent, was attempted in earnest. Pan-Africanism became identified with Nkrumah more than with any other African leader. From 1950 to 1965, the aim was to achieve political, cultural, and economic integration at the continental level.

Beginning in 1958 with the formation of the Ghana-Guinea Union, followed shortly by the Ghana-Guinea-Mali Union, Nkrumah relentlessly pursued his goal of a Union of African States. Working with leaders of other independent African countries, he convened a series of conferences to promote the Pan-African cause. Finally, a summit conference met in Addis Ababa in May 1963 to resolve the divisions, unite the leaders, and establish a common Pan-African organization.

After many proposals and counterproposals at the Addis Ababa conference, thirty African heads of states and governments signed the historic Charter of African Unity, which established the Organization of African Unity (OAU). The charter, however, fell far short of Nkrumah's ideal of African continental government. At subsequent meetings of the OAU until his overthrow in 1966, Nkrumah continued to campaign vigorously but unsuccessfully for the transformation of the OAU into a continental government of a United States of Africa. Ironically, as independent African states concentrated on domestic problems and internal developments, they found themselves compelled to strengthen ties with their former colonial rulers rather than with each other. In Ghana's case, this meant closer relations with Britain, particularly after the overthrow of Nkrumah.

In recognition of Nkrumah's stature in the Pan-Africanist cause, PNDC chairman Rawlings in June 1985 dedicated the W.E.B. DuBois Memorial Center for Pan-African Culture in Accra. The DuBois center was established to serve as a Pan-African research center and library for scholars and students of Pan-Africanism and to promote research and scholarship in the tradition of the African-American scholar, W.E.B. DuBois.

The PNDC made a determined effort to revive Ghana's historical role as a leader in the OAU and in the struggle against apartheid in South Africa. The PNDC stepped up material and financial assistance and diplomatic support to the OAU Liberation Committee, to the African National Congress in South Africa, and to the South West Africa People's Organisation in South-West Africa, now Namibia. In 1987 Ghana also became a member of the permanent steering committee of the OAU, which was charged with forging a common African position on the continent's debt problem. The same year, Ghana made a substantial financial contribution of US$5 million to the African Fund set up by the Non-Aligned Movement to assist African liberation movements and to strengthen resistance to South African destabilization activities in southern Africa. The PNDC also contributed US$1.3 million annually to the OAU budget. Ghana contributed generously to the OAU's Liberation Fund for Namibia as well as US$5 million to the African Fund for the repatriation of Namibians to enable them to participate in pre-independence elections in February 1990.

The PNDC regime sought to strengthen ties with all African countries. Good relations with the countries of eastern and southern Africa were established in the spirit of Pan-Africanism and nonalignment. In addition to visiting many West African countries, Rawlings traveled to Mozambique in October 1986 for the funeral of Samora Machel. Ghana's contribution of US$250,000 toward famine relief in Mozambique was a practical demonstration of commitment to the principles of the OAU. In late January 1989, Rawlings paid a three-day official visit to Uganda on the occasion of the third anniversary of the government's victory in a long civil war. He also visited Tanzania and Zimbabwe.

Ghana's political and diplomatic resurgence in Africa and in world affairs under PNDC leadership was evident from the number of reciprocal visits to promote bilateral ties and cooperation. Among those visiting Ghana between 1987 and 1994 were Zambia's President Kenneth Kaunda; Uganda's President Yoweri Museveni; Tanzania's former President Julius Nyerere, who received Ghana's highest state award, the Order of the Star of Ghana, in recognition of his life-long devotion to Pan-Africanism and the nonaligned movement; Libya's Colonel Muammar al Qadhafi; and Zimbabwe's President Robert Mugabe. In September 1994, President Rawlings paid a ten-day visit to Botswana, Namibia, and Zimbabwe, signing bilateral agreements in the latter two countries for political cooperation, trade, and industrial development. Ghanaian diplomats are expected to arrive in Pretoria, the Republic of South Africa, in early 1995 to open Ghana's new High Commission.

Britain and the Commonwealth

By historical tradition and choice, Ghana's political future has been bound up with that of Britain and the Commonwealth of Nations. Indeed, Nkrumah led the way for independent African states that were former British colonies to join the Commonwealth.

The close bond between Ghana and Britain was evident in 1959 when Queen Elizabeth II, the head of the Commonwealth of Nations, visited Ghana and received a warm reception. At the 1964 Commonwealth Conference, Nkrumah proposed the establishment of a permanent Commonwealth secretariat, in order, as Nkrumah put it, "to make the Commonwealth move in tune with the common aspirations of its members." According to one observer, Nkrumah believed the Commonwealth was an example of how a free association of independent states should work. The Commonwealth provided a vehicle for the transfer of technology and for economic and cultural cooperation. It also served as a place for developing the most effective methods for ending colonialism without revolution or violence and under conditions in which a former colonial territory could retain a close association with the former imperial power.

Nkrumah again took the lead in forcing South Africa out of the Commonwealth in 1961. In 1965 Ghana was forced to break diplomatic relations with Britain in order to support the OAU resolution over Rhodesia's (later, Zimbabwe) unilateral declaration of independence and imposition of a white minority government. Relations were restored the next year, however, following the overthrow of Nkrumah.

Following the 31st December 1981 Revolution, Ghana lost its membership in the Commonwealth Parliament Association, which promotes interchange and understanding among parliamentarians of member states. Ghana was readmitted to the association in September 1993, the same year it was also readmitted to the Inter-Parliamentary Union, another Commonwealth institution. With its readmission to these two bodies, Ghana became a major player in Commonwealth affairs. In May 1994, Ghana hosted a Commonwealth conference on local government that attracted participants from several West African countries. At the end of the year, Ghana remained the only West African Commonwealth country with an elected government, the other three members—Nigeria, Sierra Leone, and Gambia—all being under military rule. As a contribution toward Ghanaian democracy, the Commonwealth, along with the OAU and the Carter Center in the United States, provided international observer teams to monitor Ghana's presidential election in November 1992.

Ghana's relations with Britain continued to be generally good under the PNDC. British Minister of State for Foreign and Commonwealth Affairs, Mrs. Lynda Chalker, paid a successful official visit to Ghana in early 1987 which resulted in enhanced British aid for Ghana' economic reforms. Since the ERP began in 1983, Britain has given Ghana more than £69 million as balance of payments support. Ghana has reportedly garnered more aid from Britain than any African country except Zimbabwe. Britain, along with other Western countries and international development agencies, also provided much needed technical, logistical, and financial support for the implementation of Ghana's governmental decentralization effort, for the first District Assembly elections in 1988–89, as well as for the presidential and parliamentary elections in 1992.

The United States

Ghana has in general enjoyed good relations with the United States since independence, except for a period of strained relations during the later years of the Nkrumah regime. Ghana was the first country to which United States Peace Corps volunteers were sent in 1961. Ghana and the United States are signatories to twenty agreements and treaties covering such matters as agricultural commodities, aviation, defense, economic and technical cooperation, education,

The Kwame Nkrumah Mausoleum in Accra, dedicated in 1992
Courtesy Embassy of Ghana, Washington

extradition, postal matters, telecommunications, and treaty obligations. The refusal of the United States to join the International Cocoa Agreement, given Ghana's heavy dependence on cocoa exports to earn hard currency, is the most serious bilateral issue between the two countries.

Relations between the United States and Ghana were particularly rocky in the early 1980s, apparently because of Ghana's relations with Libya. The PNDC government restored diplomatic relations with Libya shortly after coming to power. Libya came to the aid of Ghana soon afterward by providing much-needed economic assistance. Libya also has extensive financial holdings in Ghana. Rawlings has supported Libya's position that two Libyans accused of bombing a Pan American Airlines flight over Lockerbie, Scotland, in 1988 should be tried in a neutral country rather than in Britain or the United States.

Relations between the United States and Ghana were further strained by a series of diplomatic incidents in the mid-1980s. In July 1985, a distant relative of Rawlings, Michael Soussoudis, was arrested in the United States and charged with espionage. Despite Soussoudis's conviction, he was exchanged the following December for several known United States Central Intelligence Agency (CIA) agents in Accra, but not before diplomats had been expelled in both Accra and Washington. In March 1986, a Panamanian-registered ship carrying arms and a number of mercenaries and United States veterans of the Vietnam War was seized off the coast of Brazil. The PNDC charged that the arms and soldiers were destined for Ghana and that they had been financed by a Ghanaian dissident with links to the CIA. During their trial, several crew members admitted that the charges were substantially true. Although they were convicted and imprisoned, three subsequently escaped with what the PNDC alleged was CIA assistance.

In spite of these incidents, relations between the United States and Ghana had improved markedly by the late 1980s. Former United States president Jimmy Carter visited Ghana in 1986 and again in 1988 and was warmly received by the PNDC. His Global 2000 agricultural program (see Glossary), which is quite popular with Ghanaian farmers, is helping promote good relations with the United States. In 1989 the United States forgave US$114 million of Ghana's foreign debt, part of a larger debt relief effort by Western nations. The United States has strongly favored Ghana's economic and political reform policies, and since the birth of the Fourth Republic and Ghana's return to constitutional rule, has offered assistance to help Ghana institutionalize and consolidate its steps toward democratic governance. In FY 1994, United States development aid totaled about US$38 million; in addition, the United States supplied more than US$16 million in food aid.

Other Countries

After 1981, PNDC foreign policy was designed to promote the country's economic growth and well-being by establishing friendly relations and cooperation with all countries irrespective of their economic and political philosophies or ideological orientation. PNDC policy also sought new markets for Ghana's exports, the expansion of existing markets, and new investment opportunities.

Ghana's relations with Canada were quite good under the PNDC, as were Ghana's relations with the European Community and its member countries. In 1987, as part of its cancellation of the debts of several African countries, Canada canceled a Ghanaian debt of US$77.6 million. In 1989 Germany canceled US$295 million of Ghana's foreign debt, and France canceled US$26 million.

A number of Western countries, including France and Canada, continued to cancel debts in 1991, reflecting the generally cordial relations between Ghana and Western countries and the confidence the West had in PNDC policies. In early July 1991, Rawlings paid a three-day official visit to Paris, which symbolized the close ties that had developed between the PNDC and the French government. Western countries have continued to show keen interest in, and support for, the ERP and Ghana's transition to democratic government.

In line with its commitment to the principles of nonalignment, the PNDC sought to develop close relations with the socialist regimes in Eastern Europe, Cuba, the Democratic People's Republic of Korea (North Korea), and China. In the early days of PNDC rule, Rawlings made official visits to China and Ethiopia, the latter then headed by a Marxist-Leninist regime.

During these visits, various economic, trade, and cultural agreements were concluded. Notable was the PNDC agreement with the German Democratic Republic (GDR or East Germany) for the improvement of roads in Kumasi, Ghana's second largest city, and of the Kumasi-Accra highway. The GDR also supplied Ghana with new railroad coaches. Barter trade with East European countries, especially the GDR, Romania, and Bulgaria, also increased. The PNDC established a State Committee for Economic Cooperation to ensure more effective cooperation with socialist countries and showed keen interest in developing relations with the Council for Mutual Economic Assistance.

The PNDC policy of restructuring Ghana's education system, moving from purely academic curricula to vocational and technical training, benefited from Ghana's close ties with socialist countries, notably Cuba. By 1985 Cuba was training some 1,000 Ghanaian school children and middle-level technicians. Cuba also offered Ghanaians training in political leadership for "revolutionary organs" and national security. Hundreds of Ghanaian youths left for various socialist countries to pursue professional and technical courses. The Soviet

Union, China, and other socialist countries awarded scholarships to Ghanaians for both academic and technical courses. In addition, short-term training was offered for Ghana's Committees for the Defence of the Revolution. Bulgaria provided training in political organization and leadership, and the Soviet Union furnished education in medicine, veterinary sciences, and engineering.

The PNDC believed that Cuba provided a fruitful field for cooperation in areas other than education. The PNDC agreed to a joint commission for economic cooperation and signed a number of scientific and technical agreements with Cuba ranging from cultural exchanges to cooperation in such fields as health, agriculture, and education. Cuba trained Ghana's national militia, gave advice in the creation of mass organizations such as the CDRs, and provided military advisers and medical and security officers for the PNDC leadership. The two countries also signed agreements for the renovation of Ghana's sugar industry and for three factories to produce construction materials. In 1985 Ghana and Cuba signed their first barter agreement, followed by new trade protocols in 1987 and 1988. Cuban medical brigades worked in Tamale in the Northern Region, one of the poorest areas in Ghana. Cubans coached Ghanaian boxers and athletes and taught Spanish in Ghanaian schools.

Ghana's relations with Cuba continue to be strong despite Ghana's return to multiparty democracy and the severe economic crisis in Cuba in 1993 and 1994. A joint commission for cooperation between the two countries meets biennially in the alternate venues of Accra and Havana. Cuba is helping to create a faculty of medical sciences in Ghana's new University of Development Studies at Tamale (see The Education System, ch. 2). At the end of 1994, thirty-three medical specialists were working in Ghanaian hospitals. A bilateral exchange of technology and experts in mining and agriculture was also underway. Cuba is training 600 Ghanaians, mostly in technical disciplines, including engineering, architecture, and medicine. The two countries are engaged in successful business ventures, too, including a first-class tourist resort at Ada in Greater Accra Region and a Ghana-Cuba construction company.

Economic relations between Ghana and Japan are quite cordial, having improved considerably under the PNDC. Japan offered Ghana about US$680 million toward the rehabilitation of its telephone and television services. Following the visit to

Japan of a Ghanaian delegation in early 1987, Japan pledged a total of US$70 million toward Ghana's economic development. In early 1994, Japan offered a further US$16.6 million to modernize rail transport and to improve water supplies. In October 1994, Ghana joined in urging the UN Security Council to admit Japan and Germany, two countries that in 1993 and 1994 were among Ghana's largest aid donors, in recognition of the international political and economic stature of both countries.

Ghana's relations with Arab countries were also generally good during the PNDC period, and they remained so under the new NDC administration. Considerable economic assistance flowed into Ghana from the Arab world. Ghana signed loan agreements with the Saudi Arabian Fund for Development for various development projects in Ghana, including the promotion of Islamic education. In early January 1994, loan agreements totaling US$16.5 million from the Kuwaiti Fund for Arab Economic Development were signed to fund a thermal power plant at Takoradi.

Following the peace accord between Israel and the Palestine Liberation Organization in September 1993, Ghana reestablished diplomatic relations with Israel in August 1994. Diplomatic relations between the two countries had been broken in 1973 in support of member Arab states of the OAU who were at war with Israel. In urging resumption of diplomatic ties, parliament noted that Ghana stood to gain access to Israeli technology, notably in water engineering and irrigation, sewerage construction, and agriculture.

Finally, in June 1994, a new Ghanaian ambassador presented his credentials to Russian president Boris Yeltsin in Moscow. At the time, the Ghanaian government expressed its hope that democratic restructuring in both Ghana and Russia and the advent of a market economy in Russia would lead to new and diversified bilateral trade and economic cooperation.

International Organizations

Ghana belongs to sixteen UN organizations and twenty-four other international organizations, including the Commonwealth. Nkrumah saw the UN as the most effective forum for small, poor countries such as Ghana to exert some influence in a world dominated by more powerful nations. As it had with the Commonwealth, Ghana, a leader among countries of the developing world, sought to enlarge the UN role in economic development and to make it an effective force for world peace.

Ghana was also a leader of the African countries that lobbied to advance the cause of freedom in Africa. Nkrumah made the UN Charter a plank of Ghana's foreign policy and helped to make the UN a forum for nonalignment as he maneuvered with other Afro-Asian leaders between East and West. Among Ghanaians who have achieved world prominence in the UN is Kenneth Dadzie, who from 1986 to 1994 was secretary general of the UN Conference on Trade and Development.

The PNDC preserved Ghana's commitment to the ideals and objectives of the UN. In recognition of Ghana's strong commitment to African causes and its active involvement in the General Assembly, Ghana became one of the African countries elected to a non-permanent seat in the UN Security Council during 1986–87. Ghana has also contributed troops to UN peacekeeping operations around the world, including Iraq-Kuwait (1991), Cambodia (1992–93), and Rwanda (1993–94) (see International Security Concerns, ch. 5).

The PNDC also maintained Ghana's active membership in the Non-Aligned Movement. Indeed, the diplomatic highlight of the PNDC government in 1991 was its successful hosting, in Accra in early September, of the tenth ministerial conference of the Non-Aligned Movement. The meeting attracted one of the largest contingents of foreign ministers of all recent African conferences.

Ghana also hosted a well-attended conference of nongovernmental organizations in Accra in late August 1991 as a prelude to the nonaligned conference. The conference concerned itself with economic development, peace, and a just world order.

In honor of Kwame Nkrumah, Ghana's first president and a founding member of the Non-Aligned Movement and of Pan-Africanism, the PNDC commissioned the Kwame Nkrumah Memorial Park and the Nkrumah Mausoleum in Accra on July 1, 1992. The remains of the late president were brought from Nkroful, his birthplace, and reinterred in a moving public ceremony. The park and the mausoleum fulfilled a pledge made by the PNDC in 1990 to commemorate Nkrumah's contributions to Ghana and to Africa by means of an appropriate memorial.

Future Democratic Prospects

At the end of 1994, Ghana's young democracy seemed intact and on course. Although the electoral processes of the Fourth Republic were riddled with controversy and even some violence, the prospects for multiparty democracy appeared bright. This was true despite the opposition boycott of the parliamentary elections, leading to a virtual one-party state in practice. The NDC government had so far demonstrated a willingness to abide by the strictures of the 1992 constitution; the legislature appeared unrestricted in its deliberations, which were open to public scrutiny and opposition criticism despite the absence of a formal parliamentary opposition; and the judiciary had established its independence, unfettered by executive interference in its decisions, a majority of which had gone against the government.

Another positive development since the establishment of the Fourth Republic in January 1993 has been the growing acceptance by the NDC-dominated government of the crucial distinction between the interests of a ruling party and those of the state or civil society. This distinction was virtually nonexistent under military rule or the one-party state. This development in turn has resulted in the emergence and growth of independent civic institutions and organizations.

In celebrating two years of democracy at the end of 1994, Ghanaians were not forgetful of the painful fact that each of the last two attempts at constitutional rule had come to an abrupt end after only two years. Given the record since 1992, however, there was cause for cautious optimism. It may be that the return of Jerry Rawlings in 1981 will turn out to be the coup that ended the cycle of coups and the act that led at last to a new political era in Ghana.

* * *

A rich body of literature exists on government and politics in Ghana during the colonial and early postindependence periods. Individual works range from general historical surveys to important case studies produced by Ghanaian and foreign specialists. The politics and government of the PNDC and the Fourth Republic, however, are less fully documented.

Among classic studies of the early decolonization and postindependence periods are Dennis Austin's *Politics in Ghana, 1946–1960,* David E. Apter's *Ghana in Transition,* and Maxwell Owusu's *Uses and Abuses of Political Power: A Case Study of Continuity and Change in the Politics of Ghana.* The standard works on foreign policy covering the Nkrumah period (1957–66), namely Willard S. Thompson's *Ghana's Foreign Policy, 1957–*

1966: Diplomacy, Ideology, and the New State and Michael Dei-Anang's *The Administration of Ghana's Foreign Relations, 1957–1965: A Personal Memoir,* are equally relevant for a complete understanding of foreign policy under the PNDC and the Fourth Republic, which remains basically Nkrumahist.

Zaya Yeebo's *Ghana, the Struggle for Popular Power: Rawlings, Saviour or Demagogue* and Donald I. Ray's *Ghana: Politics, Economics, and Society* are leftist and partisan but contain useful insights. *Ghana under PNDC Rule, 1982–1989,* edited by E. Gyimah-Boadi, with contributions by eleven Ghanaian academics at the University of Ghana, provides a balanced if brief overview of the years of PNDC rule. Good preliminary studies of party politics in the Fourth Republic are presented in the volume entitled *Political Parties and Democracy in Ghana's Fourth Republic,* edited by Kwame A. Ninsin and Francis K. Drah.

Jeffrey Herbst's *The Politics of Reform in Ghana, 1982–1991* is a good critical examination of the politics of economic reform under the PNDC. The most systematic and comprehensive study of the presidential and parliamentary elections of 1992 is by Richard Jeffries and Clare Thomas, "The Ghanaian Elections of 1992." Maxwell Owusu's "Custom and Coups: A Juridical Interpretation of Civil Order and Disorder in Ghana," "Rebellion, Revolution and Tradition: Reinterpreting Coups in Ghana," and "Democracy and Africa—A View From the Village" provide in-depth analysis as well as a cultural and historical perspective on the PNDC period. (For further information and complete citations, see Bibliography.)

Chapter 5. National Security

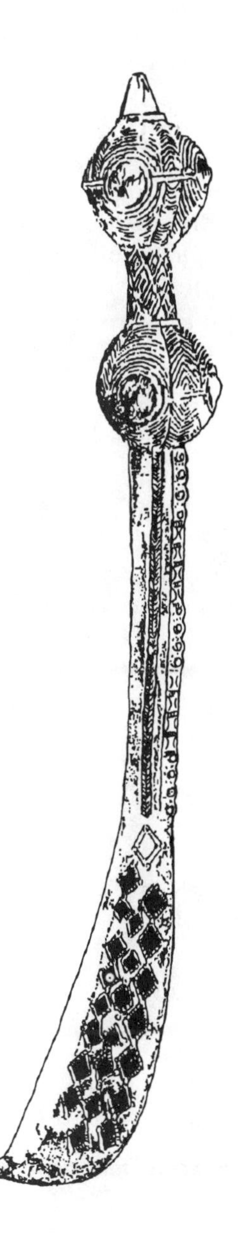

Ceremonial state sword, symbol of chiefly authority and power among the Akan

GHANA HAS A RICH AND VARIED military history. During the nineteenth century, the Asante, one of the major ethnic groups in the country, relied on military power to extend their rule throughout most of what eventually became the modern state of Ghana. The Asante also engaged in a series of military campaigns against the British (in 1873, 1896, and 1900) for control of the country's political and economic systems. After the British established a protectorate, thousands of Ghanaians served in the Royal West African Frontier Force. In the two world wars of the twentieth century, tens of thousands of Ghanaians fought with the Western allies. From 1945 until 1957, the British used the Ghanaian army to maintain internal security.

At independence in 1957, Ghana's armed forces were among the best in Africa. However, President Kwame Nkrumah (1960–66) gradually destroyed this heritage by transforming the armed forces from a traditional military organization into one that he hoped would facilitate the growth of African socialism and Pan-Africanism, would aid in the fight against neocolonialism, and would help implement Nkrumah's radical foreign policy. Nkrumah also Africanized the officer corps as rapidly as possible. In 1966 the armed forces moved to end its use as a political tool by overthrowing Nkrumah. For the next twenty-five years, the military repeatedly intervened in the political process to stabilize Ghana and to improve the country's economy. In 1992, however, Ghana's military regime presided over multiparty elections, which the regime hoped would return the country to a parliamentary system of government.

The Ghanaian military, with a personnel strength of 6,850 in 1994, helped to maintain internal security and to preserve Ghana's territorial integrity. Throughout the 1980s, the generally pro-Western armed forces relied on a variety of sources for foreign military assistance, including the United States, Italy, Libya, and the Soviet Union. Organized into a 5,000-member army, a 1,200-member air force, and a 1,000-member navy, the military was capable of performing its missions. During the 1980s and early 1990s, moreover, the Ghanaian armed forces and some police personnel participated in United Nations peacekeeping operations in Cambodia, Croatia, Western Sahara, Iraq/Kuwait, Rwanda, and Lebanon. Ghana also contributed troops to the Economic Community of West African States Monitoring Group peacekeeping force in Liberia.

International Security Concerns

As of the mid-1990s, there was no external threat against Ghana; however, Ghana has experienced periodic tensions with two West African states, Togo and Liberia, which at the time some observers believed could lead to armed conflict. The parties involved in these disputes avoided hostilities by relying on diplomacy rather than on military force to resolve their problems.

In January 1976, Ghanaian-Togolese relations deteriorated after Togo urged a readjustment of their common border in Togo's favor. Ghana rejected this demand, citing the 1956 United Nations (UN) referendum, which had given western Togoland's population the choice of staying in Togo or of joining Ghana. Nevertheless, in March 1976, the Ghanaian government banned the National Liberation Movement for Western Togoland (NLMWT). Later that month, Ghanaian security forces arrested ten people near Togo's border and charged them with subversion for contacting Ghanaian dissidents in Togo. Although the NLMWT threatened to use force against Ghana unless the UN intervened in the crisis, it failed to launch a successful guerrilla war against Ghana.

In September 1982, Ghana closed the border to prevent Ghanaian dissidents who lived in Togo from crossing into Ghana. Nevertheless, tensions between the two countries resurfaced after Flight Lieutenant Jerry John Rawlings seized power in Ghana at the end of 1981. Rawlings warned the Togolese against allowing Ghanaian dissidents to use Togo's territory as a base from which to launch attacks against Ghana. In early 1984, after Ghana had reopened the border, the Togolese government calmed Accra's fears by threatening to arrest any Ghanaian exiles who held meetings in Togo.

In 1986 relations with Togo again deteriorated after Ghanaian security forces captured a group of armed dissidents who had crossed the border from Togo. Ghana's secretary for foreign affairs protested the use of neighboring countries as bases for subversive activities against the Rawlings regime. In September 1986, Lomé claimed that Togolese dissidents, operating from Ghana, had attempted a coup against the government of Togo's president, General Gnassingbe Eyadema. As a result, Togo temporarily closed the border with Ghana and then deported 233 Ghanaians. In January 1989, relations between the two countries became strained again when Togo expelled 120 Ghanaians. After Togo reopened its land, air, and sea borders with Ghana in October 1990, relations between the two countries gradually improved.

On January 30, 1993, clashes that pitted Togolese security forces loyal to Eyadema against several opposition groups prompted approximately 55,000 refugees to flee to Ghana. Accra, which sided with Eyadema's opponents, responded by placing the Ghanaian armed forces on full alert, ostensibly to aid the refugees. Rawlings claimed that because of this trouble, he was considering a recall of all Ghanaian troops serving on missions abroad for the UN and in Liberia. After attackers stormed Eyadema's home in Lomé on March 25, 1993, the Togolese government closed its border with Ghana and accused the Rawlings regime of providing a safe haven for the raiders.

In early 1994, the two countries almost went to war following yet another incident. According to Togolese authorities, more than 100 armed Togolese crossed the border from Ghana in early January to assassinate Eyadema and to take control of the government. Togo immediately closed its border with Ghana, and each nation then accused the other's armed forces of launching cross-border raids. Although tensions eased later in the year, the Ghanaian minister of foreign affairs warned of further incidents unless Eyadema introduced basic democratic reforms.

Ghanaian-Liberian relations suffered a setback in September 1989 over rumors that Monrovia planned a forceful repatriation of resident Ghanaians following the return of more than 400 Liberians from Ghana. Although Accra denied that it had deported the Liberians, Monrovia retaliated by expelling 350 Ghanaians. A more serious problem occurred in 1990, when a rebel force known as the National Patriotic Front of Liberia reportedly seized about 2,000 Ghanaians living in Liberia. Many Ghanaians also resented the presence of approximately 6,000 Liberian refugees who had settled in a camp at Bruburam near Accra; they argued that Ghanaian security forces should halt the influx of refugees by detaining them at the border, by force if necessary.

Despite these difficulties, beginning in mid-1990 the Ghanaian government deployed three battalions of troops to Liberia as part of the Economic Community of West African States

Monitoring Group (ECOMOG) peacekeeping force. These troops served eight-month tours. In late 1994, about 1,000 Ghanaian troops were still serving in Liberia despite the government's growing impatience with the mission and the lack of progress toward a settlement of the conflict.

The ECOMOG operation was but one in a long list of international peacekeeping missions in which Ghana has participated. As early as 1978, Ghana contributed soldiers to the UN Interim Force in Lebanon; nearly 800 were still on duty there in mid-1994. Other UN missions to which Ghana has contributed include the Iraq-Kuwait Observation Mission (1991–94); Cambodia, where more than 1,000 Ghanaians served as security personnel during UN-supervised elections in 1992–93; Somalia (1994); and Rwanda, where nearly 850 Ghanaians troops were part of a 2,500-member peacekeeping force in 1994. Assignments with ECOMOG and other international peacekeeping operations were avidly sought after, in part because they presented opportunities for self-enrichment, such as black-market dealings, otherwise unavailable to the average soldier. So lucrative were UN assignments that there were reports of bribery for selecting such forces.

Internal Security Concerns

Ghana has a long history of internal division, rooted in antagonisms and conflicts among the country's various ethnic groups. For example, the Asante (also seen as Ashanti—see Glossary) in the center of the country have long been at odds with southern peoples such as the Ga, Fante, Akwapim, Nzema, and Ewe. In the seventeenth century, the Asante began conquering smaller northern states. The Asante then moved south, where they came into contact with the Fante. Conflicts between these two groups ultimately led to British intervention. For much of the nineteenth century, the British battled the Asante for control of most of the territory that became modern Ghana (see Arrival of the Europeans and The Colonial Era: British Rule of the Gold Coast, ch. 1). Even after the country gained independence as the new nation of Ghana in 1957, ethnic divisions continued to trouble Ghanaian society.

Several dissident organizations, however, most of which had been created by exiles during the 1980s, dedicated themselves to deemphasizing ethnicity and to facilitating the growth of nationalism. In April 1982, various members of Ghana's banned political parties established the Campaign for Democracy in Ghana and opened offices in Lagos and London. This group characterized the Rawlings regime as "an instrument of terror" and urged all Ghanaians to employ all legitimate means to ensure that democracy and constitutional order were restored in the country. In April 1984, J.H. Mensah, who had been the minister of finance in the Kofi Abrefa Busia government (1969–71), formed the Ghana Democratic Movement, which welcomed all citizens who believed in "the restoration of democracy in Ghana."

In the precolonial era, political opposition was tolerated only up to point, after which retribution was likely. During the colonial period in the Gold Coast, later renamed Ghana, the British jailed outspoken nationalists. Since independence, Ghana's security policy toward dissidents and political opponents has been harsh. During Kwame Nkrumah's presidency (1960–66), security personnel permeated all levels of Ghanaian society. Additionally, the Ghana Young Pioneers, created in June 1960, regularly reported all suspected dissident activities to the authorities. Nkrumah also encouraged rivalries among senior officials to discourage them from taking united action against him. Individuals who fell afoul of Nkrumah usually ended up in jail; more dangerous people received long-term sentences in the maximum security prison at Nsawam.

Since the downfall of Nkrumah, all governments except that of Hilla Limann (1979–81) have dealt harshly with any individual or organization deemed to be a threat to the established political order. Informants watched military personnel, members of political parties, academics, students, and ordinary citizens for signs of disloyalty, antigovernment activity, or coup-plotting. During the early years of the second Rawlings regime in the 1980s, the authorities also sought to prevent the emergence of prodemocracy groups. In mid-1987, for example, the police arrested members of the New Democratic Movement (NDM) and the Kwame Nkrumah Revolutionary Guards (KNRG), supposedly for plotting to overthrow the government. Gradually, however, Western and domestic pressures persuaded the Ghanaian government to permit political competition and to hold multiparty elections in late 1992.

The Armed Forces in National Life

Ghana has a rich and varied military history. The military traditions of the Asante and several other Ghanaian peoples dominated the precolonial era. During the British period, the military consisted of a modest army organized along infantry lines. At independence, Nkrumah expanded the armed forces to enhance the country's national prestige. The army grew in size and complexity, and the government established a separate air force and navy. This growth exceeded Ghana's national security requirements, however, and imposed an economic burden on the new state. In the decades since independence, Ghana has continued to maintain a comparatively large military force. By the early 1990s, it had become clear that the government would have to respond to popular demands for greater economic growth by reducing the size of the military establishment.

The Armed Forces in the Past

The armed forces have traditionally played a significant role in Ghanaian society. The most important factors associated with the growth of the military's role in national life include the emergence of Asante militarism, the British conquest, and the political activities of the armed forces following independence.

The Asante Wars

Historically, the Asante, who are members of the Twi-speaking branch of the Akan people, have exercised considerable influence in the region. The groups that constituted the core of the Asante confederacy moved north and settled in the vicinity of Lake Bosumtwi. Prior to the mid-seventeenth century, several Asante leaders, one of them Oti Akenten (r. ca. 1630–60), embarked on a program of military expansion that enabled the Asante to dominate surrounding groups, establish the most powerful state in the central forest zone, and form an alliance with neighboring states known as the Asante confederation.

In the late seventeenth century, Osei Tutu (d. 1712 or 1717) became *asantehene* (king of Asante). During his reign, the Asante confederation destroyed the influence of Denkyira, which had been the strongest state in the coastal hinterland and which had been exacting tribute from most of the other Akan groups in the central forest. Asante authorities then moved the confederation's capital to Kumasi and continued their policy of military expansion. During one southern expedition, rebels ambushed and killed Osei Tutu and most of his generals. The Asante confederation, which allowed newly conquered territories to retain their customs and chiefs, survived this catastrophe and continued to expand its boundaries, in the process transforming itself into an empire. Under succeeding leaders, Asante armies extended the empire's frontier southward. By the beginning of the nineteenth century, the Asante governed a territory as large as modern-day Ghana and were challenging the Fante states for control of the coast, where European traders had established a network of posts and fortifications.

The rapid growth of the Asante empire aroused the suspicions of the Fante, who believed that the Asante sought to subjugate the coastal states. Asante-Fante relations, therefore, remained hostile for most of the second half of the eighteenth century. Specific problems between the two Akan states included the Fante refusal to allow Asante traders direct access to the coast; a Fante law that prohibited the sale of firearms and ammunition to the Asante army; Fante support of Denkyira, Akyem, and other states in their revolts against Asante authority; and the Fante practice of granting sanctuary to refugees from the Asante empire. To resolve these problems, the Asante launched three successful military expeditions (in 1807, 1811, and 1816) against the Fante and by 1820 had become the strongest power in West Africa.

The Asante army, which achieved these and numerous other victories, relied on troops mobilized for specific campaigns rather than on a standing, professional force. Evasion of military service was punishable by death. The army, which lacked cavalry, possessed superior infantry comprising musketeers, bowmen, and spearsmen. The armed force also included scouts (*akwansrafo*); an advance guard (*twafo*); a main force (*adonten*); the king's personal bodyguard (*gyase*); a rear guard (*kyidom*); and two wings, the left (*benkum*) and the right (*nifa*). Additionally, the Asante army had a medical corps (*esumankwafo*) that treated the army's wounded and removed the dead from the battlefield.

The Asante army's success against the Fante, coupled with the Asante's determination to preserve their empire, posed a threat to the British, who also wanted to control the coast for strategic, political, and economic reasons. Britain's commitment to stopping the slave trade made it impossible for the British to maintain good relations with the Asante, who, by 1820, had become the main source of slaves on the coast. Many British policy makers believed, moreover, that it was their duty to promote Christianity and Western civilization. Some British merchants also believed that if Asante power could be destroyed, a vast market would be opened to them.

Given the differences between the British and the Asante, a military clash between them was inevitable. After the Asante executed a Fante soldier who served in a British garrison for insulting their king, the British launched a military expedition against a 10,000-member Asante force near the village of Bonsaso. The Asante not only outnumbered the British but also used superior tactics. The fighting, which began on January 22, 1824, initially favored the Asante, who encircled the British force and killed Governor Charles MacCarthy. Eventually, however, the British drove the Asante back to Kumasi.

After reorganizing and re-equipping, the Asante in 1826 again invaded the coast, attacking the British and their allies. During the fighting on the open plains of Accra, the British used Congreve rockets, which frightened Asante warriors who believed the enemy was using thunder and lightning against them. The Asante panicked and fled to Kumasi. According to a peace treaty concluded in 1831, the *asantehene* recognized the independence of the coastal states and agreed to refer all future disputes to the British for adjudication. In exchange, the coastal states promised to allow the Asante to engage in legal trade on the coast and to respect the *asantehene.* During much of the following two decades, Captain George Maclean, president of a local council of British merchants, used tact and diplomacy to enforce the peace treaty.

After the British government resumed responsibility for the administration of the coastal forts in 1843, relations with the Asante gradually deteriorated. In addition to assaults on Asante traders, the *asantehene* believed that the British and their Fante allies no longer treated him with respect. When British Governor Richard Pine refused to return an Asante chief and a runaway slave to the *asantehene,* the Asante prepared for war. In April 1863, they invaded the coast and burned thirty villages. Pine responded by deploying six companies along the Pra River, the border between states allied with the British and the Asante. The deployed force built a network of stockades and a bridge, but it returned home without engaging the enemy after inexplicably having lost its guns, ammunition, and supplies.

The Second Asante War (1873–74) began as a result of the *asantehene*'s attempt to preserve his empire's last trade outlet to the sea at the old coastal fort of Elmina, which had come into

Ghanaian infantry depart Accra for a peacekeeping mission in Liberia.
Courtesy Embassy of Ghana, Washington

British possession in 1872. In early 1873, a 12,000-member Asante army crossed the Pra River and invaded the coastal area but suffered a defeat at Elmina. The British government then appointed Major General Garnet Wolseley administrator and commander in chief and ordered him to drive the Asante from the coastal region. In December 1873, Wolseley's African levies were reinforced by the arrival of several British units.

Approximately one month later, Wolseley sent an advance party across the Pra, warning the *asantehene* that he intended to begin hostilities. Wolseley, however, also offered an armistice. When negotiations failed, both sides prepared for war.

The most significant battle of the Second Asante War occurred at Amoafo, near the village of Bekwai. Although the Asante performed admirably, superior weapons allowed the British to carry the day. Asante losses were unknown; the British lost four men and had 194 wounded. In the following days, Wolseley captured Bekwai and then Kumasi. On March 14, 1874, the two sides signed the Treaty of Fomena, which required the Asante to pay an indemnity of 50,000 ounces of gold, to renounce claims to Elmina and to all payments from the British for the use of forts, and to terminate their alliances with several other states, including Denkyira and Akyem. Additionally, the *asantehene* agreed to withdraw his troops from the coast, to keep the trade routes open, and to halt the practice of human sacrifice.

The British victory and the Treaty of Fomena ended the Asante dream of bringing the coastal states under their power. The northern states of Brong, Gonja, and Dagomba also took advantage of the Asante defeat by asserting their independence. The Asante empire was near collapse. In 1896 the British declared a protectorate over Asante and exiled the *asantehene*, Prempeh, his immediate family, and several close advisers to the Seychelles Islands.

The last Anglo-Asante war occurred in 1899–1900, when the British twice tried to take possession of the *asantehene*'s Golden Stool, symbol of Asante power and independence. In April 1900, the Asante reacted to these attempts by launching an armed rebellion and by laying siege to the Kumasi fort, where the British governor and his party had sought refuge. The British eventually defeated the Asante, both capturing and exiling the rebellion's leader, Yaa Asantewaa, and fifteen of her closest advisers. The conclusion of the last Anglo-Asante war resulted in the formal annexation of the Asante empire as a British possession.

World War I

After establishing supremacy in the Gold Coast, the British created the Gold Coast Regiment as a component of the West African Frontier Force (WAFF), which kept peace throughout the territories of the Gold Coast, Nigeria, Sierra Leone, and the Gambia. In 1928 the WAFF became the Royal West African Frontier Force (RWAFF). British officers and noncommissioned officers organized, trained, and equipped the Gold Coast Regiment. For much of the colonial period, the British recruited African enlisted personnel only from ethnic groups in the Northern Territories Protectorate, the northern third of the colony (see fig. 3). Eventually, the Gold Coast Regiment accepted a few African officers along with an increasing number of African noncommissioned officers from the south. Nevertheless, the north-south division continued to characterize the Gold Coast Regiment.

On July 31, 1914, four days before the British declaration of war on Germany, Accra mobilized its military forces. The Gold Coast Regiment included thirty-eight British officers, eleven

British warrant or noncommissioned officers, 1,584 Africans, (including 124 carriers for guns and machine guns), and about 300 reservists. Additionally, the four Volunteer Corps (Gold Coast Volunteers, Gold Coast Railway Volunteers, Gold Coast Mines Volunteers, and Ashanti Mines Volunteers) fielded about 900 men. These forces participated in the campaigns in Togo, Cameroon, and East Africa.

Deployment of the country's armed forces required the reduction of the British colonial establishment by 30 percent between 1914 and 1917 and the closure of several military installations in the Northern Territories. These actions persuaded many Gold Coast residents that British colonial rule was about to end. As a result, a series of disorders and protests against British colonial rule occurred throughout the country.

During August and September 1914, for example, riots broke out in Central Province and Ashanti, followed three years later by unrest at Old Nigo. The wartime weakening of the administrative structure in the Northern Territories also fueled opposition to chiefs who used their positions to exploit the people they ruled, to encourage military recruitment, or to advance the cause of British colonial rule. Disturbances among the Frafra at Bongo in April 1916 and in Gonja in March 1917 prompted the authorities to deploy a detachment of troops to the Northern Territories to preserve law and order.

World War II

Although many of the more radical Pan-Africanists and Marxist-Leninists hoped to enlist northern black troops and ex-servicemen in their anticolonial struggle, there was little unrest during the interwar period. During World War II, approximately 65,000 Ghanaians served in the RWAFF. The Gold Coast Regiment participated in campaigns in East Africa and Burma and in maneuvers in the Gambia.

Military service, particularly overseas, enhanced the political and economic understanding of many individual soldiers, a development that facilitated the growth of postwar nationalism. Military service, however, also underscored cultural and ethnic differences among Ghanaians. Many Asante and most southerners looked down upon northerners, who made up the majority of the Gold Coast Regiment. These divisions carried over into postwar politics and, according to some observers, have continued to prevent the development of a strong sense of national identity to the present day.

The Gold Coast also played a significant role in the Allied war effort. On June 27, 1942, the United States Army activated the Air Transport Command in Cairo under Brigadier General Shepler W. Fitzgerald. Ten days later, Fitzgerald moved his headquarters to Accra and organized the Africa-Middle East Wing. In late 1942, the United States Army expanded its presence in Accra by activating the Twelfth Ferrying Group Headquarters, the Forty-first Ferrying Squadron, and the Forty-second Ferrying Squadron. The Twelfth Ferrying Group, which was part of a transportation network reaching from the United States, via Africa, to the China-Burma-India theater of operations, ensured the movement of men and matériel through Senegal, Ghana, and Chad.

In contrast with the post-World War I era, Ghanaian veterans engaged in widespread political activities after World War II. In 1946 some former soldiers established the Gold Coast Ex-Servicemen's Union, which sought to improve economic conditions and to increase employment for veterans. During a February 1948 union-sponsored march, police killed two demonstrators and wounded several others. Unrest quickly spread throughout the country. Eventually, the union joined the United Gold Coast Convention and then became part of the Convention People's Party (CPP), which worked for independence under Nkrumah's leadership. After independence, the government passed the Ghana Legion Act, which outlawed ex-servicemen's organizations and which created instead a national Ghana Legion. Although it supposedly represented all Ghanaians, the establishment of the Ghana Legion marked the end of independent political action by ex-servicemen.

The Development of the Modern Army

After independence, Ghana opted out of the RWAFF. According to Nkrumah, this action was necessary because the RWAFF was "one of the trappings of colonialism." The Ghanaian army had grown in size and complexity, moreover, and the government created a separate air force and navy. The military's ostensible mission was to aid the national police in maintaining internal security; however, Nkrumah wanted to use the armed forces to buttress his foreign policy and Pan-Africanist goals.

British officers who served in the Ghanaian armed forces thwarted Nkrumah's plans to use the military as a political tool. As a result, in September 1961 Nkrumah dismissed all British military personnel and ordered the Africanization of the armed forces. By removing the British from command positions, Nkrumah destroyed an apolitical safeguard and exposed the military to political manipulation. However, much of the British-trained Ghanaian officer corps resisted Nkrumah's attempts to indoctrinate them with the political ideology of the CPP. Moreover, the officer corps shunned the political commissars whom Nkrumah had introduced into all units.

To break the power of the traditional Ghanaian military establishment, Nkrumah created his own private army in violation of the country's constitution. The Soviet Union supported this effort by providing military advisers and weaponry. After an unsuccessful attempt on his life, Nkrumah ordered the expansion of the presidential guard company to regimental strength. On the recommendation of Soviet security advisers, Nkrumah also added a civilian unit to the bodyguard. The military and civilian wings formed the Presidential Guard Department. In 1963 Nkrumah changed the name of this organization to the Presidential Detail Department. By February 1966, this unit's First Guard Regiment included a 1,500-member battalion, and the Second Guard Regiment was in the process of being formed and trained by Soviet advisers.

The Presidential Detail Department also supervised secret storage depots and training camps for Nkrumah's constantly expanding private army. These facilities were located at Elmina Castle, Akosombo, Afianya, and Okponglo. After Nkrumah's downfall, Ghanaian authorities discovered an array of weapons, including heavy machine guns, mortars, and artillery, at these sites. Anti-Nkrumah elements insisted that such weaponry, which exceeded the needs of the Presidential Detail Department, was destined for Nkrumah's private army.

Apart from trying to create a parallel military establishment, Nkrumah also established a multifaceted intelligence apparatus. In early 1963, one of Nkrumah's closest supporters, Ambrose Yankey, established the Special Intelligence Unit to monitor the activities of antigovernment individuals and groups. By 1966 this unit included 281 people, all of whom reportedly received training from Soviet and other communist advisers. Another intelligence unit, Department III, Military Intelligence, was not part of the Ministry of Defence. Instead, its task was to check independently on the loyalty of the regular armed forces. Department III, Military Intelligence, maintained an interrogation center at Burma Camp. The Bureau for Technical Assistance conducted espionage in other African countries. Additionally, on October 1, 1965, the bureau established an all-African intelligence service known as the Special African Service (also known as the Technical Unit), which was designed to penetrate the intelligence services of other African countries. By 1966 this organization had grown from forty to sixty-seven personnel.

The Military and the Government

The National Liberation Council, 1966–69

The officer corps of the regular armed forces viewed the activities of the Nkrumah regime with increasing alarm. As a result, on February 24, 1966, a small number of army officers and senior police officials, led by Colonel E.K. Kotoka, commander of the Second Army Brigade at Kumasi; Major A.A. Afrifa, staff officer in charge of army training and operations; Lieutenant General (retired) J.A. Ankra; and J.W.K. Harlley, the police inspector general, successfully launched a coup d'état against the Nkrumah regime. The new government, known as the National Liberation Council (NLC), justified its action by citing Nkrumah's abuse of power, widespread political repression, sharp economic decline, and rampant corruption.

On April 17, 1967, a group of junior officers of the army reconnaissance squadron based at Ho in the Volta region launched a countercoup; however, intervention by other military units and the lack of a coherent plan on the part of the mutineers saved the NLC. After an investigation, the two young lieutenants who commanded the mutiny were tried by a military court, convicted, and executed. The courts also passed lengthy prison sentences on twenty-six of the reconnaissance squadron's noncommissioned officers who supported the coup attempt.

Pro-Nkrumah elements also plotted against the NLC. In late 1968, the authorities arrested Air Marshal M.A. Otu, who had succeeded Kotoka as general officer commanding the armed forces but not as an NLC member, and his aide, a navy lieutenant, for alleged subversive activity. A military court charged both men with plans to overthrow the NLC and to return Nkrumah to power, but eventually the two were acquitted.

There were no further incidents or threats to the NLC. After a civilian government came to power in October 1969, the armed forces reverted to their traditional roles of maintaining internal security and safeguarding territorial integrity.

The Acheampong Regime, 1972–78

On January 13, 1972, the military seized control of the government for the second time under the leadership of Lieutenant Colonel I.K. Acheampong. The army justified its action by accusing the civilian government, headed by Busia, of having failed to resolve the various problems confronting the Ghanaian armed forces.

The origin of the army's disaffection lay in the 1971–72 austerity budget, according to which defense expenditures were too large for a country as small as Ghana. The subsequent reductions affected maintenance and materials. Reductions also increased the difficulties facing younger army officers. By the early 1970s, the lack of funds had forced the Ghana Military Academy to reduce the size of its annual class from about 120 to twenty-five cadets.

Many senior army officers had also complained that the 1966 coup had interrupted the normal promotion cycle. They maintained that officers who supported Kotoka received quicker promotions, whereas those whose loyalty was in question were held back. Ewe officers, who had been shunted aside since the end of the NLC regime, believed that Acheampong would restore an equitable ethnic balance to the officer corps. Lastly, the army objected to the Busia government's decision to broaden the army's mission to include such nonmilitary functions as engaging in anti-smuggling patrols, supporting anti-cholera drives, facilitating flood relief work, and participating in reconstruction projects.

To rule Ghana, Acheampong established the National Redemption Council (NRC) and acted as its chairman. Initially, the NRC consisted of six army officers and one civilian; however, Acheampong eventually broadened the NRC's membership to include officers from all the services. Newcomers included the air force and navy commanders and the inspector general of the police. Acheampong dropped the two lower-ranking army officers and the civilian member. The NRC assumed legislative and executive powers while the NRC chairman became head of state and commander in chief. The NRC chairman also was responsible for all NRC appointments and removals with the advice of not less than two-thirds of the NRC members. The NRC could remove the chairman by a unanimous decision.

The NRC appointed nine military officers who ranked from major to colonel to serve as regional commissioners. Customarily, these commissioners worked in their traditional homelands. The NRC and the regional commissioners constituted the Executive Council. The NRC and the Executive Council, which together included about thirty senior military officers, ruled Ghana. The NRC militarized Ghanaian society, moreover, by appointing senior military officers to positions in all major departments, regional bodies, state corporations, and public boards. Additionally, Acheampong wanted to change the constitution to end party politics and to create a union government composed of civilians, military personnel, and police. Such a system, Acheampong believed, would create national unity, end tribalism, and facilitate economic development.

The failure to achieve these goals and the 1975 decision to transform the NRC into the Supreme Military Council (SMC) marked the beginning of Acheampong's downfall. The government maintained that the SMC would restore the military hierarchy that the 1972 coup had destroyed. Over the next two years, the Acheampong regime gradually lost popular support because of growing corruption, economic problems, and clashes between the SMC and the general public, culminating in violent disturbances during the 1978 referendum on union government.

The Akuffo Coup, 1978

As public hostility toward the SMC increased, Ghana became increasingly ungovernable. On July 5, 1978, junior officers on the Military Advisory Committee persuaded senior officers, led by Lieutenant General Frederick W.K. Akuffo, to force Acheampong to resign. The creation of what was termed SMC II, however, failed to restore public confidence in the government, largely because Akuffo refused to abandon the idea of a union government without party politics. As a result, there were about eighty strikes in a four-month period to protest the regime's economic policies. In November 1978, when junior civil servants went on strike, the regime declared a state of emergency and dismissed more than 1,000 public employees. Akuffo eventually succumbed to this pressure by announcing that the ban on political parties would be lifted on January 1, 1979, and that free elections would be held.

The 1979 Coup and the First Rawlings Government

Ghana's third military coup was planned by a small group of disgruntled officers. On May 15, 1979, less than five weeks before the national elections, Flight Lieutenant Jerry John Rawlings and several members of the air force (junior officers and corporals) unsuccessfully tried to overthrow the government. During the court martial of the coup's seven plotters, Rawlings justified his action by claiming that official corruption had eroded public confidence in the government and had tarnished the image of the armed forces. Rawlings also charged that Syrian and Lebanese businessmen living in Ghana had gained control of the country's economy at the expense of the African majority.

On the night of June 4, 1979, a group of junior officers and enlisted personnel of the Fifth Battalion and the Reconnaissance Regiment in Burma Camp freed Rawlings and staged a coup. These individuals then formed the Armed Forces Revolutionary Council (AFRC) to rule the country. The AFRC included a cross section of ranks from private and lance corporal to staff sergeant, airman, lieutenant, and naval commander. Although the scheduled elections occurred as planned on June 18, 1979, the AFRC retained power until September 24, 1979, when President Hilla Limann and the People's National Party (PNP) assumed control of the government.

Meanwhile, the AFRC purged the senior ranks of the armed forces and executed eight officers, three of whom had been former heads of state (Acheampong, Akuffo, and Afrifa). From July to September 1979, special courts held hearings and sentenced 155 military officers, former officials, and wealthy businessmen to prison terms ranging from six months to ninety-five years. Additionally, the AFRC collected back taxes from numerous government officials and threatened to seize the assets of many others unless they refunded money to the state that they had allegedly embezzled or stolen. The AFRC also charged hundreds of military officers with corruption and sentenced them to long prison terms. Many civil servants fell victim to the purge and lost their jobs as well.

The 1981 Coup and the Second Rawlings Government

The combination of official corruption, Rawlings's continued political activities, and deteriorating economic conditions doomed the Limann government. On December 31, 1981,

Rawlings, supported by lower-ranking soldiers, most of whom served in the Reconnaissance Regiment, seized power. Rawlings then established the Provisional National Defence Council (PNDC) to rule the country, dissolved parliament, and banned all political parties. On January 21, 1982, Rawlings appointed a sixteen-member civilian government with a cabinet of secretaries and told them to "serve the people sacrificially." The PNDC also assumed control of the Ministry of Defence. The Rawlings regime further consolidated its power by promulgating PNDC Law 42, which suspended the constitution and gave the government wide powers over Ghanaian citizens.

Shortly after seizing power, Rawlings took action against individuals who had allegedly committed crimes against the Ghanaian people. In January 1982, for example, the PNDC ordered former members of the banned PNP and other undesirable elements to report to the nearest police station or army barracks. The authorities detained some of these individuals and released others after registering their names. The police and army continued this roundup by arresting allegedly corrupt individuals who had served in the Limann government, former members of parliament, businessmen suspected of trading on the black market, and alleged coup plotters. On June 30, 1982, one or more members of the PNDC and their accomplices abducted and then murdered three High Court of Justice judges and the personnel director of the Ghana Industrial Holdings Corporation.

Despite the popularity of the Rawlings regime, there were two coup attempts in late 1982 and in early 1983. On November 23, 1982, a group of soldiers tried to overthrow the regime, initiating hostilities at Gondar Barracks. Government forces, however, defeated the rebels and the police arrested more than twenty people. The second coup attempt occurred on February 27, 1983, when security forces arrested nine soldiers and two civilians in Achimota, near Accra. The authorities claimed that they also discovered heavy machine guns, rockets, ammunition, and a list of people to be assassinated. Kojo Tsikata, special adviser to the PNDC, also accused the United States embassy of involvement in the coup attempt, but the Ghanaian government never proved this allegation.

Challenges to the Rawlings regime continued throughout the 1980s. During 1985 and 1986, for example, there were at least seven coup attempts. On September 24, 1989, two days after Rawlings had assumed direct command of the armed

Lieutenant General Frederick W. K. Akuffo, head of state and chairman of the Supreme Military Council, 1978–79
Courtesy Embassy of Ghana, Washington

Armored personnel carriers of the Ghanaian army
Courtesy Embassy of Ghana, Washington

forces, the government announced that it had foiled yet another attempted coup. The attempt was led by Major Courage Quarshigah, a popular officer in the Ghanaian armed forces, former commandant of the Ghana Military Academy, and a former close ally of Rawlings. Quarshigah and four other army officers were arrested. They were accused of planning to assassinate Rawlings as part of the coup, but several of the accused allegedly favored a return to constitutional rule under a civilian government.

Despite the so-called Quarshigah Affair and other attempted coups, Rawlings remained in control of the PNDC and the armed forces, which he commanded from September 1989 until June 1990. An Economic Recovery Program (ERP), supported by the International Monetary Fund (IMF—see Glossary) and the World Bank (see Glossary), was adopted to improve the lives of Ghanaians. The Rawlings regime also acceded to popular demands for a democratic, multiparty election. Despite these accomplishments, however, corruption, authoritarianism, and the misuse of power have continued to be significant problems.

The Military and the Economy

Military costs have fluctuated widely since independence. During the Nkrumah era, the government maintained a large, relatively well-equipped military for reasons of national prestige. After the 1966 coup, the ruling NLC sought to improve the country's economy by lowering military spending. The NLC, however, was unwilling to reduce military manpower for fear of alienating the armed forces; instead, it saved money by canceling plans to purchase new equipment. To update its military inventory, Ghana strengthened links with nations such as Britain, Canada, and the United States, all of which represented possible sources of military assistance.

Since the downfall of Nkrumah, the level of Ghana's military spending has fluctuated widely, partly because of several major currency devaluations. According to the World Bank, however, Ghana's military spending has declined overall. In 1972 Ghana earmarked about 7.9 percent of total expenditures for defense, a figure that by 1989 was down to 3.2 percent. Since then, defense expenditures have declined even further. In 1992, the most recent year for which reliable figures are available, Ghana allocated about US$105 million for the armed forces, or less than 2 percent of total budgetary expenditures.

Armed Forces Mission, Organization, and Strength

Since independence, the mission of the armed forces has been twofold: to protect Ghana's territorial integrity from foreign aggression, and to maintain internal security. In the mid-1990s, ground forces held the dominant role in the defense establishment. In terms of organization, the military is composed of the army and its subordinate air and naval elements, numbering in all 6,850 active-duty personnel in 1994. The military command structure extends from the minister of defense in the national government to commanders in the field. Military units are deployed in the capital, Accra, and in Ghana's border regions. The 5,000-member Ghanaian army, which has an eastern and a western command, is organized into two brigades, with six infantry battalions; one reconnaissance regiment, with two reconnaissance squadrons; one airborne force, with one paratroop company; one artillery regiment; and one field engineer regiment.

Military equipment consists predominantly of older weapons of British, Brazilian, Swiss, Swedish, Israeli, and Finnish origin. Servicing of all types of equipment has been extremely poor, largely because of inadequate maintenance capabilities. As a result, foreign military advisers or technicians perform all major maintenance tasks. Included in the Ghanaian inventory are FV–601 Saladin and EE–9 Cascavel reconnaissance vehicles; MOWAG Piranha armored personnel carriers; 81mm and 120mm mortars; 84mm recoilless launchers; and 14.5mm ZPU–4 and 23mm ZU–23–2 air defense guns.

The 1,000-member Ghanaian air force consists of one counterinsurgency squadron equipped with MB–326K and MB–339 aircraft; three transport squadrons equipped with F–27 and F–28 Fokkers, a C–212 Aviocar, and Skyvan aircraft; and one training squadron equipped with MB–326F, Bulldog, and L–29 Delfin aircraft. The air force also has Bell, Mi–2 Hoplite, and SA–319 helicopters. It operates from bases in Accra (headquarters and main transport base), Tamale (combat and training base), Takoradi (training base), and Kumasi (support base). The air force's mission is to perform counterinsurgency operations and to provide logistical support to the army. Since independence, performance has been hindered by a lack of spare parts and by poor maintenance capabilities. On September 18, 1987, Air Force Commander J.E.A. Kotei announced plans to begin internal passenger service to supplement the efforts of Ghana Airways. Under this program, the government authorized the transformation of Tamale airport into a civil-military airport.

Ghana's navy provides coastal defense, fisheries protection, and security on Lake Volta. During World War II, the Gold Coast Volunteer Naval Force, which had been established in 1936, provided sea patrols and conducted mine-detection and neutralization operations along the coast. In 1959 the Ghanaian government established a true navy and assigned a former Royal Navy officer the duties of chief of staff with the rank of commodore. In 1961 a Ghanaian army brigadier replaced the British commodore. On July 14, 1989, the navy recommissioned two ships, *GNS Yogaga* and *GNS Dzata*, at the western naval base in Sekondi. The vessels had been refurbished by a British shipyard, Swan Hunter. In 1994 the navy was organized into an eastern command, with headquarters at Tema, and a western command, with headquarters at Sekondi. The naval inventory includes two Kromantse-class corvettes and two Achimote-class and two Dazata-class fast attack craft.

The Ghanaian navy has experienced low readiness rates because of spare parts shortages. In the late 1980s and early 1990s, budgetary constraints and a lack of serviceable equipment forced the navy to reduce its manpower from about 1,200 to approximately 850 personnel. Nevertheless, in 1990 Ghana's navy deployed some of its ships to support the Economic Community of West African States Monitoring Group (ECOMOG) mission in Liberia. In late 1992, two of the navy's ships were in France for refitting.

Paramilitary forces consist of the 5,000-member People's Militia, which serves as a home guard force and is responsible for preventing and controlling civil disturbances and insurrection. A small, elite Presidential Guard consisting of one infantry battalion provides security for the president. The Ghanaian government also has created a National Civil Defence Force (also known as the Committees for the Defence of the Revolution), which includes all citizens able to perform military service. According to the country's defense plans, the National Civil Defence Force would be required to guard important installations in times of crisis to relieve pressure on the regular armed forces.

Military Manpower, Training, and Morale

Manpower

There is a two-year national service requirement for male

Ghanaians, but military manpower levels have always been maintained by voluntary enlistment. A limited number of women also serve in the armed forces, but all women are found in administrative positions, not in operational units. Since mid-1988, all national service personnel have undergone a six-month military training program that stresses drilling, weapons handling, physical fitness, and first aid.

The armed forces offer commissions to qualified individuals from civilian life or to those who have completed cadet training. The term of service usually is five years with reserve obligations thereafter. Most technical services officers are selected from civilian life on the basis of professional qualifications. Recruits for combat or combat support branches are required to complete two years of cadet training before receiving their commissions.

Enlisted personnel are recruited for particular service branches to satisfy specific branch needs. Enlistments last up to twelve years with various active- and reserve-duty options. Reenlistments are authorized for a total of eighteen years. In addition, unit commanders are empowered to extend this term of service on a case-by-case basis. Specifically, enlisted recruits for the technical services are required to possess at least a middle school or junior secondary school education. All personnel must pass a physical examination and be at least eighteen years of age.

Training

Military training for all officer candidates of the army, air force, and navy is conducted at the Ghana Military Academy near Accra. Entrance to the academy is by examination, and the curriculum includes military and general subjects. Army cadets train for two years. At the end of the first six months, a few candidates may be selected to finish their studies at foreign institutions such as the Royal Military Academy at Sandhurst in Britain. The Ghana Military Academy, established in 1960, also provides short courses in higher military education for the officers of the three services. The best senior officers are selected periodically to attend the Army Staff College at Camberley in Britain or one of several other senior service schools in foreign countries.

The Armed Forces Training School at Kumasi trains army, air force, and navy recruits. The basic army training course lasts nine months and is followed by advanced individual training in the assigned unit. This school also provides specialist training. A parachute training school is located at Tamale and a jungle warfare school at Achiasi.

The army has conducted numerous field exercises with a variety of code names, including Hot Foot, Deep Thrust, Operation Swift Sword, Full Impact, and Starlight Stretch. These exercises test an array of skills. Full Impact 88, for example, marked the first time that Ghanaian army, air force, and navy units trained together. Deep Thrust 89 emphasized jungle warfare, junior leadership, and physical fitness. Starlight Stretch 89, which was held at Daboya in the northern region, improved low-level operations for company groups in the infantry battalion.

To enhance regional collective security, the Ghanaian army also has participated in joint exercises with Burkina Faso (Burkina, formerly Upper Volta). In November 1983 and in early 1985, the two countries sponsored joint exercises code-named Bold Union and Teamwork 85. The latter involved 5,500 troops and ninety officers from the two armed forces. These personnel engaged in maneuvers in which government soldiers defended themselves against a battalion-strong enemy force which had installed itself on Dwarf Island near the strategically critical Akosombo Dam.

The Ghanaian government subsequently pledged to help defend its neighbor in case of armed aggression. As a result of this agreement, Ghana and Burkina have continued joint exercises. In late 1986, a 3,000-member contingent of soldiers from Ghana and Burkina participated in a week-long exercise to test the combat readiness of their armed forces and security agencies. Then, in September 1987, the two countries staged a three-day exercise code-named Operation Vulcan in northern Ghana's Tamale region. During this exercise, paratroopers of the two countries parachuted into "friendly" territory to give support to ground forces under simulated enemy fire. Later that year, Ghana and Burkina concluded a three-month exercise in which four British trainers participated.

Historically, the Ghanaian air force has relied on foreign military assistance from India, Israel, Canada, Britain, and Italy for pilot training. In early 1959, Indian and Israeli officers supervised the formation of Ghana's air force. In mid-1959, an Indian air force senior air commodore established a headquarters for the service at Accra. In July 1959, Israeli air force instructors trained the first group of Ghanaian cadet fliers at

Accra International Airport. Two years later, ten Ghanaians qualified as pilots.

In late 1960, Ghana terminated the training agreement with Israel. Shortly thereafter, Accra and London signed an accord whereby 150 officers and airmen from the British Royal Air Force (RAF) assumed responsibility for training the Ghanaian air force. The commander of this RAF contingent also replaced the Indian air commodore as chief of staff of the Ghanaian air force. In mid-1961 a small group from the Royal Canadian Air Force (RCAF) supplemented the British mission. In September 1961, as part of his Africanization program, Nkrumah appointed an army brigadier as chief of staff and relieved all RAF officers of their commands. The RAF contingent remained in Ghana, however, to help develop the Ghanaian air force as part of the British Joint Services Training Mission.

In more recent years, Ghana has relied on Nigeria for air force training. In late 1989, twenty-five Ghanaian pilots and technicians graduated from various training programs in Kano, Nigeria. In 1989 Nigeria donated twelve Czech-built L–29 Delfin trainers to the Ghanaian air force. The Ghanaian and Nigerian air forces also conducted joint operations under the auspices of the ECOMOG peacekeeping force in Liberia in the early 1990s.

Naval training has concentrated on improving the skills of personnel both on shore and at sea. In addition, the Ghanaian navy regularly participates in joint air-and-sea search-and-rescue operations. The United States navy has supplemented these efforts by allowing United States ships participating in the West African Training Cruise to visit Ghana. During the 1990 training cruise, the United States donated an array of educational materials and conducted a symposium on fisheries enforcement. Inclement weather forced the cancellation of a joint amphibious exercise, however.

The paramilitary People's Militia usually receives its training during evenings, weekends, and short periods of attachment to regular army units. The Presidential Guard, which evolved from the President's Own Guard Regiment established by Nkrumah, enjoys a higher training priority and commands a greater proportion of the military's resources (see The Development of the Modern Army, this ch.).

Morale

Morale in the Ghanaian armed forces has been influenced by several factors. During the early postindependence period, military morale suffered because of ethnic tensions and the low esteem attached to the armed forces by the civilian sector. The politicization of the army and jealousy between officers and noncommissioned officers also lowered morale. During the years of military rule, morale gradually improved. In the ranks, however, esprit de corps has generally remained low because of poor pay and a lack of opportunities for education and promotion.

A 1979 purge of the armed forces reversed this trend. By the late 1980s, morale throughout the armed forces was generally good because service conditions and the public perception of the military had improved. Also, the PNDC had improved the professionalism of the army. After Ghana contributed troops to the ECOMOG peacekeeping force in Liberia in mid-1990, however, morale declined once more, especially among enlisted personnel, who opposed what they perceived to be an open-ended commitment to a war irrelevant to Ghana. Controversy arose when some individual Ghanaian soldiers exploited their position as peacekeepers to enrich themselves by engaging in black-market activities and other questionable behavior.

Uniforms, Ranks, and Insignia

Each component service has its own distinctive uniforms and insignia. At independence Ghana opted to retain the British order of military ranks and corresponding insignia. In the 1990s, Ghanaian ranks are still identical with British ranks and insignia except that Ghana has substituted a black star or the Ghanaian coat of arms for the British crown on appropriate insignia (see fig. 14; fig. 15).

Officers in the army, air force, and navy and enlisted men in the army and air force wear their insignia on the shoulder. Naval enlisted men wear their insignia as cap badges except for leading seamen and first and second class petty officers, who wear cap badges and shoulder insignia. Field uniforms of the army are olive green, those of the navy are dark blue, and those of the air force are light blue. Service caps are identical with British service caps.

Foreign Military Assistance

Like most African armed forces, the Ghanaian military has depended on foreign military assistance since independence. Initially, Ghana looked to the West, especially Britain, for equipment, training, and command support. As Ghanaian politics became radicalized and the world divided along East-West lines, Ghana's military diversified its sources of military aid by developing ties to radical states such as the former Soviet Union, China, the German Democratic Republic (GDR, or East Germany), and Libya. After the Cold War ended, Ghana again turned to the West for most of its military needs.

Britain

Between 1958 and 1961, Britain not only satisfied all Ghana's military requirements but also allowed British military personnel to serve in various command positions in the Ghanaian armed forces. By the end of 1961, the British had trained forty-three Ghanaian army cadets at Sandhurst and thirty-four at the British Officer Cadet School, Eaton Hall.

Although it initially had opposed the formation of a Ghanaian air force and navy, Britain eventually agreed to help train personnel from these services. In 1960 the British instituted an air force training and supply program on condition that the Indian and Israeli advisers who had established the air force were withdrawn. Additionally, between 1960 and 1963, Britain supplied twelve Chipmunk trainers, three Heron transports, and nine Whirlwind and Wessex helicopters.

The Ghanaian navy also benefited from British training. Each year from 1960 to 1966, four or five Ghanaian naval cadets attended the Britannia Royal Naval College at Dartmouth. By early 1967, eighty-seven Ghanaian naval officers and 740 enlisted personnel were serving in British home bases or were receiving training with the Royal Navy. There also were twenty-seven officers and forty senior enlisted personnel from the Royal Navy in Ghanaian command and training positions.

In April 1962, Accra allowed Britain to consolidate its military presence in Ghana by creating the Joint Services Training Team (JSTT). This organization, which was composed of officers and ranks from the three services under the command of a brigadier, began its work with a total personnel strength of 248 officers and men. The JSTT provided training and advisory support; some British officers also assumed command positions in the Ghanaian air force and navy. There were no British commanders in the army. The JSTT continued to function until 1971, when Ghana terminated its training agreement with Britain.

GHANAIAN RANK	2D LIEUTENANT	LIEUTENANT	CAPTAIN	MAJOR	LIEUTENANT COLONEL	COLONEL	BRIGADIER	MAJOR GENERAL	LIEUTENANT GENERAL	GENERAL	FIELD MARSHAL
ARMY											
U.S. RANK TITLE	2D LIEUTENANT	1ST LIEUTENANT	CAPTAIN	MAJOR	LIEUTENANT COLONEL	COLONEL	BRIGADIER GENERAL	MAJOR GENERAL	LIEUTENANT GENERAL	GENERAL	GENERAL OF THE ARMY
GHANAIAN RANK	PILOT OFFICER	FLYING OFFICER	FLIGHT LIEUTENANT	SQUADRON LEADER	WING COMMANDER	GROUP CAPTAIN	AIR COMMODORE	AIR VICE MARSHAL	AIR MARSHAL	AIR CHIEF MARSHAL	MARSHAL OF THE AIR FORCE
AIR FORCE										NO INSIGNIA	NO INSIGNIA
U.S. RANK TITLE	2D LIEUTENANT	1ST LIEUTENANT	CAPTAIN	MAJOR	LIEUTENANT COLONEL	COLONEL	BRIGADIER GENERAL	MAJOR GENERAL	LIEUTENANT GENERAL	GENERAL	GENERAL OF THE AIR FORCE
GHANAIAN RANK	NO RANK	SUB-LIEUTENANT	LIEUTENANT	LIEUTENANT COMMANDER	COMMANDER	CAPTAIN	COMMODORE	REAR ADMIRAL	VICE ADMIRAL	ADMIRAL	ADMIRAL OF THE FLEET
NAVY										NO INSIGNIA	NO INSIGNIA
U.S. RANK TITLE	ENSIGN	LIEUTENANT JUNIOR GRADE	LIEUTENANT	LIEUTENANT COMMANDER	COMMANDER	CAPTAIN	REAR ADMIRAL LOWER HALF	REAR ADMIRAL UPPER HALF	VICE ADMIRAL	ADMIRAL	FLEET ADMIRAL

Figure 14. Officer Ranks and Insignia, 1994

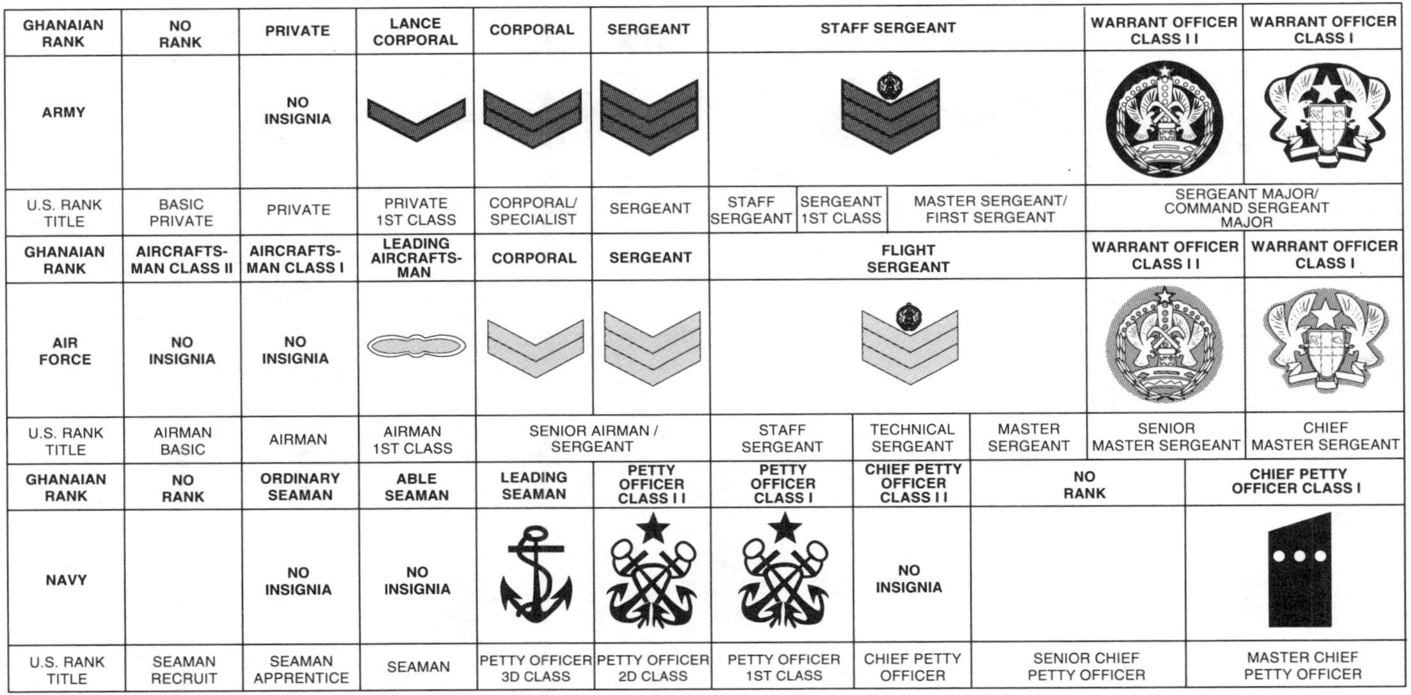

GHANAIAN RANK	NO RANK	PRIVATE	LANCE CORPORAL	CORPORAL	SERGEANT	STAFF SERGEANT			WARRANT OFFICER CLASS I I	WARRANT OFFICER CLASS I
ARMY		**NO INSIGNIA**								
U.S. RANK TITLE	BASIC PRIVATE	PRIVATE	PRIVATE 1ST CLASS	CORPORAL/ SPECIALIST	SERGEANT	STAFF SERGEANT	SERGEANT 1ST CLASS	MASTER SERGEANT/ FIRST SERGEANT	SERGEANT MAJOR/ COMMAND SERGEANT MAJOR	
GHANAIAN RANK	**AIRCRAFTS-MAN CLASS II**	**AIRCRAFTS-MAN CLASS I**	**LEADING AIRCRAFTS-MAN**	**CORPORAL**	**SERGEANT**	**FLIGHT SERGEANT**			**WARRANT OFFICER CLASS I I**	**WARRANT OFFICER CLASS I**
AIR FORCE	**NO INSIGNIA**	**NO INSIGNIA**								
U.S. RANK TITLE	AIRMAN BASIC	AIRMAN	AIRMAN 1ST CLASS	SENIOR AIRMAN / SERGEANT		STAFF SERGEANT	TECHNICAL SERGEANT	MASTER SERGEANT	SENIOR MASTER SERGEANT	CHIEF MASTER SERGEANT
GHANAIAN RANK	**NO RANK**	**ORDINARY SEAMAN**	**ABLE SEAMAN**	**LEADING SEAMAN**	**PETTY OFFICER CLASS I I**	**PETTY OFFICER CLASS I**	**CHIEF PETTY OFFICER CLASS I I**	**NO RANK**		**CHIEF PETTY OFFICER CLASS I**
NAVY		**NO INSIGNIA**	**NO INSIGNIA**				**NO INSIGNIA**			
U.S. RANK TITLE	SEAMAN RECRUIT	SEAMAN APPRENTICE	SEAMAN	PETTY OFFICER 3D CLASS	PETTY OFFICER 2D CLASS	PETTY OFFICER 1ST CLASS	CHIEF PETTY OFFICER	SENIOR CHIEF PETTY OFFICER		MASTER CHIEF PETTY OFFICER

Figure 15. Enlisted Ranks and Insignia, 1994

Even after Accra diversified its sources of foreign military assistance and Africanized the armed forces, however, Britain continued to be active in Ghana. In 1974–75 the Vosper Thornycroft shipyard refitted a corvette warship under a US$2.5 million contract. In 1978 Fairey Marine provided a Spear MK 2 Class coastal patrol boat to the Ghanaian navy. In March 1984, the British firm Plessy reported that it had arranged to furnish Ghana with equipment for air traffic control. The British also received an August 1985 contract for about US$75,000 worth of electronics equipment. A few years later, Britain agreed to refurbish four Skyvan military and VIP transports; by mid-1991, the British had completed work on two of these aircraft and delivered them to Ghana. A limited number of British military personnel also participated in joint exercises with the Ghanaian armed forces.

Canada

From 1962 to 1968, Canada maintained a significant military presence in Ghana. This relationship began on January 8, 1962, when Ottawa established a thirty-member Canadian Armed Forces Training Team (CAFTTG) to assist with the training of young Ghanaian officers. Except for pay and allowances, Ghana bore the cost of this training program. During their time in Ghana, CAFTTG personnel served at the Teshi Military Academy (later Ghana Military Academy), the Military Hospital, the Ministry of Defence, Army Headquarters, the Armed Forces Training School (Kumasi), the Air Force Station (Takoradi), the Airborne School (Tamale), and the Training School (Accra). RCAF pilots also augmented the RAF team that was training Ghanaian air force pilots. In 1969, the Canadian government decided to phase out all military assistance programs in developing countries. Ottawa later reversed this decision, however, and established a one-man CAFTTG office in Ghana until 1982, when this individual returned to Canada.

Apart from training assistance, Canada also provided a modest amount of military equipment to Ghana during the immediate postindependence period. Shortly after the Ghanaian air force was formed, Ghana purchased numerous aircraft from Canada, including fourteen Beavers, twelve Otters, and eight twin-engined Caribou transports.

Soviet Union

In January 1958, Ghana and the Soviet Union opened diplomatic relations. According to many Western observers, Moscow planned to use Ghana as a base to extend its influence and communism throughout West Africa. Nkrumah, on the other hand, hoped that close relations with the Soviet Union would enable him to diversify Ghana's sources of military assistance. Ghana temporarily achieved its goal; Moscow, however, failed to establish a communist foothold in West Africa.

The two countries maintained a multifaceted military relationship. In 1961 Ghana purchased eight Ilyushin–18s, on credit, at more than US$1.5 million each. High operating coats forced the Ghanaian government to return four of these aircraft to the Soviet Union and to transfer the other four to Ghana Airways. Two years later, Moscow presented an Mi–4 helicopter to Nkrumah as a personal gift. In 1965, after a year of internal unrest and several assassination attempts against him, Nkrumah concluded an arms deal with the Soviet Union for the purchase of weapons for the presidential guard. The shipment included twenty-four light artillery pieces, twenty-one medium mortars, fifteen antiaircraft guns, twenty heavy machine guns, and a large amount of ammunition.

Apart from these military sales and the gift of a helicopter, the Soviet Union deployed an array of military, security, and technical advisers to Ghana in the 1960s. In 1964, for example, Soviet crews manned four patrol boats based at Tema; according to anti-Nkrumah elements, these patrol boats cruised the coast of Ghana and carried arms to opposition groups in nearby countries. By early 1966, the Soviet Union had begun construction of a new air base near Tamale in northern Ghana. Soviet instructors worked at secret Bureau of African Affairs camps, at the Kwame Nkrumah Ideological Institute in Winneba, and at numerous other security and military training facilities. Additionally, at least seventy-six Ghanaian army officer cadets attended military schools in the Soviet Union. Ghana Young Pioneers also received training at Komsomol schools in the Soviet Union.

After the downfall of Nkrumah in 1966, up to 1,100 Soviet personnel were expelled from Ghana. The new government broke diplomatic relations with Moscow and terminated all military assistance agreements. In the following years, Soviet-Ghanaian cooperation was minimal. In the mid-1980s, Ghana unsuccessfully petitioned the Soviet Union to reactivate some of the projects that had been abandoned after Nkrumah was overthrown. In late 1986, Ghana's National Secretariat of Committees for the Defence of the Revolution reportedly signed an agreement with the Soviet Union for assistance in training national cadres. At the end of the 1980s, an unknown number of secret service personnel and commandos received training in the Soviet Union. As of late 1994, there was no indication that Ghana and Russia, the most powerful of the successor states of the former Soviet Union, had concluded any military assistance agreements.

German Democratic Republic

Like other major communist powers, East Germany sought to exploit Kwame Nkrumah's radicalism to erode Western influence in Ghana and to use Ghana as a base for spreading communism throughout West Africa. The relationship between the two countries began in 1964, when Ghana's Bureau of African Affairs approached the East German Trade Mission in Accra and requested intelligence training for its staff. Subsequently, two East German officers who worked for the Ministry of State Security traveled to Ghana to assess the bureau's training requirements. One of these officers remained in Ghana and inaugurated a "Secret Service and Intelligence Work" course for seven members of the Bureau of African Affairs. This officer later offered an "Intelligence Work Under Diplomatic Cover" course for six other people who worked in the Bureau of African Affairs and who eventually were assigned to posts in Zambia, Nigeria, Kenya, Sierra Leone, Tanzania, and Burundi. East Germany also helped the Ghanaian government to create an intelligence section in the Bureau of African Affairs. These activities ended after Nkrumah's downfall.

China

Next to the former Soviet Union, China was the most active communist nation in Ghana. Chinese activities began in October 1962, when Beijing provided a loan for the construction of two arms factories; Ghana, however, never used the funds. Two years later, the two countries signed a secret agreement for the provision of military equipment and advisers for Ghana's "freedom fighters." In late 1964, a five-member team of Chinese guerrilla warfare experts arrived at Half Assini Training Camp. Shortly thereafter, this team inaugurated a twenty-day course that consisted of training in the manufacture and the use of explosives, guerrilla tactics, and "basic guiding and thinking on armed struggle." Other Chinese instructors offered another course at Obenimase Camp in Ashanti Region on strategy and tactics, explosives, weapons use, telecommunications, and battlefield first aid. An unknown number of Ghanaians also attended a three-month espionage training course in China. Students from many other African nations, including Zaire, Niger, Cameroon, Fernando Po, Tanzania, Zambia, Rwanda, Togo, Côte d'Ivoire, Burkina, Gabon, Nigeria, and Guinea, also received intelligence training from the Chinese in Ghana.

After the 1966 change of government, Ghana expelled 430 Chinese nationals, including three intelligence officers and thirteen guerrilla warfare specialists. Although they resumed diplomatic relations in 1972, Ghana and China never re-initiated significant military ties.

Israel

In April 1959, Israel, with help from India, supervised the establishment of the Ghanaian air force. A small Israeli team also trained aircraft maintenance personnel and radio technicians at the Accra-based Air Force Trade Training School. Although the British persuaded Nkrumah to withdraw Israeli advisers from Ghana in 1960, Ghanaian pilots continued to receive some training at aviation schools in Israel. After Nkrumah's overthrow, Israeli military activities in Ghana ended.

United States

Military relations between Ghana and the United States have been minimal and have been concentrated in the International Military Education and Training (IMET) program, which includes professional military education, management, and technical training. Between fiscal year (FY) 1950 and FY 1990, the value of training under the IMET program amounted to US$3.5 million. Estimated IMET figures for FY 1991 were US$252,000; for FY 1992, US$175,000; and for FY 1993, US$250,000. No credits under the United States Foreign Military Sales program were given to Ghana after 1955; in FY 1995, however, $300,000 in credits was reportedly made available. Private United States companies received about US$905,000 worth of commercial export licenses for Ghanaian arms purchases from FY 1950 to FY 1990.

Italy

Since independence, Ghana has relied on Italy for an array of military aircraft. In early 1966, the Ghanaian air force established a jet fighter/ground-attack squadron, which was composed of seven Italian Aermacchi MB–326s (within two years, three of these aircraft crashed and were later replaced). A small group of Italian Air Force instructors supervised this squadron. In 1983 and 1984, the Ghanaian air force accepted delivery of eight SIAI–Marchetti SF–260TP turboprop trainers. In mid-1987, Ghana ordered two Aermacchi MB–339 jet trainers from Italy.

Libya

Little is known about the Ghanaian-Libyan military relationship. An unknown number of Libyan military personnel have participated in Ghanaian military exercises as observers. During the second Rawlings regime, an undetermined number of Libyan soldiers received jungle warfare training in Ghana. In May 1983, the Ghanaian government acknowledged that it had received unspecified quantities of military equipment, mostly artillery pieces and ammunition, as gifts from Libya. To all appearances, Accra's ties to Libya weakened after Ghana moved closer to the West in the late 1980s.

State Security Services

The origins of Ghana's police force lie in efforts by the British council of merchants to protect trading routes and depots. In 1830 the committee hired numerous guards and escorts. Fourteen years later, the British established the 120-member Gold Coast Militia and Police (GCMP). The authorities disbanded this force in 1860 and created a ninety-member corps called the Queen's Messengers. Military units assumed the GCMP's paramilitary duties.

During the Asante wars, the Queen's Messengers joined the Hausa Constabulary, imported from Nigeria, and formed the Gold Coast Armed Police Force. In 1876 the British reorganized this unit into the Gold Coast Constabulary, which was divided into two forces in 1901, with the paramilitary mission assigned to the Gold Coast Regiment and the police functions given to the Gold Coast Police Force. The Northern Territories Constabulary, which the British created in 1907, joined the Gold Coast Police Force shortly after World War I. This left the Gold Coast with one police force, a situation that prevailed until independence.

Ghanaian air force personnel on parade
Contingent of the Ghanaian navy on parade
Courtesy Embassy of Ghana, Washington

During the 1950s, the British instituted several changes in the Gold Coast Police Force to modernize, enlarge, and better equip the force. Of greater importance was Britain's decision to Africanize the police. During the first decade of this century, the British had restricted access to senior positions in all branches of the colonial administration. This restriction became a major concern of Ghanaian nationalists, who agitated against it, an action that gradually caused a reduction in the number of British officers. In 1951, for example, sixty-four of eighty senior police officers were foreigners; however, by 1958, only eleven of 128 senior officers were foreigners.

This Africanization continued under Nkrumah. In 1958 Nkrumah appointed the first Ghanaian police commissioner, E.R.T. Madjitey. By the early 1960s, the only expatriates who remained on the force were a few technical advisers and instructors. Nkrumah, however, distrusted the police. After an unsuccessful assassination attempt against Nkrumah in 1964 by a police constable, he disarmed the police, discharged nine senior officers, detained eight others, and removed the Border Guards unit from the police and placed it under military control. Nkrumah also reduced the size of the police force from 13,247 in 1964 to 10,709 in 1965.

After the demise of the Nkrumah regime, the size of the police force increased from 17,692 in 1966 to 19,895 in 1968. The government also restored the Border Guards unit to police control (in 1972 this unit again became an autonomous unit). By the early 1980s, the police enjoyed respect from most Ghanaians because, for the most part, they were not involved with government attempts to suppress political dissidents or to punish those suspected of trying to overthrow the Rawlings regime, duties normally assigned to the armed forces.

In 1993 Ghana's law enforcement establishment consisted of 351 police officers, 649 inspectors, and 15,191 personnel in other grades distributed among 479 stations. The national headquarters are in Accra; they operate under command of an inspector general. An eight-member Police Council, established in 1969, advises the inspector general on all personnel and policy matters. The inspector general supervises ten police regions, each commanded by an assistant commissioner of police. The police regions in turn are divided into districts, stations, and posts. The police service is composed of General Administration, Criminal Investigations Department, Special Branch, Police Hospital, and National Ambulance Service.

Recruitment into the police is conducted at the rank-and-file and the commissioned-officer levels. All recruits must be between eighteen and thirty-four years of age, must pass a medical examination, and must have no criminal record. Escort Police applicants must have at least basic facility in spoken English, General Police applicants must have completed middle school or junior secondary school, and officer corps applicants must hold a university degree.

Training for rank-and-file personnel in the Escort and the General Police forces is conducted at the Elmina police depot; Escort Police also have been trained at several regional depots. Since 1975 recruits have attended a nine-month course of instruction in physical training and drill, firearms use, unarmed combat, and first aid. Escort Police are given general education and instruction in patrol and escort duties. General Police are trained in criminal law and procedures, methods of investigation, current affairs, and social sciences.

The Accra Police College, established in 1959, offers a nine-month officer cadet course and two- to six-week refresher courses in general and technical subjects. Police officers staff the college; guest lecturers come from the police, other government agencies, and universities. The officer cadet course offers instruction in criminal law and procedures, laws of evidence, police administration, finance, social sciences, practical police work, and physical fitness. Upon graduation, cadets are sworn in and promoted to assistant superintendent.

Since the early 1990s, the reputation of the police has improved, primarily because fewer individual officers have used their positions to extort money from civilians. Moreover, an increasing number of police have been deployed overseas to support Ghana's commitment to international peacekeeping operations. In 1992–93, for example, a police contingent served with the United Nations Transitional Authority in Cambodia. In addition to supervising local police and maintaining law and order, this contingent also tried to prevent gross violations of human rights and fundamental freedoms.

Criminal Justice

Prior to the advent of British imperial rule, traditional law, which sought to maintain social equilibrium and to ensure communal solidarity, governed social relations among Ghana's peoples. Among the Talensi ethnic group of northern Ghana, for example, homicide was viewed as a transgression against the earth, one's ancestors, and the victim's lineage. Deterrence from crime or rehabilitation of an offender were not objectives of the legal system. Among the Asante, the same concern with social equilibrium and communal solidarity prevailed. Serious crimes such as murder, unintentional homicide, suicide, sexual offenses, treason, cowardice in war, witchcraft, and crimes against the chief were termed *oman akyiwade,* offenses that threatened the mystical communion between the community on the one hand and one's ancestors and Asante gods on the other. The authorities punished such behavior with a sentence of death in the case of murder or by the sacrifice of an appropriate animal in the case of lesser offenses. *Efisem,* or minor crimes, did not rupture this relationship; hence, an offender could repay his debt to society with a ritual *impata,* or compensation.

The British imposed upon Ghana's traditional societies criminal laws and penal systems designed to "keep the multitude in order" rather than to preserve the equilibrium between the human and spiritual worlds. The development of penal law, however, was uneven. From 1828 to 1842, a council of merchants exercised criminal jurisdiction in and around British forts on the coast. The council often abused this power, thereby alienating many Ghanaians. After creating the Gold Coast Colony in 1874, the British gradually reformed and improved the legal and the penal systems. After more than a century of legal evolution, the application of traditional law to criminal acts disappeared. Since 1961 the criminal law administered by the court system has been statutory and based on a Criminal Code. This code is founded on British common law, doctrines of equity, and general statutes which were in force in Britain in 1874, as amended by subsequent Ghanaian ordinances.

Criminal Code and Courts

Two of the three categories of offenses cited in the Criminal Code concern transgressions against the individual. The third category includes a series of offenses against public order, health and morality, and the security of the state, as well as piracy, perjury, rioting, vagrancy, and cruelty to animals. Several offenses reflect Ghana's traditional laws, including drumming with the intent to provoke disorder, cocoa smuggling, and settlement of private disputes by methods of traditional ordeal.

Criminal Court procedure is guided by the Criminal Procedure Code of 1960 as subsequently amended. As in British law, habeas corpus is allowed, and the courts are authorized to release suspects on bail. Ghana's legal system does not use grand juries, but, in accordance with constitutionally guaranteed fundamental rights, defendants charged with a criminal offense are entitled to a trial by jury.

Five degrees of offenses are recognized in Ghana. Capital offenses, for which the maximum penalty is death by hanging, include murder, treason, and piracy. First-degree felonies punishable by life imprisonment are limited to manslaughter, rape, and mutiny. Second-degree felonies, punishable by ten years' imprisonment, include intentional and unlawful harm to persons, perjury, and robbery. Misdemeanors, punishable by various terms of imprisonment, include assault, theft, unlawful assembly, official corruption, and public nuisances. Increased penalties apply to individuals with a prior criminal record. Corporal punishment is not permitted. Punishments for juveniles are subject to two restrictions: no death sentence may be passed against a juvenile, and no juvenile under age seventeen may be imprisoned. Regulations and laws such as these are not applied equitably. Indeed, defendants habitually resort to one or another measure to avoid or ameliorate punishment.

The Ghanaian court system is a multifaceted organization. The Supreme Court of Ghana, which consists of the chief justice and four other justices, is the final court of appeal and has jurisdiction over matters relating to the enforcement or the interpretation of constitutional law. The Court of Appeal, which includes the chief justice and not fewer than five other judges, has jurisdiction to hear and to determine appeals from any judgment, decree, or High Court of Justice order. The High Court of Justice, which consists of the chief justice and not fewer than twelve other justices, has jurisdiction in all matters, civil and criminal, other than those involving treason.

Before mid-1993, lower courts consisted of circuit courts, which had jurisdiction in civil matters and in all criminal cases except offenses in which the maximum punishment was death or the offense was treason; district or magistrate courts, with jurisdiction over civil suits and criminal cases except first-degree felonies; and juvenile courts, empowered to hear charges against persons under seventeen years of age. In 1982 the PNDC created a parallel hierarchy of special courts called public tribunals, which exercised only criminal jurisdiction, including some offenses under the Criminal Code (see The Judiciary, ch. 4). Members of the public tribunals and their panels were mostly lay people who sat with lawyers. Proceedings were often swift and could result in death sentences. There were no provisions for appeals until 1984, when the PNDC established the National Public Tribunal, which consisted of three to five members, to receive appeals from lower tribunals. Its decisions, however, were final and could not be appealed. In 1982 a five- to seven-member Special Military Tribunal was also established to handle crimes committed by military personnel.

In July 1993, the Parliament of the Fourth Republic incorporated the public tribunals into the existing lower courts system, except for the National Public Tribunal, which was abolished. A new hierarchy of lower courts was established consisting of community tribunals, circuit tribunals, and regional tribunals. The tribunals have original jurisdiction in both civil and criminal cases, and decisions can be appealed through higher courts. In late 1994, indications were that the new tribunals had not yet begun to function in many parts of the country, at least partly for lack of funds.

Prison System

There was no prison system in traditional Ghanaian societies. In the mid-nineteenth century, the British council of merchants established a network of harsh prisons in forts such as Cape Coast Castle. By 1850 four such prisons could hold up to 129 prisoners. Convicts usually worked on road gangs. The Prisons Ordinance of 1860 outlined regulations for the safe-keeping of prisoners. Later ordinances further defined the nature of the colony's prison regimen, or "separate system," which required solitary confinement by night, penal labor, and a minimum diet. By the early 1900s, British colonial officials administered the country's prisons and employed Europeans to work as guards in the prisons. After World War II, Ghanaians gradually replaced these individuals. By 1962 Ghanaians staffed all positions in the prison system.

Under Nkrumah the government showed little concern for reform and modernization of the penal system. After Nkrumah's overthrow, the National Liberation Council (NLC) authorized a civilian commission to investigate the prison system and to make recommendations for improvements. The commission's report, issued in 1968, revealed numerous problems. Of the country's twenty-nine prisons, nine were judged unfit for human habitation, two were suitable only for police lockups, and thirteen were appropriate only for short-term detainment. Because of corruption and incompetence, however, the NLC failed to act upon the commission's recommendations. As a result, prison conditions continued to be substandard, with poor ventilation, sanitation, and food-preparation facilities.

Ministerial responsibility for the prison system has shifted periodically since independence, but the operation of prisons is fixed by statute and is divided into adult and juvenile correction. The former is governed by the Prisons Ordinance, which outlines rules for prison operation and treatment of prisoners. The constitution of 1969 established a Prison Service, the director of which is appointed by the chief executive and is responsible to the minister of interior. The Criminal Procedure Code determines procedures for handling young offenders.

The Prisons Service Board formulates prison policy and regulations and administers the country's prisons. The board consists of a Public Services Commission member as chairman, the prison services director, a medical officer of the Ghana Medical Association, a representative of the attorney general, the principal secretary of the Ministry of Employment and Social Welfare, and three other appointed members, one of whom must be a woman and two of whom must be representatives of religious organizations.

To ensure the welfare and the proper treatment of prisoners, the constitution requires the Prisons Service Board to ensure that prison conditions are reviewed at intervals of not less than two years. Reports of unjustified treatment of prisoners and recommendations for reform measures are required of the board.

The prisons service is a career establishment with a promotion system based on training and merit; its members have retirement privileges similar to those of other public services. Prisons service standards require one staff member for every three prisoners, but the ratio in many institutions has risen to one to five or more.

Although understaffing has been a long-standing problem, the quality of prison officers and guards has improved over the years. Women are included in both categories. Although recruited from all over the country, prison personnel largely come from the Ewe and Ga ethnic groups. The prisons service maintains a training school and depot at Mamobi, near Accra. This facility offers a six-month training course for senior staff members, special courses for matrons, and preparatory courses for promotion examinations.

In 1992, the most recent year for which data were available, the prison system consisted of twenty-seven institutions, including six central prisons for men at Accra (Ussher Fort and James Fort), Sekondi, Kumasi, Tamale, and Nsawam; two for women at Ekuasi (near Sekondi) and at Ho; fifteen local prisons sited throughout the country, six of which have annexes for women; and two "open" prisons, one at James Camp near Accra, and the other at Ankaful near Cape Coast. About 70 percent of commitments are for less than six months. Outside the criminal justice system, the Ministry of Employment and Social Welfare operates probation homes in Accra and Jakobu Ashanti for boys and in Kumasi for girls; detention centers in Accra, Sekondi, Cape Coast, and Kumasi handle juveniles of both sexes.

Persons convicted and sentenced to a period of police supervision (parole) rather than imprisonment are subject to a licensing arrangement. Violations of the license terms are punishable by one-year imprisonment. Upon convicting an offender of any age, a court may release that individual on probation for six months to three years. Failure to comply with the terms of the probation can result in the probationer's having to serve the sentence for the original offense. Probation has been used mainly for young persons.

Human Rights

Ever since the Nkrumah government of the late 1950s and early 1960s, successive Ghanaian governments have devised policies to contain or to eliminate political opposition. Observers, both domestic and international, point to the Preventive Detention Act of 1958 as the first major official act of human rights infringement. Subsequently, international human rights organizations such as Amnesty International and Africa Watch have reported many cases of abuse.

The NLC, which ousted Nkrumah in 1966, used authoritarian tactics against real and imagined adversaries. The Busia government, which followed the NLC, also employed harsh measures against its opponents. Beginning in 1972 when Acheampong seized power, respect for the state and its institutions and laws withered, a development that in turn caused an

President Jerry John Rawlings, on an official visit to Washington in March 1995, discussed Ghana's role in international peacekeeping, regional stability in West Africa, trade, and mutual cooperation with President William J. Clinton.
Courtesy The White House

increase in human rights violations. In 1979 Jerry Rawlings sought to redress this situation by launching an army mutiny, which led to several executions, including those of three former heads of state.

Following a second coup on December 31, 1981, Rawlings promised to put power in the hands of the people by revolutionizing the country's political and economic system. To achieve this goal, Rawlings suspended the constitution, banned political parties, and arrested numerous party leaders. On February 18, 1983, the Rawlings government promulgated PNDC Law 42, the Provisional National Defence Council (Establishment) Proclamation (Supplementary and Consequential Provisions) Law, which was retroactive to December 31, 1981. According to Amnesty International, this law gave the PNDC and its chairman, Rawlings, "wide and apparently arbitrary power over the citizens of Ghana." Additionally, Amnesty International voiced concern about the establishment of public tribunals to try political criminals, the detention without trial of suspected government opponents, the imprisonment after an unfair trial of such people, reports of arbitrary killings by armed forces personnel, and the beating and ill treatment of political opponents and criminals by armed forces personnel.

Since the late 1980s, Ghana has continued to experience human rights problems. These include restrictions on such basic rights as freedom of speech, freedom of the press, freedom of religion, and freedom of assembly; the right of citizens to change their government; and due process of law. In June 1989, Ghanaian authorities established regulations for registering all religious organizations, froze the assets of four churches, and expelled expatriate missionaries who were Jehovah's Witnesses or Mormons. Additionally, the PNDC detained the president and the secretary general of the Ghana Bar Association without charge for more than a week after the association announced its intention to hold a conference commemorating the 1982 murder of three judges by soldiers. After the association canceled its plans, the government released the president and the secretary general.

Ghanaian authorities also arrested numerous American citizens who belonged to a religious group known as the Black Hebrews and held them without charge for lengthy periods. In September 1989, the Ministry of Defence ordered the imprisonment of Major Courage Quarshigah and four others for "their alleged involvement in activities which could have compromised the security of the state," that is, for having attempted a coup. Eventually, the government detained another group of five people in connection with the so-called Quarshigah Affair. By the end of 1989, there were about 200 political detainees and prisoners. The government failed to respond to appeals by Amnesty International to investigate reported mistreatment of these detainees and prisoners.

Significant restrictions on personal freedoms continued in 1990. Summary arrests and detention without formal charges were also numerous. Additionally, Lebanese and other resident foreign businessmen were jailed and held without formal charges and without benefit of trial. In August 1990, authorities charged the chairman and other officials of the Movement for Freedom and Justice, a political group that advocated greater respect for human rights and democratization, with conspiracy and publication of a false statement regarding their detention. The movement's officials later retracted their charge of illegal detention and apologized to the government.

According to Africa Watch, the Ghanaian government in 1991 continued to hold at least seventy-six political prisoners and other detainees. In a radio interview on May 31, 1991, Secretary for Foreign Affairs Obed Asamoah claimed that some of these detainees were subversives. If they were brought to trial, Asamoah added, they would be convicted and executed. In late

1991, the PNDC arrested several opposition leaders for criticizing the Rawlings regime. Human-rights advocates also reported various examples of mistreatment of prisoners, such as keeping them in isolation for long periods and in dark, small cells without clothes or bedding. During political demonstrations, the police were often accused of using excessive force against antigovernment elements.

With the introduction of the 1992 constitution, observers hoped that Ghana's human rights record would improve because the new constitution contains a system of checks and balances, it guarantees basic human rights and freedoms, and it provides for an autonomous organization called the Commission on Human Rights and Administrative Justice. This commission, established in September 1993, is empowered to investigate alleged human rights violations, and it may take action to remedy proven abuses.

When the commission uncovers a human rights violation, it can seek resolution through negotiation, report the incident to the attorney general or auditor general, or institute proceedings. As of late 1994, the commission had received some 2,500 complaints and petitions from Ghanaians with human rights grievances against present and past governments, of which about 1,000 had been dealt with.

Another prominent human rights organization is the Ghana Committee on Human and People's Rights. Established in early 1991 specifically to watch for and to publicize violations of basic freedoms, it was credited with contributing to an improved human rights climate in the early 1990s.

Military Trends

Like many African militaries, the Ghanaian armed forces are in a state of transition. In the past, the military was an important instrument of state power, the purposes of which were to defend the country's national security, to suppress domestic dissidents, and, when necessary, to assume the reins of government. In the 1990s, growing popular demands for a better material life, for democratization, and for respect for human rights are slowly changing the nature of Ghana's military establishment.

After seizing power in 1981, the Rawlings regime assigned a high priority to economic development, and it downplayed the necessity for a large, traditional military. As part of an international financial and economic aid program, the World Bank and the IMF forced Ghana to keep its military budget low. For this reason, there have been no major weapons purchases for at least a decade, and many of Ghana's more sophisticated weapons systems have fallen into disrepair. By the late 1980s, it had also become evident that most Ghanaians favored a multiparty, rather than a military, form of government and that they opposed the use of the armed forces as an instrument to silence political debate.

These trends are likely to continue for the foreseeable future. By the beginning of the twenty-first century, additional budget cuts doubtless will have further reduced the size of the Ghanaian armed forces. Moreover, the government will be increasingly unwilling or unable to finance the high costs of acquiring, operating, and maintaining advanced weapons.

Despite the inevitable downsizing of the Ghanaian military establishment, Accra undoubtedly will maintain and perhaps will increase its commitment to international peacekeeping forces. Ghana also is likely to support efforts to persuade the Organization of African Unity to take up the role of peacekeeper on the African continent. The success of Ghana's future participation in peacekeeping operations will depend on the ability of its armed forces to adapt to highly demanding service in far-off countries.

* * *

Historically, the Ghanaian armed forces have played a significant role in the life of the country. As a result, there is abundant literature about the growth and the development of the Ghanaian military. Useful historical works include Henry Brackenbury's *The Ashanti War: A Narrative,* Mary Alice Hodgson's *The Siege of Kumassi,* Alan Lloyd's *The Drums of Kumasi: The Story of the Ashanti Wars,* and Frederick Myatt's *The Golden Stool: An Account of the Ashanti War of 1900.*

The best account of the military during the colonial period is *The History of the Royal West African Frontier Force* by A. Haywood and F.A.S. Clarke. Other important studies of this era include Hugh Charles Clifford's *The Gold Coast Regiment in the East African Campaign* and Sir Charles Prestwood Lucas's *The Gold Coast and the War.*

The postindependence evolution of the Ghanaian armed forces is examined in Simon Baynham's *The Military and Politics in Nkrumah's Ghana,* Robert Pickney's *Ghana under Military*

Rule, 1966–1969, Albert Kwesi Ocran's *Politics of the Sword: A Personal Memoir on Military Involvement in Ghana and of Problems of Military Government,* and *Politicians and Soldiers in Ghana, 1966–1972,* edited by Dennis Austin and Robin Luckham.

Material about Ghana's military is also available in a variety of periodical sources, including *West Africa, African Defence Journal, Africa Research Bulletin,* and *Africa Confidential.* Other useful publications include *New African, Africa Events,* and *The Journal of Modern African Studies.* Two International Institute for Strategic Studies annuals, *The Military Balance* and *Strategic Survey,* are essential for anyone wishing to understand the evolution of Ghana's security forces. The same is true of three other annuals: *Africa Contemporary Record, Africa South of the Sahara,* and *World Armaments and Disarmament.* The last is published by the Stockholm International Peace Research Institute. (For further information and complete citations, see Bibliography.)

Appendix

Table

Table 1. *Metric Conversion Coefficients and Factors*

When you know	Multiply by	To find
Millimeters	0.04	inches
Centimeters	0.39	inches
Meters	3.3	feet
Kilometers	0.62	miles
Hectares (10,000^2)	2.47	acres
Square kilometers	0.39	square miles
Cubic meters	35.3	cubic feet
Liters	0.26	gallons
Kilograms	2.2	pounds
Metric tons	0.98	long tons
....	1.1	short tons
....	2,204	pounds
Degrees Celsius (Centigrade)	1.8 and add 32	degrees Fahrenheit

Table 2. *Population Distribution by Region, 1960, 1970, and 1984*[1] (in thousands)

Region	1960	1970	1984
Ashanti	1,109.1	1,481.7	2,090.1
Brong-Ahafo	587.9	766.5	1,206.6
Central	751.4	890.1	1,142.3
Eastern	777.3	1,209.8	1,680.9
Greater Accra	491.8[2]	903.4	1,431.1
Northern	531.6	727.6	1,164.6
Upper East	—[3]	542.9	772.7
Upper West	757.3[3]	319.9	438.[illegible]
Volta	1,094.2	947.3	1,211.9
Western	626.2	770.1	1,157.8
TOTAL	6,726.8	8,559.3	12,296.0

[1] Latest available data. Ghana's 1994 population is estimated at 17.2 million, but no regional breakdown is available.
[2] Represents only Accra administrative area. The rest of what is now Greater Accra Region was part of Eastern Region in 1960.
[3] In 1960 Upper East and Upper West regions were combined in Upper Region.

Source: Based on information from Ghana, *Monthly Economic Bulletin*, Accra, 3, May 1970, 2; Ghana, Statistical Service, *Quarterly Digest of Statistics*, Accra, December 1991, Table 95; and United States, Central Intelligence Agency, *The World Factbook*, Washington, 1994, 151.

Table 3. Population Density, Growth Rate, and Rural-Urban Distribution by Region, 1970-84

Region	Area[4]	Population Density[1]		Growth Rate[2]	Population Distribution[3]	
		1970	1984		Rural	Urban
Ashanti	24,389	61	86	2.5	67.5	32.5
Brong-Ahafo	39,557	19	31	3.3	73.4	26.6
Central	9,826	91	116	1.8	71.2	28.8
Eastern	19,323	63	87	2.4	72.3	27.7
Greater Accra	3,245	278	441	3.3	17.0	83.0
Northern	70,384	10	17	3.4	74.8	25.2
Upper East	8,842	61	87	2.6	87.1	12.9
Upper West	18,476	17	24	2.3	89.1	10.9
Volta	20,570	46	59	1.8	79.5	20.5
Western	23,921	32	48	3.0	77.4	22.6
GHANA	238,533	36	52	2.6	68.0	32.0

[1] Persons per square kilometer.
[2] Average annual compound rate for 1970–84 period, in percentages.
[3] In percentages, for 1984; towns with 5,000 or more inhabitants.
[4] In square kilometers.

Source: Based on information from Ghana, Statistical Service, *Quarterly Digest of Statistics,* Accra, December 1991, Tables 94, 95, and 96.

Table 4. Medical and Paramedical Personnel in Government Institutions by Region, 1989[1]

Region	Physicians	Medical Assistants	Dentists	Dental Assistants	Nurses[2]	Nurses[3]	Midwives	Pharmacists	Dispensary Assistants
Ashanti	24	35	2	3	163	379	136	5	108
Brong-Ahafo	19	23	2	5	65	703	74	3	62
Central	16	37	5	5	226	730	103	4	74
Eastern	50	41	4	6	318	1,240	287	4	135
Greater Accra	60	39	12	14	1,078	1,138	335	10	123
Northern	18	36	—[4]	3	275	544	110	6	44
Upper East	15	17	—	4	109	414	90	2	47
Upper West	9	16	—	—	138	283	131	3	27
Volta	35	30	2	5	277	901	156	6	69
Western	43	40	4	8	394	563	89	5	76
Komfo Anokye Teaching Hospital[5]	121	1	5	9	306	292	170	11	47
Korle-Bu Hospital[5]	218	—	3	8	649	623	55	8	62
TOTAL	628	315	39	70	3,998	7,810	1,736	67	874

[1] Latest available data. Figures do not include medical personnel working in quasi-governmental institutions.
[2] Includes registered nurses and nurse anesthetists.
[3] Includes community health nurses.
[4] — means negligible.
[5] Korle-Bu Hospital in Accra and Komfo Anokye Teaching Hospital in Kumasi are both teaching hospitals.

Source: Based on information from Ghana, Statistical Service, *Quarterly Digest of Statistics*, Accra, December 1991, Table 85.

Table 5. Enrollment and Gender Breakdown by Education Level, Selected Academic Years, 1980-81 to 1990-91

Education Level	1980–81		1985–86		1989–90		1990–91	
	Student Enrollment	Gender Breakdown[1]	Student Enrollment	Gender Breakdown[1]	Student Enrollment	Gender Breakdown[1]	Student Enrollment	Gender Breakdown[1]
Primary								
Males	766,406	56	718,173	55	939,010	55	991,877	55
Females	611,328	44	577,727	45	764,064	45	811,271	45
Total primary	1,377,734	100	1,295,900	100	1,703,074	100	1,803,148	100
Middle[2]								
Males	316,063	60	315,253	58	62,117	60	n.a.	n.a.
Females	213,632	40	224,670	42	40,951	40	n.a.	n.a.
Total middle	529,695	100	539,923	100	103,068	100	n.a.	n.a.
Junior secondary[2]								
Males	n.a.	n.a.	n.a.	n.a.	366,830	59	377,108	62
Females	n.a.	n.a.	n.a.	n.a.	258,188	41	232,235	38
Total junior secondary	n.a.	n.a.	n.a.	n.a.	625,018	100	609,343	100
Senior secondary								
Males	78,017	69	89,220	69	112,542	67	133,581	67
Females	35,140	31	40,787	31	55,458	33	65,679	33
Total senior secondary	113,157	100	130,007	100	168,000	100	199,260	100

Table 5. Enrollment and Gender Breakdown by Education Level, Selected Academic Years, 1980–81 to 1990–91

Education Level	1980–81		1985–86		1989–90		1990–91	
	Student Enrollment	Gender Breakdown[1]	Student Enrollment	Gender Breakdown[1]	Student Enrollment	Gender Breakdown[1]	Student Enrollment	Gender Breakdown[1]
Polytechnics[3]								
Males	n.a.	n.a.	7,203[4]	72[4]	8,403	73	n.a.	n.a.
Females	n.a.	n.a.	2,785[4]	28[4]	3,065	27	n.a.	n.a.
Total polytechnics	n.a.	n.a.	9,988[4]	100[4]	1,468	100	n.a.	n.a.
University of Ghana								
Males	3,098	84	2,807	81	3,269	81	3,076	76
Females	607	16	645	19	771	19	976	24
Total University of Ghana	3,705	100	3,452	100	4,040	100	4,052	100
University of Science and Technology								
Males	2,432	86	2,702	84	2,902	83	3,099	82
Females	384	14	500	16	575	17	697	18
Total University of Science and Technology	2,816	100	3,202	100	3,477	100	3,796	100
University of Cape Coast								
Males	1,139	81	1,259	82	1,387	80	n.a.	n.a.
Females	266	19	280	18	347	20	n.a.	n.a.

Table 5. Enrollment and Gender Breakdown by Education Level, Selected Academic Years, 1980–81 to 1990–91

Education Level	1980–81		1985–86		1989–90		1990–91	
	Student Enrollment	Gender Breakdown[1]	Student Enrollment	Gender Breakdown[1]	Student Enrollment	Gender Breakdown[1]	Student Enrollment	Gender Breakdown[1]
Total University of Cape Coast	1,405	100	1,539	100	1,734	100	n.a.	n.a.
Total university enrollment								
Males	6,669	84	6,768	83	7,558	81	6,175[5]	79[5]
Females	1,257	16	1,425	17	1,693	19	1,673[5]	21
Total university enrollment	7,926	100	8,193	100	9,251	100	7,848[5]	100[5]

[1] In percentages.
[2] As a result of education reforms of the mid-1980s, middle schools were phased out and junior secondary schools were phased in.
[3] Full-time and part-time students.
[4] 1986–87 figures.
[5] Enrollment in the University of Ghana and in the University of Science and Technology only.

n.a.—not available.

Source: Based on information from Ghana, Statistical Service, *Quarterly Digest of Statistics*, Accra, December 1991, Tables 69, 70, 72, 73, 74, 75, 76, and 77; and World Bank, various sources.

Table 6. Gross Domestic Product (GDP) at Market Prices, Selected Years, 1986–92[1]

	1986	1988	1990	1992
Total GDP (in billions of cedis)[2]				
At current prices	511	1,051	2,032	3,009
At constant 1987 prices	713	787	854	934
Real change (in percentages)	5.1	5.5	3.3	3.9
In billions of United States dollars	4.62	5.11	5.55	6.06
Per capita GDP (in thousands of cedis)				
At current prices	38.8	74.8	135.5	188.5
At constant 1987 prices	54.2	56.0	56.9	58.5
Real change (in percentages)	1.7	2.2	0.0	0.9
In United States dollars	352	364	369	380

[1] Latest available data.
[2] For value of the cedi—see Glossary.

Source: Based on information from Ghana, Statistical Service, *Quarterly Digest of Statistics*, Accra, December 1991, Table 87; and Economist Intelligence Unit, *Country Profile: Ghana, 1994-95*, London, 1994, 16.

Table 7. Gross Domestic Product (GDP) by Sector, 1983 and 1991[1]

Sector	1983 Value[2]	1983 Percentage	1991 Value[2]	1991 Percentage
Agriculture				
Agriculture and livestock	92,047	50.0	873,493	33.9
Cocoa production and marketing	10,227	5.6	244,602	9.5
Forestry and logging	5,609	3.0	99,986	3.9
Fishing	2,044	1.1	33,942	1.3
Total agriculture	109,927	59.7	1,252,024	48.6
Industry				
Mining and quarrying	1,944	1.1	45,587	1.8
Manufacturing	7,101	3.9	225,078	8.7
Electricity and water	358	0.2	51,950	2.0
Construction	2,796	1.5	89,195	3.5
Total industry	12,199	6.6	411,811	16.0
Services				
Transportation and communications	7,663	4.2	114,688	4.5
Wholesale and retail trade	43,120	23.4	442,787	17.2
Finance and insurance	3,311	1.8	107,391	4.2
Government and other	8,670	4.7	243,456	9.4
Total services	62,764	34.1	908,322	35.3
Less imputed bank service charges	-2,259	-1.2	-35,461	-1.4
Import duties	1,407	0.8	38,077	1.5
GDP at market prices	184,038	100.0	2,574,774	100.0

[1] Figures may not add to totals because of rounding.
[2] At current prices, in millions of cedis (for value of the cedi—see Glossary).

Source: Based on information from Ghana, Statistical Service, *Quarterly Digest of Statistics*, Accra, 1987, Table 74; and Economist Intelligence Unit, *Country Profile: Ghana*, 1994-95, London, 1994, 15.

Table 8. External Debt, Selected Years, 1986–92[1]
(in millions of United States dollars)

	1986	1988	1990	1992
External debt				
Long-term	1,754	2,214	2,705	3,131
Short-term	187	72	312	404
IMF credit[2]	786	762	745	740
Total external debt	2,726	3,048	3,761	4,275
Public disbursed debt				
Official creditors	1,464	1,892	2,483	2,894
Private creditors	252	290	189	202
Total public disbursed debt	1,716	2,182	2,672	3,096
Debt service				
Principal	112	424	250	185
Interest	111	128	105	115
Total debt service	223	552	356	300

[1] Figures may not add to totals because of rounding.
[2] IMF—see Glossary.

Source: Based on information from Economist Intelligence Unit, *Country Profile: Ghana,* 1994–95, London, 1994, 34.

Table 9. Public Finance, Selected Years, 1988–94
(in millions of cedis)[1]

	1988	1990	1992	1994
Revenue	153,791	267,347	400,000	1,078,069
Current expenditure	-111,004	-198,193	-283,000	-742,376
Balance	42,787	69,154	117,000	335,693
Development expenditure	-32,893	-56,280	-157,000	-174,200
Net lending[2]	-5,983	-9,487	n.a.[3]	-93,457
Overall balance	3,911	3,387	n.a.	68,036
Financing				
Domestic	-6,166	-27,977	n.a.	-151,813
External	2,255	24,590	n.a.	83,777

[1] For value of the cedi—see Glossary.
[2] Net loans, advances, and investment in public boards, corporations, and companies.
[3] n.a.—not available.

Source: Based on information from Ghana, Statistical Service, *Quarterly Digest of Statistics,* Accra, December 1991, Table 33; and Economist Intelligence Unit, *Country Profile: Ghana, 1994–95,* London, 1994, 28.

Table 10. Balance of Payments, Selected Years, 1986-94[1]
(in millions of United States dollars)

	1986	1988	1990	1992	1994[2]
Merchandise exports	773	881	891	986	1,246
Merchandise imports	-713	-993	-1,199	-1,457	-1,760
Trade balance	61	-112	-308	-470	-514
Exports of services	45	78	93	129	n.a.[3]
Imports of services	-344	-400	-429	-505	n.a.
Net private transfers	72	172	202	255	n.a.
Net official transfers	123	196	214	214	n.a.
Current account balance	-43	-66	-228	-378	-190
Direct investment	4	5	15	22	n.a.
Other capital	59	204	310	299	n.a.
Capital account balance	63	209	325	321	n.a.

[1] Figures may not add to totals because of rounding.
[2] Estimated.
[3] n.a.—not available.

Source: Based on information from Economist Intelligence Unit, *Country Profile: Ghana, 1993-94,* London, 1993, 32; Economist Intelligence Unit, *Country Report: Ghana* [London], No. 3, 1994, 6; and Economist Intelligence Unit, *Country Profile: Ghana, 1994-95,* London, 1994, 32.

Table 11. Major Political Parties and Military Regimes, 1897-1994

Period	Description
1897–1920s	British West Africa Aborigine Rights Protection Society. Founded by small urban elite to protect property rights from British encroachment. Became limited vehicle for later tribal leader protest as well.
1920s	National Congress of British West Africa. Regional educated elites' first effort to influence British to provide some elected voice for Africans.
1947–55	United Gold Coast Convention (UGCC). Postwar movement of educated Africans demanding a voice in government. Brought Kwame Nkrumah back from Britain as its secretary.
1949–66	Convention People's Party (CPP). Founded by Nkrumah. Served as main force for independence, then as his vehicle to power and rule. Governing party, 1957–66. Abolished after 1966 coup.
1954–56	National Liberation Movement (NLM). Conservative, federalist opposition to CPP in crucial 1956 election. Largely Asante-based. Joined United Party (UP).
1955–1960s	United Party (UP). Led by Kofi A. Busia. Unified NLM and other CPP opponents as CPP's primary opposition. Gradually crushed by government.
1966–70	National Liberation Council (NLC). Name adopted by army and police leaders of coup that overthrew Nkrumah. Dedicated to return to democratic civilian rule.
1969–72	Progress Party (PP). Led by Busia and consisting of former UP supporters. Won 1969 election. Lost support of people and army through efforts to impose order on country's economy.
	National Alliance of Liberals (NAL). Led by K.A. Gbedemah and consisting of other followers of CPP's right wing. Defeated by PP in 1969. Joined others in opposition Justice Party (JP).
1972–75	National Redemption Council (NRC). Name adopted by Lieutenant Colonel Ignatius K. Acheampong and associates after overthrow of Busia government. Ruled country without civilian input, with soldiers assigned to every organization.
1975–79	Supreme Military Council (SMC). Created by Acheampong out of the NRC. After ouster of Acheampong in 1978, began steps toward civilian rule, calling for elections in June 1979. On eve of elections, overthrown by junior officers of Armed Forces Revolutionary Council (AFRC).
1978–81	People's National Party (PNP). Created to contest 1979 election. Attracted former NAL members and others. Chose Hilla Limann as its candidate and won election by slim majority.
	Popular Front Party (PFP). Party of former Busia supporters. Formed opposition in new parliament.
1979	Armed Forces Revolutionary Council (AFRC). Name adopted by Flight Lieutenant Jerry Rawlings and associates after Ghana's first violent coup. Without concrete platform except to punish corruption. Withdrew in favor of elected Limann government after four months in power.
1982–92	Provisional National Defence Council (PNDC). Composed of leaders of Rawlings's second coup. With considerable evolution of personnel and objectives, continued until 1992 to be sole center of political power in Ghana.
1992–94	National Democratic Congress (NDC), National Independence Party (NIP), New Patriotic Party (NPP), People's Heritage Party (PHP), and People's National Convention (PNC) were major parties organized to contest 1992 presidential election. NDC party of Rawlings and PNDC; NPP largely Asante-based, nominated Adu Boahen; NIP, PHP, and PNC all Nkrumahists. NDC

Table 11. Major Political Parties and Military Regimes, 1897-1994

Period	Description
1992–94	elected, formed first government under Fourth Republic; remaining parties formed opposition. In 1993 NIP and PHP formed (new) People's Convention Party (PCP).

Table 12. Voting Patterns in the District Assembly Elections by Region, 1988-89

Region	District	Candidates	Registered Voters	Votes Cast	Percentage Turnout
Ashanti	18	2,211	950,222	577,735	60.8
Brong-Ahafo	13	1,629	650,143	391,489	60.2
Central	12	1,421	549,564	307,668	56.0
Eastern	15	1,825	744,160	452,449	60.8
Greater Accra	5	693	792,012	350,861	44.3
Northern	13	1,471	508,560	308,191	60.6
Upper East	6	822	358,174	222,068	62.0
Upper West	5	458	212,192	143,017	67.4
Volta	12	1,343	568,590	334,445	58.6
Western	11	969	589,221	328,479	55.3
GHANA	110	12,842	5,922,838	3,416,402	58.9

Source: Based on information from Ghana, *Local Government Information Digest*, Special Editions I and II, Nos. 4-5, Accra, 1989.

Bibliography

Chapter 1

Afrifa, Akwasi A. *The Ghana Coup*. London: Frank Cass, 1966.

Agbodeka, Francis. *African Politics and British Policy in the Gold Coast, 1868–1900*. Evanston, Illinois: Northwestern University Press, 1971.

Alexander, H.T. *African Tightrope: My Two Years as Nkrumah's Chief of Staff*. New York: Praeger, 1966.

Allman, Jean Marie. *The Quills of the Porcupine: Asante Nationalism in an Emergent Ghana*. Madison: University of Wisconsin Press, 1993.

Anquandah, James. "The Archaeological Evidence for the Emergence of Akan Civilization," *Tarikh* [Ibadan], 7, No. 2, 1982, 9–21.

Anquandah, James. *Rediscovering Ghana's Past*. Essex: Longman, 1982.

Apter, David E. *The Gold Coast in Transition*. Princeton: Princeton University Press, 1955. Reprint. *Ghana in Trnsition* (2d rev. ed.) Princeton: Princeton University Press, 1972.

Arhin, Kwame. "The Structure of Greater Ashanti," *Journal of African History* [Cambridge], 7, No. 1, 1976, 65–85.

Austin, Dennis. "Opposition in Ghana, 1947–67," *Government and Opposition* [London], 2, No. 4, October 1967, 539–55.

Austin, Dennis. "Return to Ghana," *African Affairs* [Oxford], 69, No. 274, January 1970, 67–71.

Austin, Dennis. "The Ghana Armed Forces and Ghanaian Society," *Third World Quarterly* [London], 7, No. 1, January 1985, 90–101.

Austin, Dennis, and Robin Luckham. *Politicians and Soldiers in Ghana, 1966–1972*. London: Frank Cass, 1975.

Boahen, A. Adu. *The Ghanaian Sphinx: Reflections on the Contemporary History of Ghana, 1972–1987*. Accra and New York: Ghana Democratic Movement, 1989.

Bretton, Henry L. *The Rise and Fall of Kwame Nkrumah: A Study of Personal Rule in Africa*. New York: Praeger, 1966.

Busia, Kofi Abrefa. *The Position of the Chief in the Modern Political System of Ashanti.* London: Oxford University Press, 1951.

Chazan, Naomi. *An Anatomy of Ghanaian Politics: Managing Political Recession, 1969–1982.* Boulder, Colorado: Westview Press, 1983.

Chazan, Naomi. "Liberalization, Governance, and Political Space in Ghana." Pages 121–41 in Goran Hyden and Michael Bratton (eds.), *Governance and Politics in Africa.* Boulder, Colorado: Lynne Rienner, 1992.

Chazan, Naomi. "The Political Transformation of Ghana under the PNDC." Pages 21–47 in Donald Rothchild (ed.), *Ghana: the Political Economy of Recovery.* Boulder, Colorado: Lynne Rienner, 1991.

Claridge, William Walton. *A History of the Gold Coast and Ashanti.* (2 vols.) London: J. Murray, 1915.

Cooper, Frederick. "The Problem of Slavery in African Studies," *Journal of African History* [Cambridge], 20, No. 1, 1979, 103–25.

Crowder, Michael, and J.F. Ade Ajayi (eds.). *History of West Africa.* New York: Columbia University Press, 1972.

Curtin, Philip D. *The Atlantic Slave Trade: A Census.* Madison: University of Wisconsin Press, 1969.

Davidson, Basil. *Black Star: A View of the Life and Times of Kwame Nkrumah.* Boulder, Colorado: Westview Press, 1989.

Decalo, Samuel. *Coups and Army Rule in Africa: Studies in Military Style.* New Haven: Yale University Press, 1976.

Edsman, Bjorn M. *Lawyers in Gold Coast Politics, ca. 1900–1945.* Uppsala: University of Uppsala, 1979.

Fage, J.D. *A History of West Africa: An Introductory Survey.* (4th ed.) London: Cambridge University Press, 1969.

Fage, J.D. "Slavery and the Slave Trade in the Context of West African History," *Journal of African History* [Cambridge], 10, No. 3, 1969, 393–404.

Fage, J.D. "Reflections on the Early History of the Mossi-Dagomba Group of States." Pages 177–92 in Jan Vansina, et al. (eds.), *The Historian in Tropical Africa.* London: Oxford University Press, 1964.

Finley, Moses I. *Ancient Slavery and Modern Ideology.* Middlesex, United Kingdom: Penguin Books, 1980.

Fitch, Robert Beck, and Mary Oppenheimer. *Ghana: End of an Illusion.* New York: Monthly Review Press, 1966.

Forde, Daryll, and P.M. Kaberry (eds.). *West African Kingdoms in the Nineteenth Century.* London: Oxford University Press for the International African Institute, 1967.

Fynn, John K. *Asante and Its Neighbours, 1700–1807.* London: Longman, 1971.

Ghana. Supreme Military Council. Office of the Press Secretary. *Fourth Year in Office of Colonel Ignatius Kutu Acheampong, 13th January 1975–12th January 1976.* Accra: Office of the Press Secretary of the SMC, 1976.

Ghana. *General Kutu Acheampong: The Fifth Milestone, 13 January 1976–12 January 1977.* Accra: Office of the Press Secretary of the SMC, 1977.

Goldsworthy, David. "Ghana's Second Republic: A Post Mortem," *African Affairs* [Oxford], 72, No. 286, 1973, 8–25.

Hailey, William M. *Native Administration in the British African Territories, Part III: West Africa.* London: HMSO, 1951.

Hargreaves, John D. *The End of Colonial Rule in West Africa.* New York: Barnes and Noble, 1979.

Harrell-Bond, Barbara E. *Ghana's Troubled Transition to Civilian Government.* (American Universities Field Staff, Fieldstaff Reports, No. 48.) Hanover, New Hampshire: AUFS, 1979.

Harrell-Bond, Barbara E. *Diary of a Revolution 'Which Might Have Been.'* (American Universities Field Staff, Fieldstaff Reports, Nos. 24–25.) Hanover, New Hampshire: AUFS, 1980.

Haynes, Jeff. "Human Rights and Democracy in Ghana: The Record of the Rawlings Regime," *African Affairs* [Oxford], 90, No. 360, July 1991, 407–25.

Haynes, Jeff. "The PNDC and Political Decentralization in Ghana, 1981-91," *Journal of Commonwealth and Comparative Politics* [London], 29, No. 3, November 1991, 283–307.

Howard, Rhoda. *Colonialism and Underdevelopment in Ghana.* New York: Africana, 1978.

Hyden, Goran, and Michael Bratton (eds.). *Governance and Politics in Africa.* Boulder, Colorado: Lynne Rienner, 1992.

International Monetary Fund. *Ghana: Adjustment and Growth, 1983–1991.* Washington: 1991.

Jeffries, Richard. "Rawlings and the Political Economy of Underdevelopment in Ghana," *African Affairs* [Oxford], 81, No. 324, July 1982, 307–17.

Jeffries, Richard. "The Ghanaian Elections of 1979," *African Affairs* [Oxford], 79, No. 316, July 1980, 397–414.

Kimble, David. *A Political History of Ghana, 1850-1928.* London: Clarendon Press, 1963.

Kraus, Jon. "Arms and Politics in Ghana." Pages 154–221 in Claude E. Welch, Jr. (ed.), *Soldier and State in Africa: A Comparative Analysis of Military Intervention and Political Change.* Evanston, Illinois: Northwestern University Press, 1970.

Ladouceur, Paul Andre. *Chiefs and Politicians: The Politics of Regionalism in Northern Ghana.* London: Longman, 1979.

Lawrence, Arnold Walter. *Trade, Castles, and Forts of West Africa.* Stanford: Stanford University Press, 1964.

Lawrence, Arnold Walter. *Fortified Trade-posts: The English in West Africa, 1645–1822.* London: Jonathan Cape, 1969.

LeVine, Victor T. *Political Corruption: The Ghana Case.* Stanford: Hoover Institution Press, 1975.

Levtzion, Nehemia. *Muslims and Chiefs in West Africa.* Oxford: Clarendon Press, 1968.

Lugard, Frederick. *The Dual Mandate in British Tropical Africa.* Edinburgh: Blackwood, 1922.

Lystad, Robert. *The Ashanti.* New Brunswick: Rutgers University Press, 1958.

McCaskie, Thomas. "Komfo Anokye of Asante: Meaning, History and Philosophy in an African Society," *Journal of African History* [Cambridge], 27, No. 2, 1986, 315–39.

McCaskie, Thomas. *State and Society in Precolonial Asante.* Cambridge: Cambrige University Press, 1995.

Makepeace, Margaret. "English Traders on the Gold Coast, 1657–1668: An Analysis of the East India Company Archives," *History in Africa,* 16, 1989, 237–84.

Martin, Eveline Christiana. *The British West African Settlements, 1750–1821.* London: Longmans, Green, for the Royal Colonial Institute, 1927.

Mbaeyi, Paul Mmegha. *British Military and Naval Forces in West African History, 1807–1874.* New York: Nok, 1978.

Metcalfe, George E. *Maclean of the Gold Coast.* London: Oxford University Press, 1962.

Meyerowitz, Eva L.R. *The Early History of the Akan States of Ghana.* London: Red Candle Press, 1974.

Ninsin, Kwame. "Ghanaian Politics After 1981: Revolution or Evolution?" *Canadian Journal of African Studies* [Ottawa], 21, No.1, 1987, 17–37.

Ninsin, Kwame, and F.K. Drah (eds.). *The Search for Democracy in Ghana: A Case Study of Political Instability in Africa.* Accra: Asempa, 1987.

Nkrumah, Kwame. *Consciencism: Philosophy and Ideology of Decolonization and Development with Particular Reference to the African Revolution.* London: Heinemann, 1964. Reprint. New York: Monthly Review Press, 1970.

Nkrumah, Kwame. *Africa Must Unite.* New York: Praeger, 1963.

Nkrumah, Kwame. *I Speak of Freedom: A Statement of African Ideology.* London: Heinemann, 1961.

Nkrumah, Kwame. *Neo-Colonialism: The Last Stage of Imperialism.* London: Nelson, 1965.

Omari, T. Peter. *Kwame Nkrumah: Anatomy of an African Dictatorship.* New York: Africana, 1970.

Owusu, Maxwell. "Ghana: What Went Wrong, A Response," *Africa Today,* 19, No. 2, 1972, 77–80.

Owusu, Maxwell. "Politics Without Parties: Reflections on the Union Government Proposals in Ghana," *African Studies Review,* 22, No. 1, April 1979, 89–108.

Owusu, Maxwell. "The Search for Solvency: Background to the Fall of Ghana's Second Republic, 1969–1972," *Africa Today,* 19, No. 1, 1972, 52–60.

Owusu-Ansah, David. *Islamic Talismanic Tradition in Nineteenth-Century Asante.* Lewiston, New York: Edwin Mellen Press, 1991.

Owusu-Ansah, David. "The Provisional National Defence Council of Ghana: A Move Toward Consolidation," *International Third World Studies Journal and Review,* 1, No. 1, 1989, 213–18.

Owusu-Ansah, David, and Daniel M. McFarland. *Historical Dictionary of Ghana.* (2d ed.) Metuchen, New Jersey: Scarecrow Press, 1995.

Pellow, Deborah, and Naomi Chazan. *Ghana: Coping with Uncertainty.* Boulder, Colorado: Westview Press, 1986.

Pinkney, Robert. *Ghana under Military Rule: 1966–1969.* London: Methuen, 1972.

Rathbone, Richard (ed.). *British Documents on the End of Empire. Series B, Volume 1, Ghana, Part 1, 1941–1952; Part II, 1952–1957.* London: HMSO for the Institute of Commonwealth Studies, 1992.

Rattray, Robert, S. *Ashanti Law and Constitution.* London: Clarendon Press, 1929.

Robertson, Claire C., and Martin Klein. *Women and Slavery in Africa.* Madison: University of Wisconsin Press, 1983.

Rodney, Walter. *How Europe Underdeveloped Africa.* Washington: Howard University Press, 1982.

Rothchild, Donald (ed.). *Ghana: The Political Economy of Recovery.* Boulder, Colorado: Lynne Rienner, 1991.

Schildkrout, Enid. *The Golden Stool: Studies of the Asante Center and Periphery.* (Anthropological Papers of the American Museum of Natural History, Vol. 65, Part 1.) New York: American Museum of Natural History, 1987.

Schleh, Eugene P. A. "The Post-War Careers of Ex-Servicemen in Ghana and Uganda," *Journal of Modern African Studies* [Cambridge], 6, No. 2, August 1968, 203–20.

Shillington, Kevin. *Ghana and the Rawlings Factor.* New York: St. Martin's Press, 1992.

Smith, Robert S. *Warfare and Diplomacy in Pre-Colonial West Africa.* London: Methuen, 1976.

Stride, G.T., and Caroline Ifeka. *Peoples and Empires of West Africa: 1000–1800.* New York: Africana, 1971.

Vansina, Jan, et al. (eds.). *The Historian in Tropical Africa.* London: Oxford University Press, 1964.

Vogt, John. *Portuguese Rule on the Gold Coast, 1469–1682.* Athens, Georgia: University of Georgia Press, 1979.

Ward, William Ernest. *A History of Ghana.* London: Allen and Unwin, 1958.

Welch, Claude E., Jr. (ed.). *Soldier and State in Africa: A Comparative Analysis of Military Intervention and Political Change.* Evanston, Illinois: Northwestern University Press, 1970.

Wilks, Ivor G. *Asante in the Nineteenth Century: The Structure and Evolution of a Political Order.* London: Cambrige University Press, 1975. Reprint. Cambridge: Cambridge University Press, 1989.

Wilks, Ivor G. *Forests of Gold: Essays on the Akan and the Kingdom of Asante.* Athens: Ohio University Press, 1993.

Wilks, Ivor G. "The Mossi and Akan States, 1500–1800." Pages 344–86 in Michael Crowder and J.F. Ade Ajayi (eds.), *History of West Africa.* New York: Columbia University Press, 1972.

Wilks, Ivor G. "The State of the Akan and the Akan State: A Discussion," *Cahier d'Études Africaines* [Paris], 22, Nos. 3–4, 1982, 231–49.

Wilks, Ivor, Nehemia Levtzion, and Bruce M. Haight. *Chronicles from Gonja: A Tradition of West African Muslim Historiography.* Cambridge: Cambridge University Press, 1986.

Wraith, R.E. *Guggisberg.* London: Oxford University Press, 1967.

Yarak, Larry W. *Asante and the Dutch.* London: Oxford University Press, 1990.

Young, Crawford. *Ideology and Development in Africa.* New Haven: Yale University Press, 1982.

Young, Crawford. *Politics in the Congo.* Evanston, Illinois: Northwestern University Press, 1968.

(Various issues of the following publications were also used in the preparation of this chapter: *Africa Report, Current History, Ghanaian Times* [Accra], *People's Daily Graphic* [Accra], and *Workers' Banner* [Accra].)

Chapter 2

Amedekey, E.Y. *The Culture of Ghana: A Bibliography.* Accra: Ghana Universities Press, 1970.

Amonoo, Reginald F. *Language and Nationhood: Reflections on Language Situations with Particular Reference to Ghana.* Accra: Ghana Academy of Arts and Sciences, 1989.

Anquandah, James. *Rediscovering Ghana's Past.* Essex: Longman, 1982.

Arhin, Kwame. *West African Traders in Ghana in the Nineteenth and Twentieth Centuries.* London: Longman, 1979.

Arhin, Kwame. *Traditional Rule in Ghana: Past and Present.* Accra: Sedco, 1985.

Awoonor, Kofi Nyidevu. *Ghana: A Political History from Pre-European to Modern Times.* Accra: Sedco and Woeli, 1990.

Beecham, John. *Ashantee and the Gold Coast.* London, John Mason, 1841. Reprint. New York: Johnson Reprint Corp., 1970.

Belcher, Wendy Laura. *Honey from the Lion: An African Journey.* New York: Dutton, 1988.

Boahen, A. Adu. *The Ghanaian Sphinx: Reflections on the Contemporary History of Ghana, 1972–1987.* New York: Greenwood Press, 1989.

Boahen, A. Adu. *Ghana: Evolution and Change in the Nineteenth and Twentieth Centuries.* London: Longman, 1975.

Boateng, E. A. *A Geography of Ghana.* (2d ed.) Cambridge: Cambridge University Press, 1966.

Bos, Eduard, My T. Vu, Ann Levin, and Rodolfo A. Bulatao. *World Population Projections, 1992–93 Edition: Estimates and Projections with Related Demographic Statistics.* Baltimore: Johns Hopkins University Press, 1992.

Busia, Kofi Abrefa. *The Position of the Chief in the Modern Political System of Ashanti.* London: Oxford University Press, 1951.

Chazan, Naomi. *An Anatomy of Ghanaian Politics: Managing Political Recession, 1969–82.* Boulder, Colorado: Westview Press, 1983.

Clark, J.D., and S.A. Brandt (eds.). *From Hunters to Farmers: The Courses and Consequences of Food Production in Africa.* Berkeley: University of California Press, 1984.

Cobbe, James. "The Political Economy of Education Reform in Ghana." Pages 101–15 in Donald Rothchild (ed.), *Ghana: The Political Economy of Recovery.* Boulder, Colorado: Lynne Rienner, 1991.

Crossland, L.B. "Traditional Textile Industry in Northwest Brong Ahafo, Ghana—The Archeological and Contemporary Evidence," *Sankofa* [Legon], 1, 1975, 69–73.

Dickson, Kwamina B. *A Historical Geography of Ghana.* Cambridge: Cambridge University Press, 1971.

Dzobo, N.K. "Introduction to the Indigenous Ethic of the Ewe of West Africa," *The Oguaa Educator* [Cape Coast], 6, No. 1, 1975, 82–97.

Effah-Gyamfi, Kwaku. *Bono Manso: An Archaeological Investigation into Early Akan Urbanism.* Calgary: University of Calgary Press, 1985.

Ehret, C., and M. Posnansky (eds.). *The Archaeological and Linguistic Reconstruction of African History.* Berkeley: University of California Press, 1982.

Field, Margaret J. *Social Organization of the Ga People.* Accra: Crown Agents for the Colonies, 1940.

Garrard, Timothy F. *Akan Weights and the Gold Trade.* London: Longman, 1980.

Ghana. Central Bureau of Statistics. *Preliminary Report on the 1984 Census.* Accra: 1985.

Ghana. Statistical Service. *1984 Population Census of Ghana: Demography and Economic Characteristics.* 11 vols. Accra: 1990.

Goody, Jack. *Literacy in Traditional Societies.* London: Cambridge University Press, 1968.

Goody, Jack. *Production and Reproduction: A Comparative Study of the Domestic Domain.* Cambridge and New York: Cambridge University Press, 1976.

Goody, Jack. *The Social Organization of the Lo Wiili.* London: Oxford University Press for the International African Institute, 1967.

Hansen, Emmanuel, and Kwame A. Ninsin (eds.). *The State, Development, and Politics in Ghana.* London: Codesria, 1989.

Johnson, Marion. "Ashanti East of the Volta," *Transactions of the Historical Society of Ghana* [Legon], 8, 1965, 33–59.

Johnson, Marion. "The Population of Asante, 1817–1921: A Reconsideration," *Asantesem,* 8, 1978, 22–27.

Kiyaga-Mulindwa, David. "Archaeological and Historical Research in the Birim Valley," *Sankofa* [Legon], 2, 1976, 90–91.

Kropp Dakubu, M.E. "Linguistic, Prehistoric and Historical Reconstruction of the Ga-Dangbe Migration," *Transactions of the Historical Society of Ghana* [Legon], 13, 1972, 87–111.

Kropp Dakubu, M.E. (ed.). *The Languages of Ghana.* London: Kegan Paul for the International African Institute, 1988.

Manoukian, Madeline. *Akan and Ga-Adangme Peoples of the Gold Coast.* London: Oxford University Press, 1950.

Martin, Bradford G. "Arabic Materials for Ghanaian History," *Research Review* [Legon], 2, No. 1, 1965, 74–83.

Meillassoux, Claude. *The Development of Indigenous Trade and Markets in West Africa.* London: Oxford University Press, 1971.

Mikell, Gwendolyn. "Equity Issues in Ghana's Rural Development." Pages 85–100 in Donald Rothchild (ed.), *Ghana: The*

Political Economy of Recovery. Boulder, Colorado: Lynne Rienner, 1991.

Morrison, Minion. *Ethnicity and Political Integration: The Case of Ashanti, Ghana.* Syracuse: Maxwell School of Citizenship and Public Affairs, 1981.

Ninsin, Kwame, and F.K. Drah (eds.). *The Search for Democracy in Ghana: A Case Study of Political Instability in Africa.* Accra: Asempa, 1987.

Nketia, Kwabena J.H. "The Musical Traditions of the Akan," *Tarikh* [Ibadan], 7, No. 2, 1982, 47–59.

Oppenheim, Mason. *The Status of Women: A Review of Its Relationship to Fertility and Mortality.* New York: Rockefeller Foundation, 1984.

Oppong, Christine, and Katharine Abu. *Seven Roles of Women: Impact of Education, Migration and Employment on Ghanaian Mothers.* Geneva: International Labour Office, 1987.

Owusu, Maxwell. *Uses and Abuses of Political Power: A Case Study of Continuity and Change in the Politics of Ghana.* Chicago: University of Chicago Press, 1970.

Owusu-Ansah, David. *Islamic Talismanic Tradition in Nineteenth-Century Asante.* Lewiston, New York: Edwin Mellen Press, 1991.

Owusu-Ansah, David, and Daniel M. McFarland. *Historical Dictionary of Ghana.* (2d ed.) Metuchen, New Jersey: Scarecrow Press, 1995.

Plass, Margaret Webster. *African Miniatures: The Goldweights of the Ashanti.* London: Lund Humphries, 1967.

Posnansky, Merrick. "Archaeological and Linguistic Reconstruction in Ghana." Pages 256–66 in C. Ehret and M. Posnansky (eds.), *The Archaeological and Linguistic Reconstruction of African History.* Berkeley: University of California Press, 1982.

Posnansky, Merrick. "Early Agricultural Societies in Ghana." Pages 147–51 in J.D. Clark and S.A. Brandt (eds.), *From Hunters to Farmers: The Courses and Consequences of Food Production in Africa.* Berkeley: University of California Press, 1984.

Quarcoo, Alfred K. "The Ancestors in Ghanaian Religious and Social Behavior," *Research Review* [Legon], 3, No. 2, 1967, 39–50.

Rattray, Robert S. *Akan-Ashanti Folk-Tales.* London: Oxford University Press, 1930.

Rattray, Robert S. *Ashanti Law and Constitution.* London: Clarendon Press, 1929.

Rattray, Robert S. *Ashanti Proverbs.* Oxford: Clarendon Press, 1916.

Rattray, Robert S. *Religion and Art in Ashanti.* Oxford: Clarendon Press, 1923.

Robertson, Claire. "Economic Women in Africa: Profit-Making Techniques of Accra Market Women," *Journal of Modern African Studies,* 12, No. 4, 1974, 657–64.

Robertson, Claire, and Martin Klein. *Women and Slavery in Africa.* Madison: University of Wisconsin Press, 1983.

Rothchild, Donald (ed.). *Ghana: The Political Economy of Recovery.* Boulder, Colorado: Lynne Rienner, 1991.

Sarfoh, Joseph A. *Population, Urbanization, and Rural Settlement in Ghana: A Bibliographic Survey.* New York: Greenwood Press, 1987.

Sarpong, Peter K. *Ghana in Retrospect: Some Aspects of Ghanaian Culture.* Tema: Ghana Publishing, 1974.

Sarpong, Peter K. *The Sacred Stools of the Akan.* Tema: Ghana Publishing, 1971.

Schildkrout, Enid. *People of the Zongo: The Transformation of Ethnic Identities in Ghana.* New York: Cambridge University Press, 1978.

Schildkrout, Enid (ed.). *The Golden Stool: Studies of the Asante Center and Periphery.* (Anthropological Papers of the American Museum of Natural History, Vol. 65, Part 1.) New York: American Museum of Natural History, 1987.

Shinnie, Peter L. "Archaeology in Gonja and Asante Connections." Pages 23–28 in Enid Schildkrout (ed.), *The Golden Stool: Studies of the Asante Center and Periphery.* (Anthropological Papers of the American Museum of Natural History, Vol. 65, Part 1.) New York: American Museum of Natural History, 1987.

Shinnie, Peter L. *Archaeology of Gonja, Ghana: Excavations at Daboya.* Calgary: Calgary University Press, 1989.

Sillah, Mohammed-Bassiru. *African Coup d'Etat: A Case Study of Jerry Rawlings in Ghana.* Lawrenceville, Virginia: Brunswick, 1984.

Silverman, Raymond, and David Owusu-Ansah. "The Presence of Islam among the Akan of Ghana: A Bibliographic Essay," *History in Africa*, 16, 1989, 325–39.

United Nations. *Demographic Yearbook, 1991*. New York: 1992.

United Nations. *Statistical Yearbook, 1990–91*. New York: 1993.

United States. Central Intelligence Agency. *The World Factbook, 1994*. Washington: GPO, 1994.

University of Ghana. Regional Institute for Population Studies. *Population of Ghana: An Annotated Bibliography, 1980–1988*. Addis Ababa: Population Division, United Nations Economic Commission for Africa, 1988.

Vansina, Jan, et al. (eds.). *The Historian in Tropical Africa*. London: Oxford University Press, 1964.

Wilks, Ivor G. *Asante in the Nineteenth Century: The Structure and Evolution of a Political Order.* London: Cambridge University Press, 1975. Reprint. Cambridge: Cambridge University Press, 1989.

Yankah, Kwesi. *Woes of a Kwatriot: Reflections on the Ghanaian Situation*. Accra: Woeli, 1990.

Zedlitz, Albrecht von. *Ethnisch-nationale Integration und Erziehung in Ghana: Ethnische und Nationale Einstellungen unter den Fante, Asante, Dagbamba und Ewe*. Hohenschaftlarn: K. Renner, 1984.

(Various issues of the following publications were also used in the preparation of this chapter: *Ghanaian Times* [Accra]; *Monthly Economic Bulletin* [Accra]; *People's Daily Graphic* [Accra]; *Quarterly Digest of Statistics* [Accra]; and *West Africa* [London].)

Chapter 3

Africa South of the Sahara, 1995. (24th ed.) London: Europa, 1994.

Adhikari, R., C. Kirkpatrick, and J. Weiss (eds.). *Industrial and Trade Policy Reform in Developing Countries*. Manchester: Manchester University Press, 1992.

Agbodeka, Francis. *An Economic History of Ghana from the Earliest Times*. Legon: Ghana Universities Press, 1993.

Akuoko-Frimpong, H. "Ghana: Capacity Building for Policy Change." Pages 19–36 in Louis A. Picard and Michele Garrity (eds.), *Policy Reform for Sustainable Development in Africa: The Institutional Imperative.* Boulder, Colorado: Lynne Rienner, 1994.

Anin, T.E. *Essays on the Political Economy of Ghana.* Accra: Selwyn, 1991.

Anyemedu, Kwasi. "Export Diversification Under the Economic Recovery Program." Pages 209–20 in Donald Rothchild (ed.), *Ghana: The Political Economy of Recovery.* Boulder, Colorado: Lynne Rienner, 1991.

Aryeetey, Ernest. "Private Investment Under Uncertainty in Ghana," *World Development* [Oxford] 22, No. 8, August 1994, 1211–21.

Bank of Ghana. "Ghana's Stabilisation Measures and the IMF: A Case Study," *Africa Development* [Dakar]," 10, 1985.

Beckman, Bjorn. *Organizing the Farmers: Cocoa Politics and National Development in Ghana.* Uppsala: Scandinavian Institute of African Studies, 1976.

Chand, Sheetal K., and Reinold van Til. "Ghana: Toward Successful Stabilization and Recovery," *Finance and Development,* 25, No. 1, March 1988, 32–35.

Cohen, Robin, and Harry Goulbourne (eds.). *Democracy and Socialism in Africa.* Boulder, Colorado: Westview Press, 1991.

Cruise O'Brien, Donal B., John Dunn, and Richard Rathbone (eds.). *Contemporary West African States.* Cambridge: Cambridge University Press, 1989.

Daaku, Kwame Yeboah. *Trade and Politics on the Gold Coast, 1600–1720: A Study of the African Reaction to European Trade.* London: Clarendon, 1970.

Duncan, Alex, and John Howell. *Structural Adjustment and the African Farmer.* London: Overseas Development Institute, 1992.

Ewusi, Kodwo. *Structural Adjustment and Stabilization Policies in Developing Countries: A Case Study of Ghana's Experience, 1983–1986.* Tema: Ghana Publishing, 1987.

Fontaine, Jean-Marc. "Bias Overkill? Removal of Anti-export Bias and Manufacturing Investment: Ghana, 1983–89." Pages 120–34 in R. Adhikari, C. Kirkpatrick, and J. Weiss (eds.), *Industrial and Trade Policy Reform in Developing Countries.* Manchester: Manchester University Press, 1992.

Ghana. *Economic Recovery Programme, 1984–1986: Review of Progress in 1984 and Goals for 1985, 1986: Report.* Accra: 1983.

Ghana. *National Programme for Economic Development, Revised, Wednesday, 1st July 1987.* Accra: 1987.

Ghana. *Programme of Action to Mitigate the Social Costs of Adjustment.* Accra: 1987.

Green, Reginald H. *Stabilization and Adjustment Policies and Programs: Country Study 1: Ghana.* Helsinki: World Institute for Development Economics Research of the United Nations University, 1987.

Gyimah-Boadi, E. "State Enterprises Divestiture: Recent Ghanaian Experiences." Pages 193–208 in Donald Rothchild, (ed.), *Ghana: The Political Economy of Recovery.* Boulder, Colorado: Lynne Rienner, 1991.

Hansen, Emmanuel, and Kwame A. Ninsin (eds.). *The State, Development, and Politics in Ghana.* London: Codesria, 1989.

Haynes, Jeff. "Inching Towards Democracy: The Ghanaian 'Revolution,' the International Monetary Fund, and the Politics of the Possible." Pages 142–64 in Robin Cohen and Harry Goulbourne (eds.), *Democracy and Socialism in Africa.* Boulder, Colorado: Westview Press, 1991.

Herbst, Jeffrey. *The Politics of Reform in Ghana, 1982–1991.* Berkeley: University of California Press, 1993.

Hill, Polly. *The Migrant Cocoa-Farmers of Southern Ghana: A Study in Rural Capitalism.* Cambridge: Cambridge University Press, 1963.

Howard, Rhoda E. *Colonialism and Underdevelopment in Ghana.* London: Croom Helm, 1978.

Huq, M.M. *The Economy of Ghana: The First 25 Years Since Independence.* New York: St. Martin's Press, 1989.

Hutchful, Eboe. *The IMF and Ghana: The Confidential Record.* London: Institute for African Alternatives, 1987.

International Monetary Fund. *Ghana: Adjustment and Growth, 1983–1991.* Washington: 1991.

Jakobeit, Cord. "Reviving Cocoa: Policies and Perspectives on Structural Adjustment in Ghana's Key Agricultural Sector." Pages 221–32 in Donald Rothchild (ed.), *Ghana: The Political Economy of Recovery.* Boulder, Colorado: Lynne Rienner, 1991.

Jebuni, C.D., A.D. Oduro, and K.A. Tutu. "Trade and Payments Regime and the Balance of Payments in Ghana," *World Development* [Oxford], 22, No. 8, August 1994, 1161–73.

Jeffries, Richard. "Ghana: The Political Economy of Personal Rule." Pages 75–98 in Donal B. Cruise O'Brien, John Dunn, and Richard Rathbone (eds.), *Contemporary West African States*. Cambridge: Cambridge University Press, 1989.

Killick, Tony. *Development Economics in Action: A Study of Economic Policies in Ghana*. London: Heinemann, 1978.

Kraus, Jon. "The Political Economy of Stabilization and Structural Adjustment in Ghana." Pages 119–56 in Donald Rothchild (ed.), *Ghana: The Political Economy of Recovery*. Boulder, Colorado: Lynne Rienner, 1991.

Martin, Matthew. "Negotiating Adjustment and External Finance: Ghana and the International Community, 1982–1989." Pages 235–63 in Donald Rothchild (ed.), *Ghana: The Political Economy of Recovery*. Boulder, Colorado: Lynne Rienner, 1991.

Mikell, Gwendolyn. *Cocoa and Chaos in Ghana*. New York: Paragon House, 1989.

Nugent, Paul. "Educating Rawlings: The Evolution of Government Strategy Toward Smuggling." Pages 69–84 in Donald Rothchild (ed.), *Ghana: The Political Economy of Recovery*. Boulder, Colorado: Lynne Rienner, 1991.

Pearce, Richard. "Ghana." Pages 14–47 in Alex Duncan and John Howell (eds.), *Structural Adjustment and the African Farmer*. London: Overseas Development Institute, 1992.

Picard, Louis A., and Michele Garrity (eds.). *Policy Reform for Sustainable Development in Africa: The Institutional Imperative*. Boulder, Colorado: Lynne Rienner, 1994.

Price, Robert M. "Neo-colonialism and Ghana's Economic Decline: A Critical Assessment," *Canadian Journal of African Studies* [Ottawa], 18, No. 1, 1984, 163–94.

Ray, Donald. *Ghana: Politics, Economics and Society*. Boulder, Colorado: Lynne Rienner, 1986.

Reynolds, Edward. *Trade and Economic Change on the Gold Coast, 1807–1874*. London: Longman, 1974.

Rimmer, Douglas. *Staying Poor: Ghana's Political Economy, 1950–1990*. New York: Pergamon, 1992.

Rodney, Walter. *How Europe Underdeveloped Africa.* Washington: Howard University Press, 1982.

Roe, Alan, and Hartmut Schneider, with Graham Pyatt. *Adjustment and Equity in Ghana.* (Adjustment and Equity in Developing Countries series.) Paris: Organisation for Economic Co-operation and Development, 1992.

Rothchild, Donald. "Ghana and Structural Adjustment: An Overview." Pages 3–17 in Donald Rothchild (ed.), *Ghana: The Political Economy of Recovery.* Boulder, Colorado: Lynne Rienner, 1991.

Rothchild, Donald (ed.). *Ghana: The Political Economy of Recovery.* Boulder, Colorado: Lynne Rienner, 1991.

Sarris, Alexander, and Hadi Shams. *Ghana Under Structural Adjustment: The Impact on Agriculture and the Rural Poor.* New York: New York University Press for the International Fund for Agricultural Development, 1991.

World Bank. *Ghana 2000 and Beyond: Setting the Stage for Accelerated Growth and Poverty Reduction.* Washington: 1992.

World Bank. *Ghana: Financial Sector Review: Bringing Savers and Investors Together.* Washington: 1994.

Yankson, P.W.K. "The Growth and Development of Petty Commodity Enterprises in the Urban Economy: The Cases of Tema and Tamale, Ghana," *African Urban Quarterly* [Nairobi], 6, Nos. 3–4, 1991, 217–27.

(Various issues of the following publications were also used in the preparation of this chapter: *Africa Economic Digest* [London]; *Africa Research Bulletin* (Economic Series) [Oxford]; *African Business* [London]; Economist Intelligence Unit, *Country Report: Ghana* (1990–94) and *Country Profile: Ghana* (1992–93, 1993–94, 1994–95) [London]; and Ghana, Statistical Service, *Quarterly Digest of Statistics, Ghana in Figures,* and *Statistical Newsletter* [Accra].)

Chapter 4

Abdulai, David. "Rawlings 'Wins' Ghana's Presidential Elections: Establishing a New Constitutional Order," *Africa Today,* 39, No. 4, 1992, 66–71.

Adjetey, Peter Ala. "Ghana Bar Association's Presidential Address, 1987," *Ghana Bar Bulletin* [Accra], 1, No. 1, June 1988, 41–51.

Afari-Gyan, Kwadwo. *Public Tribunals and Justice in Ghana.* Accra: Asempa, 1988.

Ahiakpor, James C. W. "Rawlings, Economic Policy Reform, and the Poor: Consistency or Betrayal?" *The Journal of Modern African Studies* [Cambridge], 29, No. 4, December 1991, 583–600.

Apter, David E. *Ghana in Transition.* (2d rev. ed.) Princeton: Princeton University Press, 1972.

Arhin, Kwame (ed.). *The Life and Work of Kwame Nkrumah.* Trenton, New Jersey: Africa World Press, 1993.

Aryee, Joseph R.A. "The Provisional National Defence Council's 'Blue Book' on District Political Authority and the Future of Local Government in Ghana," *The Journal of Management Studies, Third Series* [Legon], 4, January–December 1988, 25–39.

Asamoah, Obed. "Nkrumah's Foreign Policy, 1951–1966." Pages 231–47 in Kwame Arhin (ed.), *The Life and Work of Kwame Nkrumah.* Trenton, New Jersey: Africa World Press, 1993.

Asante, S.K.B., and David Chanaiwa. "Pan-Africanism and Regional Integration." Pages 724–43 in Ali A. Mazrui and C. Wondji (eds.), *Unesco General History of Africa, VIII: Africa since 1935.* London: Heinemann, 1993.

Asmah, Kobena Annan. *Ghana's Revolution: The PNDC's Politics of Pragmatic Ideology.* (Contemporary National Affairs, Series No. 2.) Accra: Kakabaah, 1986.

Atta, William Ofori. *Ghana: A Nation in Crisis. The J.B. Danquah Memorial Lectures.* (Eighteenth Series, February 1985.) Accra: Ghana Academy of Arts and Sciences, 1988.

Austin, Dennis. *Politics in Ghana, 1946–1960.* (Issued under auspices of the Royal Institute of International Affairs.) London: Oxford University Press, 1970.

Awoonor, Kofi Nyidevu. *Ghana: A Political History from Pre-European to Modern Times.* Accra: Sedco and Woeli, 1990.

Barber, Benjamin, and Patrick Watson. *The Struggle For Democracy.* Boston: Little, Brown, 1988.

Boateng, Oti E., et al. "A Poverty Profile of Ghana, 1987–88," *Journal of African Economies* [Oxford], 7, No. 1, March 1992, 25–58.

Brittain, Victoria. "Africa: A Political Audit," *Race and Class* [London], 34, No. 1, July-September 1992, 41–49.

Brydon, Lynne. "Ghanaian Responses to the Nigerian Expulsions of 1983," *African Affairs* [Oxford], 84, No. 337, October 1985, 561–85.

Callaghy, Thomas M., and Ernest J. Wilson III. "Africa: Policy, Reality, or Ritual?" Pages 179–230 in Raymond Vernon (ed.), *The Promise of Privatization: A Challenge For American Foreign Policy.* New York: Council on Foreign Relations, 1988.

Chazan, Naomi. "Ghana." Pages 94–121 in Timothy M. Shaw and Olajide Aluko, (eds.), *The Political Economy of African Foreign Policy: Comparative Analysis.* New York: St. Martin's Press, 1984.

Chazan, Naomi. "Planning Democracy in Africa: A Comparative Perspective on Nigeria and Ghana," *Policy Sciences* [Dordrecht, The Netherlands], 22, 1989, 325–57.

Chazan, Naomi. "The Republic of Ghana." Pages 408–12 in George E. Delury (ed.), *World Encyclopedia of Political Systems and Parties, 1.* (2d ed.) New York: Facts on File, 1989.

Davidson, Basil. *The Black Man's Burden: Africa and The Curse of the Nation-State.* New York: Times Books, 1992.

Dei-Anang, Michael. *The Administration of Ghana's Foreign Relations, 1957–1965: A Personal Memoir.* London: Athlone Press, 1975.

Delury, George E. (ed.). *World Encyclopedia of Political Systems and Parties,* 1. (2d ed.) New York: Facts on File, 1989.

Diaz-Briquets, Sergio (ed.). *Cuban Internationalism in Sub-Saharan Africa.* Pittsburgh: Duquesne University Press, 1989.

Djoleto, Amu. *Hurricane of Dust.* Harlow, United Kingdom: Longman, 1991.

Du Sautoy, Peter. *Choice: Lessons From The Third World.* (IEA Occasional Paper No. 22.) London: Institute of Economic Affairs, 1968.

Freire, Paulo. *Pedagogy of the Oppressed.* New York: Herder and Herder, 1970.

Ghana. *Committee For the Defence of the Revolution: Guidelines, 1986.* Accra: Nsamankow Press, 1986.

Ghana. *The Constitution of the Republic of Ghana.* Accra: Ghana Publishing, 1992.

Ghana. *The Constitution of the Republic of Ghana, 1979.* Accra: Ghana Publishing, 1988.

Ghana. *Evolving A True Democracy.* (Report Presented to the PNDC, Issued by The National Commission For Democracy, Accra, March 25, 1991.) Tema: Tema Press, 1991.

Ghana. *NCD's Role in The Transformation of Ghana. (NCD Educational Series No. 2, National Commission For Democracy.)* Accra: Information Services Department, 1989.

Ghana. *Outlines of the Decentralization Plan of the Provisional National Defence Council.* Accra: Information Services Department, 1988.

Ghana. *Picking Up the Pace of Progress. Selected Speeches of Flt. Lt. J.J. Rawlings, Chairman of the PNDC, January 1–December 31, [1987], 6.* Accra: Information Services Department, 1987.

Ghana. *Report of the Committee of Experts (Constitution) on Proposals for a Draft Constitution of Ghana, Presented to the PNDC, July 31, 1991.* Tema: Tema Press, 1991.

Ghana. *Towards A Greater Tomorrow. Selected Speeches of Flt. Lt. Jerry John Rawlings, Chairman of the PNDC, 1st January–31st December, 1988, 7.* Accra: Information Services Department, 1989.

Ghana. *Unity Is Strength: Selected Speeches of Flt. Lt. Jerry John Rawlings, Chairman of the PNDC, 1st January–31st December, 1989, 8.* Accra: Information Services Department, 1990.

Gyimah-Boadi, E. "Associational Life, Civil Society, and Democratization in Ghana." Pages 125–48 in John W. Harbeson, Donald Rothchild, and Naomi Chazan (eds.), *Civil Society and the State in Africa.* Boulder, Colorado: Lynne Rienner, 1994.

Gyimah-Boadi, E. "Notes on Ghana's Current Transition to Constitutional Rule," *Africa Today,* 38, No. 4, 1992, 5–17.

Gyimah-Boadi, E. (ed.). *Ghana Under PNDC Rule, 1982–1989.* Dakar: Codesria, 1993.

Hansen, Emmanuel. *Ghana Under Rawlings.* Oxford: Malthouse, 1991.

Hansen, Emmanuel, and Kwame A. Ninsin (eds.). *The State, Development, and Politics in Ghana.* London: Codesria, 1989.

Harbeson, John W., Donald Rothchild, and Naomi Chazan (eds.). *Civil Society and the State in Africa.* Boulder, Colorado: Lynne Rienner, 1994.

Haynes, Jeff. "Human Rights and Democracy in Ghana: The Record of the Rawlings' Regime," *African Affairs* [Oxford] 90, No. 360, July 1991, 407–25.

Herbst, Jeffrey. *The Politics of Reform in Ghana, 1982–1991.* Berkeley: University of California Press, 1993.

Jeffries, Richard. "Urban Popular Attitudes Towards The Economic Recovery Programme and the PNDC Government in Ghana," *African Affairs* [Oxford], 91, No. 363, 207–26.

Jeffries, Richard, and Clare Thomas. "The Ghanaian Elections of 1992," *African Affairs* [Oxford], 92, No. 368, July 1993, 331–66.

Kodjo, Edem, and David Chanaiwa. "Pan-Africanism and Liberation." Pages 744–66 in Ali A. Mazrui and C. Wondji (eds.), *Unesco General History of Africa, VIII: Africa since 1935.* London: Heinemann, 1993.

Krafona, Kwesi (ed.). *Organization of African Unity: 25 Years On: Essays in Honour of Kwame Nkrumah.* London: Afroworld, 1988.

Kraus, Jon. "Building Democracy in Africa," *Current History,* 90, No. 556, May 1991, 209–12.

Kraus, Jon. "Ghana's Shift from Radical Populism," *Current History,* 86, No. 520, May 1987, 205–08, 227–28.

Limann, Hilla. *Limann Speaks: "The Way Ahead." Address by His Excellency President Hilla Limann at the Annual Congress of the People's National Party (29th May to 1st June 1980) at the Prempeh Assembly Hall, Kumasi.* Accra: People's National Party, 1980.

Lowy, Michael J. "A Good Name Is Worth More than Money: Strategies of Court Use in Urban Ghana." Pages 181–208 in Laura Nader and Harry F. Todd, Jr., (eds.), *The Disputing Process: Law in Ten Societies.* New York, Columbia University Press, 1978.

Loxley, John. "Structural Adjustment Programmes in Africa: Ghana and Zambia," *Review of African Political Economy* [Sheffield, United Kingdom], No. 47, Spring 1990, 8–27.

McColm, Bruce R., et al. "Ghana." Pages 216–18 in *Freedom in the World: Political Rights and Civil Liberties, 1991–1992.* New York: Freedom House, 1992.

Mazrui, Ali A., and C. Wondji (eds.). *Unesco General History of Africa, VIII: Africa since 1935.* London: Heinemann, 1993.

Mills, Pierre Landell. "Governance, Cultural Change and Empowerment," *The Journal of Modern African Studies* [Cambridge], 30, No. 4, December 1992, 543–67.

Mireku, Ebenezer. *Which Way Ghana?* Accra: Asuo Peabo, 1991.

Nader, Laura, and Harry F. Todd, Jr., (eds.). *The Disputing Process: Law in Ten Societies.* New York: Columbia University Press, 1978.

Ninsin, Kwame A. *Political Parties and Democracy in Ghana's Fourth Republic: Proceedings of a Seminar Organized by the Department of Political Science, University of Ghana, Legon, on 2nd and 3rd July 1992.* Accra: Woeli, 1993.

Ninsin, Kwame A. *The Search For Democracy in Ghana: A Case Study of Political Instability in Africa.* Accra: Asempa, 1987.

Ninsin, Kwame A., and Francis K. Drah (eds.). *Ghana's Transition to Constitutional Rule: Proceedings of a Seminar Organized by the Department of Political Science, University of Ghana, Legon.* Accra: Ghana Universities Press, 1991.

Nkrumah, Kwame. *Africa Must Unite.* London: Heinemann, 1963.

Nkrumah, Kwame. *I Speak of Freedom: A Statement of African Ideology.* London: Heinemann, 1961.

Okeke, Barbara E. *4 June: A Revolution Betrayed.* Enugu, Nigeria: Ikenga, 1982.

Overseas Development Administration. *Britain and Ghana: Partners in Development.* London: 1989.

Owusu, Maxwell. "Custom and Coups: A Juridical Interpretation of Civil Order and Disorder in Ghana," *The Journal of Modern African Studies* [Cambridge], 24, No. 1, March 1986, 69–99.

Owusu, Maxwell. "Democracy and Africa—A View from the Village," *The Journal of Modern African Studies* [Cambridge], 30, No. 3, September 1992, 369–96.

Owusu, Maxwell. "Evolution in the Revolution: Nkrumah, Ghana, and African Socialism," *Africa Today*, 26, No. 2, 1979, 71–76.

Owusu, Maxwell. "Kingship in Contemporary Asante Society." Pages 161–72 in Enid Schildkrout (ed.), *The Golden Stool: Studies of the Asante Center and Periphery.* (Anthropological Papers of the American Museum of Natural History, Vol. 65, Part 1.) New York: American Museum of National History, 1987.

Owusu, Maxwell. "Peace in the Coup. Chiefs, Courts, and Civil Order." Pages 150–70 in Mario D. Zamora, Bjorn B. Erring, and Anthony L. Laruffa (eds.), *The Anthropology of War and Peace.* Nueva Vizcaya, Philippines: St. Mary's College of Bayombong, 1990.

Owusu, Maxwell. "Politics Without Parties: Reflections on the Union Government Proposals in Ghana," *African Studies Review,* 22, No. 1, April 1979, 89–108.

Owusu, Maxwell. "Rebellion, Revolution, and Tradition: Re-Interpreting Coups in Ghana," *Comparative Studies in Society and History* [London and New York], 31, No. 2, April 1989, 372–97.

Owusu, Maxwell. *Uses and Abuses of Political Power: A Case Study of Continuity and Change in the Politics of Ghana.* Chicago: University of Chicago Press, 1970.

Owusu-Ansah, David. "The Provisional National Defence Council of Ghana: A Move Toward Consolidation," *International Third World Studies Journal and Review,* 1, No. 1, 1989, 213–18.

Pare, Osei. *Towards a Better Ghana.* Accra: Pare, 1988.

Ramphal, Shridath S. "The Legacy of Kwame Nkrumah." Pages 4–14 in Kwesi Krafona (ed.), *Organization of African Unity: 25 Years On: Essays in Honour of Kwame Nkrumah.* London: Afroworld, 1988.

Ray, Donald I. *Ghana: Politics, Economics, and Society.* Boulder, Colorado: Lynne Rienner, 1986.

Rothchild, Donald (ed.). *Ghana: The Political Economy of Recovery.* Boulder, Colorado: Lynne Rienner, 1991.

Schildkrout, Enid (ed.). *The Golden Stool: Studies of the Asante Center and Periphery.* (Anthropological Papers of the American Museum of Natural History, Vol. 65, Part 1.) New York: American Museum of Natural History, 1987.

Shaw, Timothy M., and Olajide Aluko (eds.). *The Political Economy of African Foreign Policy: Comparative Analysis.* New York: St. Martin's Press, 1984.

Shillington, Kevin. *Ghana and the Rawlings Factor.* New York: St. Martin's Press, 1992.

Tangri, Roger. "The Politics of State Divestiture in Ghana," *African Affairs* [Oxford], 90, No. 361, 523–36.

Thompson, Willard S. *Ghana's Foreign Policy, 1957–1966: Diplomacy, Ideology, and the New State.* Princeton: Princeton University Press, 1969.

Twumasi, P.K. *Criminal Law in Ghana.* Tema: Ghana Publishing, 1985.

Vernon, Raymond (ed.). *The Promise of Privatization: A Challenge for American Foreign Policy.* New York: Council on Foreign Relations, 1988.

Yankah, Kojo. *The Trial of J.J. Rawlings.* Accra: Ghana Publishing, 1987.

Yankah, Kwesi. *Woes of A Kwatriot. Reflections on the Ghanaian Situation.* Accra: Woeli, 1990.

Yeebo, Zaya. *Ghana: The Struggle For Popular Power. Rawlings: Saviour or Demagogue?* Boston: New Beacon Books, 1992.

Zamora, Mario D., Bjorn B. Erring, and Anthony L. Laruffa (eds.). *The Anthropology of War and Peace.* Nueva Vizcaya, Philippines: St. Mary's College of Bayombong, 1990.

Ziorklui, Emmanuel Doe. *Ghana: Nkrumah to Rawlings.* (Em-zed Historical Series, Vol. 1.) Accra: Em-zed Books Centre, 1988.

(Various issues of the following publications were also used in the preparation of this chapter: *Africa Contemporary Record* [New York and London], *The Christian Chronicle* [Accra], *Christian Messenger* [Accra], *The Free Press* [Accra], *Ghanaian Times* [Accra], *The Ghanaian Voice* [Accra], *Home Front Ghanaian News and Views* [Accra], *Local Government Information Digest* [Accra], *The Mirror* [Accra], *New African* [London], *People's Daily Graphic* [Accra], *The Pioneer* [Accra], *Talking Drums* [London], *The Verdict: Journal of the Revolutionary Organs* [Accra], *Weekly Spectator* [Accra], and *West Africa* [London].)

Chapter 5

Adekson, J. Bayo. "Army in a Multi-Ethnic Society: The Case of Nkrumah's Ghana, 1957–1966," *Armed Forces and Society,* 2, No. 2, Winter 1976, 251–72.

Africa Watch. *Abuse of Legal System Under PNDC.* New York: Africa Watch, 1992.

Africa Watch. *Government Denies Existence of Political Prisoners: Minister Says Detainees "Safer" in Custody.* New York: Africa Watch, 1991.

Afrifa, A.A. *The Ghana Coup, 24th February 1966.* London: Frank Cass, 1966.

Agyeman-Duah, Baffour. "Global Transformation and Democratic Reforms in Ghana." Pages 193–208 in Eileen McCarthy-Arnolds, David R. Penna, and Debra Joy Cruz Sobrepena (eds.), *Africa, Human Rights, and the Global System: The Political Economy of Human Rights in a Changing World.* Westport, Connecticut: Greenwood Press, 1994.

Akyempim, Owusu. *The Native Court and Its Functions.* Kumasi: Adom Press, 1955.

Alexander, H.T. *African Tightrope: My Two Years as Nkrumah's Chief of Staff.* New York: Praeger, 1966.

Allot, Antony Nicholas. *Essays in African Laws, with Special Reference to the Law of Ghana.* London: Butterworths, 1960.

Amdoh, A.S.Y. "The Asante National Liberation Movement of the 1950s." Pages 173–83 in Enid Schildkrout (ed.), *The Golden Stool: Studies of the Asante Center and Periphery.* (Anthropological Papers of the American Museum of Natural History, Vol. 65, Part 1.) New York: American Museum of Natural History, 1987.

Amnesty International. *Ghana: Political Imprisonment and the Death Penalty.* London: 1991.

Ankrah, Joseph A. "The Future of the Military in Ghana," *Africa Forum* [London], 2, No. 1, Summer 1966, 5–16.

Arakan Assignment: The Story of the 82nd West African Division. New Delhi: Roxy Press, 1946.

Armitage, Cecil Hamilton, and A.F. Montanaro. *The Ashanti Campaign of 1900.* London: Sands, 1901.

Arnold, Guy. "Ghana: Will It Be Rule by Army and Chiefs?," *New African Development* [London], No. 128, April 1978, 28–29.

Austin, Dennis. "The Ghana Armed Forces and Ghanaian Society," *Third World Quarterly* [London], 7, No. 1, January 1985, 90–101.

Austin, Dennis, and Robin Luckham (eds.). *Politicians and Soldiers in Ghana, 1966–1972.* London: Frank Cass, 1976.

Baden Powell, Robert S.S. *The Downfall of Prempeh: A Diary of Life with the Native Levy in Ashanti, 1895–96.* London: Methuen, 1896.

Barker, Peter. *Operation Cold Chop: The Coup That Toppled Nkrumah.* (2d ed.) Accra: Ghana Publishing, 1979.

Baynham, Simon. "Civil-Military Relations in Ghana's Second Republic," *Journal of Contemporary African Studies* [Pretoria], 4, Nos. 1–2, October 1984–April 1985, 71–88.

Baynham, Simon. "Civilian Rule and the Coup d'Etat: The Case of Busia's Ghana," *Journal of the Royal United Services Institute for Defence Studies* [London], 123, No. 3, September 1978, 27–33.

Baynham, Simon. *The Military and Politics in Nkrumah's Ghana.* Boulder, Colorado: Westview Press, 1988.

Baynham, Simon. "Soldier and State in Ghana," *Armed Forces and Society,* 5, No. 1, Fall 1978, 155–68.

Bebler, Anton. *Military Rule in Africa: Dahomey, Ghana, Sierra Leone, and Mali.* New York: Praeger, 1973.

Bennett, Valerie Plave. "The Motivation for Military Intervention: The Case of Ghana," *The Western Political Quarterly,* 26, No. 4, December 1973, 659–74.

Biss, Harold C.J. *The Relief of Kumasi.* London: Methuen's Colonial Library, 1901.

Boahen, A. Adu. "A Nation in Exile: The Asante on the Seychelles Islands, 1900–24." Pages 146–60 in Enid Schildkrout (ed.), *The Golden Stool: Studies of the Asante Center and Periphery.* (Anthropological Papers of the American Museum of Natural History, Vol. 65, Part 1.) New York: American Museum of Natural History, 1987.

Boyle, Frederick. *Through Fanteeland to Coomassie: A Diary of the Ashantee Expedition.* London: Chapman and Hall, 1874.

Brackenbury, Henry. *The Ashanti War: A Narrative.* (2 vols.) Edinburgh and London: Blackwood, 1874. Reprint. London: Frank Cass, 1968.

Clayton, Anthony, and David Killingray. *Khaki and Blue: Military and Police in British Colonial Africa.* Athens: Ohio University Center for International Studies, 1989.

Clifford, Hugh Charles. *The Gold Coast Regiment in the East African Campaign.* London: John Murray, 1920.

Crowder, Michael (ed.). *West African Resistance: The Military Response to Colonial Occupation.* New York: Africana, 1972.

Dare, L.O. "The Patterns of Military Entrenchment in Ghana and Nigeria," *Africa Quarterly* [New Delhi], 16, No. 3, 1977, 28–41.

Ekoko, Edho. "British War Plans Against Germany in West Africa, 1903–14," *The Journal of Strategic Studies* [London], 7, No. 4, December 1984, 441–56.

Farwell, Byron. *Queen Victoria's Little Wars.* New York: Harper and Row, 1972.

Feit, Edward. "Military Coups and Political Development: Some Lessons from Ghana and Nigeria," *World Politics,* 20, No. 2, April 1967, 179–93.

Feit, Edward. "The Rule of the Iron Surgeons: Military Government in Spain and Ghana," *Comparative Politics,* 1, No. 4, July 1969, 485–97.

Fynn, John K. "Ghana-Asante (Ashanti)." Pages 19–52 in Michael Crowder (ed.), *West African Resistance: The Military Response to Colonial Occupation.* New York: Africana, 1972.

Gillespie, W.H. *The Gold Coast Police, 1844–1938.* Accra: Government Printer, 1938.

Gorges, Edmund. *The Great War in West Africa.* London: Hutchinson, 1930.

Great Britain. *Correspondence Relating to the Ashanti War, 1900.* London: HMSO, 1901.

Great Britain. *Further Papers Relating to the Ashantee Invasion.* London: HMSO, 1874.

Great Britain. *Papers Relating to the Ashantee Invasion (Gold Coast).* London: HMSO, 1873(?).

Gutteridge, W.F. "Military Elites in Nigeria and Ghana," *Africa Forum* [London], 2, No. 1, Summer 1966, 31–41.

Haynes, Jeff. "Human Rights and Democracy in Ghana: The Record of the Rawlings' Regime," *African Affairs* [Oxford], 90, No. 360, July 1991, 407–25.

Haywood, A., and F.A.S. Clarke. *The History of the Royal West African Frontier Force.* Aldershot: Gale and Polden, 1964.

Hettne, Björn. "The Ghanaian Experiments with Military Rule." Pages 145–70 in Peter Wallensteen, Johan Galtung, and Carlos Portales (eds.), *Global Militarization.* Boulder, Colorado: Westview Press, 1985.

Hodgson, Mary Alice. *The Siege of Kumassi.* London: C. Arthur Pearson, 1901.

Holbrook, Wendell P. "British Propaganda and the Mobilization of the Gold Coast War Effort, 1939–1945," *Journal of African History* [Cambridge], 26, No. 4, 1985, 347–61.

Holbrook, Wendell P. "Oral History and the Nascent Historiography for West Africa and World War II: A Focus on Ghana," *International Journal of Oral History,* 3, No. 3, November 1982, 149–66.

Hunt, G.D. "Recollections of the Canadian Armed Forces Training Team in Ghana, 1961–1968," *Canadian Defence Quarterly* [Ottawa], 18, No. 5, 1989, 43–50.

Hutchful, Eboe. "The Development of the Army Officer Corps in Ghana, 1956–1966," *Journal of African Studies,* 12, No. 3, Fall 1985, 163–73.

Hutchful, Eboe. "Organizational Instability in African Military Forces: The Case of the Ghanaian Army," *International Social Science Journal* [Paris], 31, No. 4, 1979, 606–18.

Hutchful, Eboe. "A Tale of Two Regimes: Imperialism, the Military, and Class in Ghana," *Review of African Political Economy* [Sheffield, United Kingdom], No. 14, January-April 1979, 36–55.

Israel, Adrienne M. "Ex-Servicemen at the Crossroads: Protest and Politics in Post-War Ghana," *Journal of Modern African Studies* [Cambridge], 30, No. 2, June 1992, 359–68.

Kea, R.A. "Firearms and Warfare on the Gold and Slave Coasts from the Sixteenth to the Nineteenth Centuries," *Journal of African History* [Cambridge], 12, No. 2, 1971, 185–213.

Killingray, David. "Military and Labour Policies in Gold Coast during the First World War." Pages 152–70 in Melvin E. Page (ed.), *Africa and the First World War.* London: Macmillan, 1987.

Killingray, David. "Military and Labour Recruitment in the Gold Coast during the Second World War," *Journal of African History* [Cambridge], 23, No. 1, 1982, 83–95.

Killingray, David. "The Mutiny of the West African Regiment in the Gold Coast, 1901," *International Journal of African Historical Studies,* 16, No. 3, 1983, 441–54.

Killingray, David. "Soldiers, Ex-Servicemen and Politics in the Gold Coast, 1939–1950," *The Journal of Modern African Studies* [Cambridge], 21, No. 3, September 1983, 523–34.

Kraus, Jon. "Arms and Politics in Ghana." Pages 154–221 in Claude E. Welch, Jr. (ed.), *Soldier and State in Africa: A Comparative Analysis of Military Intervention and Political Change.* Evanston, Illinois: Northwestern University Press, 1970.

Lefever, Ernest W. *Spear and Scepter: Army, Police, and Politics in Tropical Africa.* Washington: The Brookings Institution, 1970.

Lloyd, Alan. *The Drums of Kumasi: The Story of the Ashanti Wars.* London: Longman, 1964.

Lucas, Charles Prestwood. *The Gold Coast and the War.* London: Milford, 1920.

McCarthy-Arnolds, Eileen, David R. Penna, and Debra Joy Cruz Sobrepena (eds.). *Africa, Human Rights, and the Global System: The Political Economy of Human Rights in a Changing World.* Westport, Connecticut: Greenwood Press, 1994.

McInnes, I. *Ashanti, 1895–96.* London: Picton, 1987.

Maier, D.J.E. "Asante War Aims in the 1896 Invasion of Ewe." Pages 232–44 in Enid Schildkrout (ed.), *The Golden Stool: Studies of the Asante Center and Periphery.* (Anthropological Papers of the American Museum of Natural History, Vol. 65, Part 1.) New York: American Museum of Natural History, 1987.

"Military Training Assistance to Ghana," *External Affairs* [Ottawa], 14, No. 4, April 1962, 136–37.

Milner, Alan (ed.). *African Penal Systems.* London: Routledge and Kegan Paul, 1969.

Moberly, Frederick James. *History of the Great War: Military Operations, Togoland and the Cameroons, 1914–1916.* London: HMSO, 1931.

Myatt, Frederick. *The Golden Stool: An Account of the Ashanti War of 1900.* London: William Kimber, 1966.

Nkrumah, Kwame. *Dark Days in Ghana.* London: Lawrence and Wishart, 1968.

Ocran, Albert Kwesi. *A Myth Is Broken: An Account of the Ghana Coup d'Etat of 24th February 1966.* New York: Humanities Press, 1968.

Ocran, Albert Kwesi. *Politics of the Sword: A Personal Memoir on Military Involvement in Ghana and of Problems of Military Government.* London: Rex Collings, 1977.

Ofusu-Appiah, L.H. *The Life of Lt. Gen. E.K. Kotoka.* Accra: Waterville Publishing, 1972.

Okeke, Barbara E. *4 June: A Revolution Betrayed.* Enugu, Nigeria: Ikenga, 1982.

Owusu, Maxwell. "Rebellion, Revolution, and Tradition: Reinterpreting Coups in Ghana," *Comparative Studies in Society and History* [London and New York], 31, No. 2, April 1989, 372–97.

Page, Melvin E. (ed.). *Africa and the First World War.* London: Macmillan, 1987.

Pieterse, Jan. "Rawlings and the 1979 Revolt in Ghana," *Race and Class* [London], 23, No. 4, Spring 1982, 9–18.

Pinkney, Robert. *Ghana Under Military Rule, 1966–1969.* London: Methuen, 1972.

Price, Robert M. "Military Officers and Political Leadership: The Ghanaian Case," *Comparative Politics,* 3, No. 3, April 1971, 361–79.

Price, Robert M. "A Theoretical Approach to Military Rule in New States: Reference Group Theory and the Ghanaian Case," *World Politics,* 23, No. 3, April 1971, 399–430.

Reynolds, Edward. "Asante Wars of the 19th Century and Direct Access to the Coast." Pages 225–31 in Enid Schildkrout (ed.), *The Golden Stool: Studies of the Asante Center and Periphery.* (Anthropological Papers of the American Museum of Natural History, Vol. 65, Part 1.) New York: American Museum of Natural History, 1987.

Rothchild, Donald. "Military Regime Performance: An Appraisal of the Ghana Experience, 1972–78," *Comparative Politics,* 12, No. 4, July 1980, 459–70.

Schildkrout, Enid (ed.). *The Golden Stool: Studies of the Asante Center and Periphery.* (Anthropological Papers of the American Museum of Natural History, Vol. 65, Part 1.) New York: American Museum of Natural History, 1987.

Schleh, Eugene P.A. "The Post-War Careers of Ex-Servicemen in Ghana and Uganda," *Journal of Modern African Studies* [Cambridge], 6, No. 2, August 1968, 203–20.

Seidman, Robert B. "The Ghana Prison System: An Historical Perspective." Pages 431–72 in Alan Milner (ed.), *African Penal Systems.* London: Routledge and Kegan Paul, 1969.

Seidman, Robert B., and J.D. Abaka Eyison. "Ghana." Pages 59–87 in Alan Milner (ed.), *African Penal Systems.* London: Routledge and Kegan Paul, 1969.

Sillah, Mohammed-Bassiru. *African Coup d'Etat: A Case Study of Jerry Rawlings in Ghana.* Lawrenceville, Virginia: Brunswick, 1984.

Stanley, Henry Morton. *Coomassie and Magdala: The Story of Two British Campaigns in Africa.* London: Low, Marston, Low and Searle, 1874.

Stanley, Henry Morton. *Coomassie: The Story of the Campaign in Africa, 1873–4.* London: Low, Marston and Company, 1896.

Tenkorang, S. "The Importance of Firearms in the Struggle between Ashanti and the Coastal States, 1708–1807," *Transactions of the Historical Society of Ghana* [Legon], 9, 1968, 1–16.

Terry, E. "Asante Imperialism and Gyaman Resistance: Forms, Motivations, Trends." Pages 245–51 in Enid Schildkrout (ed.), *The Golden Stool: Studies of the Asante Center and Periphery.* (Anthropological Papers of the American Museum of Natural History, Vol. 65, Part 1.) New York: American Museum of Natural History, 1987.

Thomas, Roger G. "Military Recruitment in the Gold Coast during the First World War," *Cahiers d'Études Africaines* [Paris], 15, No. 1, 1975, 57–83.

Thomas, Roger G. "The 1916 Bongo 'Riots' and Their Background: Aspects of Colonial Administration and African Response in Eastern Upper Ghana," *Journal of African History* [Cambridge], 24, No. 1, 1983, 57–75.

Ukpabi, S.C. "The British Colonial Office Approach to the Ashanti War of 1900," *African Studies Review,* 13, No. 3, December 1970, 363–80.

Wallensteen, Peter, Johan Galtung, and Carlos Portales (eds.). *Global Militarization.* Boulder, Colorado: Westview Press, 1985.

Wasserman, B. "The Ashanti War of 1900: A Study in Cultural Conflict," *Africa* [Edinburgh], 31, April 1961, 167–78.

Welch, Claude E., Jr. (ed.). *Soldier and State in Africa: A Comparative Analysis of Military Intervention and Political Change.* Evanston, Illinois: Northwestern University Press, 1970.

Zeff, Eleanor Elwell. "New Directions in Understanding Military and Civilian Regimes in Ghana," *African Studies Review,* 24, No. 1, March 1981, 49–72.

(Various issues of the following publications were also used in the preparation of this chapter: *Africa Confidential* [London], *Africa Contemporary Record* [New York and London], *Africa Events* [London], *Africa Research Bulletin* (Political Series) [Oxford], *Africa South of the Sahara* [London], *African Defence Journal* [Paris], *The Army Quarterly and Defence Journal* [London], *Current History, Ghana Armed Forces Magazine* [Accra], *Journal of the African Society* [London], *The Military Balance* [London], *New African* [London], *Strategic Survey* [London], *West Africa* [London], and *World Armaments and Disarmament* [Stockholm].)

Glossary

asafo—Traditional warrior organization of the Akan and other coastal peoples of southern Ghana, originating in the early seventeenth century or earlier. Traditionally, the *asafo* served as an independent outlet for popular dissatisfaction, and they had a voice in the enthronement (enstoolment) and dethronement (destoolment) of chiefs. Among other tasks, the *asafo* performed police and militia duties, collected tribute, and built roads. People's Defence Committees and Committees for the Defence of the Revolution of the Provisional National Defence Council era were inspired in part by the *asafo* tradition.

Asante/Ashanti—Terms used interchangeably to refer to what are probably the best-known people and state among the Akan. *Asante* is the original Akan term. *Ashanti*, according to popular accounts, is a corruption that originated early in the colonial period. Although Asante is now preferred, Ashanti remains in use in contemporary Ghana, for example, Ashanti Region.

cedi (pl. cedis; ¢ or c)—Ghanaian unit of currency, composed of 100 pesewas. Introduced after independence by Kwame Nkrumah, it has undergone several devaluations, including one that proved politically unpopular in December 1971. In 1982 the value of the cedi was US$1.00 = 2.75 cedis. In October 1983, the Provisional National Defence Council further devalued the cedi, which produced an exchange rate of US$1.00 = 90 cedis in March 1986. Beginning in September 1986, the cedi was freed to float against other currencies, which yielded an exchange rate of US$1.00 = 326 cedis by 1990 and US$1.00 = 1,040 cedis by late 1994.

clan—A group whose members are descended in the male line from a putative common male ancestor (patriclan) or in the female line from a putative common female ancestor (matriclan). Clans may be divided into subclans organized on the same principle or into lineages (*q. v.*) believed to be linked by descent from a common ancestor less remote than the founding ancestor of the clan.

fiscal year (FY)—An annual period established for accounting purposes. In Ghana, the government's fiscal year is the same as the calendar year.

Global 2000—Program founded and chaired by Jimmy Carter, former president of the United States, to deliver agricultural assistance to farmers in the developing world. Provides improved seedlings, financial assistance, and extension services, and has as its goal the attainment of agricultural self-sufficiency in participating countries. Ghana became a member country in the mid-1980s.

gross domestic product (GDP)—A measure of the total value of goods and services produced by the domestic economy during a given period, usually one year. Obtained by adding the value contributed by each sector of the economy in the form of profits, compensation to employees, and depreciation (consumption of capital). The income arising from investments and possessions owned abroad is not included, hence the use of the word *domestic* to distinguish GDP from gross national product (*q.v.*).

gross national product (GNP)—Total market value of all final goods and services produced by an economy during a year. Obtained by adding the gross domestic product (*q.v.*) and the income received from abroad by residents minus payments remitted abroad to nonresidents.

International Monetary Fund (IMF)—Established on July 22, 1944, the IMF began operating along with the World Bank (*q.v.*) on December 27, 1945. The IMF is a specialized agency affiliated with the United Nations that takes responsibility for stabilizing international exchange rates and payments. The IMF's main business is the provision of loans to its members when they experience balance-of-payments difficulties. These loans often carry conditions that require substantial internal economic adjustments by the recipients.

lineage—A group whose members are descended through males from a common male ancestor (patrilineage) or through females from a common female ancestor (matrilineage). Such descent can in principle be traced. Lineages vary in genealogical depth from the lineage ancestor to living generations; the more extensive ones often are internally segmented. A lineage is generally a branch of a clan (*q.v.*).

matriclan—A group of men and women who are descended in the female line from a putative common female ancestor.

matrilineage—A group of male and female descendants of a

female ancestor, each of whom is related to the common ancestor through female forebears.

patriclan—A group of men and women who are descended in the male line from a putative common male ancestor.

patrilineage—A group of male and female descendants of a male ancestor, each of whom is related to the common ancestor through male forebears.

Shia (also Shiite, from Shiat Ali, the Party of Ali)—A member of the smaller of the two great divisions of Islam. In the mid-seventh century, the Shia supported the hereditary claim of Ali, the Prophet Muhammad's cousin and son-in-law, and of his descendants to presumptive right to the Islamic caliphate and leadership of the Muslim community. On this issue, they divided from the Sunnis, the larger of the two great divisions of Islam.

World Bank—Informal name used to designate a group of four affiliated international institutions: the International Bank for Reconstruction and Development (IBRD), the International Development Association (IDA), the International Finance Corporation (IFC), and the Multilateral Investment Guarantee Agency (MIGA). The IBRD, established in 1945, has the primary purpose of providing loans to developing countries for productive projects. The IDA, a legally separate loan fund administered by the staff of the IBRD, was set up in 1960 to furnish credits to the poorest developing countries on much easier terms than those of conventional IBRD loans. The IFC, founded in 1956, supplements the activities of the IBRD through loans and assistance specifically designed to encourage the growth of productive private enterprises in the less developed countries. The MIGA, founded in 1988, insures private foreign investment in developing countries against various noncommercial risks. The president and certain senior officers of the IBRD hold the same positions in the IFC. The four institutions are owned by the governments of the countries that subscribe their capital. To participate in the World Bank group, member states must first belong to the International Monetary Fund (IMF—*q.v.*).

Index

Contributors

LaVerle Berry is Senior Research Specialist for Africa with the Federal Research Division, Library of Congress.

Nancy L. Clark is Associate Professor of History at California Polytechnic State University.

James L. McLaughlin is a retired United States Army colonel who has written numerous articles on Africa and the Middle East.

Thomas P. Ofcansky is Senior African Analyst with the Department of Defense.

Maxwell Owusu is Professor of Anthropology at the University of Michigan.

David Owusu-Ansah is Associate Professor of History at James Madison University.

Published Country Studies

(Area Handbook Series)

550–65	Afghanistan
550–98	Albania
550–44	Algeria
550–59	Angola
550–73	Argentina
550–111	Armenia, Azerbaijan, and Georgia
550–169	Australia
550–176	Austria
550–175	Bangladesh
550–112	Belarus and Moldova
550–170	Belgium
550–66	Bolivia
550–20	Brazil
550–168	Bulgaria
550–61	Burma
550–50	Cambodia
550–166	Cameroon
550–159	Chad
550–77	Chile
550–60	China
550–26	Colombia
550–33	Commonwealth Carib-bean, Islands of the
550–91	Congo
550–90	Costa Rica
550–69	Côte d'Ivoire (Ivory Coast)
550–152	Cuba
550–22	Cyprus
550–158	Czechoslovakia
550–36	Dominican Republic and Haiti
550–52	Ecuador
550–43	Egypt
550–150	El Salvador
550–28	Ethiopia
550–167	Finland
550–173	Germany, East
550–155	Germany, Fed. Rep. of
550–153	Ghana
550–87	Greece
550–78	Guatemala
550–174	Guinea
550–82	Guyana and Belize
550–151	Honduras
550–165	Hungary
550–21	India
550–154	Indian Ocean
550–39	Indonesia
550–68	Iran
550–31	Iraq
550–25	Israel
550–182	Italy
550–30	Japan
550–34	Jordan
550–56	Kenya
550–81	Korea, North
550–41	Korea, South
550–58	Laos
550–24	Lebanon
550–38	Liberia

550–85	Libya
550–172	Malawi
550–45	Malaysia
550–161	Mauritania
550–79	Mexico
550–76	Mongolia
550–49	Morocco
550–64	Mozambique
550–35	Nepal and Bhutan
550–88	Nicaragua
550–157	Nigeria
550–94	Oceania
550–48	Pakistan
550–46	Panama
550–156	Paraguay
550–185	Persian Gulf States
550–42	Peru
550–72	Philippines
550–162	Poland
550–181	Portugal
550–160	Romania
550–37	Rwanda and Burundi
550–51	Saudi Arabia
550–70	Senegal
550–180	Sierra Leone
550–184	Singapore
550–86	Somalia
550–93	South Africa
550–95	Soviet Union
550–179	Spain
550–96	Sri Lanka
550–27	Sudan
550–47	Syria
550–62	Tanzania
550–53	Thailand
550–89	Tunisia
550–80	Turkey
550–74	Uganda
550–97	Uruguay
550–71	Venezuela
550–32	Vietnam
550–183	Yemens, The
550–99	Yugoslavia
550–67	Zaire
550–75	Zambia
550–171	Zimbabwe